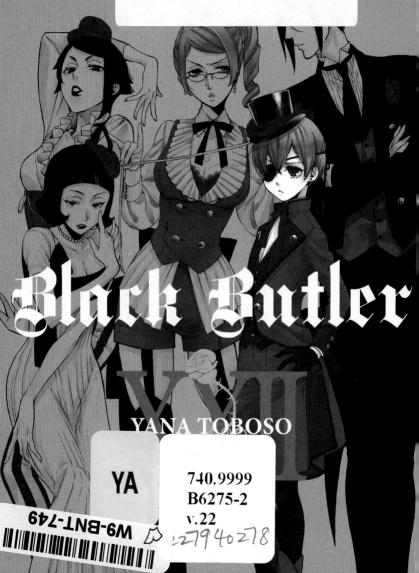

Black Butler

XXII

YANA TOBOSO

Contents

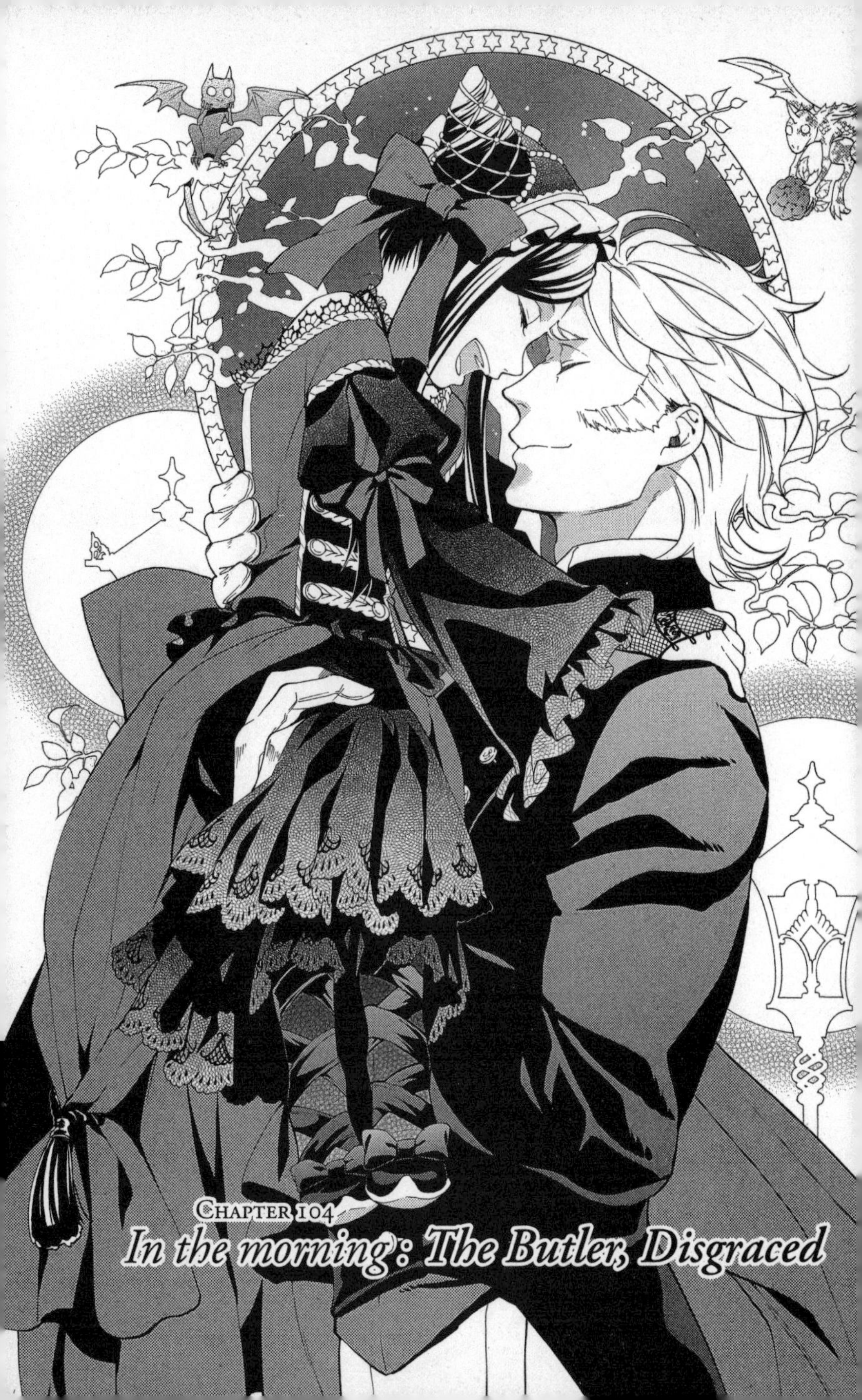

Chapter 104
In the morning: The Butler, Disgraced

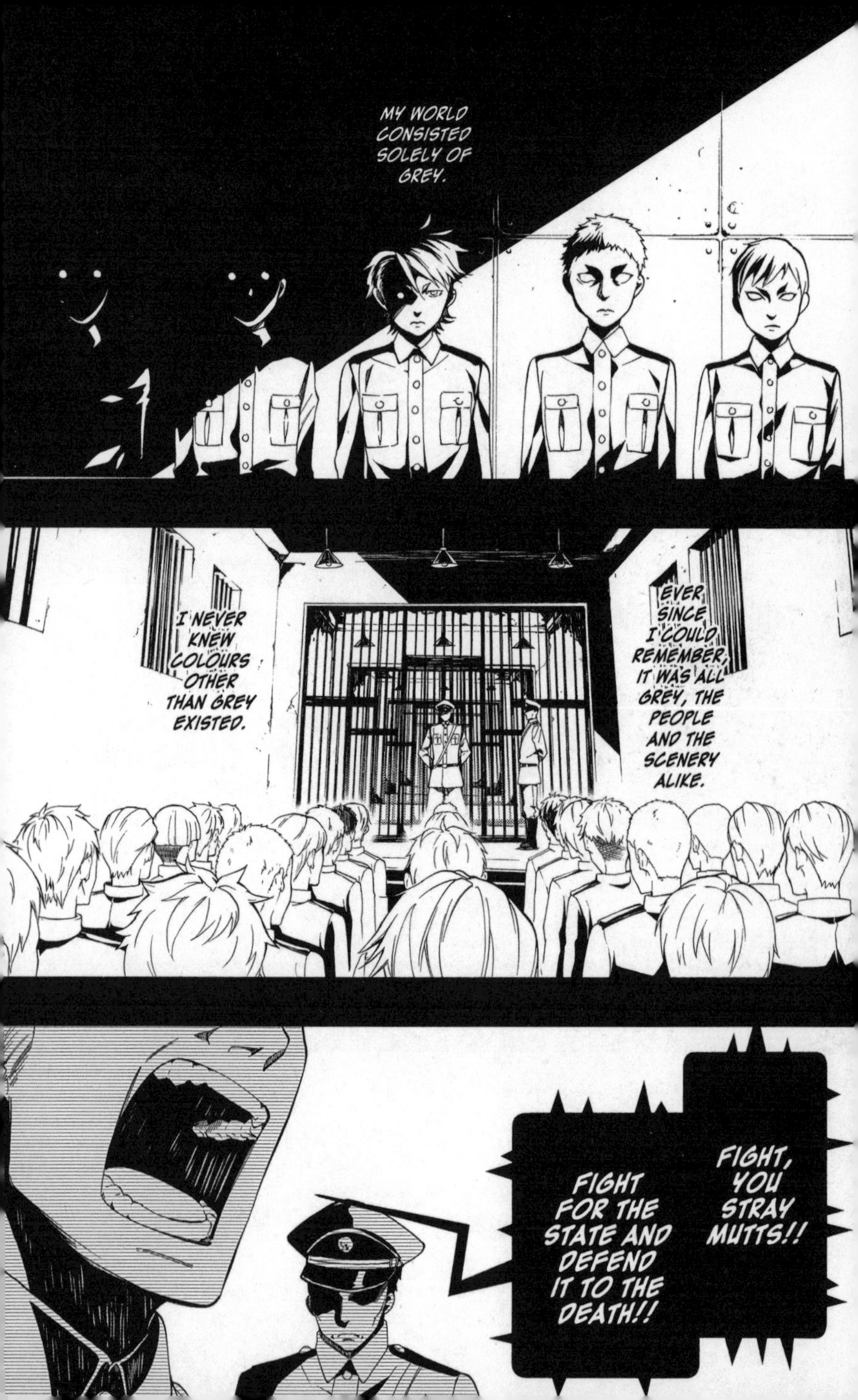
MY WORLD CONSISTED SOLELY OF GREY.
EVER SINCE I COULD REMEMBER, IT WAS ALL GREY, THE PEOPLE AND THE SCENERY ALIKE.
I NEVER KNEW COLOURS OTHER THAN GREY EXISTED.
FIGHT, YOU STRAY MUTTS!!
FIGHT FOR THE STATE AND DEFEND IT TO THE DEATH!!

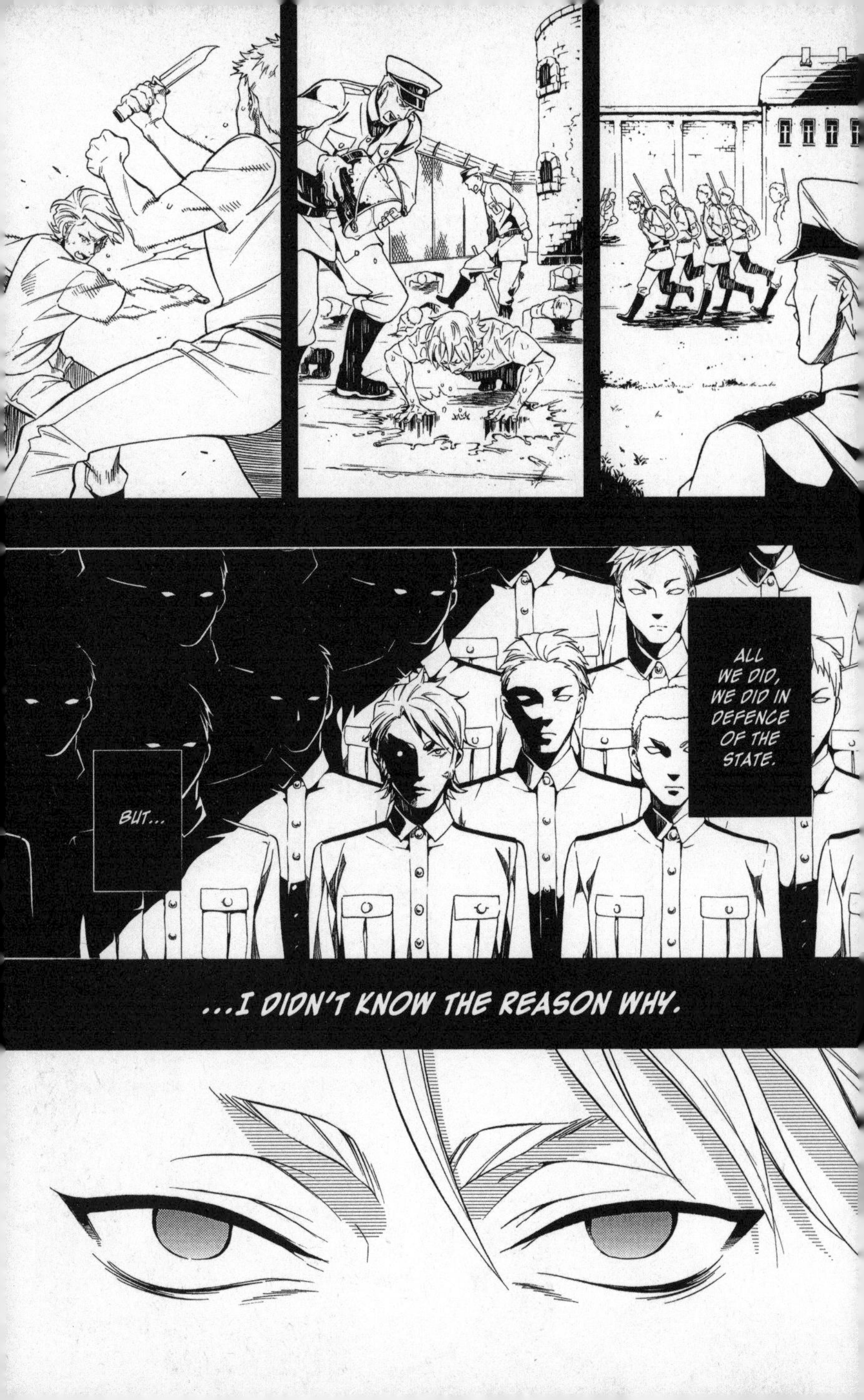
ALL WE DID, WE DID IN DEFENCE OF THE STATE.
BUT...
...I DIDN'T KNOW THE REASON WHY.

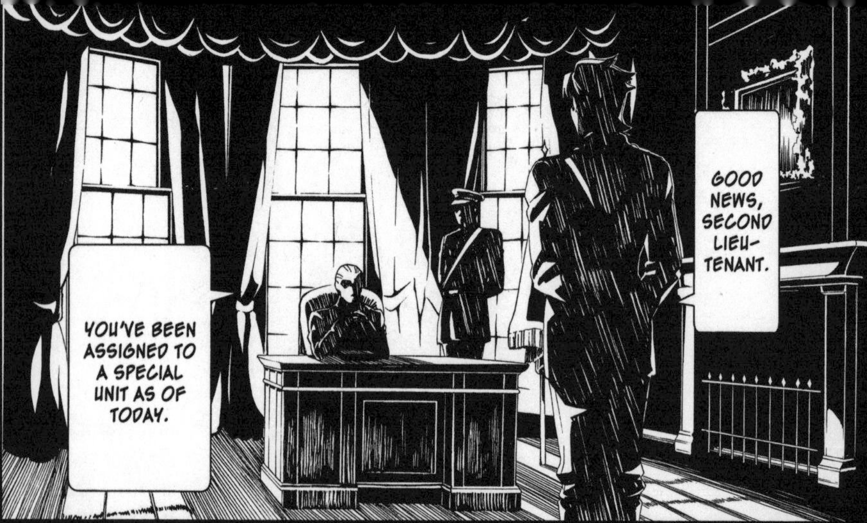
GOOD NEWS, SECOND LIEU-TENANT.
YOU'VE BEEN ASSIGNED TO A SPECIAL UNIT AS OF TODAY.

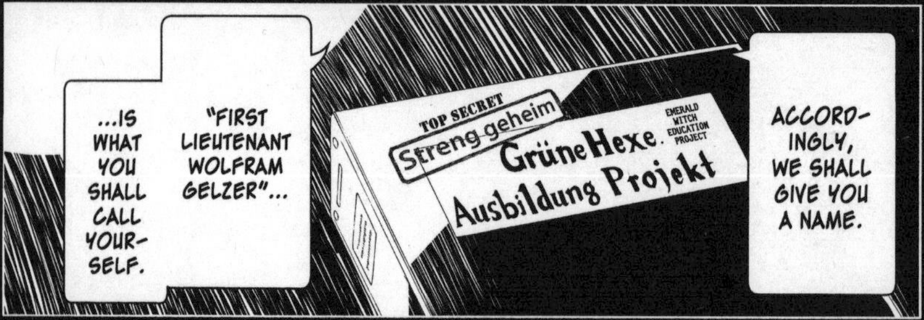
ACCORD-INGLY, WE SHALL GIVE YOU A NAME.
TOP SECRET
Streng geheim
EMERALD WITCH EDUCATION PROJECT
GrüneHexe. Ausbildung Projekt
"FIRST LIEUTENANT WOLFRAM GELZER"...
...IS WHAT YOU SHALL CALL YOUR-SELF.

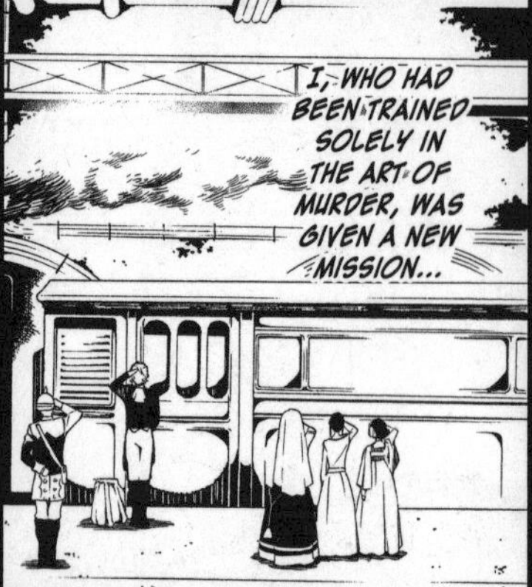
I, WHO HAD BEEN TRAINED SOLELY IN THE ART OF MURDER, WAS GIVEN A NEW MISSION...

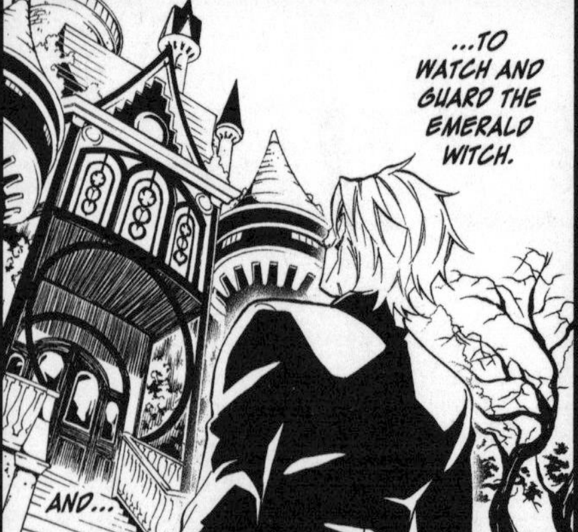
...TO WATCH AND GUARD THE EMERALD WITCH.
AND...

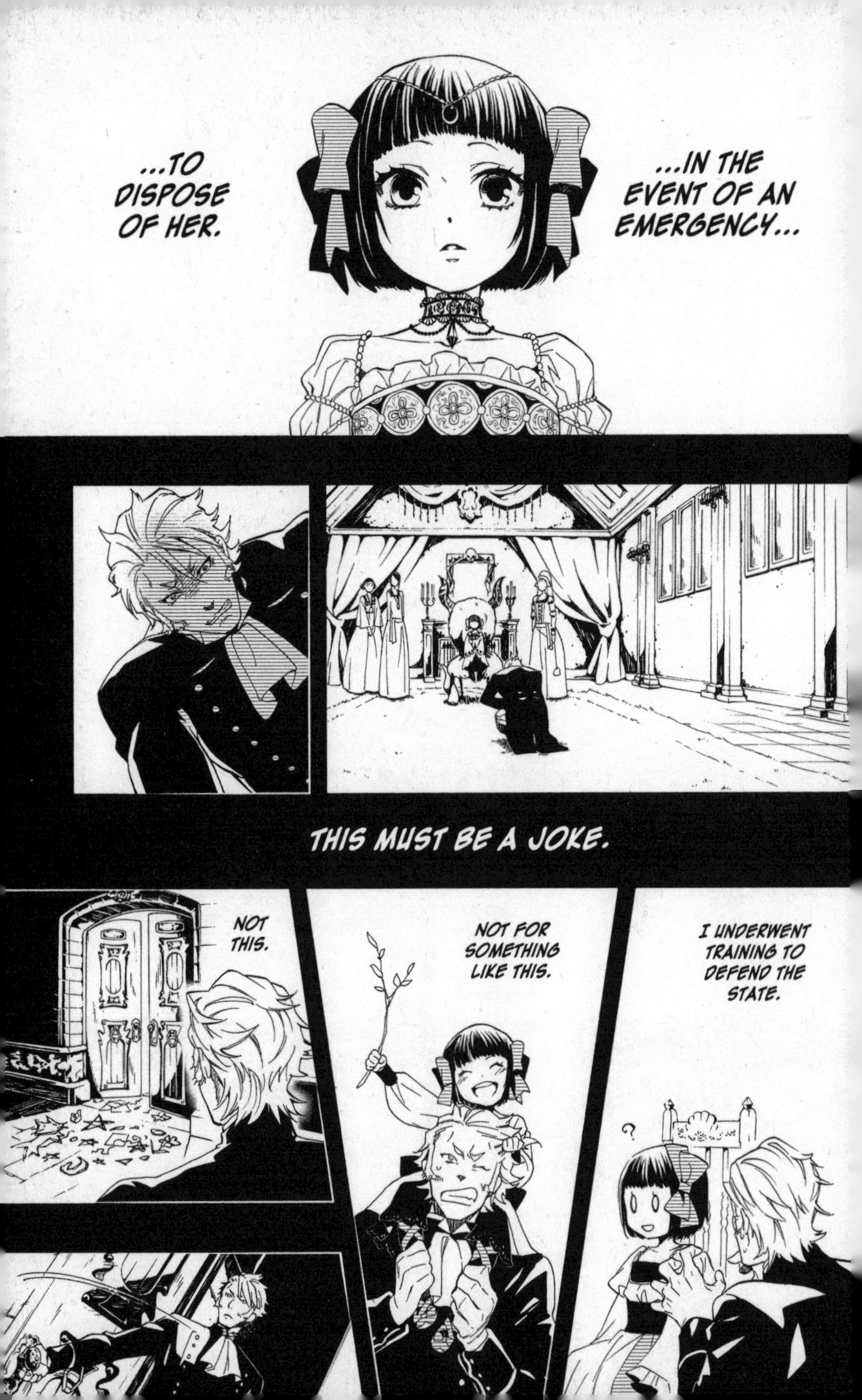
...IN THE EVENT OF AN EMERGENCY...
...TO DISPOSE OF HER.
THIS MUST BE A JOKE.
I UNDERWENT TRAINING TO DEFEND THE STATE.
NOT FOR SOMETHING LIKE THIS.
NOT THIS.

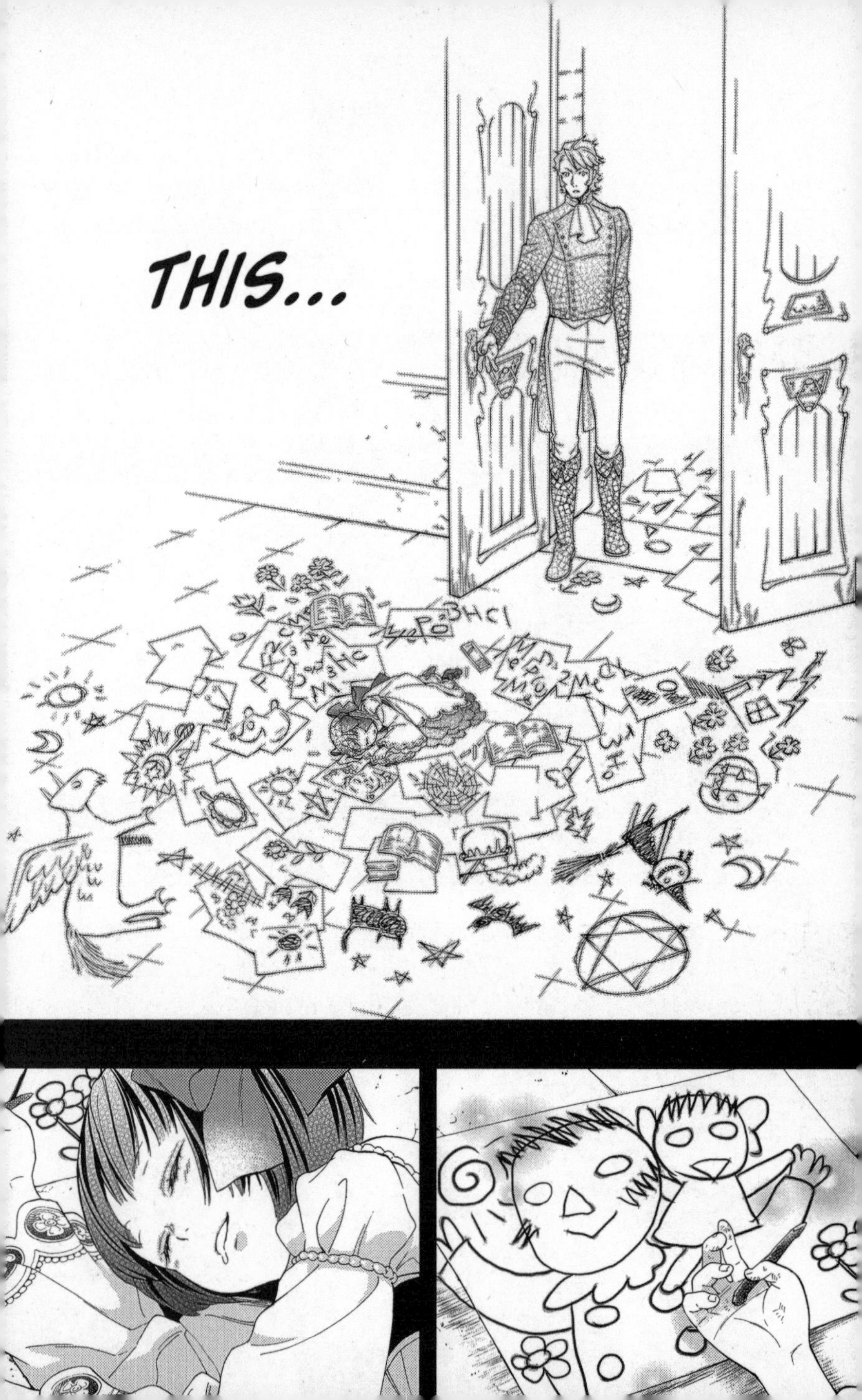
THIS...

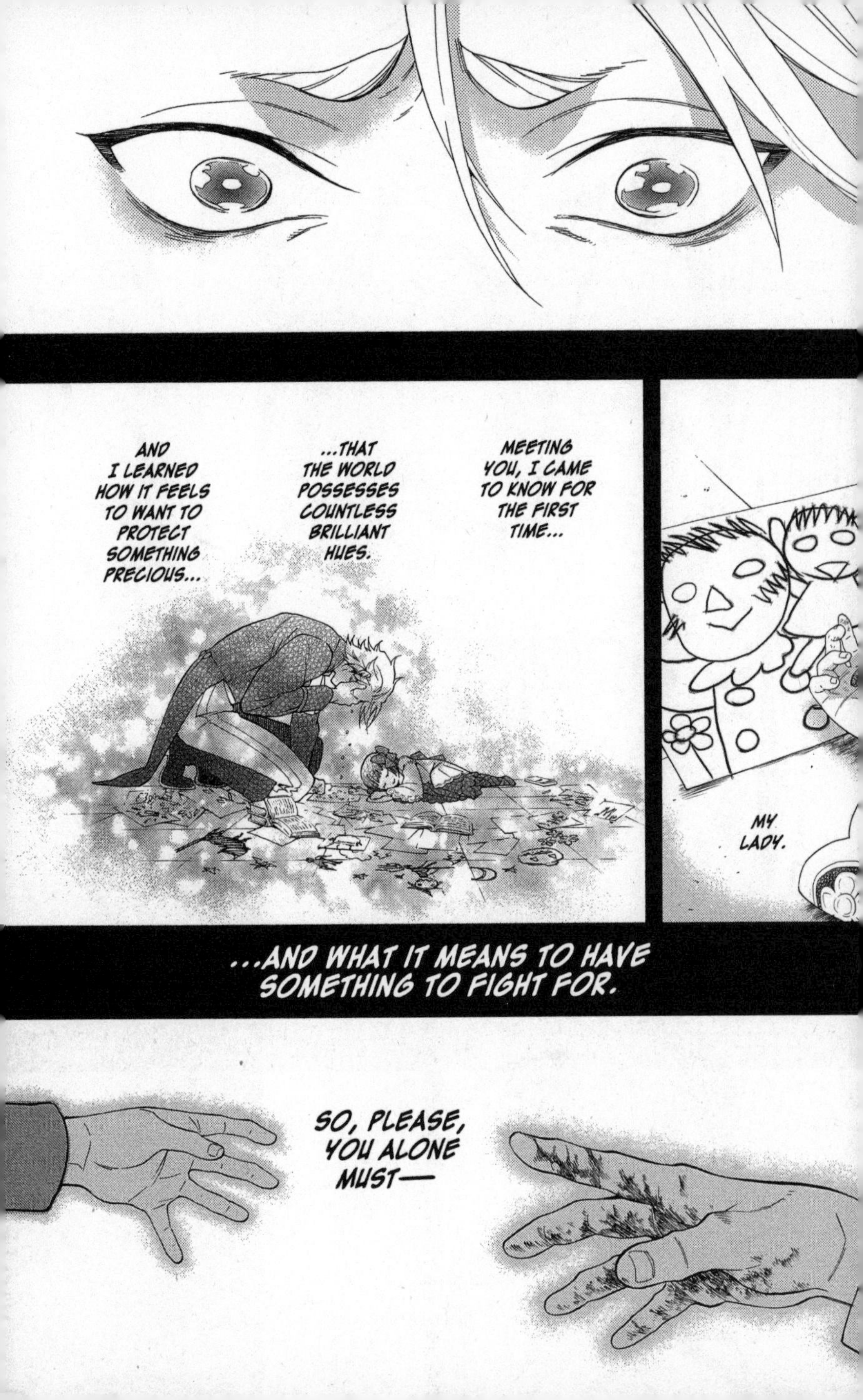
MY LADY.
MEETING YOU, I CAME TO KNOW FOR THE FIRST TIME...
...THAT THE WORLD POSSESSES COUNTLESS BRILLIANT HUES.
AND I LEARNED HOW IT FEELS TO WANT TO PROTECT SOMETHING PRECIOUS...
...AND WHAT IT MEANS TO HAVE SOMETHING TO FIGHT FOR.
SO, PLEASE, YOU ALONE MUST—

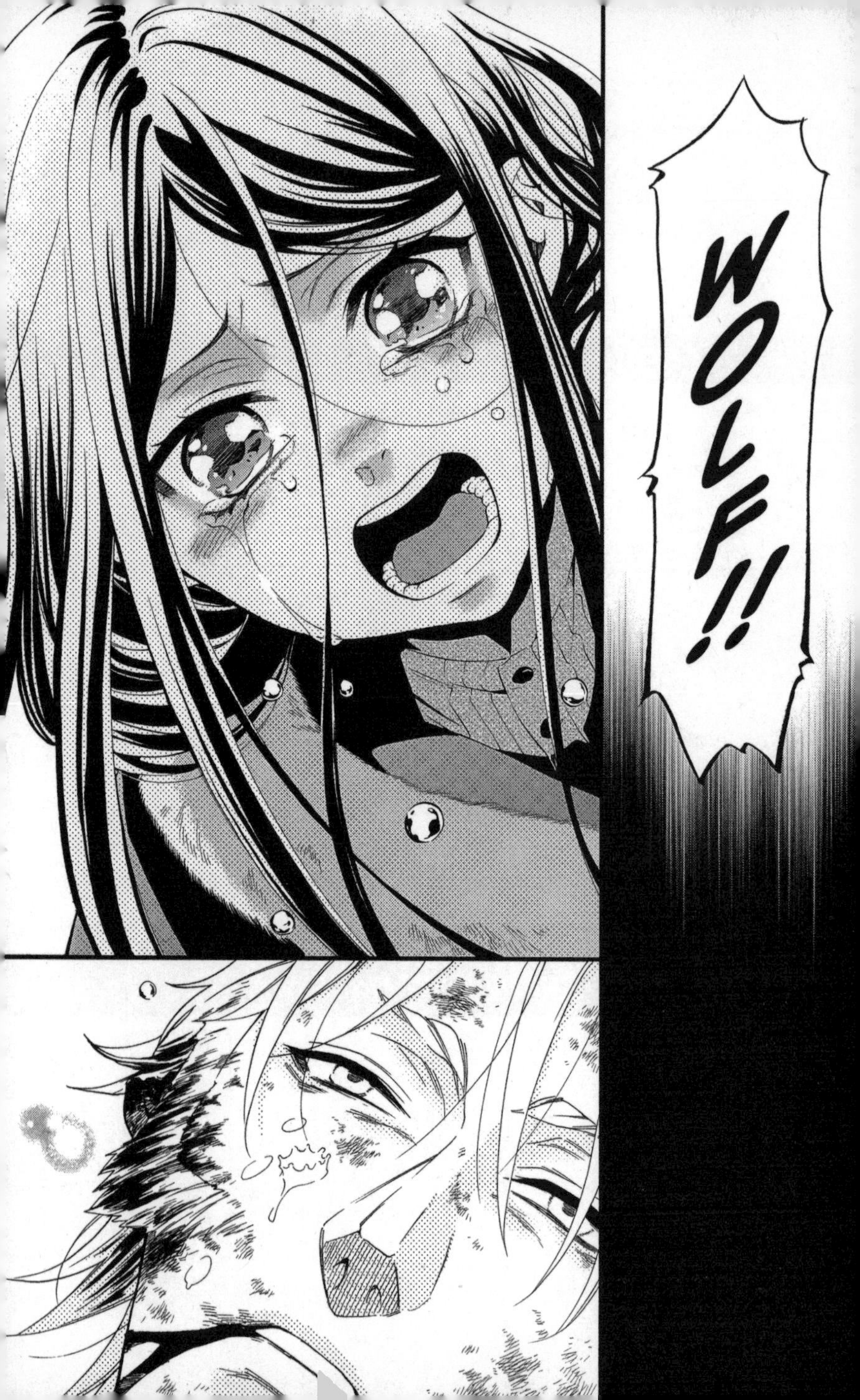
WOLF!!

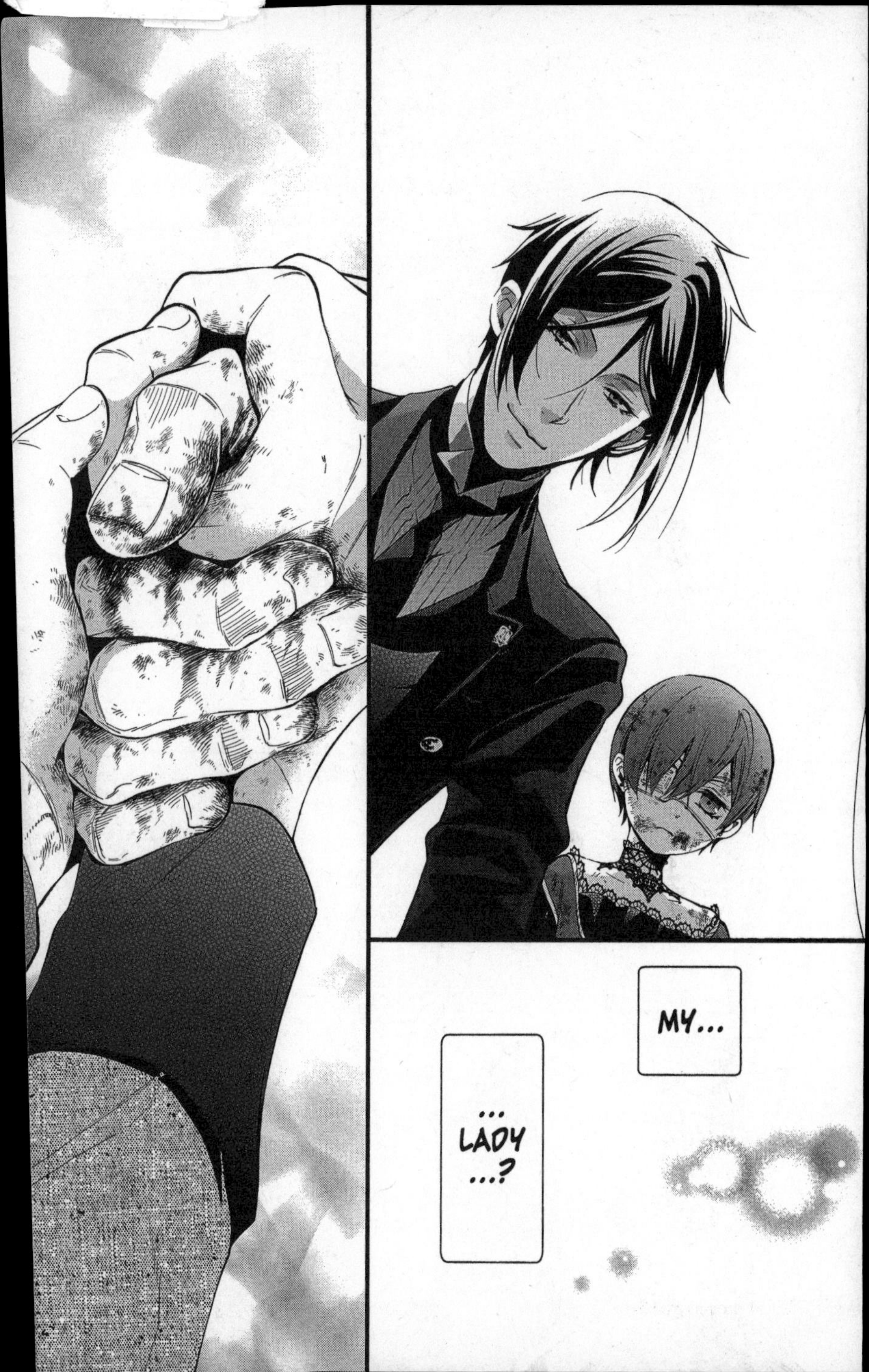
MY...
...LADY...?

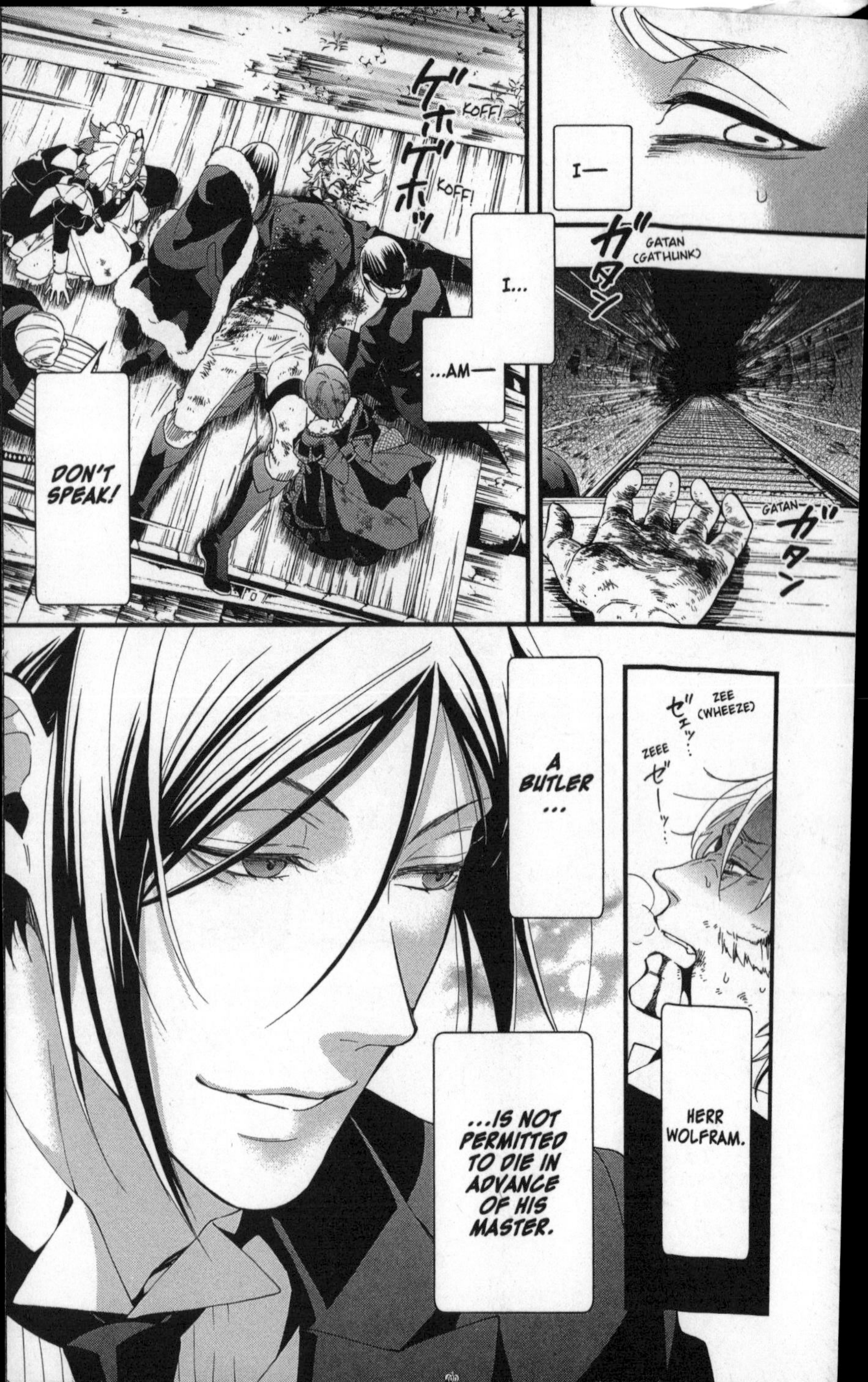
I—
ガタン
GATAN (GATHUNK)
ガタン
GATAN—
ゲホゲホッ
KOFF!
KOFF!
I...
...AM—
DON'T SPEAK!
ゼェッ…
ZEE (WHEEZE)
ゼーッ…
ZEEE
HERR WOLFRAM.
A BUTLER ...
...IS NOT PERMITTED TO DIE IN ADVANCE OF HIS MASTER.

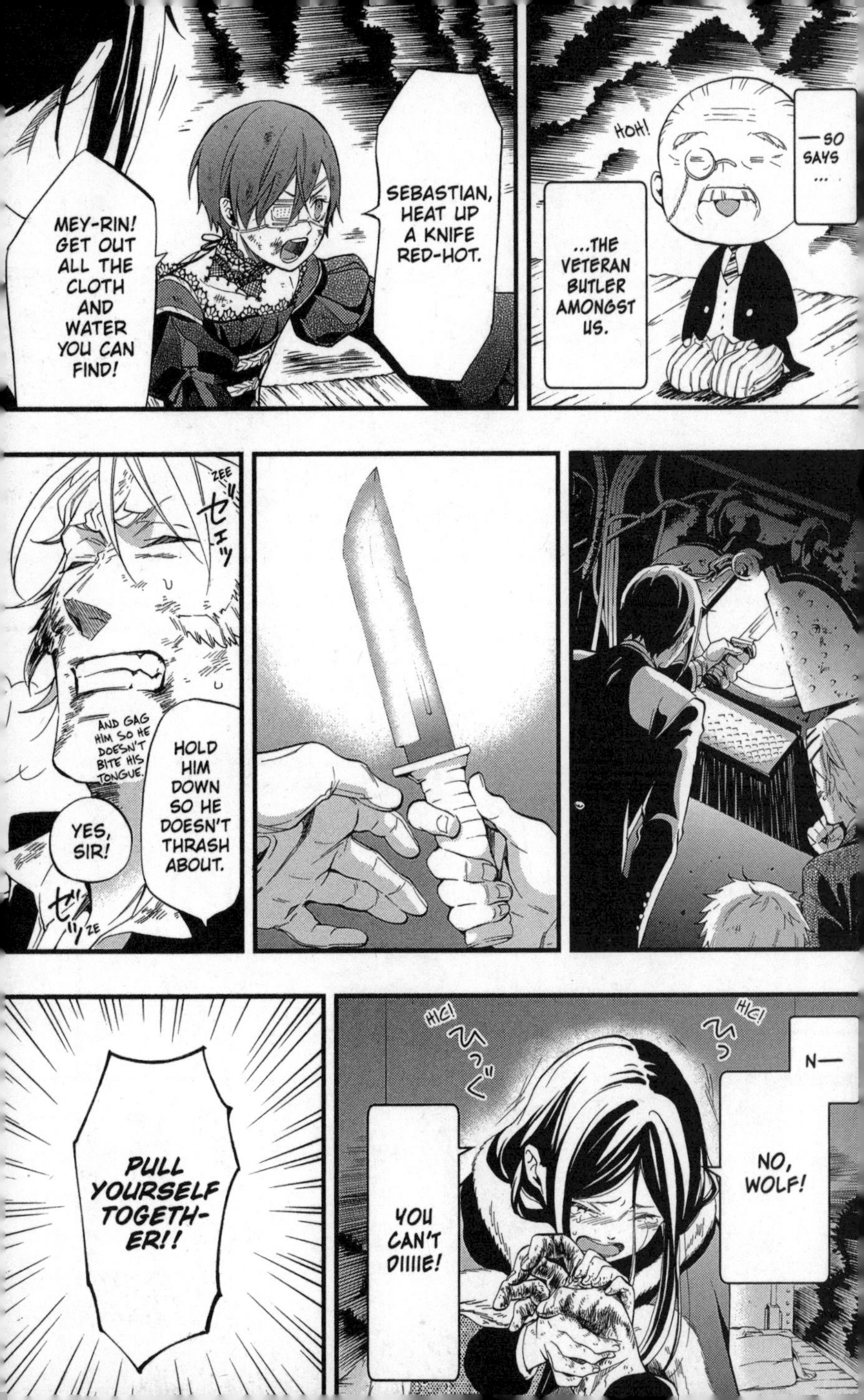
—SO SAYS ...
HOH!
...THE VETERAN BUTLER AMONGST US.
SEBASTIAN, HEAT UP A KNIFE RED-HOT.
MEY-RIN! GET OUT ALL THE CLOTH AND WATER YOU CAN FIND!
ZEE
HOLD HIM DOWN SO HE DOESN'T THRASH ABOUT.
AND GAG HIM SO HE DOESN'T BITE HIS TONGUE.
YES, SIR!
ZE
HIC!
HIC!
N—
NO, WOLF!
YOU CAN'T DIIIIE!
PULL YOURSELF TOGETH-ER!!

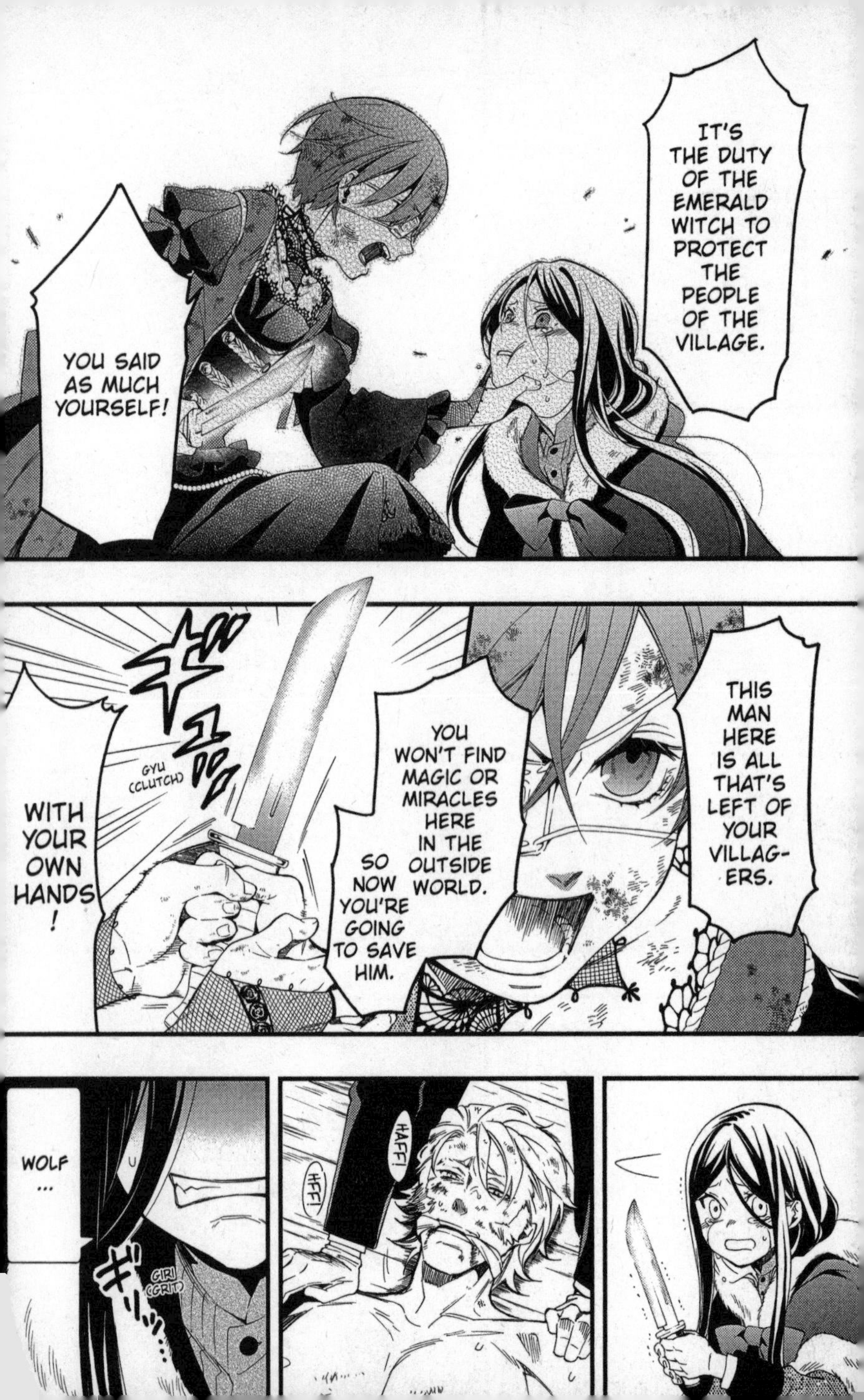
IT'S THE DUTY OF THE EMERALD WITCH TO PROTECT THE PEOPLE OF THE VILLAGE.
YOU SAID AS MUCH YOURSELF!
THIS MAN HERE IS ALL THAT'S LEFT OF YOUR VILLAG-ERS.
YOU WON'T FIND MAGIC OR MIRACLES HERE IN THE OUTSIDE WORLD.
SO NOW YOU'RE GOING TO SAVE HIM.
GYU (CLUTCH)
WITH YOUR OWN HANDS!
HAFF!
HFF!
WOLF ...
GIRI (GRIT)

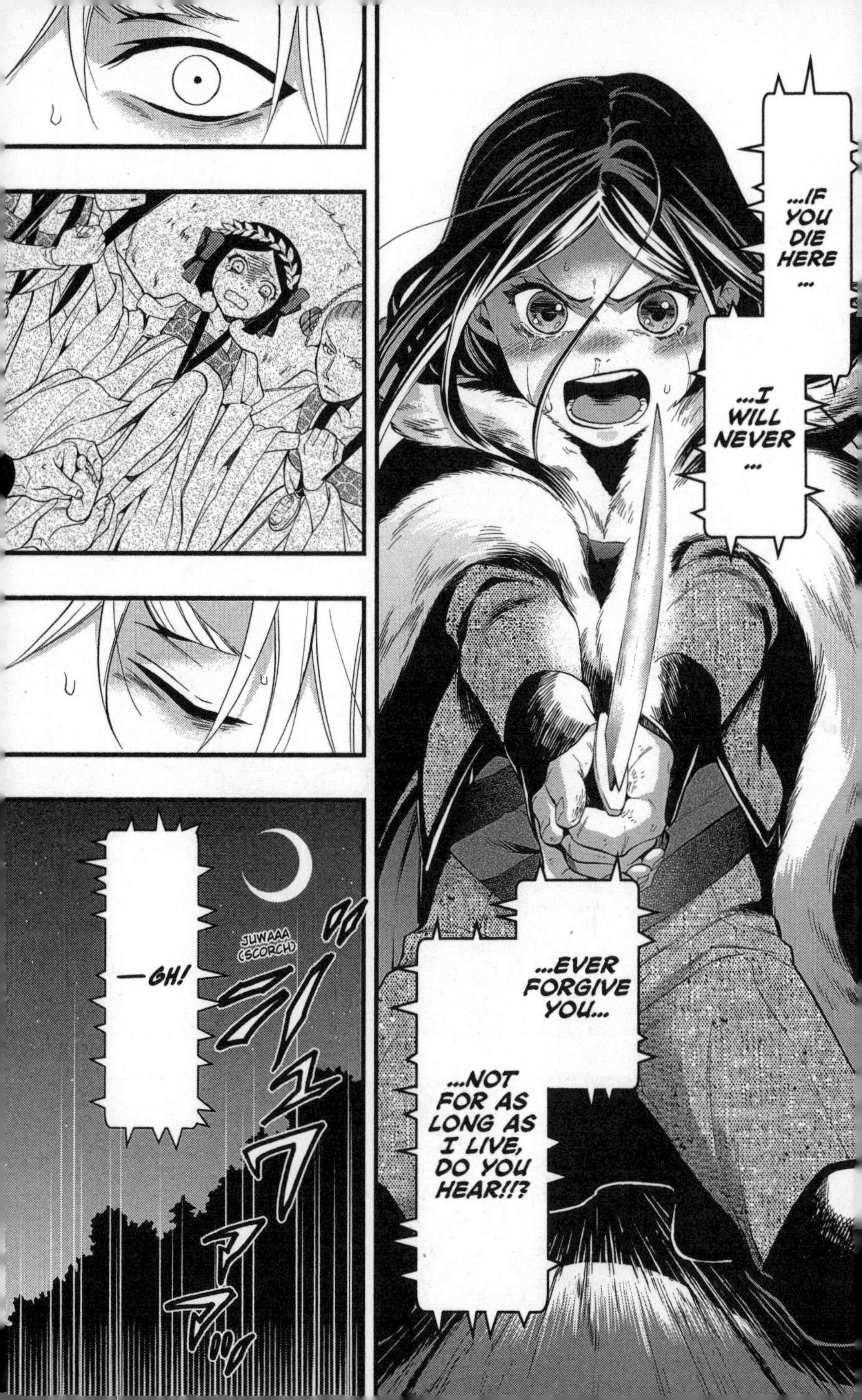
...IF YOU DIE HERE ...
...I WILL NEVER ...
...EVER FORGIVE YOU...
...NOT FOR AS LONG AS I LIVE, DO YOU HEAR!!?
—GH!
JUWAAA (SCORCH)

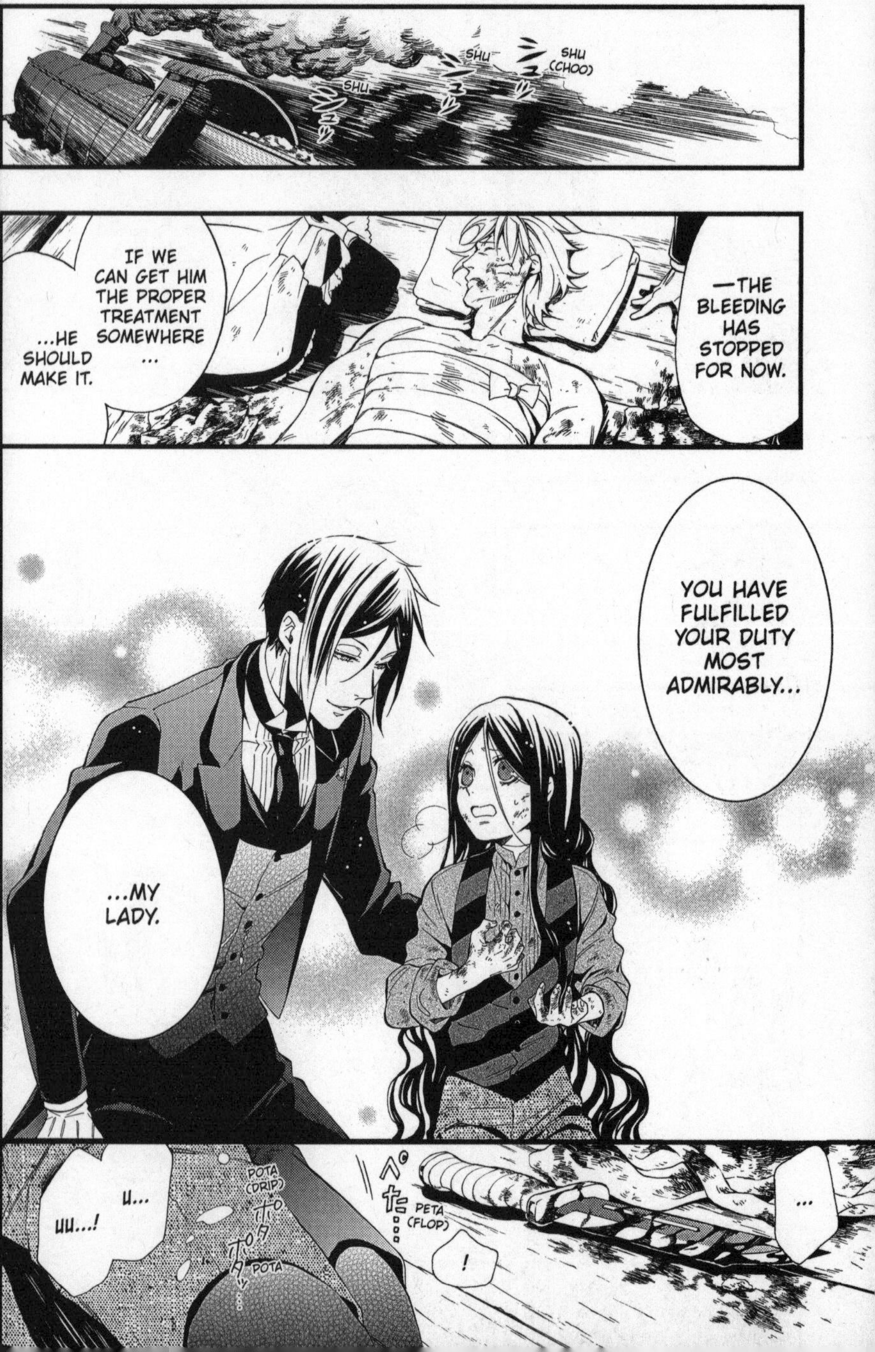
SHU (CHOO)
SHU
SHU
—THE BLEEDING HAS STOPPED FOR NOW.
IF WE CAN GET HIM THE PROPER TREATMENT SOMEWHERE ...
...HE SHOULD MAKE IT.
YOU HAVE FULFILLED YOUR DUTY MOST ADMIRABLY...
...MY LADY.
...
!
PETA (FLOP)
POTA (DRIP)
POTA
U...
UU...!

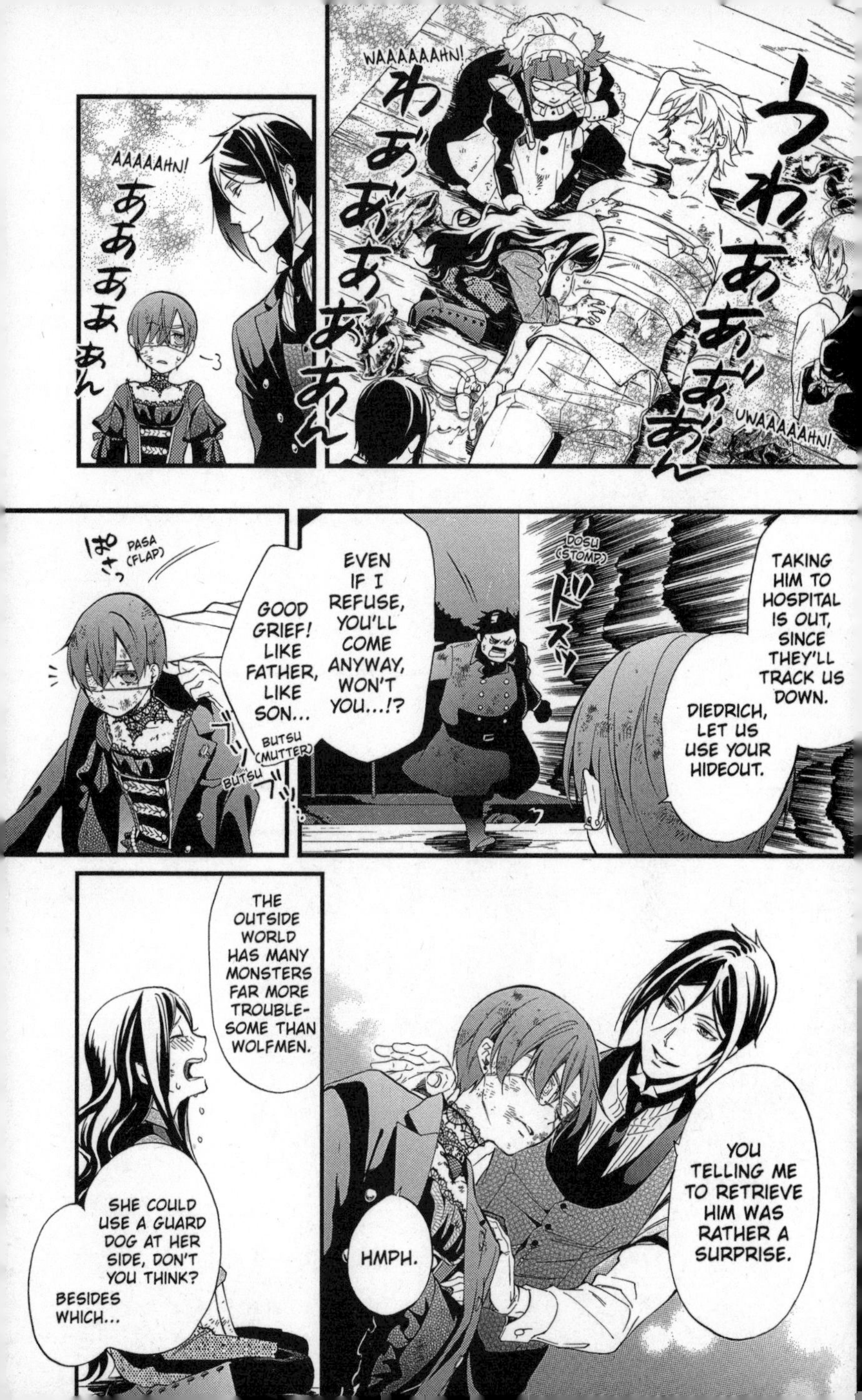
うわああ゛あ゛あん
UWAAAAAAHN!
わあ゛あ゛あああん
WAAAAAAHN!
ああああん
AAAAAHN!
TAKING HIM TO HOSPITAL IS OUT, SINCE THEY'LL TRACK US DOWN.
DIEDRICH, LET US USE YOUR HIDEOUT.
ドスッ
DOSU (STOMP)
EVEN IF I REFUSE, YOU'LL COME ANYWAY, WON'T YOU...!?
GOOD GRIEF! LIKE FATHER, LIKE SON...
ぱさっ
PASA (FLAP)
ブツ ブツ
BUTSU (MUTTER) BUTSU
YOU TELLING ME TO RETRIEVE HIM WAS RATHER A SURPRISE.
HMPH.
THE OUTSIDE WORLD HAS MANY MONSTERS FAR MORE TROUBLE-SOME THAN WOLFMEN.
SHE COULD USE A GUARD DOG AT HER SIDE, DON'T YOU THINK?
BESIDES WHICH...

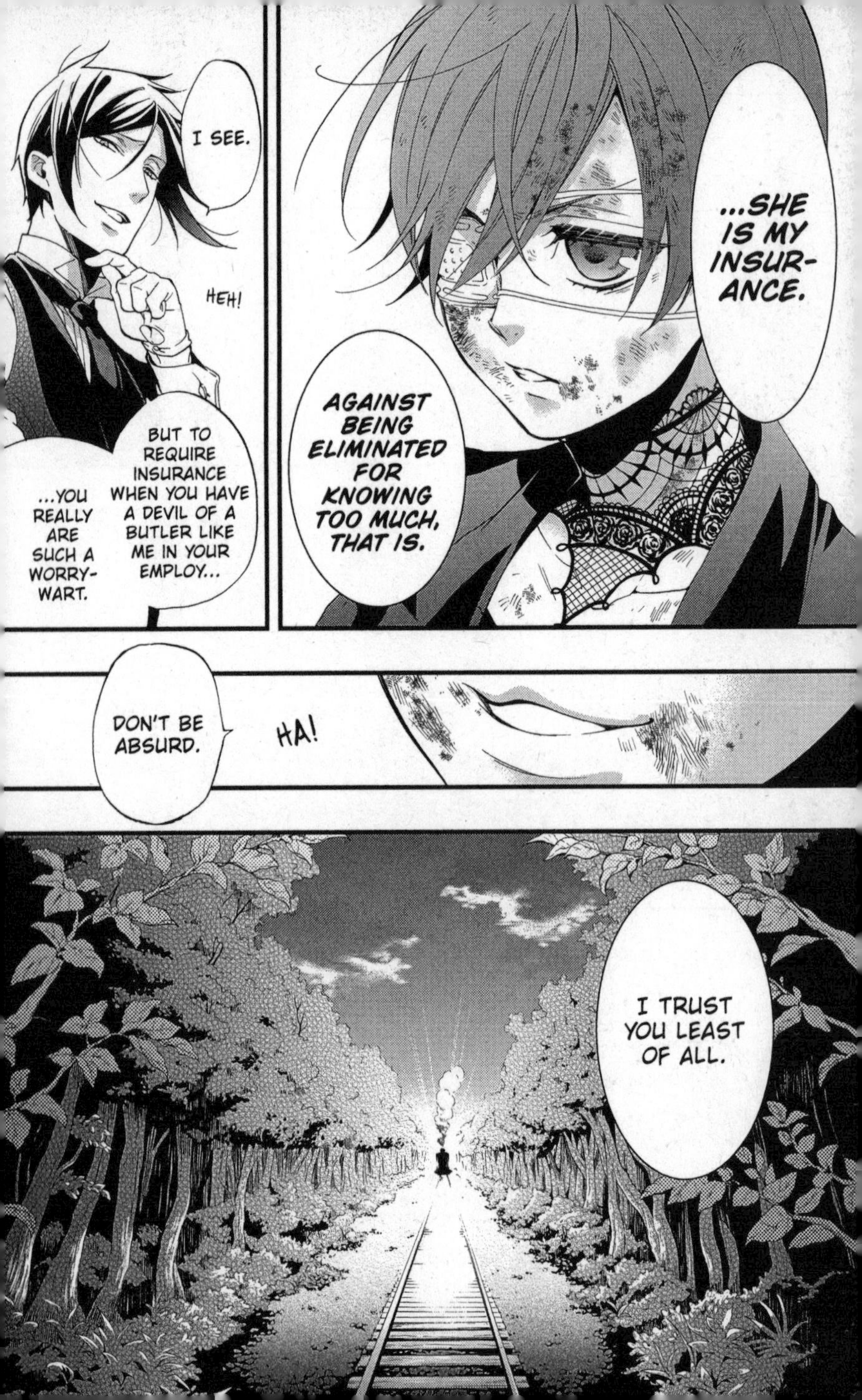
...SHE IS MY INSURANCE.
AGAINST BEING ELIMINATED FOR KNOWING TOO MUCH, THAT IS.
I SEE.
HEH!
BUT TO REQUIRE INSURANCE WHEN YOU HAVE A DEVIL OF A BUTLER LIKE ME IN YOUR EMPLOY...
...YOU REALLY ARE SUCH A WORRY-WART.
HA!
DON'T BE ABSURD.
I TRUST YOU LEAST OF ALL.

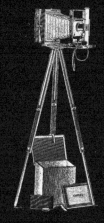

Black Butler

Chapter 105
At noon : The Butler, Dropping In

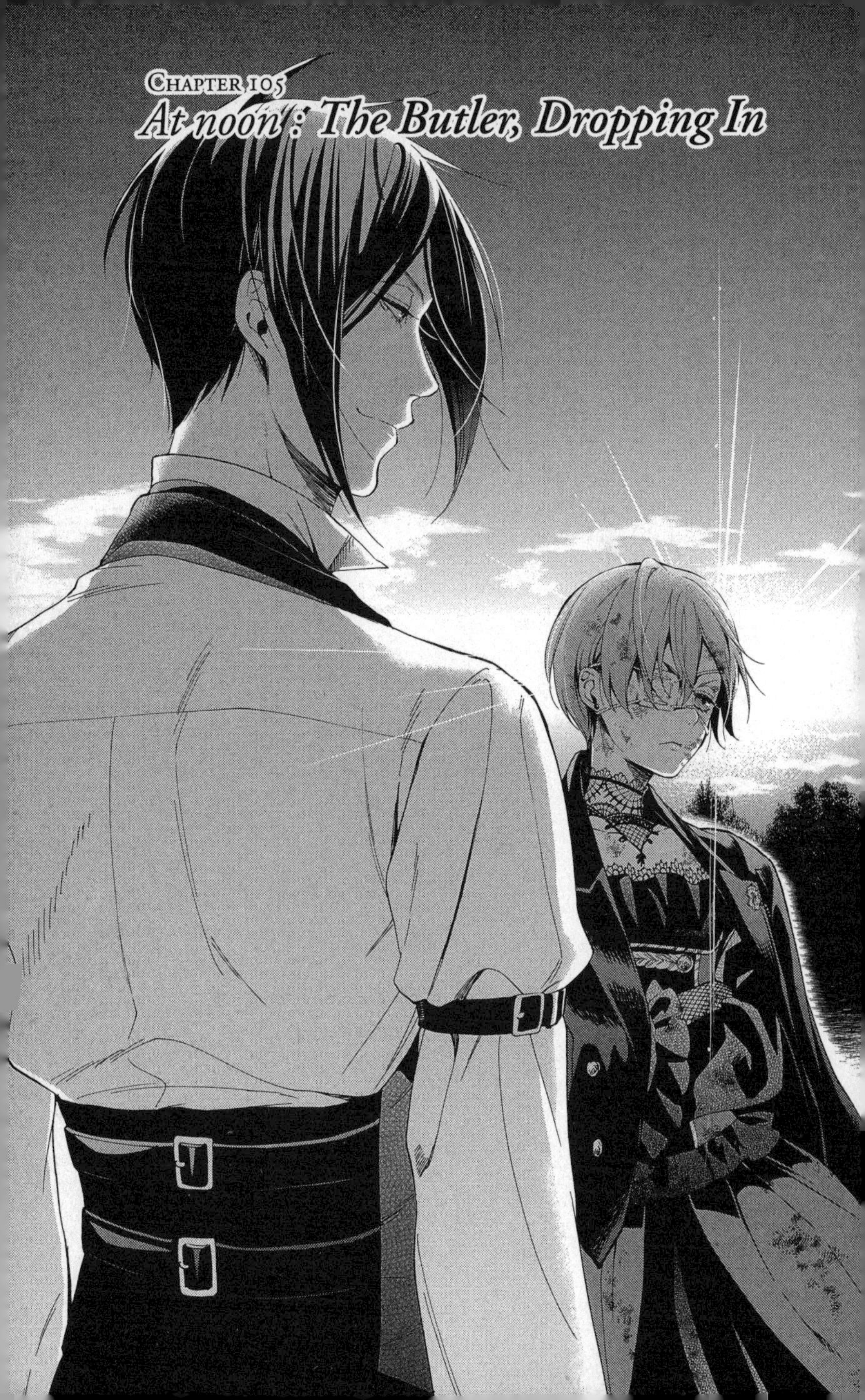

Black Butler

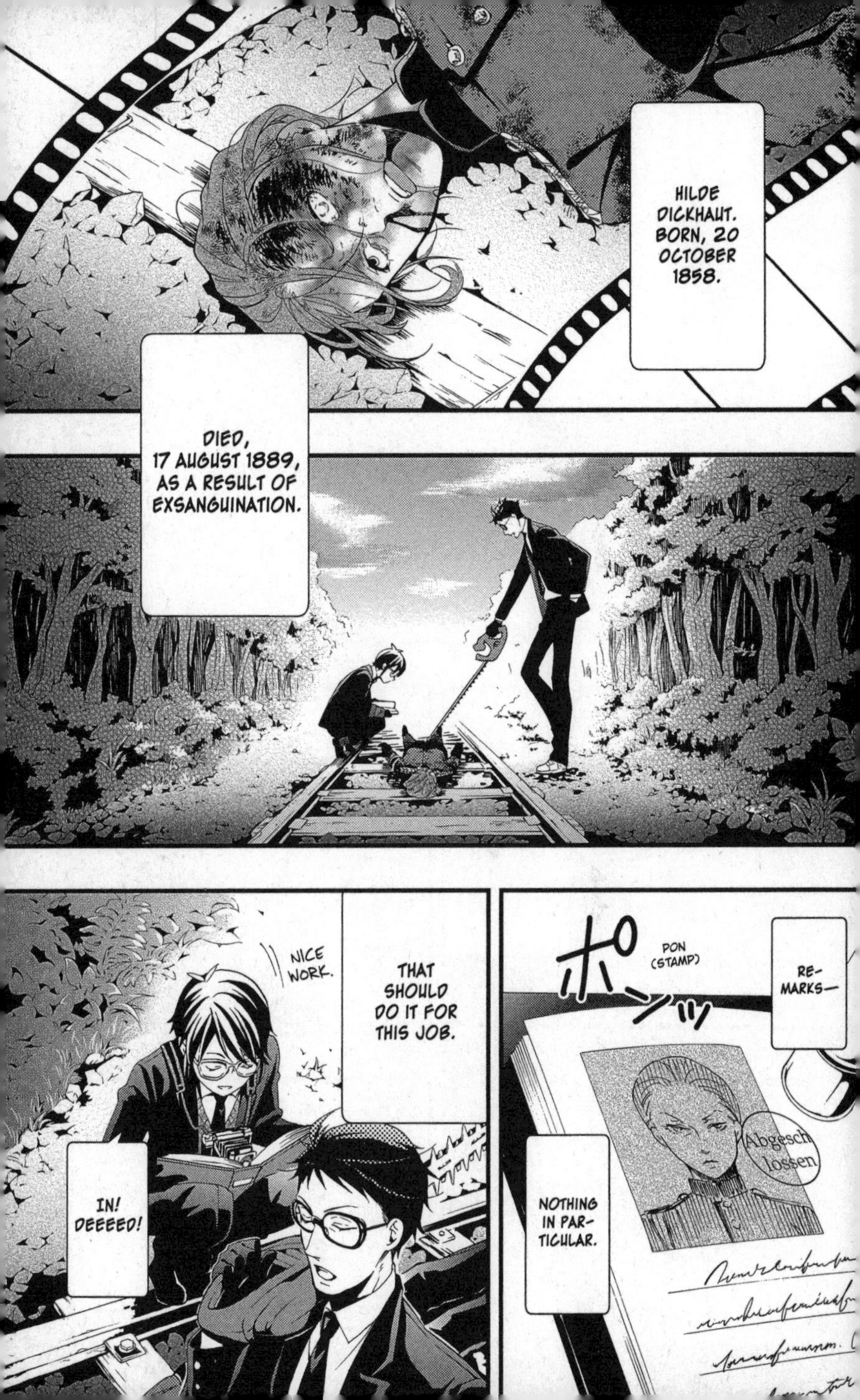
HILDE DICKHAUT. BORN, 20 OCTOBER 1858.
DIED, 17 AUGUST 1889, AS A RESULT OF EXSANGUINATION.
ポーッ
PON (STAMP)
RE-MARKS—
NOTHING IN PAR-TICULAR.
Abgeschlossen
THAT SHOULD DO IT FOR THIS JOB.
NICE WORK.
IN! DEEEED!

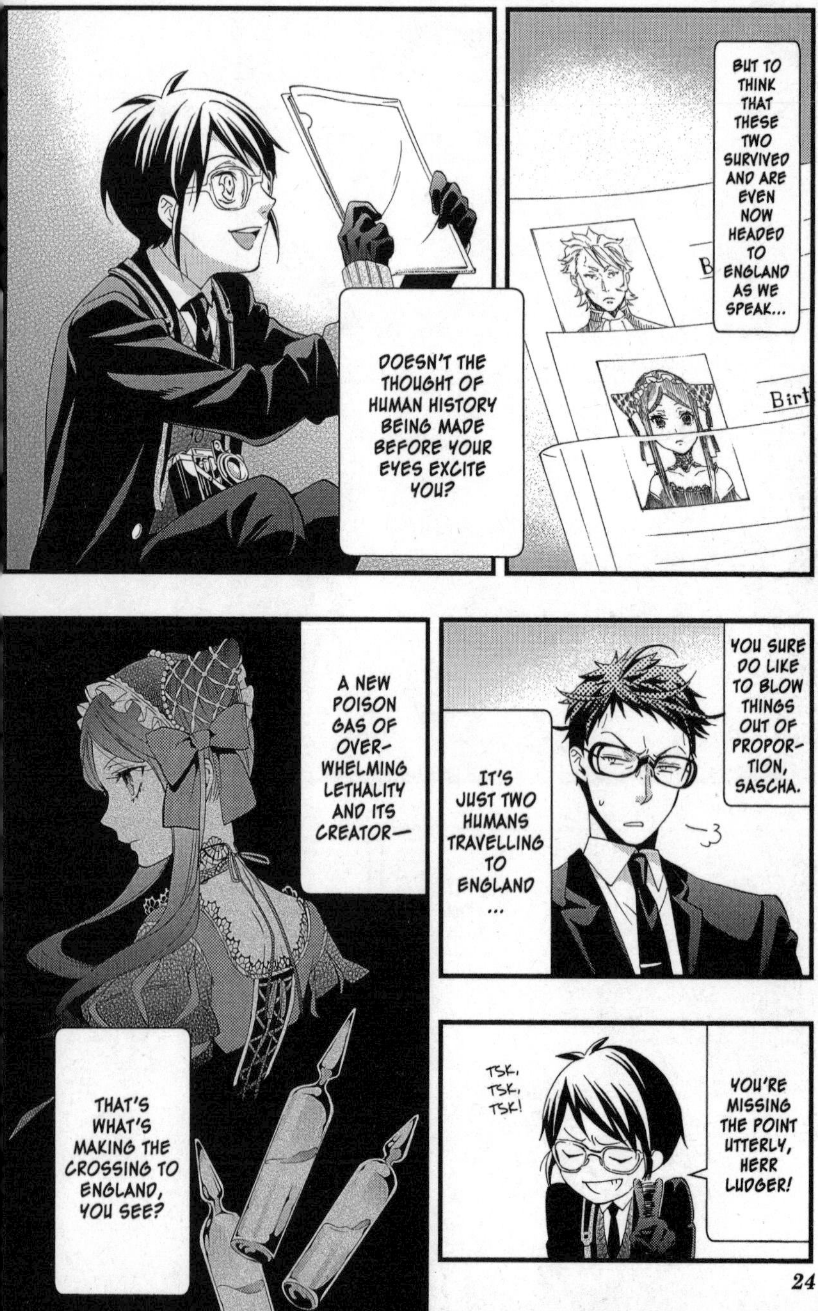
BUT TO THINK THAT THESE TWO SURVIVED AND ARE EVEN NOW HEADED TO ENGLAND AS WE SPEAK...
DOESN'T THE THOUGHT OF HUMAN HISTORY BEING MADE BEFORE YOUR EYES EXCITE YOU?
YOU SURE DO LIKE TO BLOW THINGS OUT OF PROPORTION, SASCHA.
IT'S JUST TWO HUMANS TRAVELLING TO ENGLAND ...
TSK, TSK, TSK!
YOU'RE MISSING THE POINT UTTERLY, HERR LUDGER!
A NEW POISON GAS OF OVERWHELMING LETHALITY AND ITS CREATOR—
THAT'S WHAT'S MAKING THE CROSSING TO ENGLAND, YOU SEE?

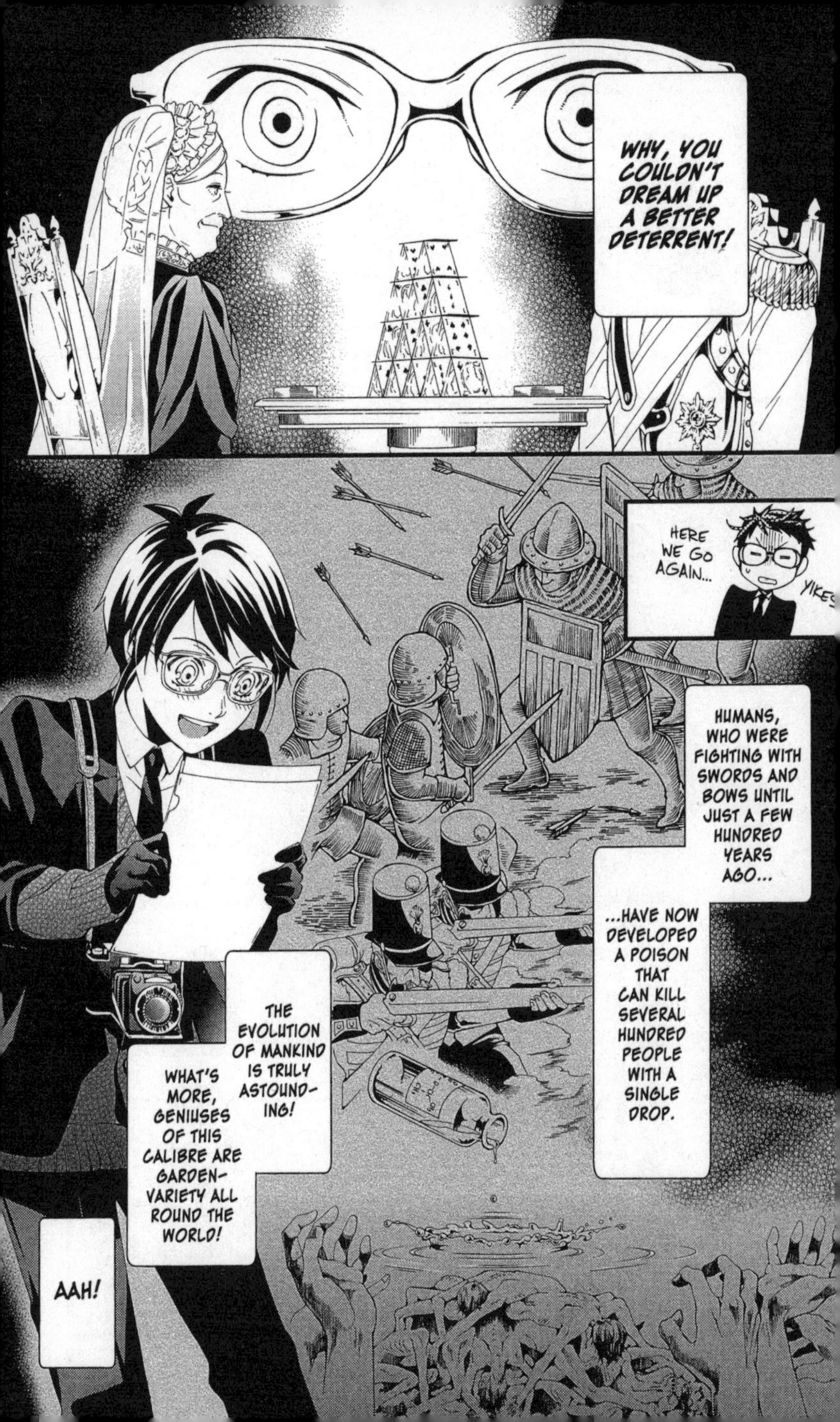
WHY, YOU COULDN'T DREAM UP A BETTER DETERRENT!
HERE WE GO AGAIN...
YIKES
HUMANS, WHO WERE FIGHTING WITH SWORDS AND BOWS UNTIL JUST A FEW HUNDRED YEARS AGO...
...HAVE NOW DEVELOPED A POISON THAT CAN KILL SEVERAL HUNDRED PEOPLE WITH A SINGLE DROP.
THE EVOLUTION OF MANKIND IS TRULY ASTOUND-ING!
WHAT'S MORE, GENIUSES OF THIS CALIBRE ARE GARDEN-VARIETY ALL ROUND THE WORLD!
AAH!

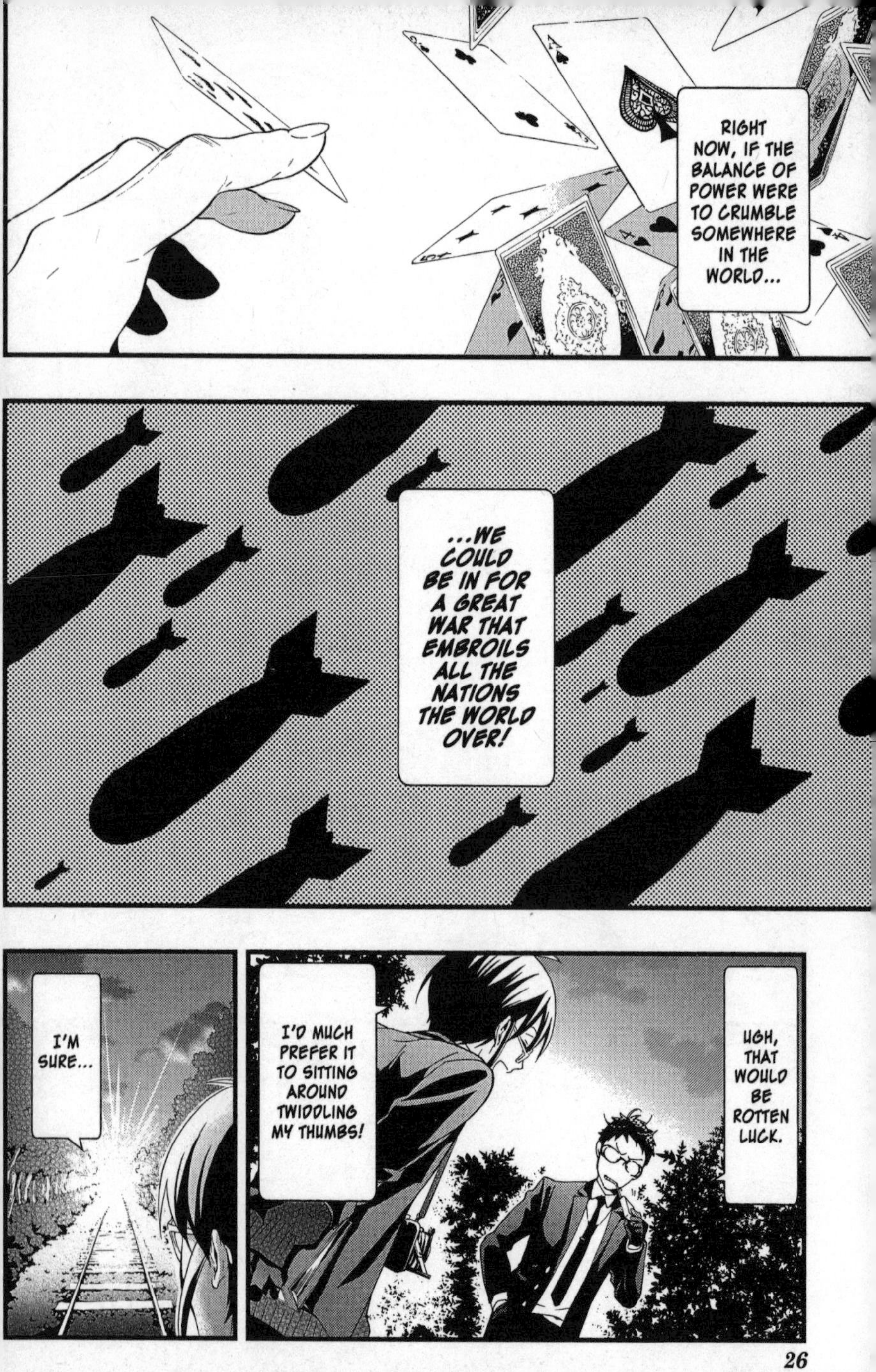
RIGHT NOW, IF THE BALANCE OF POWER WERE TO CRUMBLE SOMEWHERE IN THE WORLD...
...WE COULD BE IN FOR A GREAT WAR THAT EMBROILS ALL THE NATIONS THE WORLD OVER!
UGH, THAT WOULD BE ROTTEN LUCK.
I'D MUCH PREFER IT TO SITTING AROUND TWIDDLING MY THUMBS!
I'M SURE...

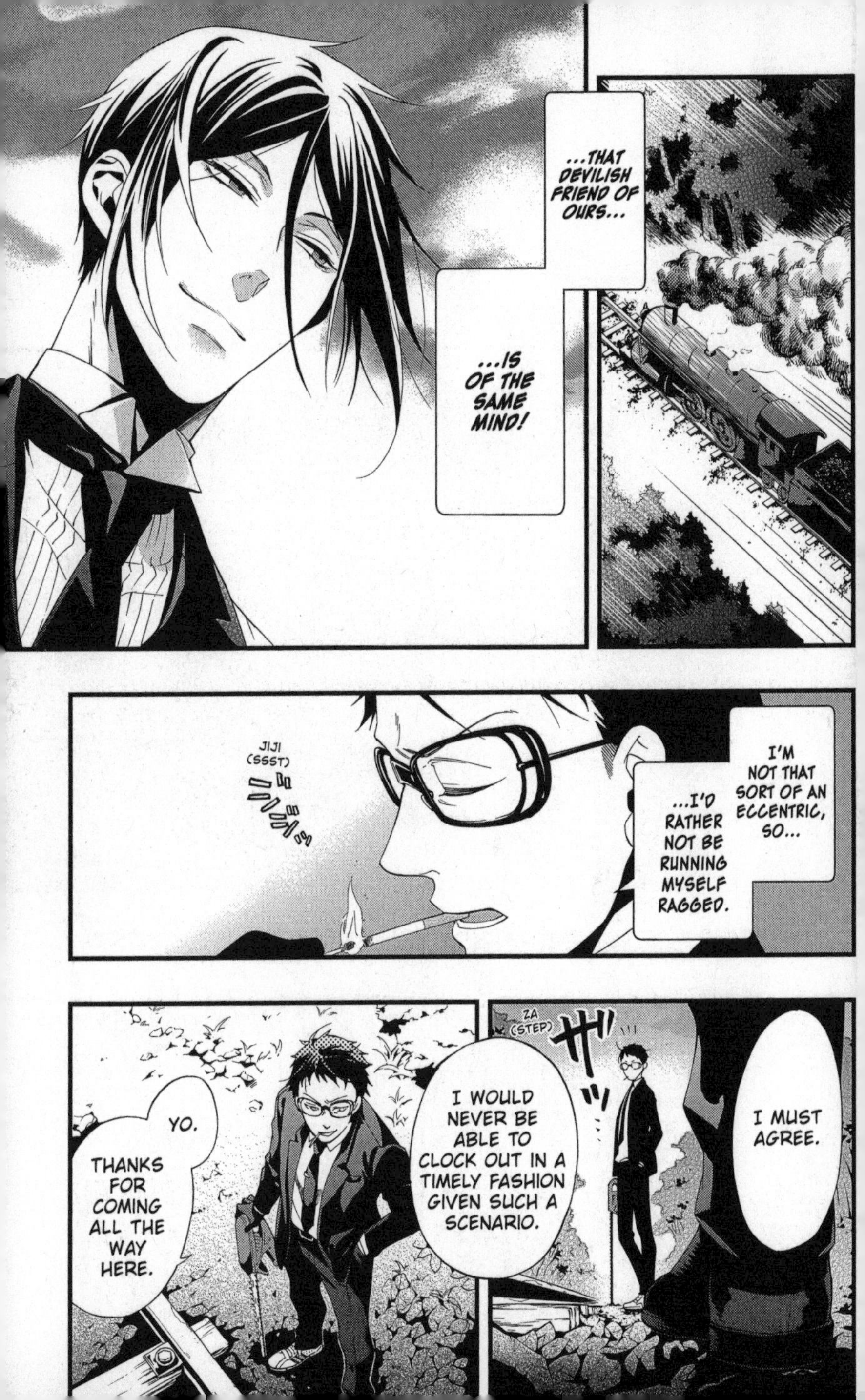
...THAT DEVILISH FRIEND OF OURS...
...IS OF THE SAME MIND!
I'M NOT THAT SORT OF AN ECCENTRIC, SO...
...I'D RATHER NOT BE RUNNING MYSELF RAGGED.
JIJI (SSST)
ZA (STEP)
I MUST AGREE.
I WOULD NEVER BE ABLE TO CLOCK OUT IN A TIMELY FASHION GIVEN SUCH A SCENARIO.
YO.
THANKS FOR COMING ALL THE WAY HERE.

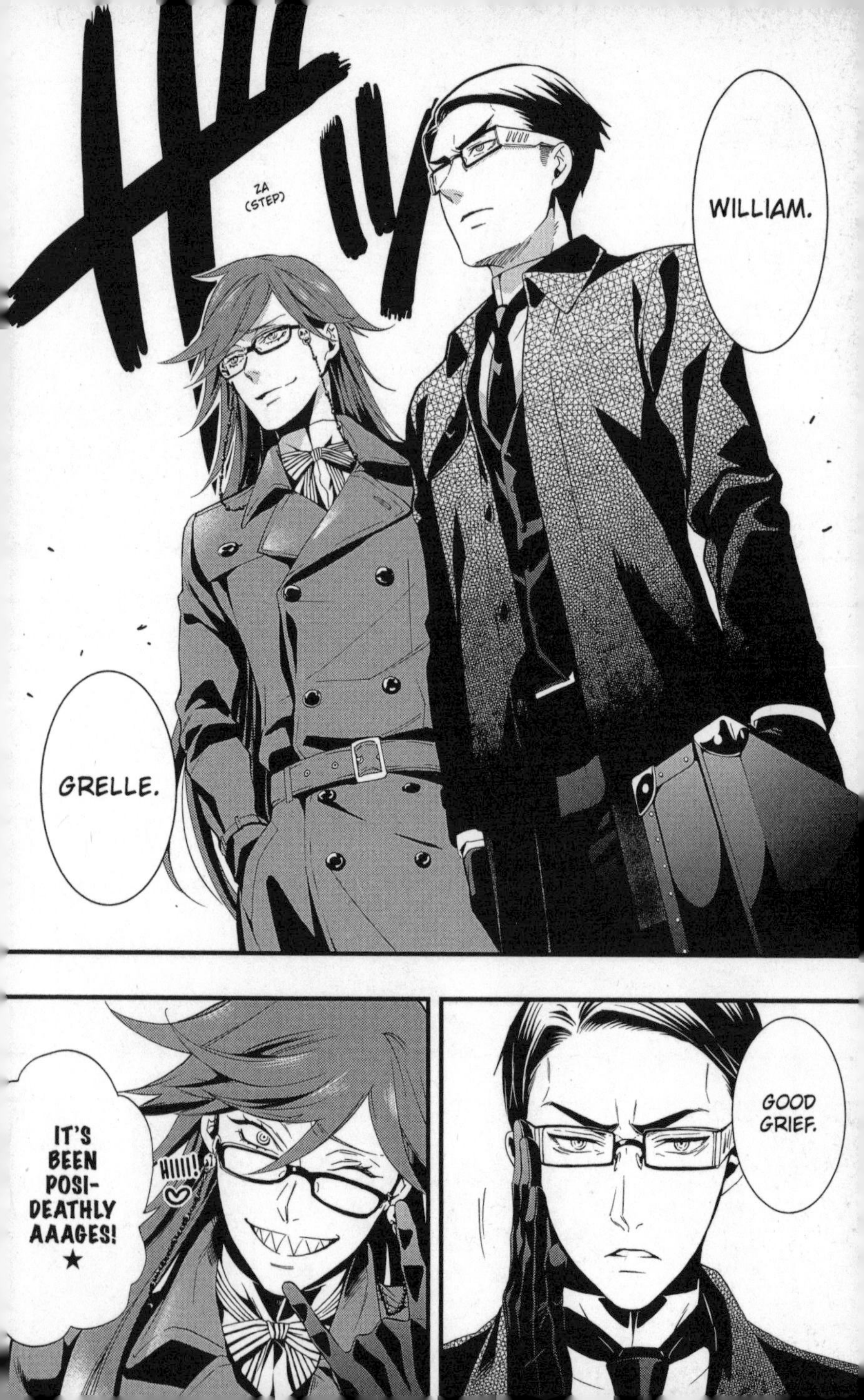
WILLIAM.
ZA (STEP)
GRELLE.
GOOD GRIEF.
HIIII! ♡
IT'S BEEN POSI-DEATHLY AAAGES! ★

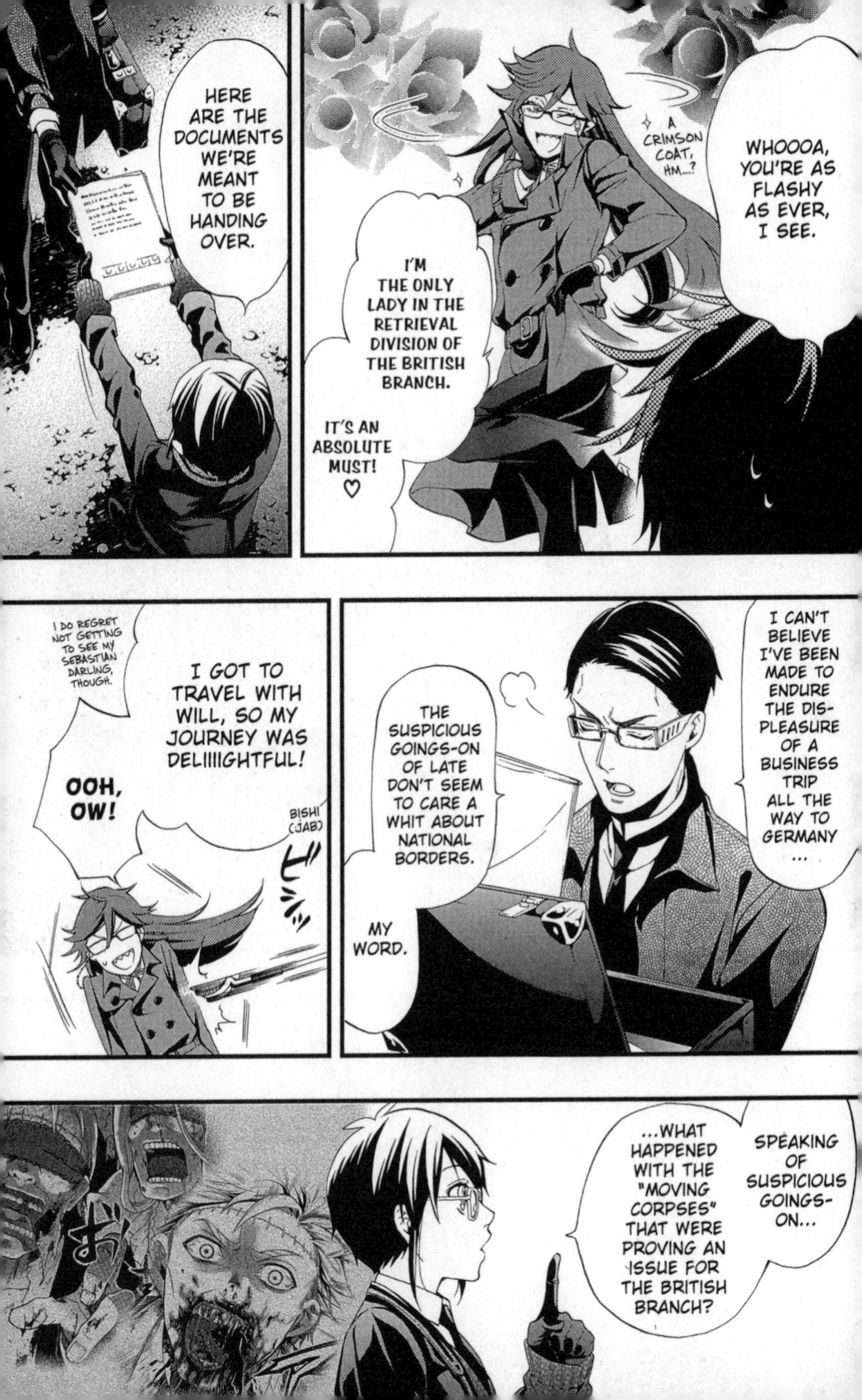
WHOOOA, YOU'RE AS FLASHY AS EVER, I SEE.
A CRIMSON COAT, HM...?
I'M THE ONLY LADY IN THE RETRIEVAL DIVISION OF THE BRITISH BRANCH.
IT'S AN ABSOLUTE MUST! ♡
HERE ARE THE DOCUMENTS WE'RE MEANT TO BE HANDING OVER.
I CAN'T BELIEVE I'VE BEEN MADE TO ENDURE THE DIS-PLEASURE OF A BUSINESS TRIP ALL THE WAY TO GERMANY...
THE SUSPICIOUS GOINGS-ON OF LATE DON'T SEEM TO CARE A WHIT ABOUT NATIONAL BORDERS.
MY WORD.
I GOT TO TRAVEL WITH WILL, SO MY JOURNEY WAS DELIIIIGHTFUL!
I DO REGRET NOT GETTING TO SEE MY SEBASTIAN DARLING, THOUGH.
BISHI (JAB)
OOH, OW!
SPEAKING OF SUSPICIOUS GOINGS-ON...
...WHAT HAPPENED WITH THE "MOVING CORPSES" THAT WERE PROVING AN ISSUE FOR THE BRITISH BRANCH?

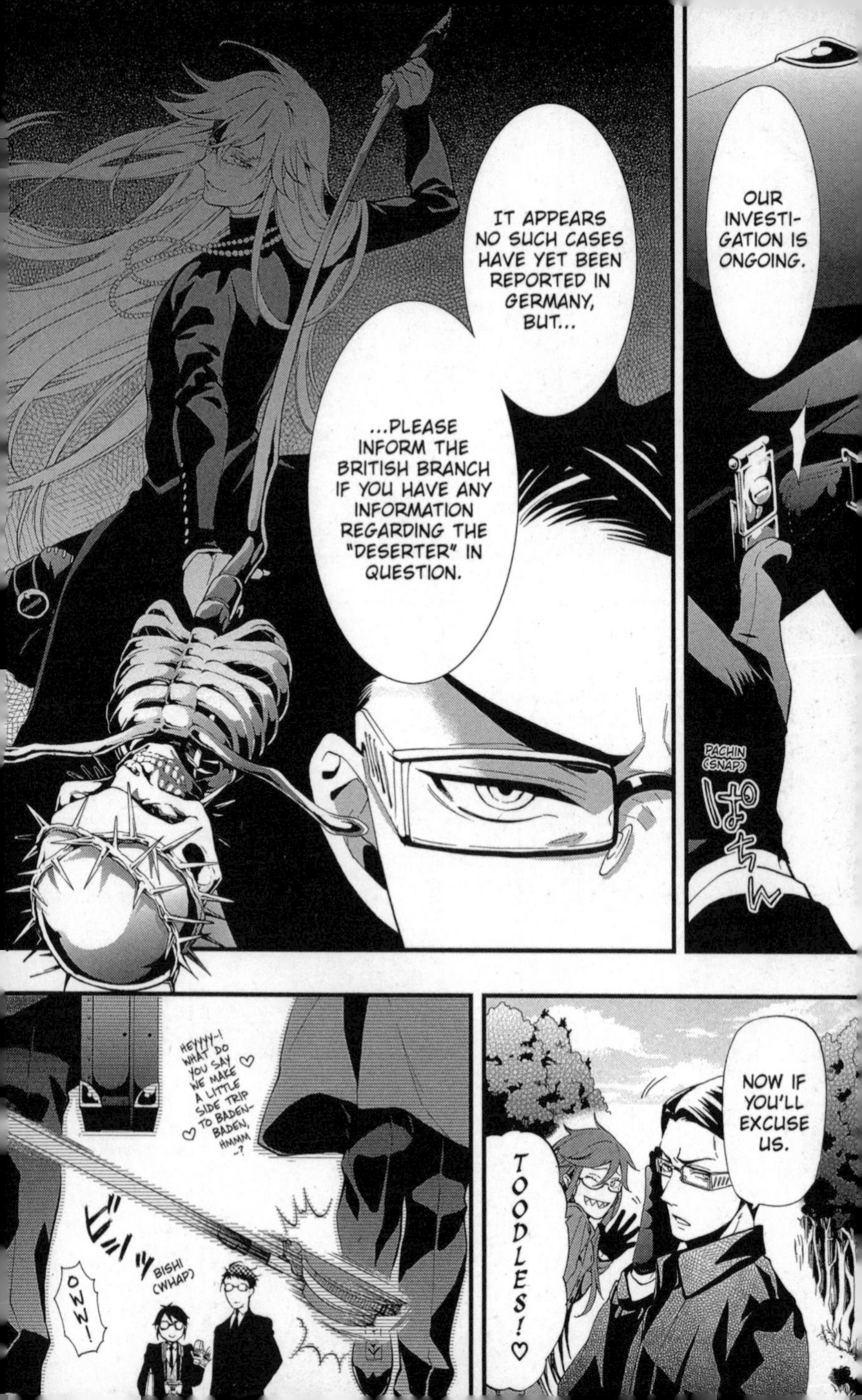
OUR INVESTIGATION IS ONGOING.
PACHIN (SNAP)
ぱちん
IT APPEARS NO SUCH CASES HAVE YET BEEN REPORTED IN GERMANY, BUT...
...PLEASE INFORM THE BRITISH BRANCH IF YOU HAVE ANY INFORMATION REGARDING THE "DESERTER" IN QUESTION.
NOW IF YOU'LL EXCUSE US.
TOODLES!♡
HEYYYY-! WHAT DO YOU SAY WE MAKE A LITTLE SIDE TRIP TO BADEN-BADEN, HMMM-? ♡
ビシッ
BISHI (WHAP)
OWW!

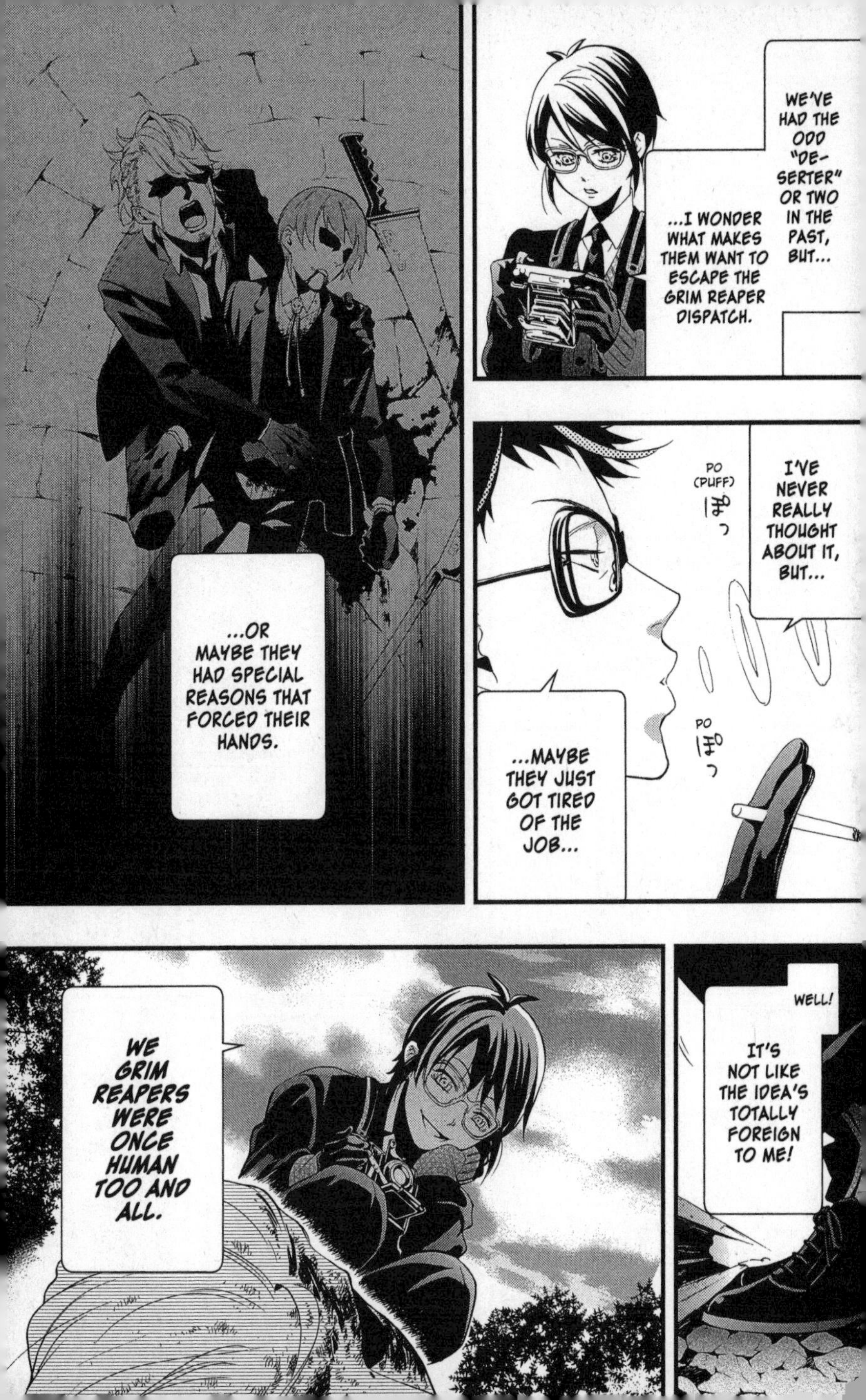
WE'VE HAD THE ODD "DE-SERTER" OR TWO IN THE PAST, BUT...
...I WONDER WHAT MAKES THEM WANT TO ESCAPE THE GRIM REAPER DISPATCH.
I'VE NEVER REALLY THOUGHT ABOUT IT, BUT...
PO (PUFF) ぽっ
PO ぽっ
...MAYBE THEY JUST GOT TIRED OF THE JOB...
...OR MAYBE THEY HAD SPECIAL REASONS THAT FORCED THEIR HANDS.
WELL!
IT'S NOT LIKE THE IDEA'S TOTALLY FOREIGN TO ME!
WE GRIM REAPERS WERE ONCE HUMAN TOO AND ALL.

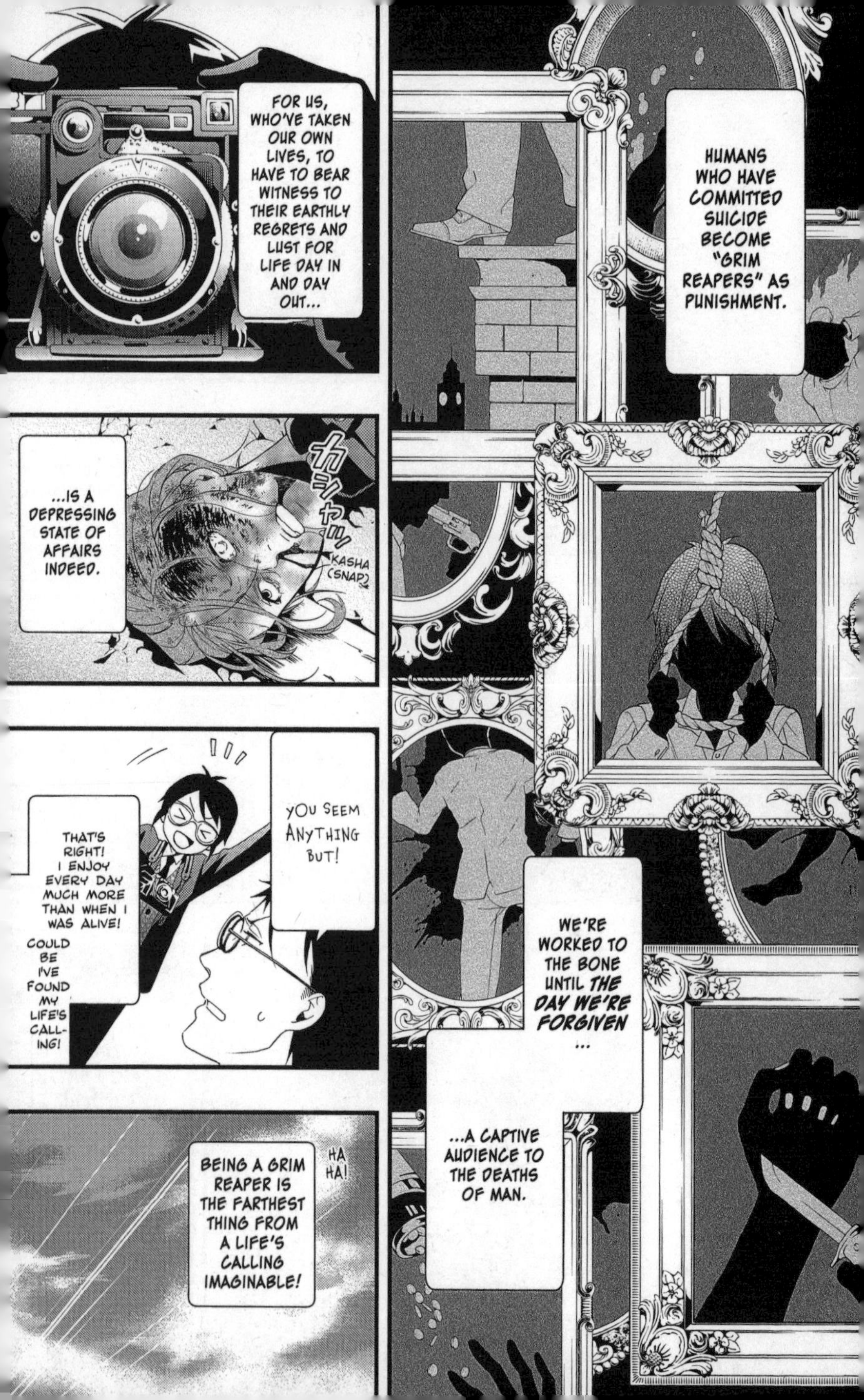
HUMANS WHO HAVE COMMITTED SUICIDE BECOME "GRIM REAPERS" AS PUNISHMENT.
WE'RE WORKED TO THE BONE UNTIL *THE DAY WE'RE FORGIVEN*...
...A CAPTIVE AUDIENCE TO THE DEATHS OF MAN.
FOR US, WHO'VE TAKEN OUR OWN LIVES, TO HAVE TO BEAR WITNESS TO THEIR EARTHLY REGRETS AND LUST FOR LIFE DAY IN AND DAY OUT...
KASHA (SNAP)
...IS A DEPRESSING STATE OF AFFAIRS INDEED.
YOU SEEM ANYTHING BUT!
THAT'S RIGHT! I ENJOY EVERY DAY MUCH MORE THAN WHEN I WAS ALIVE!
COULD BE I'VE FOUND MY LIFE'S CALL-ING!
HA HA!
BEING A GRIM REAPER IS THE FARTHEST THING FROM A LIFE'S CALLING IMAGINABLE!

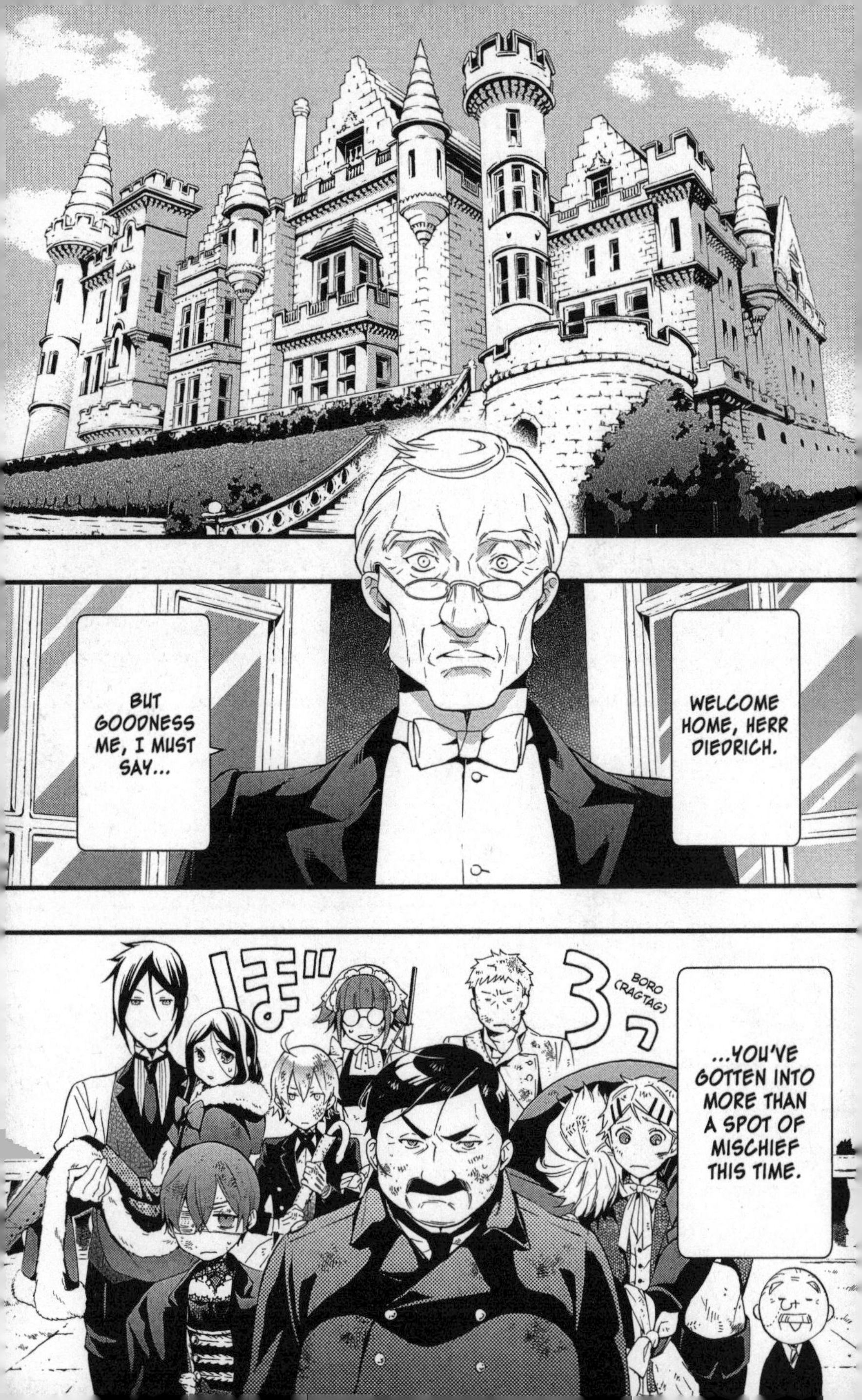
WELCOME HOME, HERR DIEDRICH.
BUT GOODNESS ME, I MUST SAY...
...YOU'VE GOTTEN INTO MORE THAN A SPOT OF MISCHIEF THIS TIME.
BORO (RAGTAG)
ぼろっ

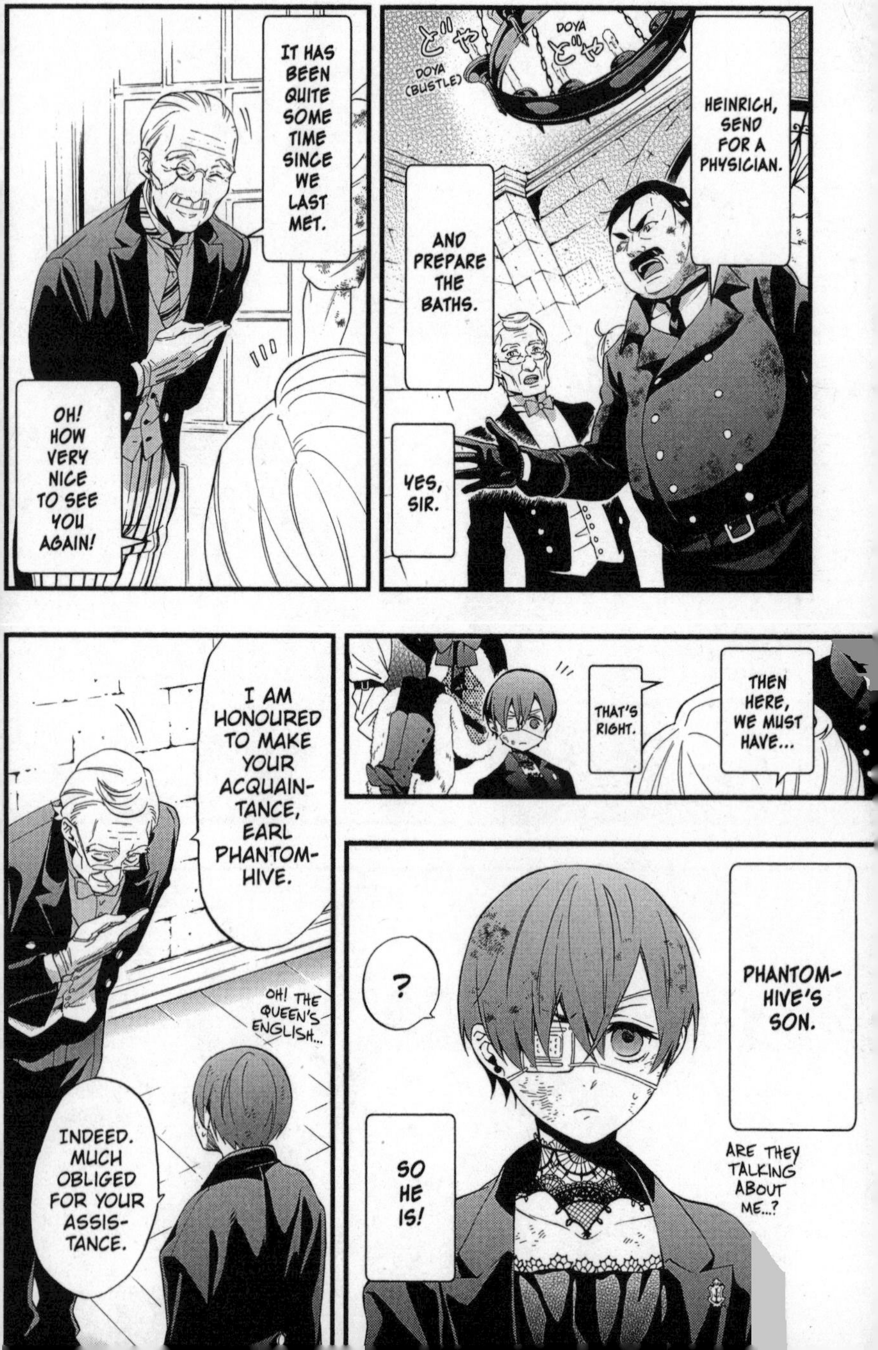
どや
DOYA (BUSTLE)
どや
DOYA
HEINRICH, SEND FOR A PHYSICIAN.
AND PREPARE THE BATHS.
YES, SIR.
IT HAS BEEN QUITE SOME TIME SINCE WE LAST MET.
OH! HOW VERY NICE TO SEE YOU AGAIN!
THEN HERE, WE MUST HAVE...
THAT'S RIGHT.
PHANTOM-HIVE'S SON.
ARE THEY TALKING ABOUT ME...?
?
SO HE IS!
I AM HONOURED TO MAKE YOUR ACQUAIN-TANCE, EARL PHANTOM-HIVE.
OH! THE QUEEN'S ENGLISH...
INDEED. MUCH OBLIGED FOR YOUR ASSIS-TANCE.

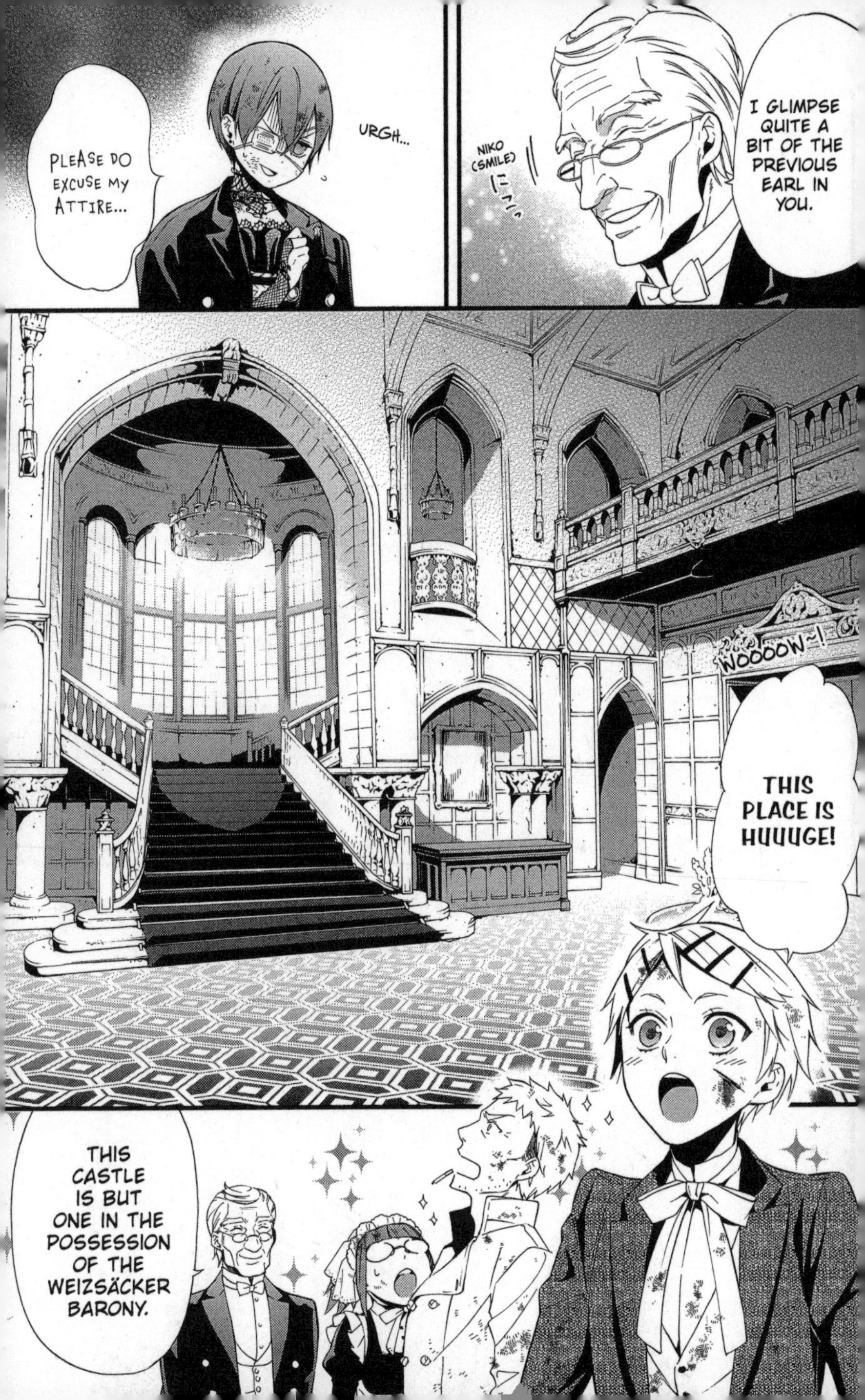
I GLIMPSE QUITE A BIT OF THE PREVIOUS EARL IN YOU.
NIKO (SMILE)
URGH...
PLEASE DO EXCUSE MY ATTIRE...
WOOOOW~!
THIS PLACE IS HUUUGE!
THIS CASTLE IS BUT ONE IN THE POSSESSION OF THE WEIZSÄCKER BARONY.

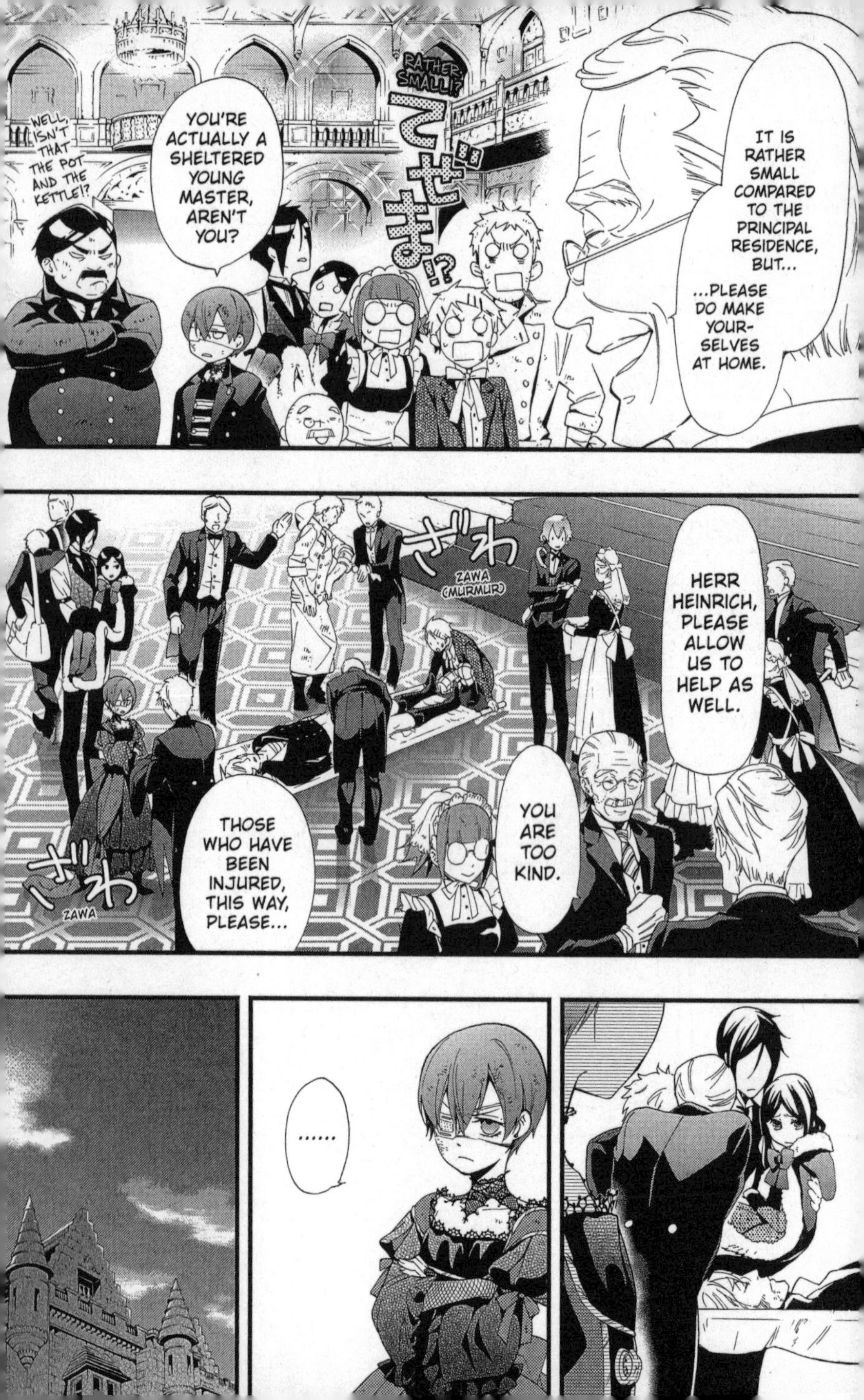
IT IS RATHER SMALL COMPARED TO THE PRINCIPAL RESIDENCE, BUT...
...PLEASE DO MAKE YOURSELVES AT HOME.
RATHER SMALL!?
てぜま!?
YOU'RE ACTUALLY A SHELTERED YOUNG MASTER, AREN'T YOU?
WELL, ISN'T THAT THE POT AND THE KETTLE!?
HERR HEINRICH, PLEASE ALLOW US TO HELP AS WELL.
ざわ
ZAWA (MURMUR)
YOU ARE TOO KIND.
THOSE WHO HAVE BEEN INJURED, THIS WAY, PLEASE...
ざわ
ZAWA
......

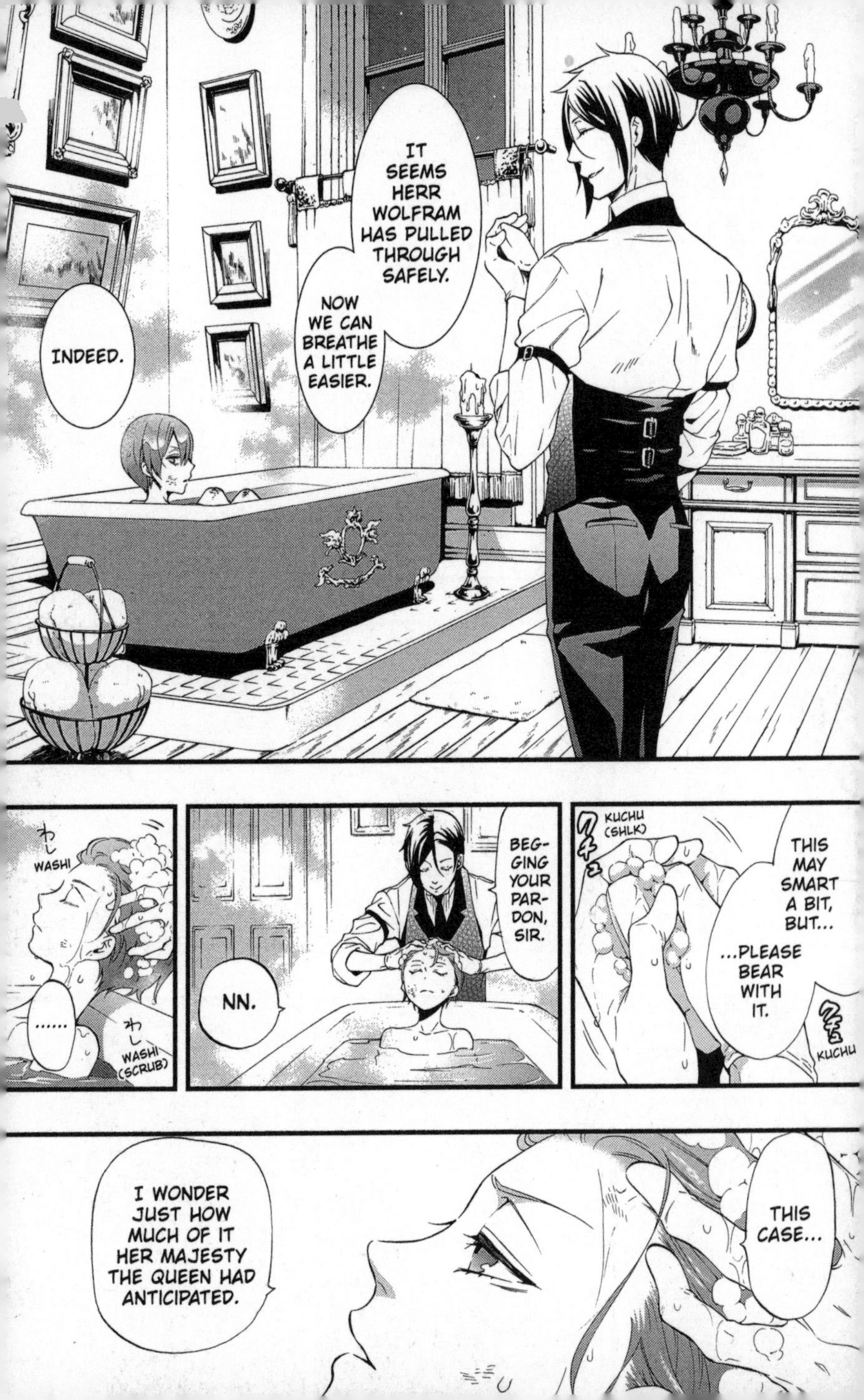
IT SEEMS HERR WOLFRAM HAS PULLED THROUGH SAFELY.
NOW WE CAN BREATHE A LITTLE EASIER.
INDEED.
KUCHU (SHLK)
THIS MAY SMART A BIT, BUT...
...PLEASE BEAR WITH IT.
KUCHU
BEG-GING YOUR PAR-DON, SIR.
NN.
わし
WASHI
......
わし
WASHI (SCRUB)
THIS CASE...
I WONDER JUST HOW MUCH OF IT HER MAJESTY THE QUEEN HAD ANTICIPATED.

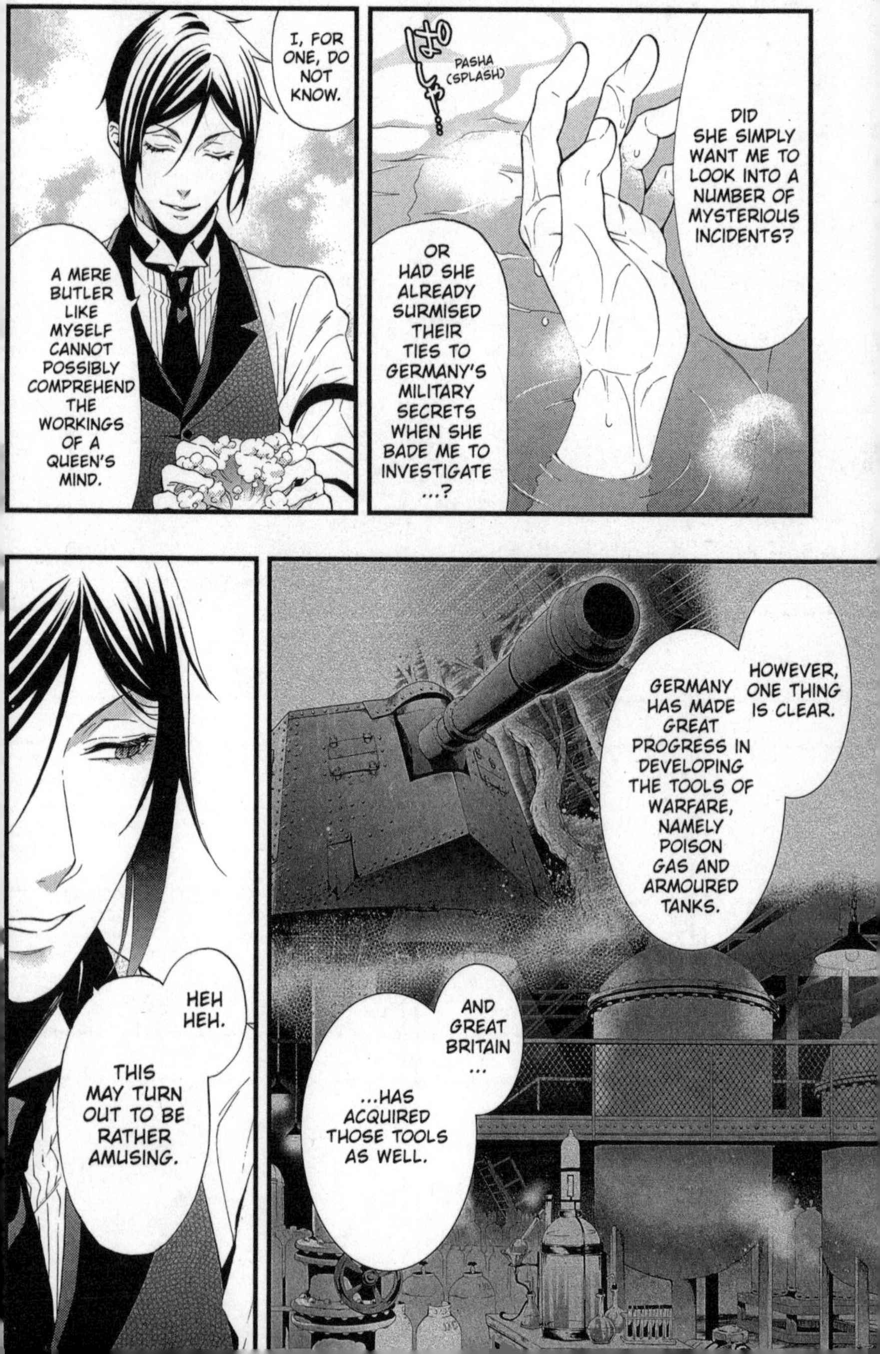
ぱしゃ…
PASHA (SPLASH)
DID SHE SIMPLY WANT ME TO LOOK INTO A NUMBER OF MYSTERIOUS INCIDENTS?
OR HAD SHE ALREADY SURMISED THEIR TIES TO GERMANY'S MILITARY SECRETS WHEN SHE BADE ME TO INVESTIGATE ...?
I, FOR ONE, DO NOT KNOW.
A MERE BUTLER LIKE MYSELF CANNOT POSSIBLY COMPREHEND THE WORKINGS OF A QUEEN'S MIND.
HOWEVER, ONE THING IS CLEAR.
GERMANY HAS MADE GREAT PROGRESS IN DEVELOPING THE TOOLS OF WARFARE, NAMELY POISON GAS AND ARMOURED TANKS.
AND GREAT BRITAIN ...
...HAS ACQUIRED THOSE TOOLS AS WELL.
HEH HEH.
THIS MAY TURN OUT TO BE RATHER AMUSING.

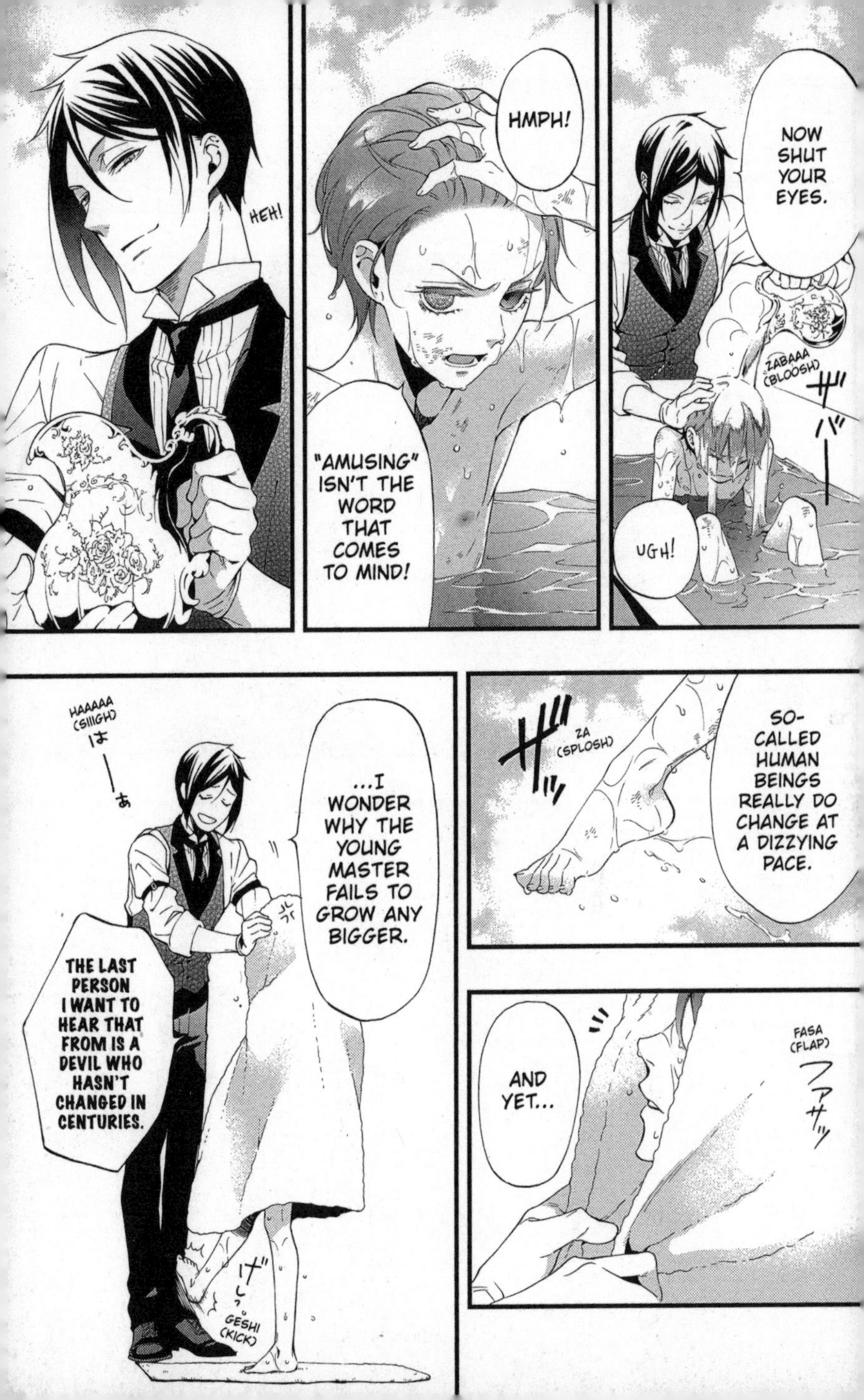
NOW SHUT YOUR EYES.
ZABAAA (BLOOSH)
ザバー
UGH!
HMPH!
"AMUSING" ISN'T THE WORD THAT COMES TO MIND!
HEH!
SO-CALLED HUMAN BEINGS REALLY DO CHANGE AT A DIZZYING PACE.
ZA (SPLOSH)
ザッ
AND YET...
FASA (FLAP)
ファサッ
...I WONDER WHY THE YOUNG MASTER FAILS TO GROW ANY BIGGER.
HAAAAA (SIIIGH)
はーあ
THE LAST PERSON I WANT TO HEAR THAT FROM IS A DEVIL WHO HASN'T CHANGED IN CENTURIES.
げしっ
GESHI (KICK)

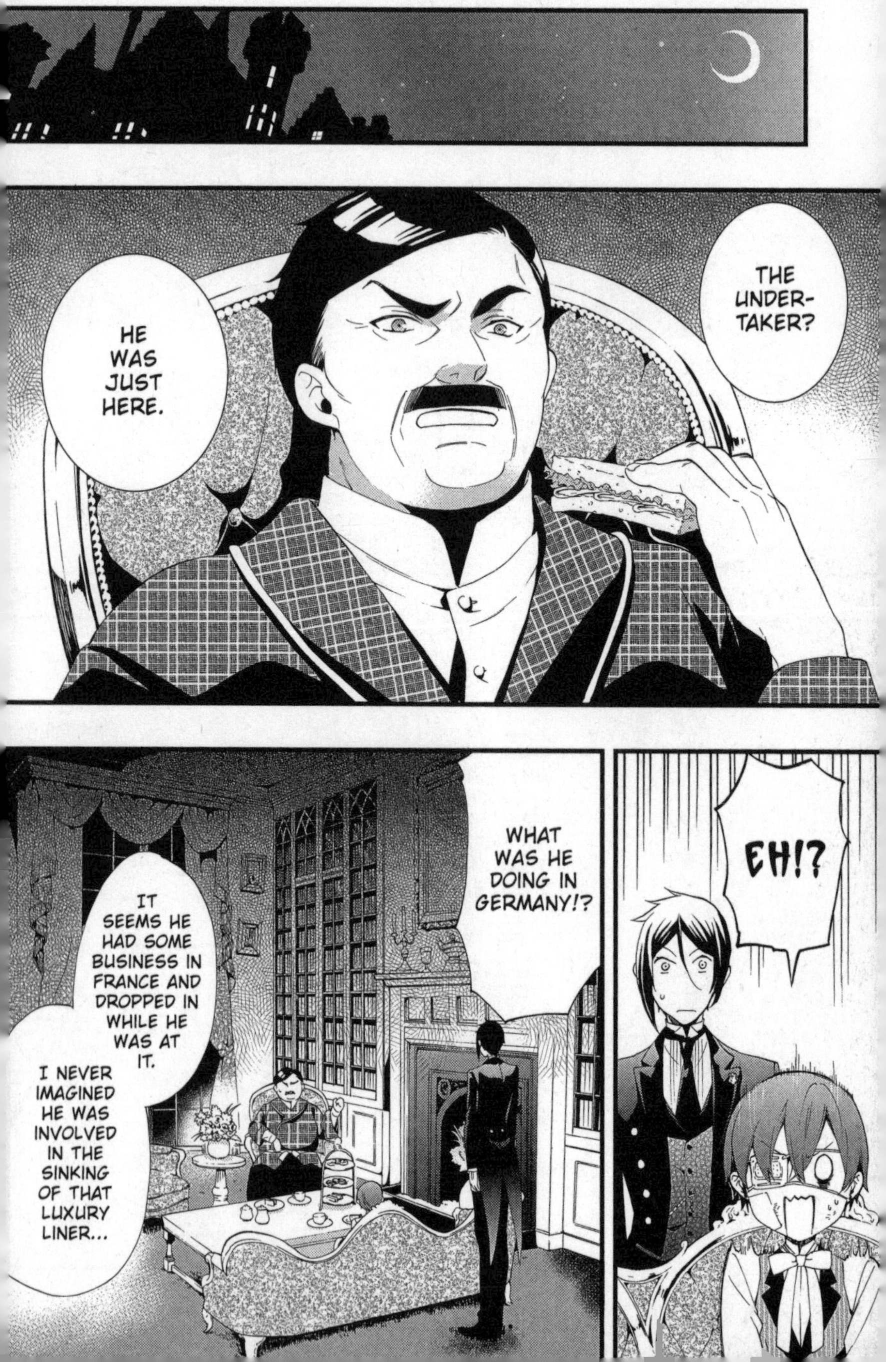
THE UNDER-TAKER?
HE WAS JUST HERE.
EH!?
WHAT WAS HE DOING IN GERMANY!?
IT SEEMS HE HAD SOME BUSINESS IN FRANCE AND DROPPED IN WHILE HE WAS AT IT.
I NEVER IMAGINED HE WAS INVOLVED IN THE SINKING OF THAT LUXURY LINER...

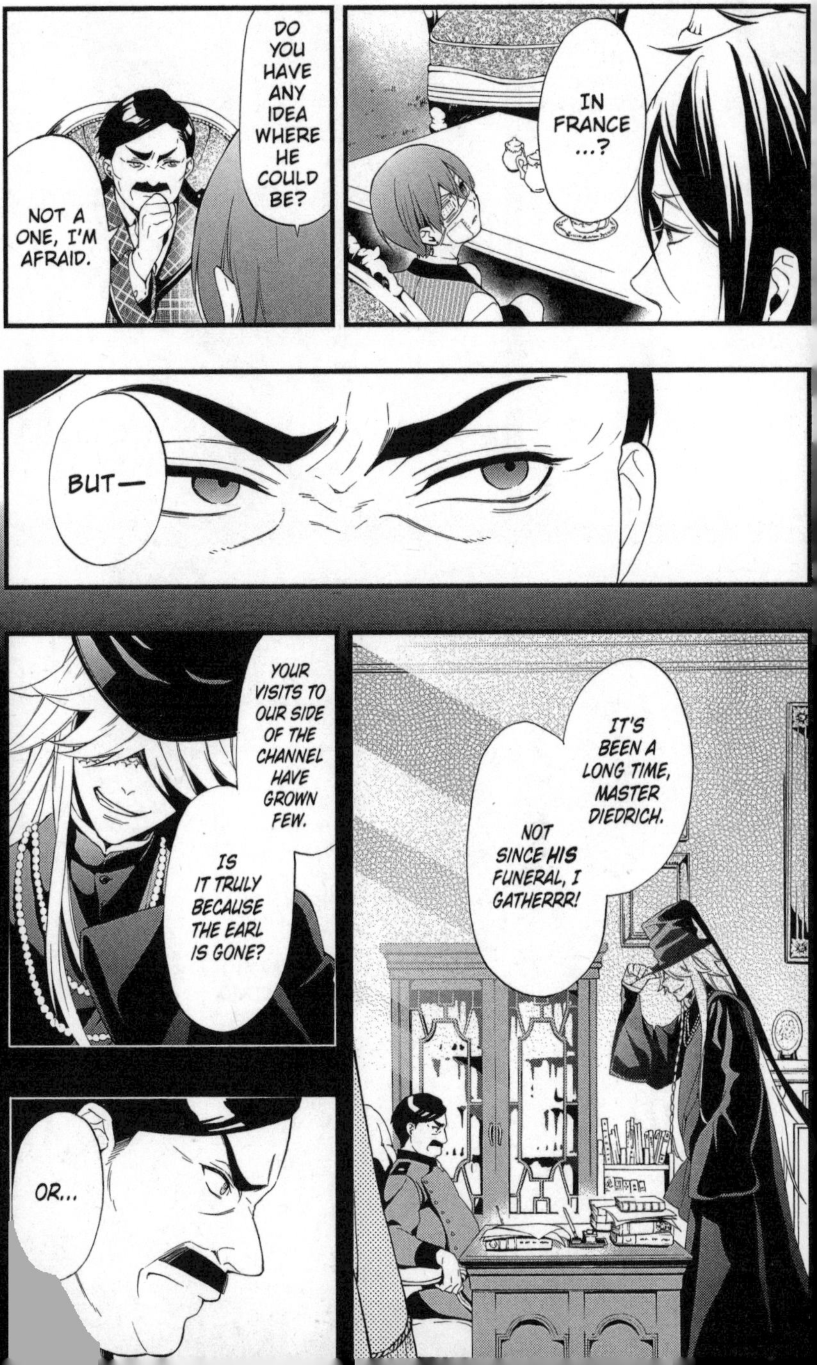
IN FRANCE ...?
DO YOU HAVE ANY IDEA WHERE HE COULD BE?
NOT A ONE, I'M AFRAID.
BUT—
IT'S BEEN A LONG TIME, MASTER DIEDRICH.
NOT SINCE HIS FUNERAL, I GATHERRR!
YOUR VISITS TO OUR SIDE OF THE CHANNEL HAVE GROWN FEW.
IS IT TRULY BECAUSE THE EARL IS GONE?
OR...

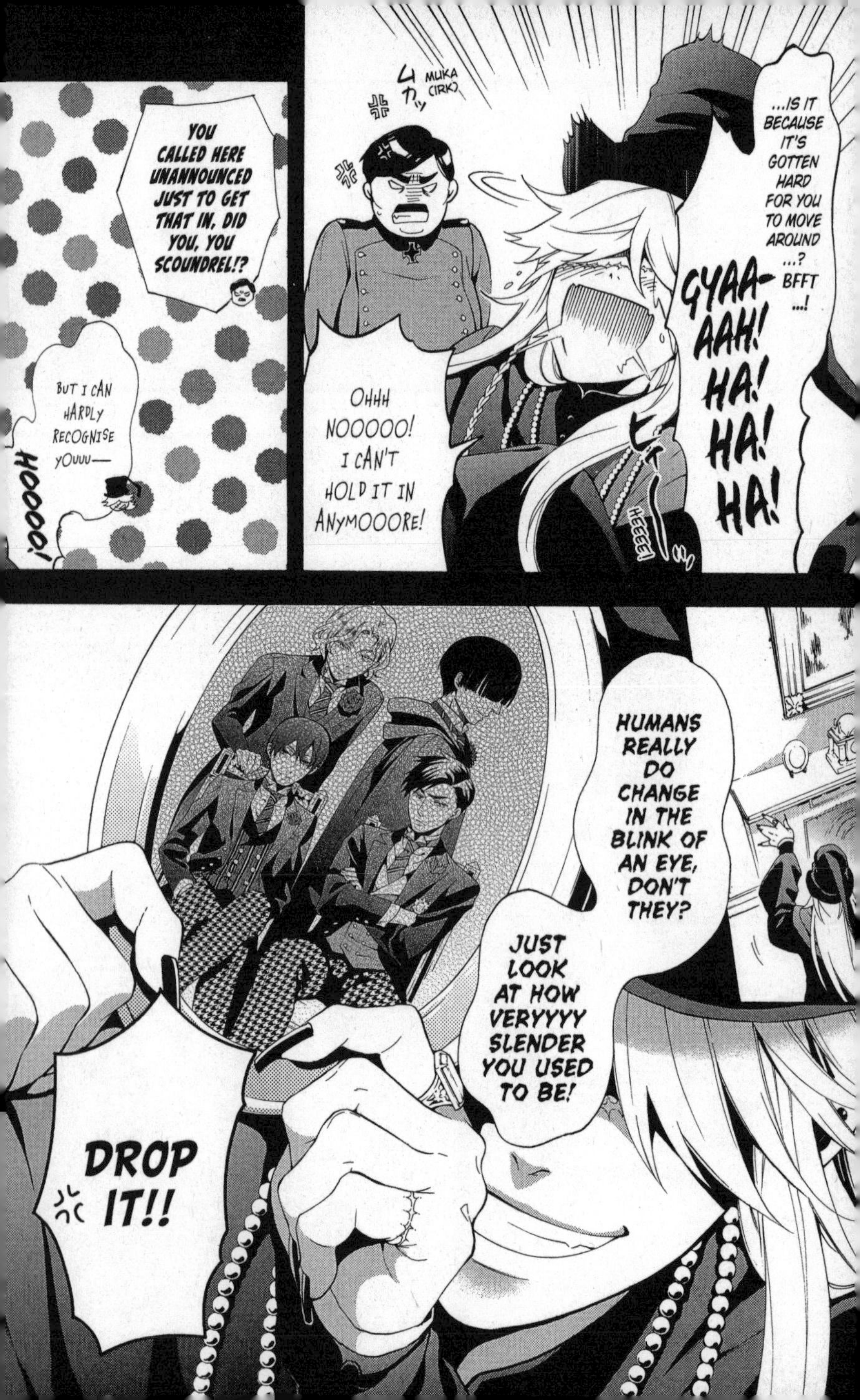
...IS IT BECAUSE IT'S GOTTEN HARD FOR YOU TO MOVE AROUND ...? BFFT ...!
ムカッ MUKA (IRK)
GYAA-AAH! HA! HA! HA!
OHHH NOOOOO! I CAN'T HOLD IT IN ANYMOOORE!
HEEEE!
YOU CALLED HERE UNANNOUNCED JUST TO GET THAT IN, DID YOU, YOU SCOUNDREL!?
BUT I CAN HARDLY RECOGNISE YOUUU——
HOOOO!
HUMANS REALLY DO CHANGE IN THE BLINK OF AN EYE, DON'T THEY?
JUST LOOK AT HOW VERYYYY SLENDER YOU USED TO BE!
DROP IT!!

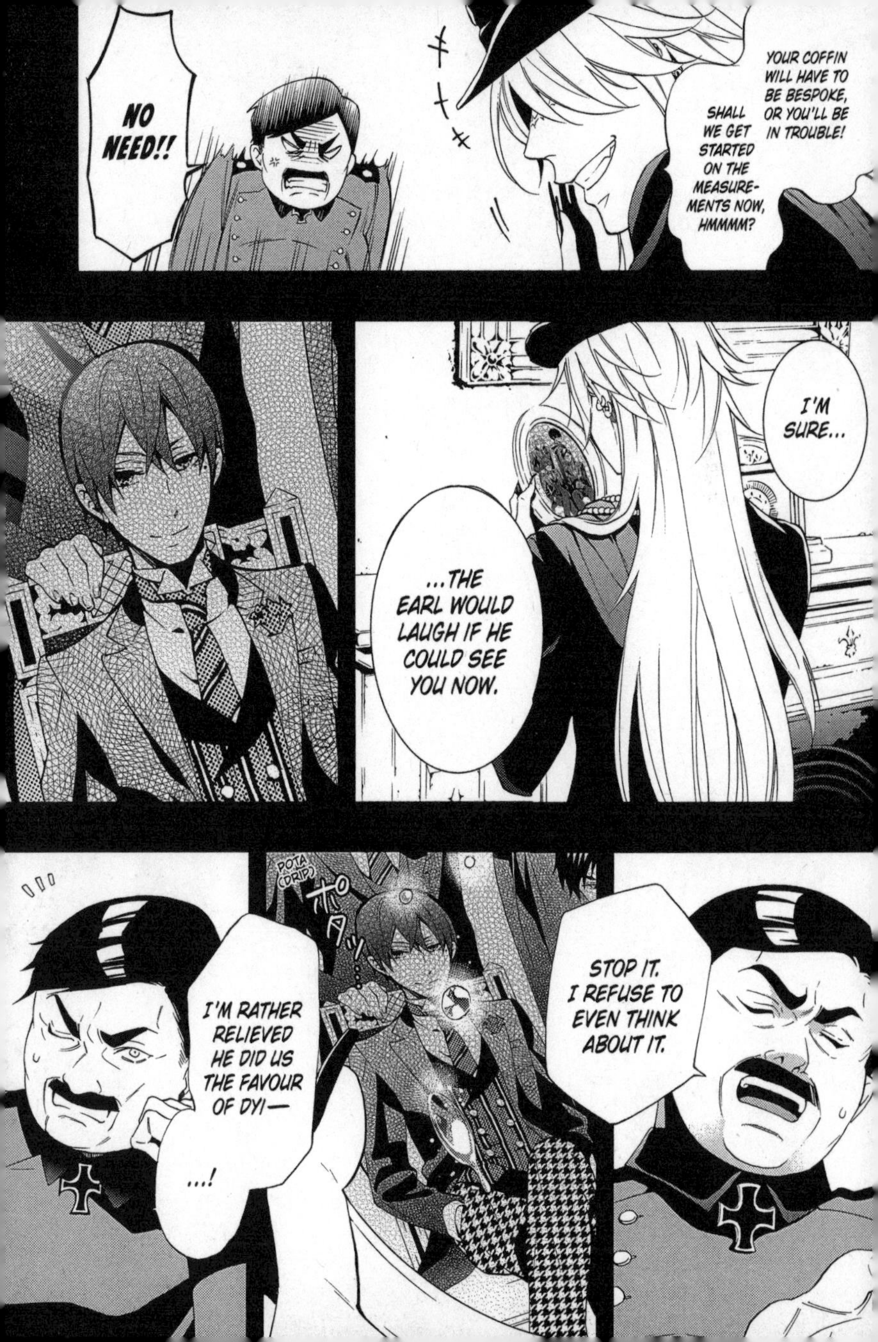
YOUR COFFIN WILL HAVE TO BE BESPOKE, OR YOU'LL BE IN TROUBLE!
SHALL WE GET STARTED ON THE MEASUREMENTS NOW, HMMMM?
NO NEED!!
I'M SURE...
...THE EARL WOULD LAUGH IF HE COULD SEE YOU NOW.
STOP IT. I REFUSE TO EVEN THINK ABOUT IT.
POTA (DRIP)
I'M RATHER RELIEVED HE DID US THE FAVOUR OF DYI—
...!

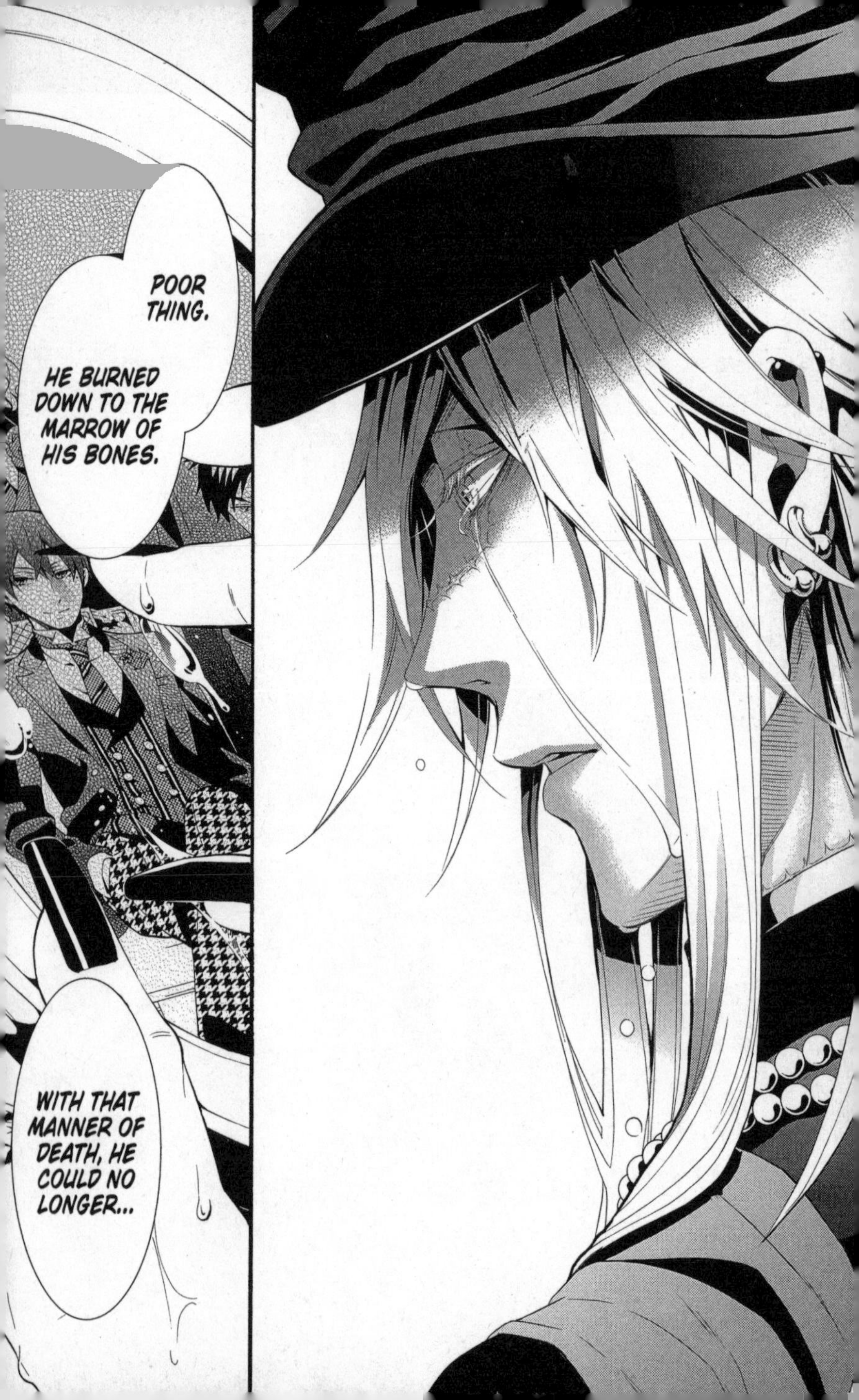
POOR THING.
HE BURNED DOWN TO THE MARROW OF HIS BONES.
WITH THAT MANNER OF DEATH, HE COULD NO LONGER...

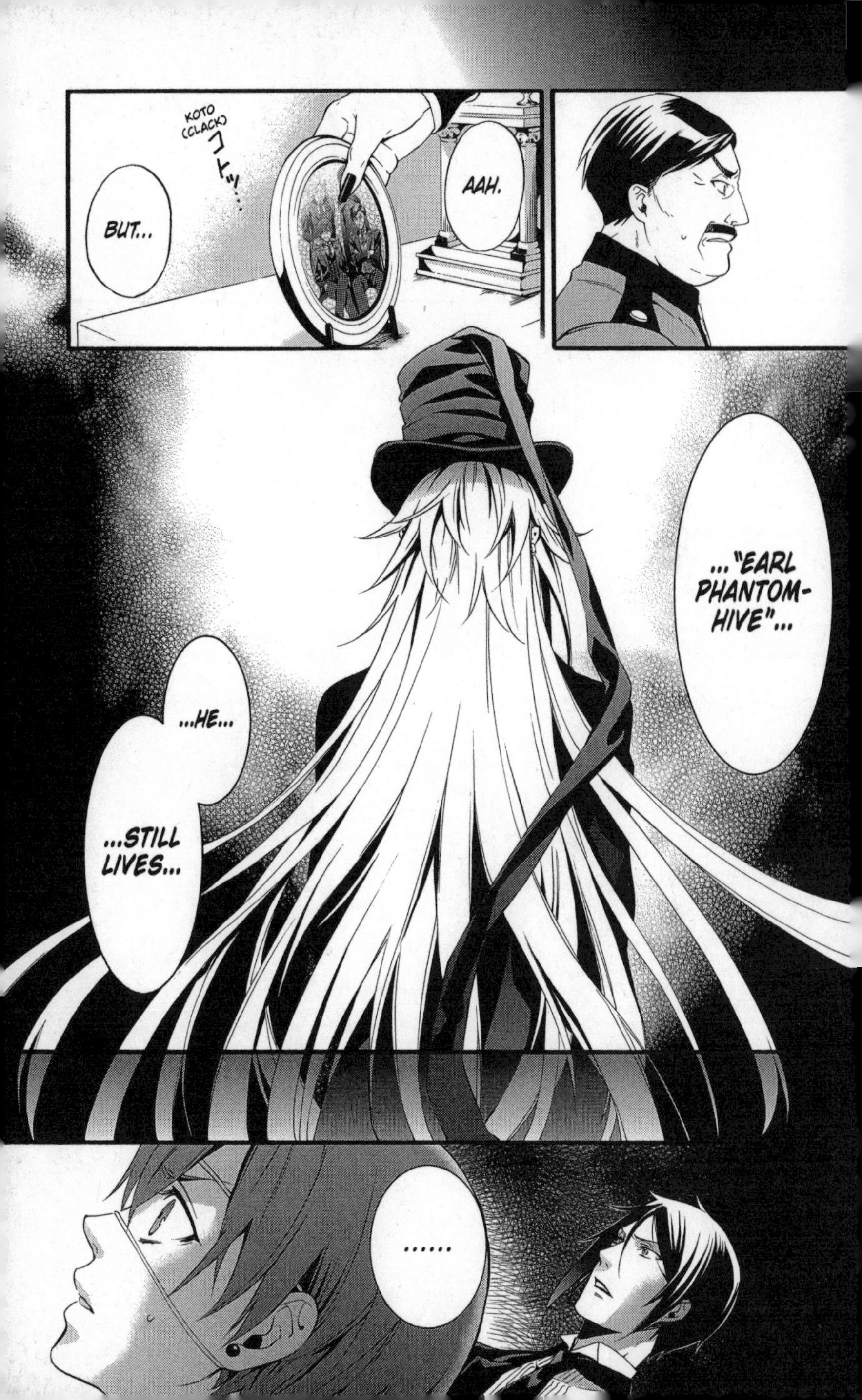
AAH.
KOTO (CLACK)
コトッ...
BUT...
..."EARL PHANTOM-HIVE"...
...HE...
...STILL LIVES...
......

"STILL LIVES"...

...HM?

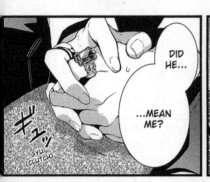

DID HE...

...MEAN ME?

GYU
(CLUTCH)

I CAN NEVER UNDER- STAND A WORD THAT FELLOW SAYS, SO...

...I HADN'T GIVEN IT MUCH THOUGHT, BUT...

OR—

Black Butler

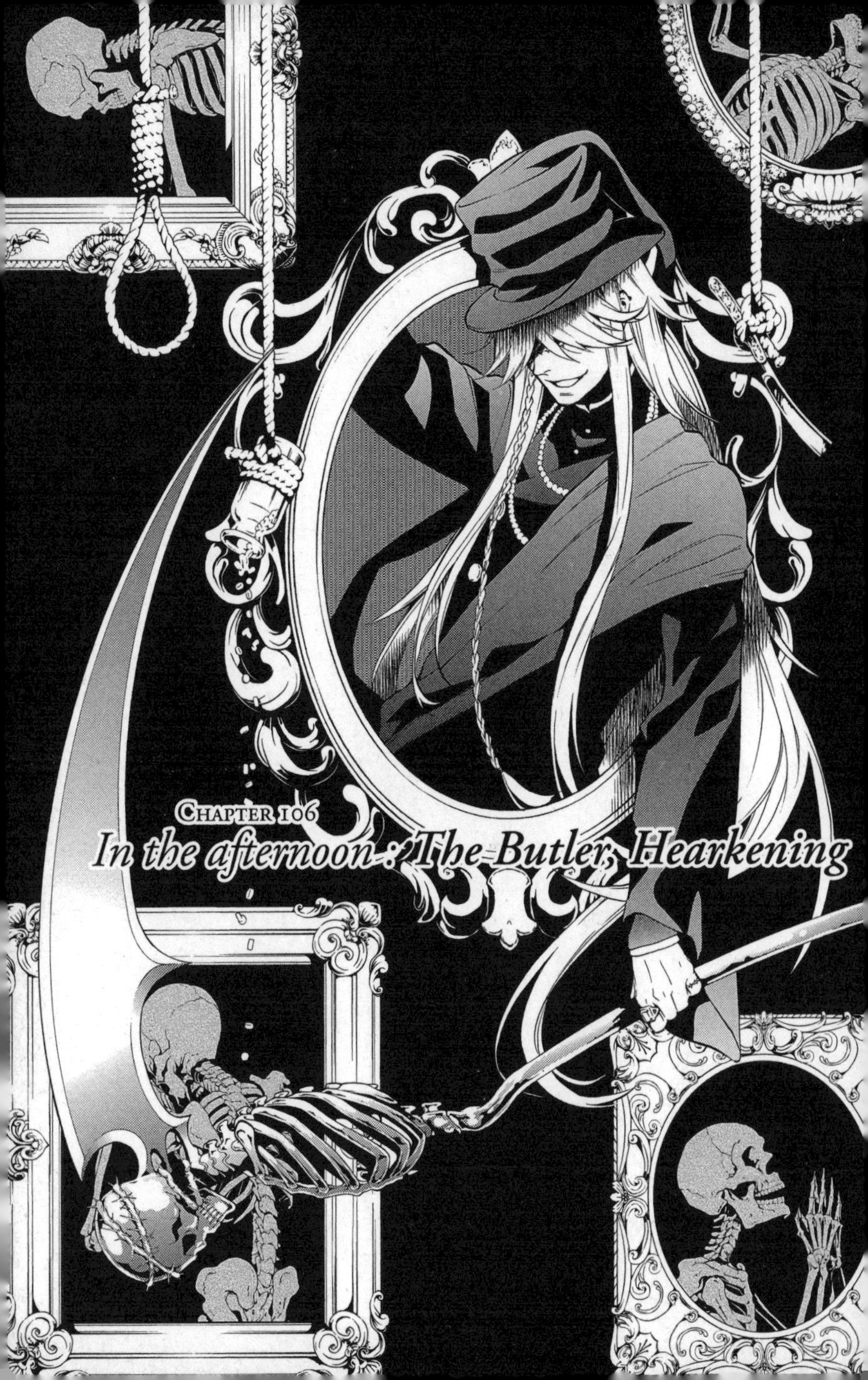
Chapter 106
In the afternoon : The Butler, Hearkening

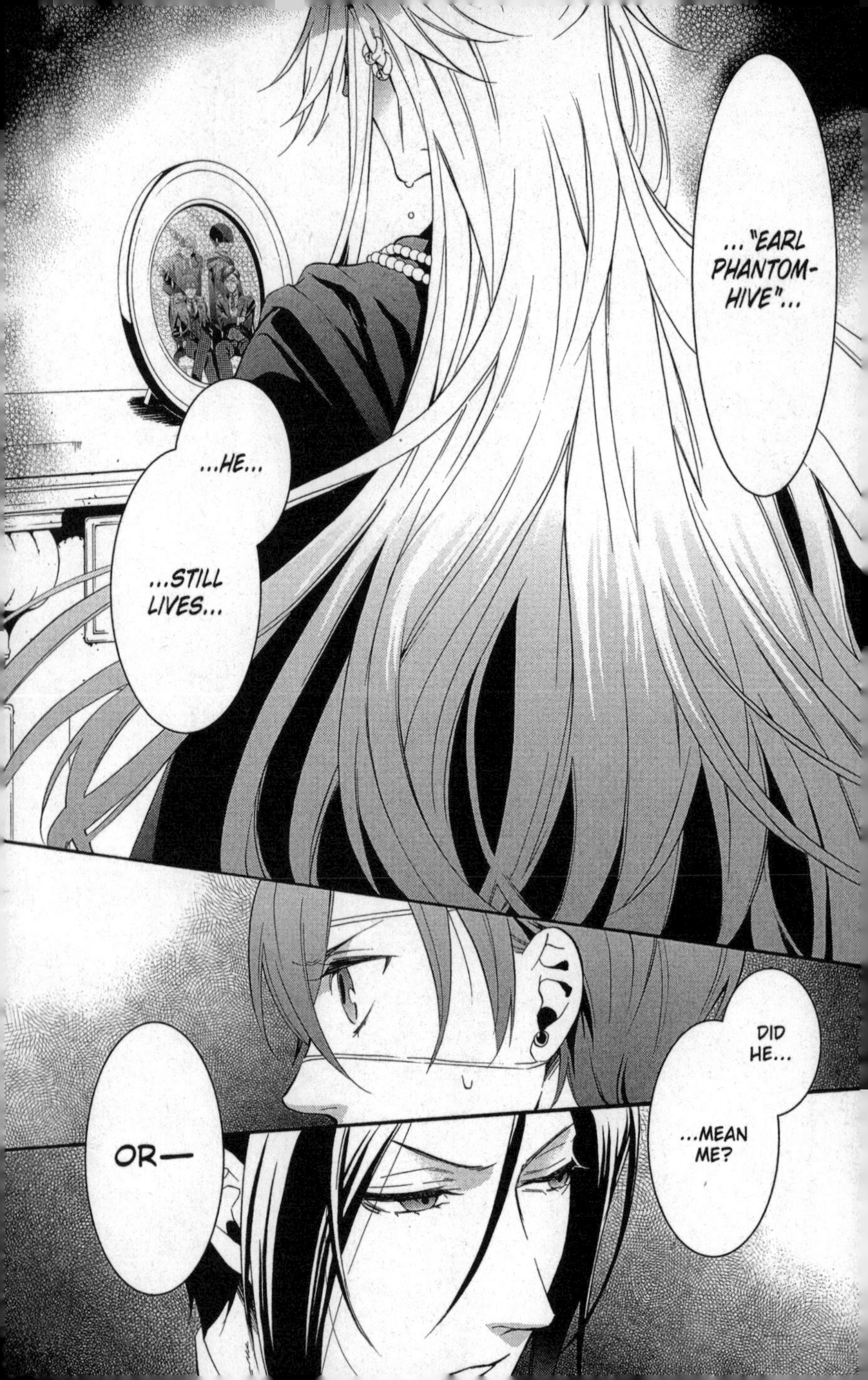
..."EARL PHANTOM-HIVE"...
...HE...
...STILL LIVES...
DID HE...
...MEAN ME?
OR—

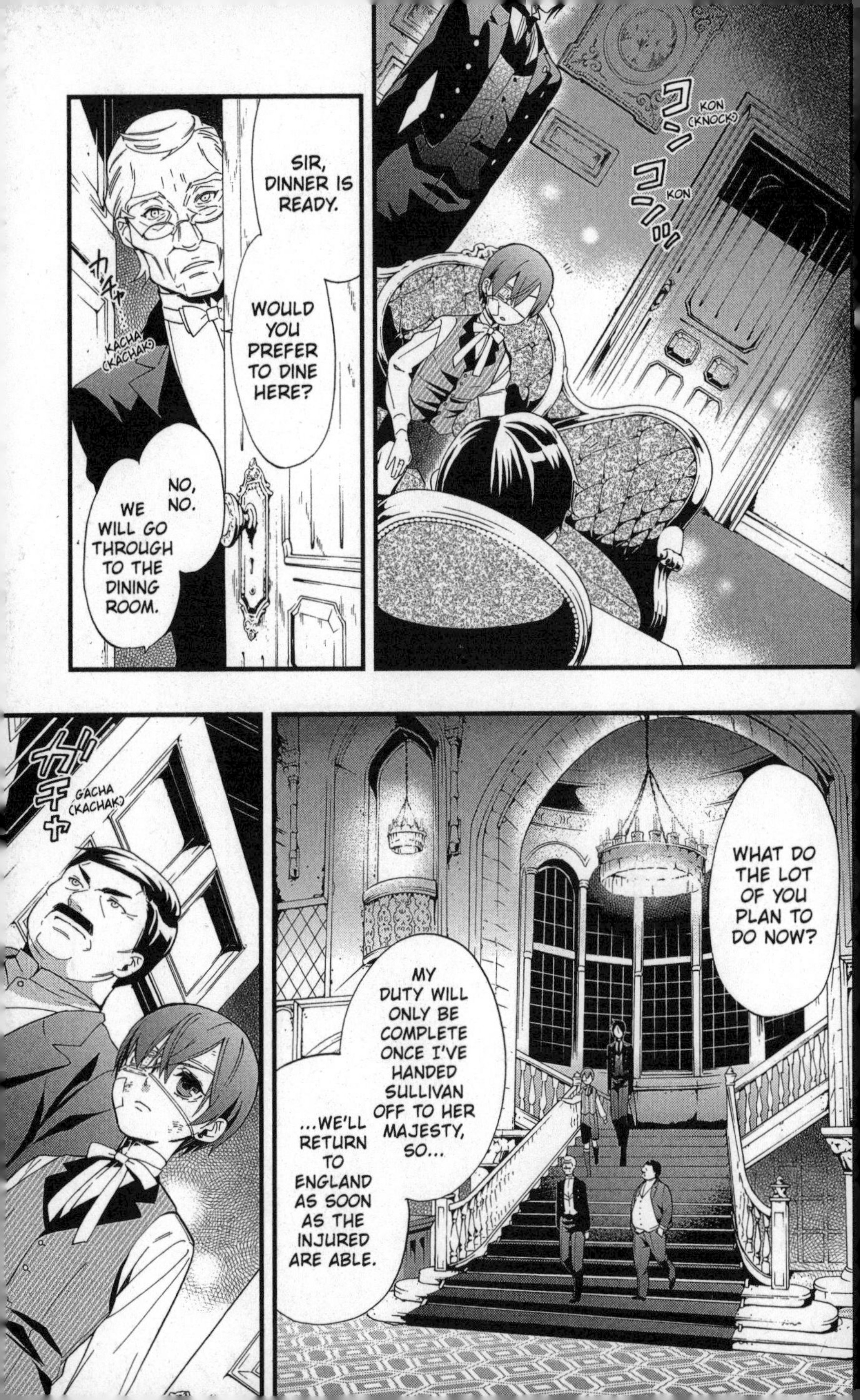
KON (KNOCK)
KON
KACHA (KACHAK)
SIR, DINNER IS READY.
WOULD YOU PREFER TO DINE HERE?
NO, NO. WE WILL GO THROUGH TO THE DINING ROOM.
WHAT DO THE LOT OF YOU PLAN TO DO NOW?
MY DUTY WILL ONLY BE COMPLETE ONCE I'VE HANDED SULLIVAN OFF TO HER MAJESTY, SO...
...WE'LL RETURN TO ENGLAND AS SOON AS THE INJURED ARE ABLE.
GACHA (KACHAK)

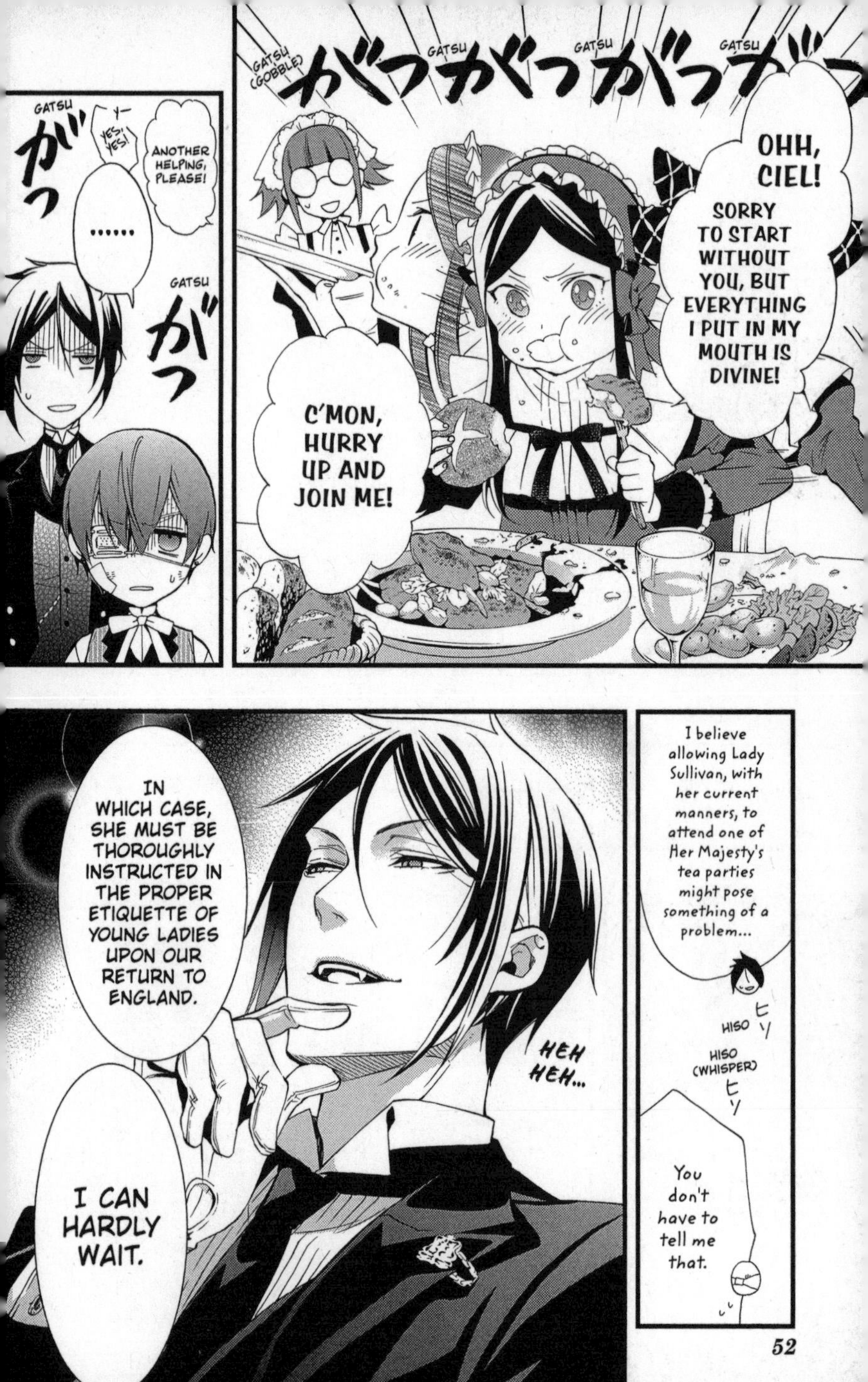
GATSU (GOBBLE)
GATSU
GATSU
GATSU
がつがつがつがつ
OHH, CIEL!
SORRY TO START WITHOUT YOU, BUT EVERYTHING I PUT IN MY MOUTH IS DIVINE!
C'MON, HURRY UP AND JOIN ME!
ANOTHER HELPING, PLEASE!
Y- YES! YES!
GATSU
がっ
......
GATSU
がっ
I believe allowing Lady Sullivan, with her current manners, to attend one of Her Majesty's tea parties might pose something of a problem...
HISO
ヒソ
HISO (WHISPER)
ヒソ
You don't have to tell me that.
IN WHICH CASE, SHE MUST BE THOROUGHLY INSTRUCTED IN THE PROPER ETIQUETTE OF YOUNG LADIES UPON OUR RETURN TO ENGLAND.
HEH HEH...
I CAN HARDLY WAIT.

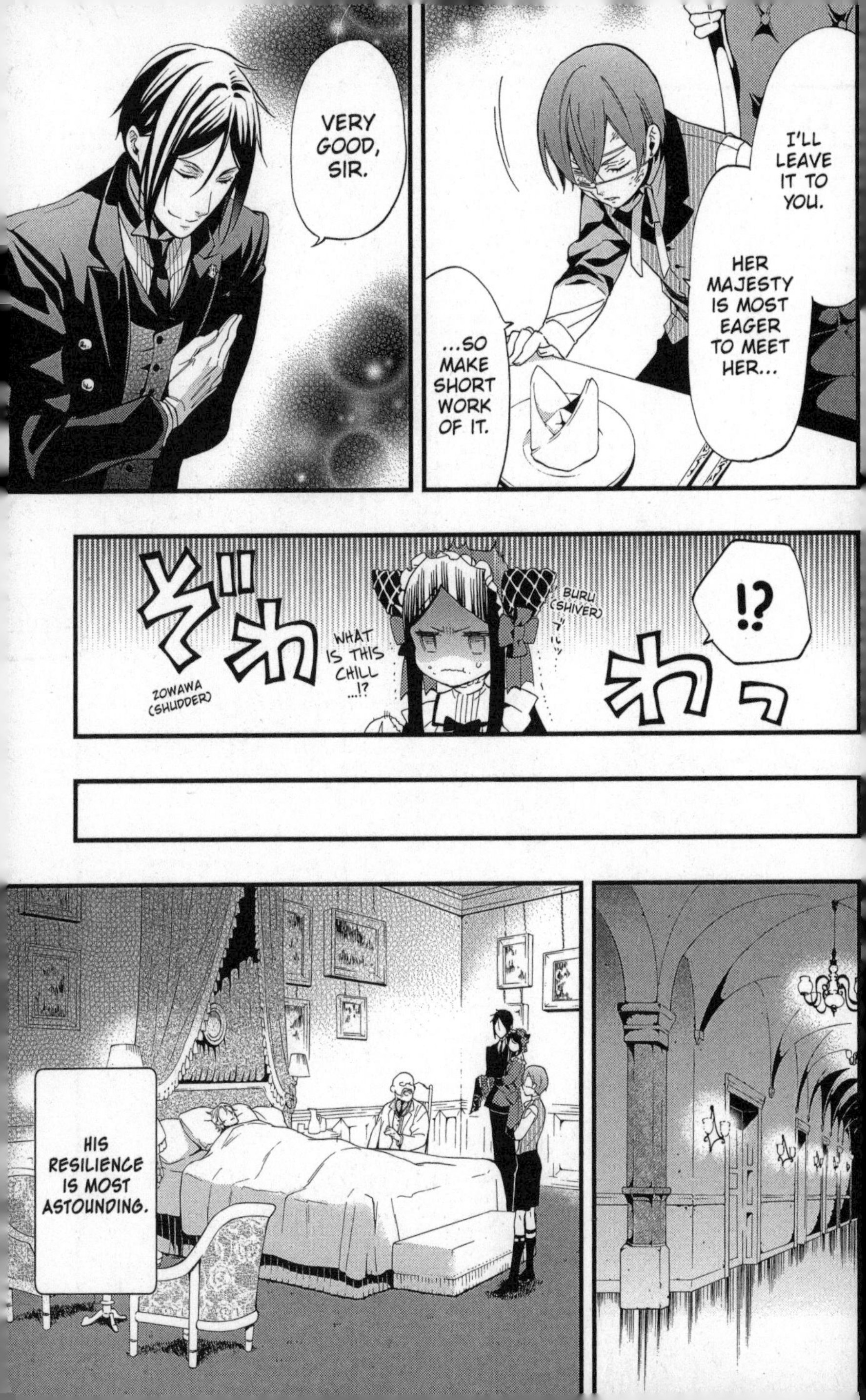
I'LL LEAVE IT TO YOU.
HER MAJESTY IS MOST EAGER TO MEET HER...
...SO MAKE SHORT WORK OF IT.
VERY GOOD, SIR.
!?
わっ
BURU (SHIVER)
ブルッ
WHAT IS THIS CHILL ...!?
ぞわ
ZOWAWA (SHUDDER)
HIS RESILIENCE IS MOST ASTOUNDING.

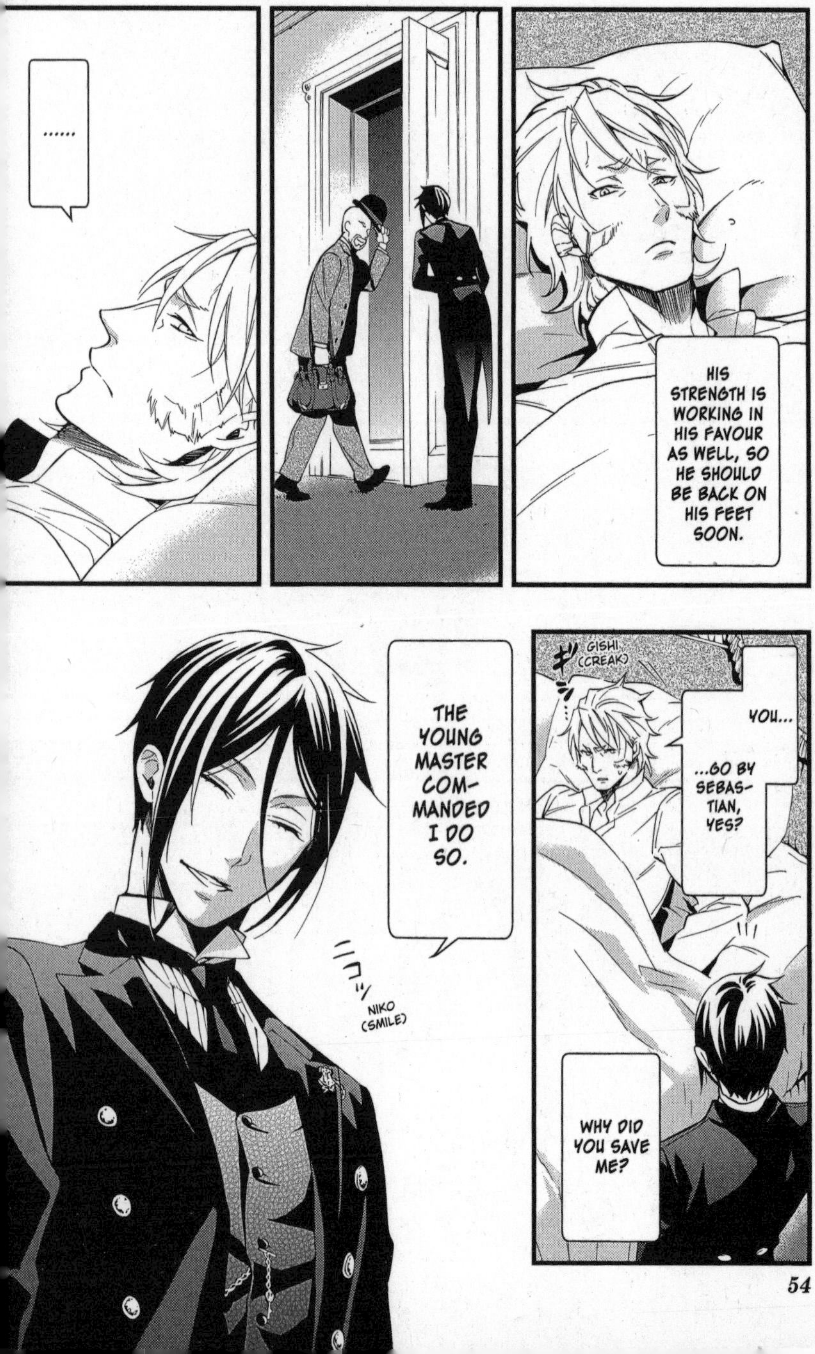
HIS STRENGTH IS WORKING IN HIS FAVOUR AS WELL, SO HE SHOULD BE BACK ON HIS FEET SOON.
......
GISHI (CREAK)
YOU...
...GO BY SEBASTIAN, YES?
WHY DID YOU SAVE ME?
THE YOUNG MASTER COMMANDED I DO SO.
NIKO (SMILE)

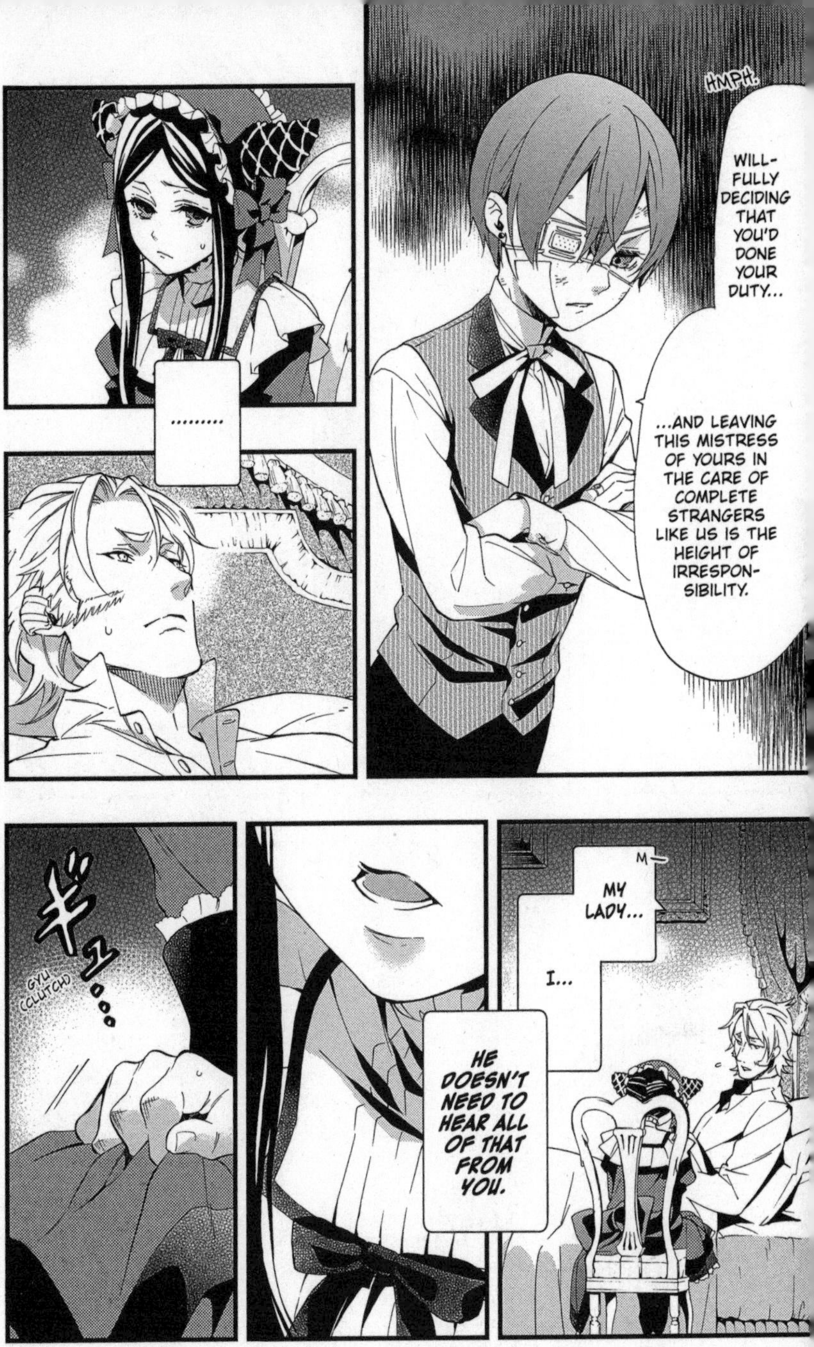
HMPH.
WILL-FULLY DECIDING THAT YOU'D DONE YOUR DUTY...
...AND LEAVING THIS MISTRESS OF YOURS IN THE CARE OF COMPLETE STRANGERS LIKE US IS THE HEIGHT OF IRRESPON-SIBILITY.
....
M—
MY LADY...
I...
HE DOESN'T NEED TO HEAR ALL OF THAT FROM YOU.
GYU (CLUTCH)

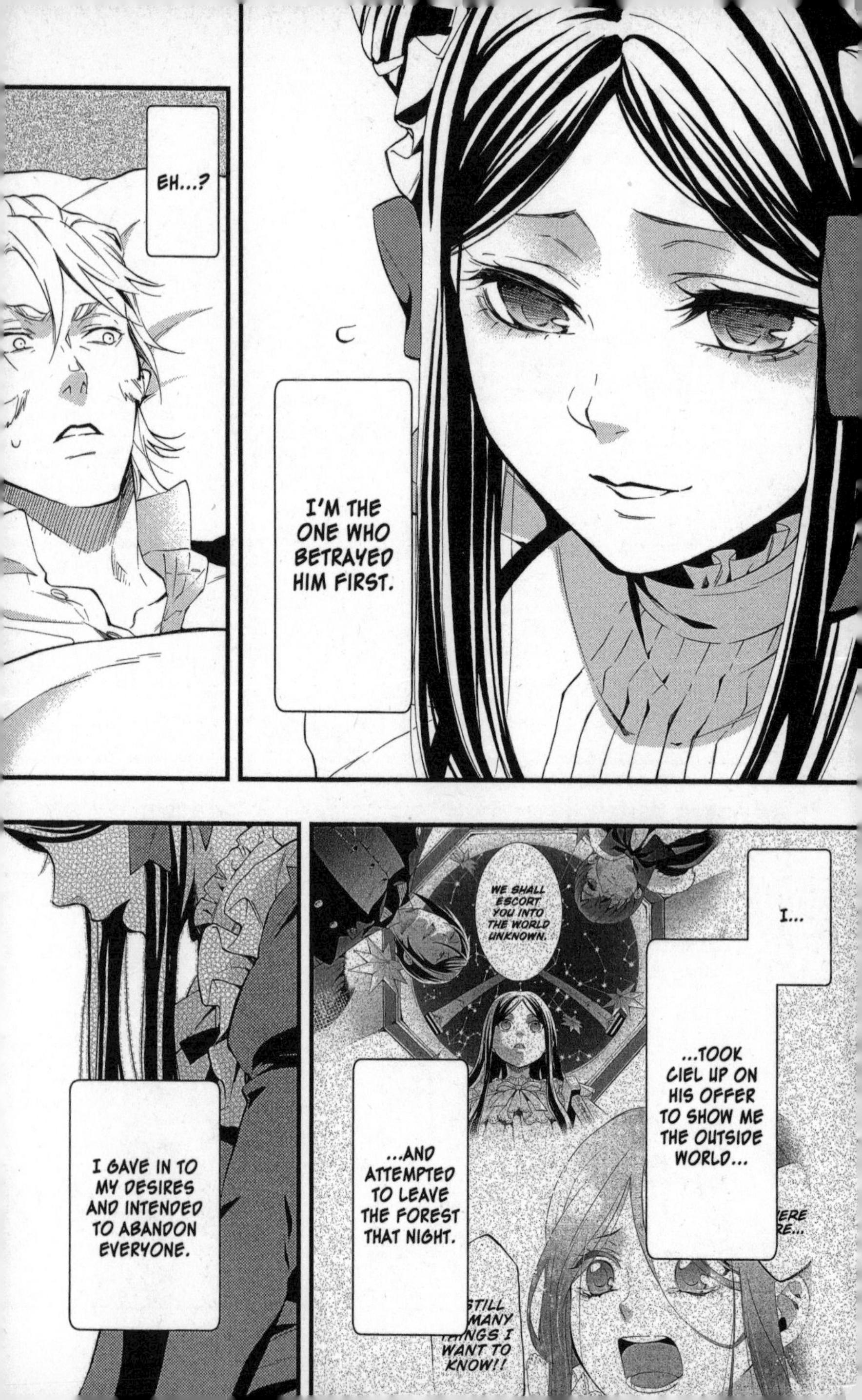
I'M THE ONE WHO BETRAYED HIM FIRST.
EH...?
I...
...TOOK CIEL UP ON HIS OFFER TO SHOW ME THE OUTSIDE WORLD...
WE SHALL ESCORT YOU INTO THE WORLD UNKNOWN.
...AND ATTEMPTED TO LEAVE THE FOREST THAT NIGHT.
STILL MANY THINGS I WANT TO KNOW!!
I GAVE IN TO MY DESIRES AND INTENDED TO ABANDON EVERYONE.

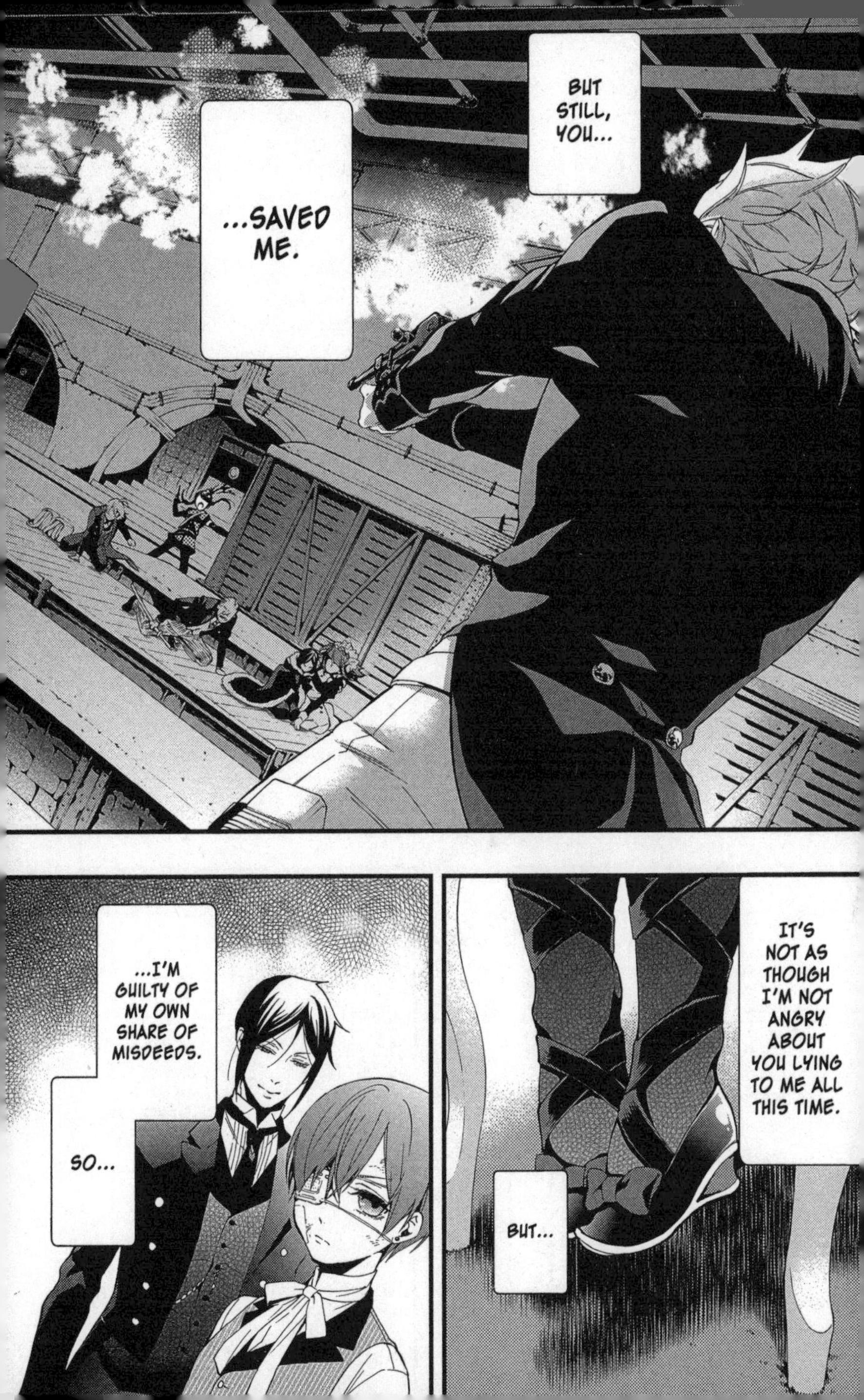
BUT STILL, YOU...
...SAVED ME.
IT'S NOT AS THOUGH I'M NOT ANGRY ABOUT YOU LYING TO ME ALL THIS TIME.
BUT...
...I'M GUILTY OF MY OWN SHARE OF MISDEEDS.
SO...

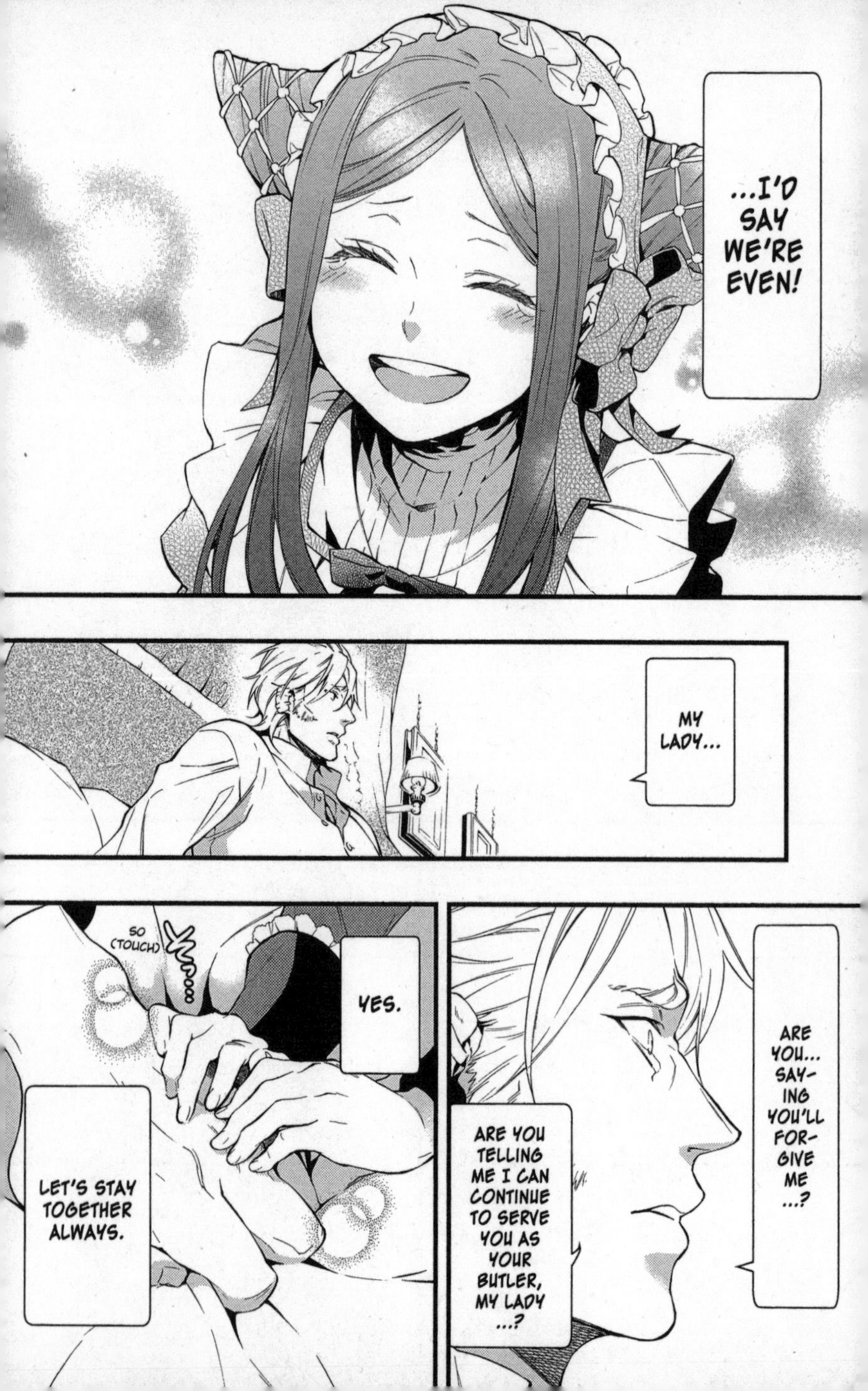

...I'D SAY WE'RE EVEN!
MY LADY...
ARE YOU... SAYING YOU'LL FORGIVE ME ...?
ARE YOU TELLING ME I CAN CONTINUE TO SERVE YOU AS YOUR BUTLER, MY LADY ...?
YES.
SO (TOUCH)
LET'S STAY TOGETHER ALWAYS.

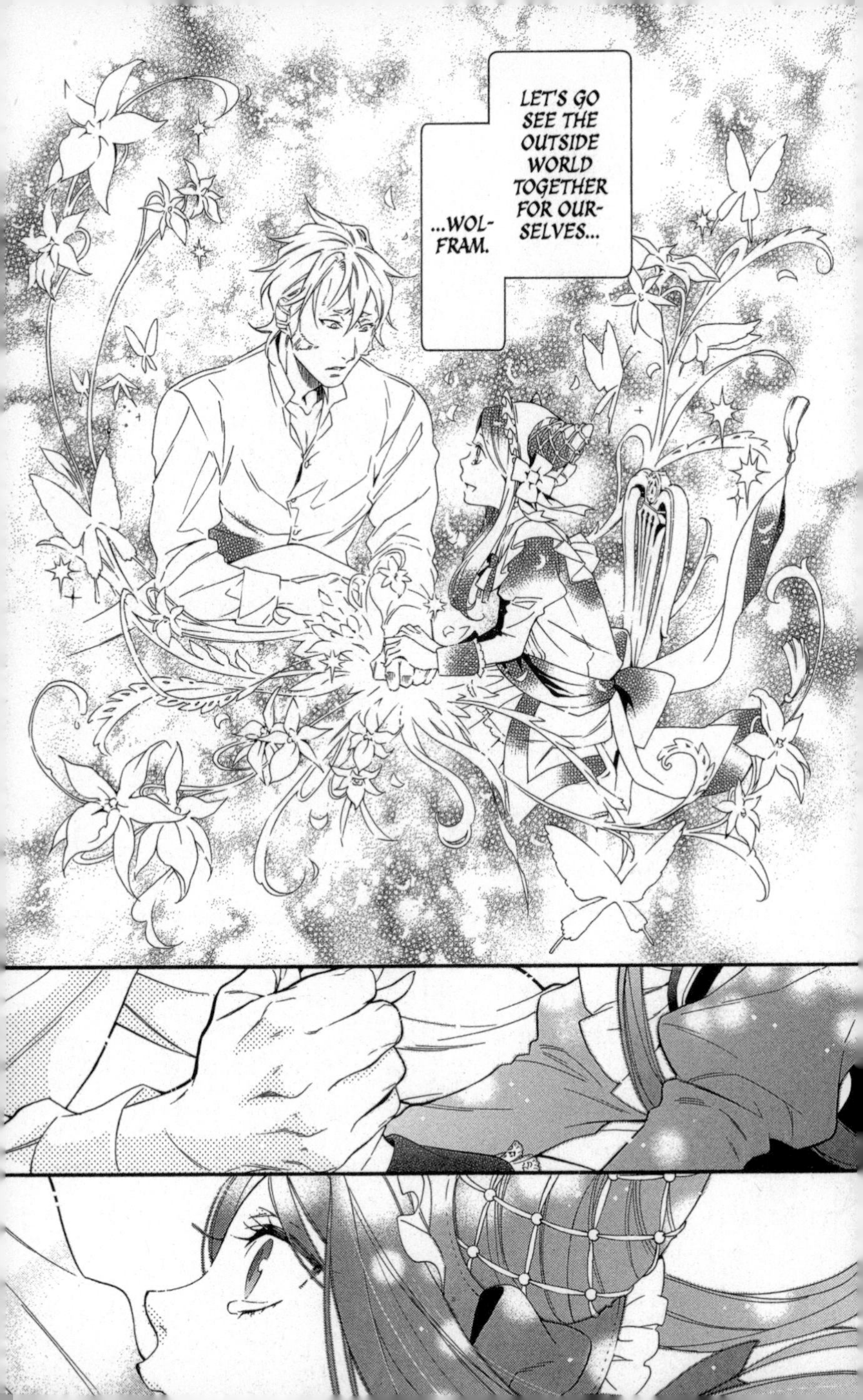
LET'S GO SEE THE OUTSIDE WORLD TOGETHER FOR OURSELVES...
...WOLFRAM.

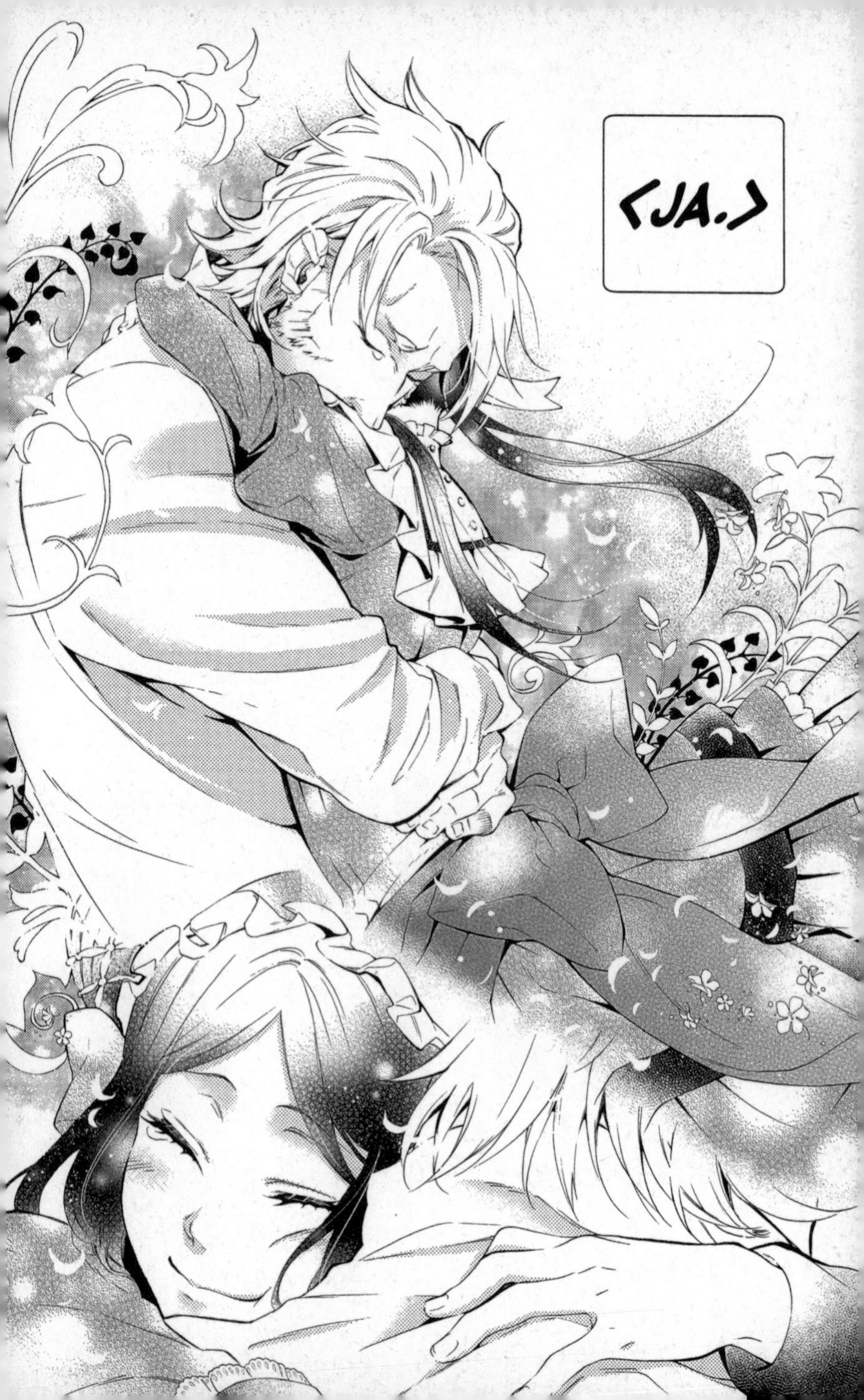
<JA.>

Black Butler

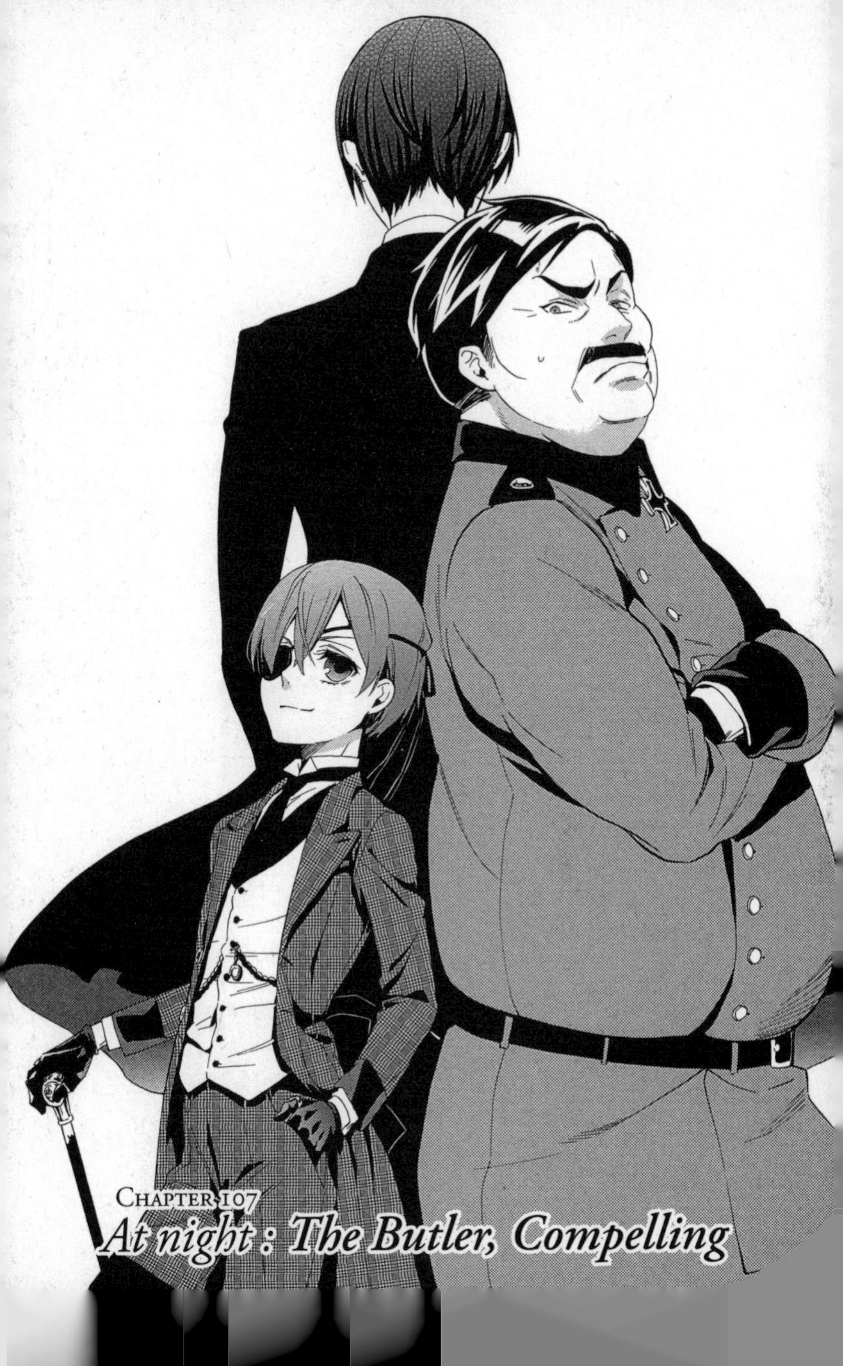
Chapter 107
At night : The Butler, Compelling

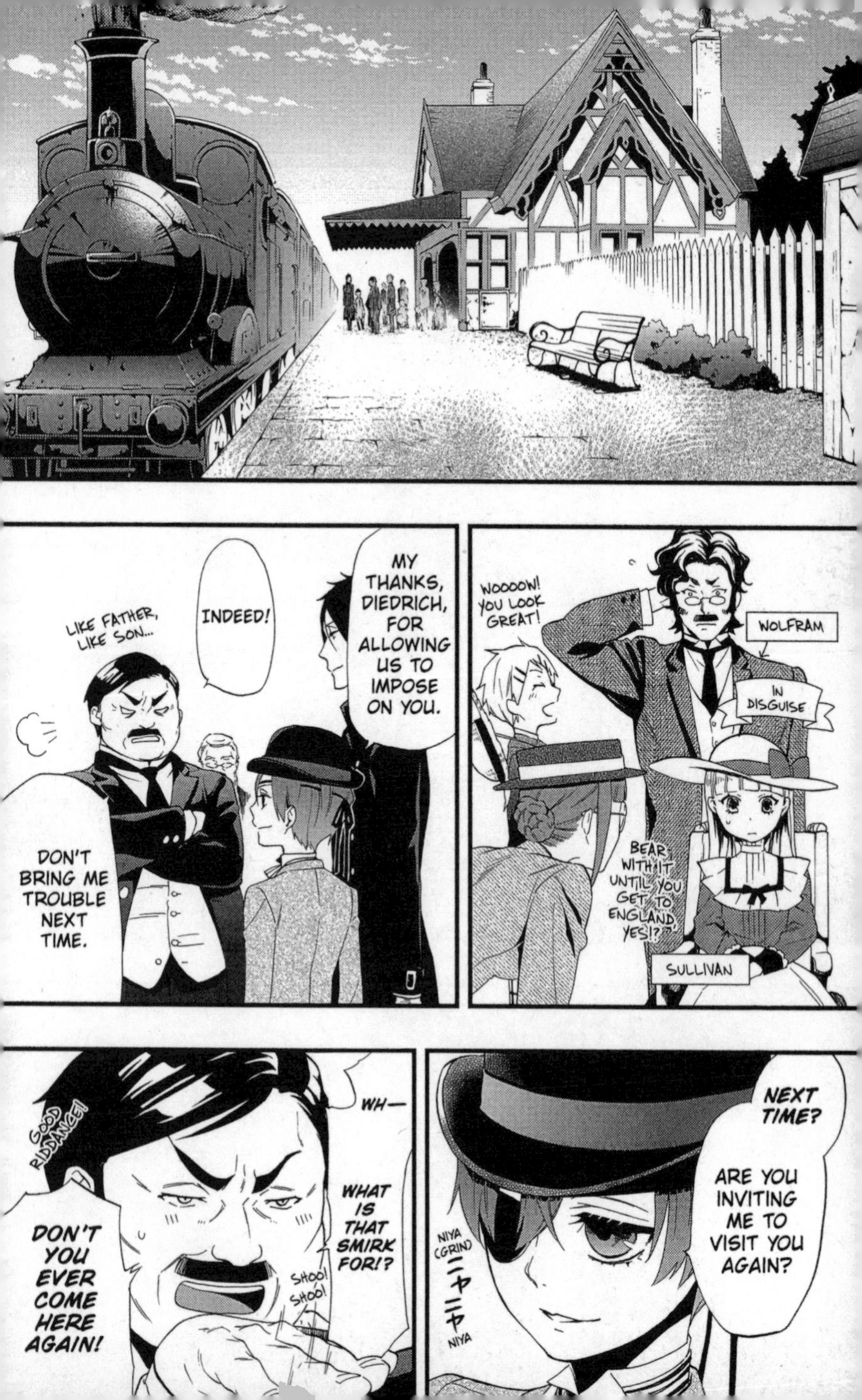
WOOOOW! YOU LOOK GREAT!
WOLFRAM
IN DISGUISE
BEAR WITH IT UNTIL YOU GET TO ENGLAND, YES!?
SULLIVAN
MY THANKS, DIEDRICH, FOR ALLOWING US TO IMPOSE ON YOU.
INDEED!
LIKE FATHER, LIKE SON...
DON'T BRING ME TROUBLE NEXT TIME.
NEXT TIME?
ARE YOU INVITING ME TO VISIT YOU AGAIN?
NIYA (GRIN) ニヤニヤ NIYA
WH—
WHAT IS THAT SMIRK FOR!?
GOOD RIDDANCE!
DON'T YOU EVER COME HERE AGAIN!
SHOO! SHOO!

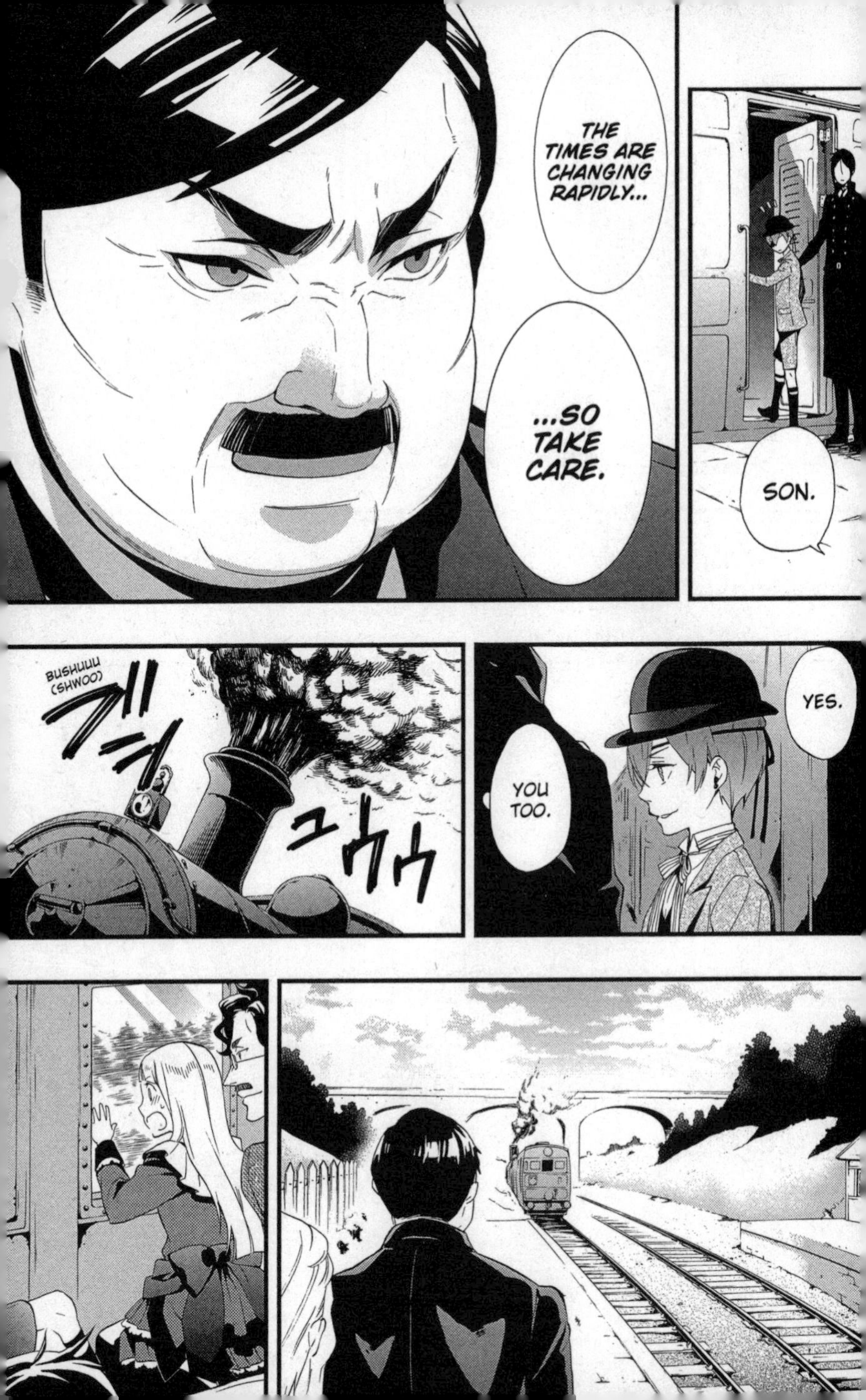
SON.
THE TIMES ARE CHANGING RAPIDLY...
...SO TAKE CARE.
YES.
YOU TOO.
BUSHUUU (SHWOO)

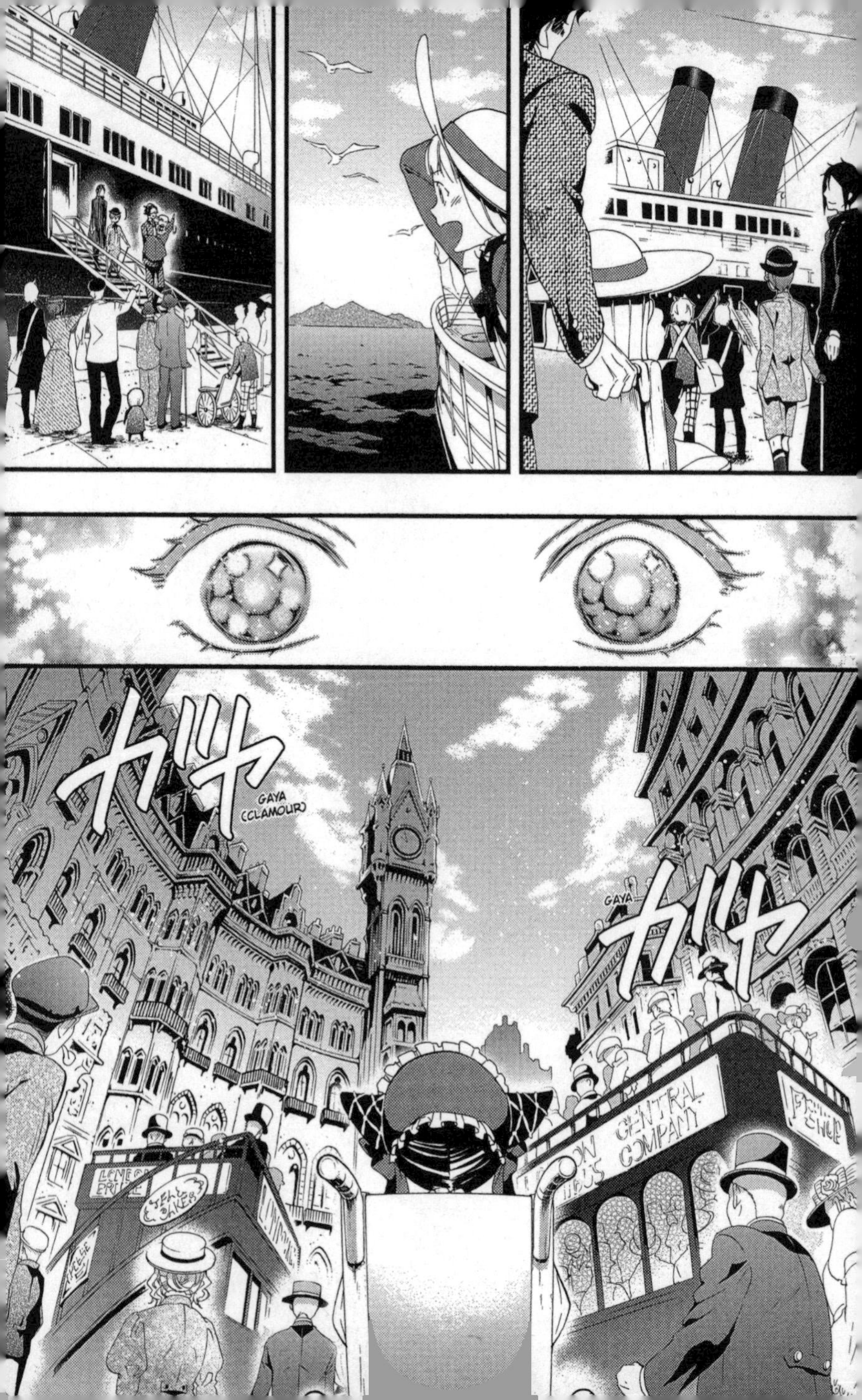
GAYA (CLAMOUR)
GAYA
GENERAL
COMPANY

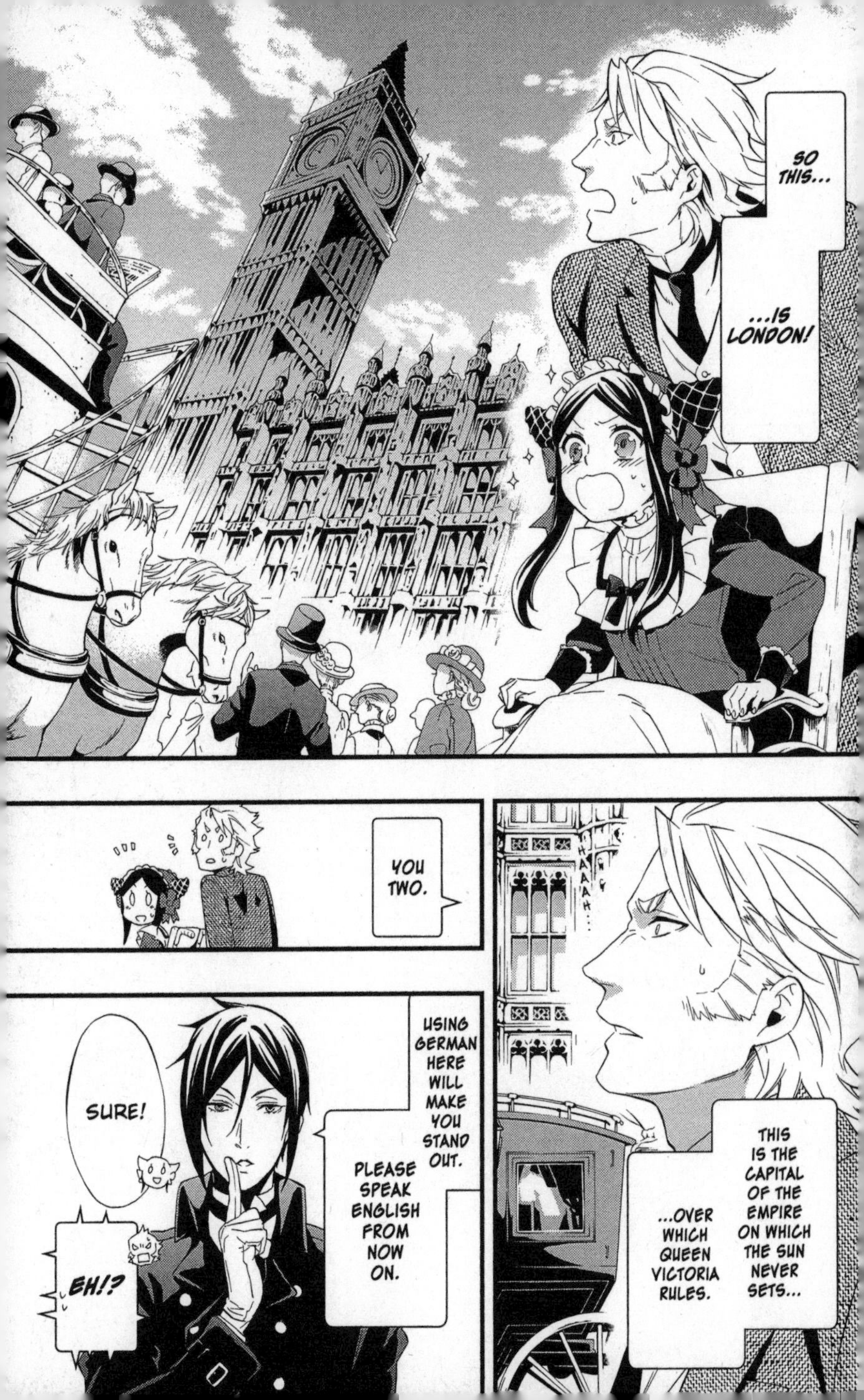
SO THIS...
...IS LONDON!
THIS IS THE CAPITAL OF THE EMPIRE ON WHICH THE SUN NEVER SETS...
...OVER WHICH QUEEN VICTORIA RULES.
YOU TWO.
USING GERMAN HERE WILL MAKE YOU STAND OUT.
PLEASE SPEAK ENGLISH FROM NOW ON.
SURE!
EH!?

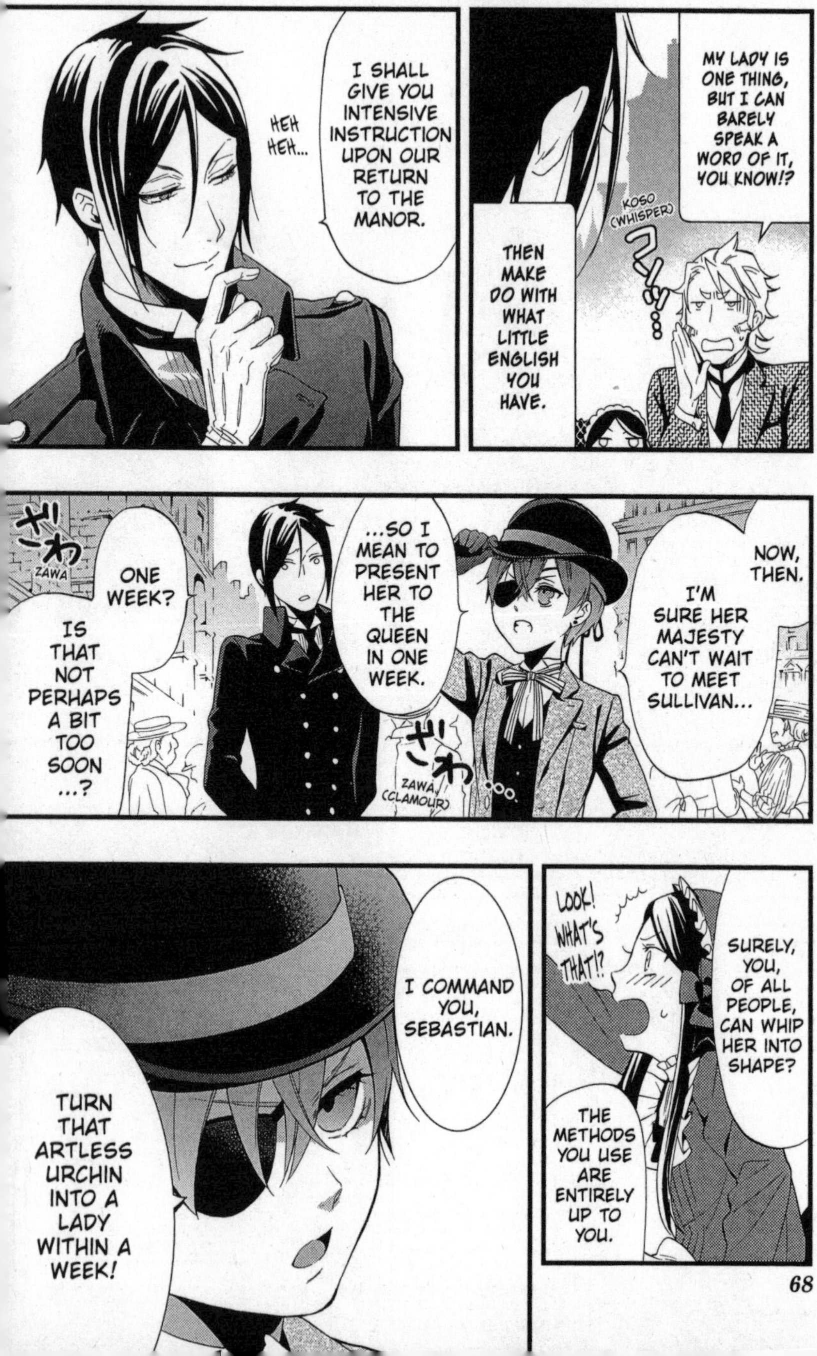
MY LADY IS ONE THING, BUT I CAN BARELY SPEAK A WORD OF IT, YOU KNOW!?
KOSO (WHISPER)
THEN MAKE DO WITH WHAT LITTLE ENGLISH YOU HAVE.
I SHALL GIVE YOU INTENSIVE INSTRUCTION UPON OUR RETURN TO THE MANOR.
HEH HEH...
NOW, THEN.
I'M SURE HER MAJESTY CAN'T WAIT TO MEET SULLIVAN...
...SO I MEAN TO PRESENT HER TO THE QUEEN IN ONE WEEK.
ZAWA (CLAMOUR)
ONE WEEK?
IS THAT NOT PERHAPS A BIT TOO SOON ...?
ZAWA
LOOK! WHAT'S THAT!?
SURELY, YOU, OF ALL PEOPLE, CAN WHIP HER INTO SHAPE?
THE METHODS YOU USE ARE ENTIRELY UP TO YOU.
I COMMAND YOU, SEBASTIAN.
TURN THAT ARTLESS URCHIN INTO A LADY WITHIN A WEEK!

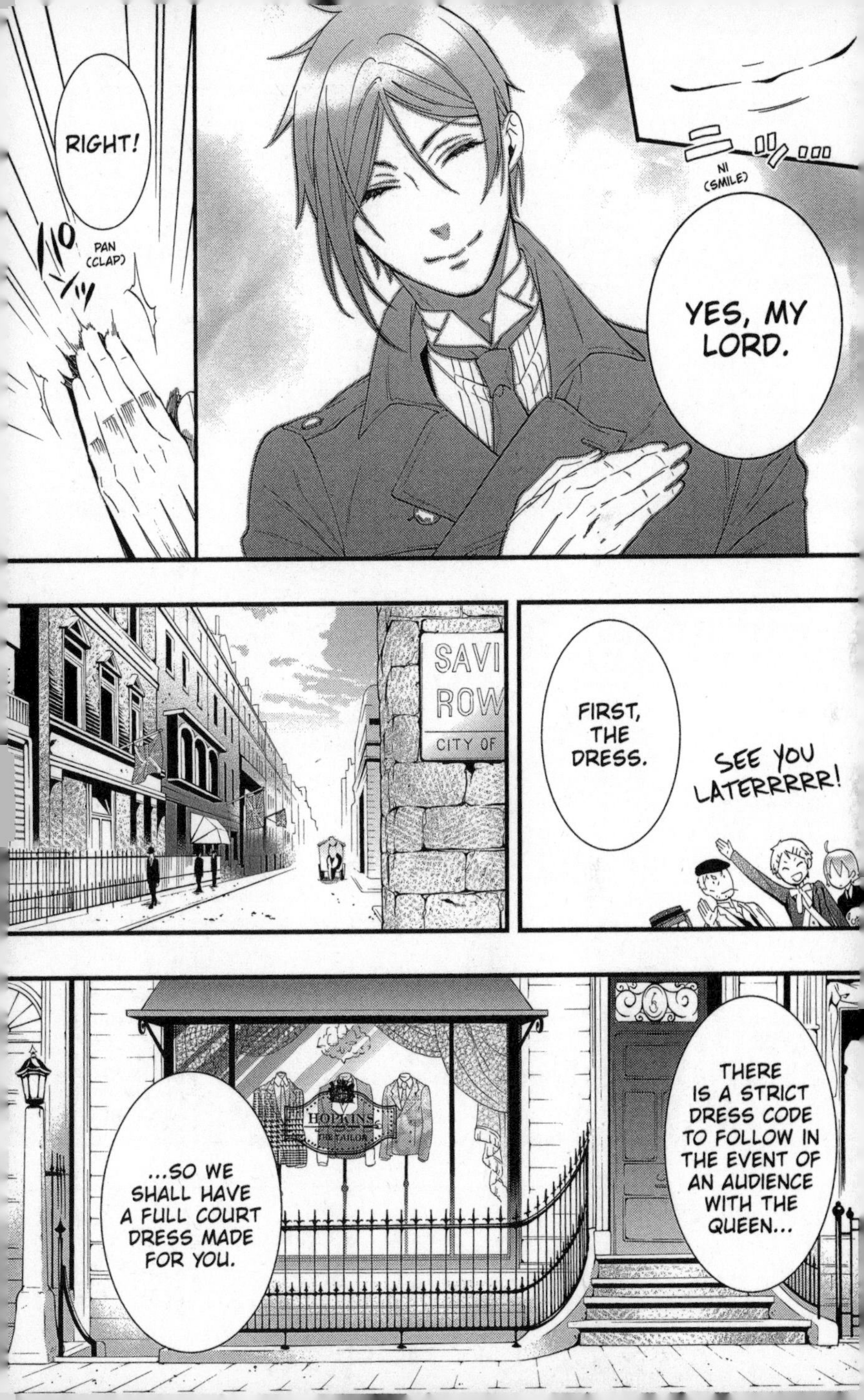
NI (SMILE)
YES, MY LORD.
RIGHT!
PAN (CLAP)
FIRST, THE DRESS.
SEE YOU LATERRRRR!
SAVI ROW
CITY OF
THERE IS A STRICT DRESS CODE TO FOLLOW IN THE EVENT OF AN AUDIENCE WITH THE QUEEN...
...SO WE SHALL HAVE A FULL COURT DRESS MADE FOR YOU.
HOPKINS
THE TAILOR

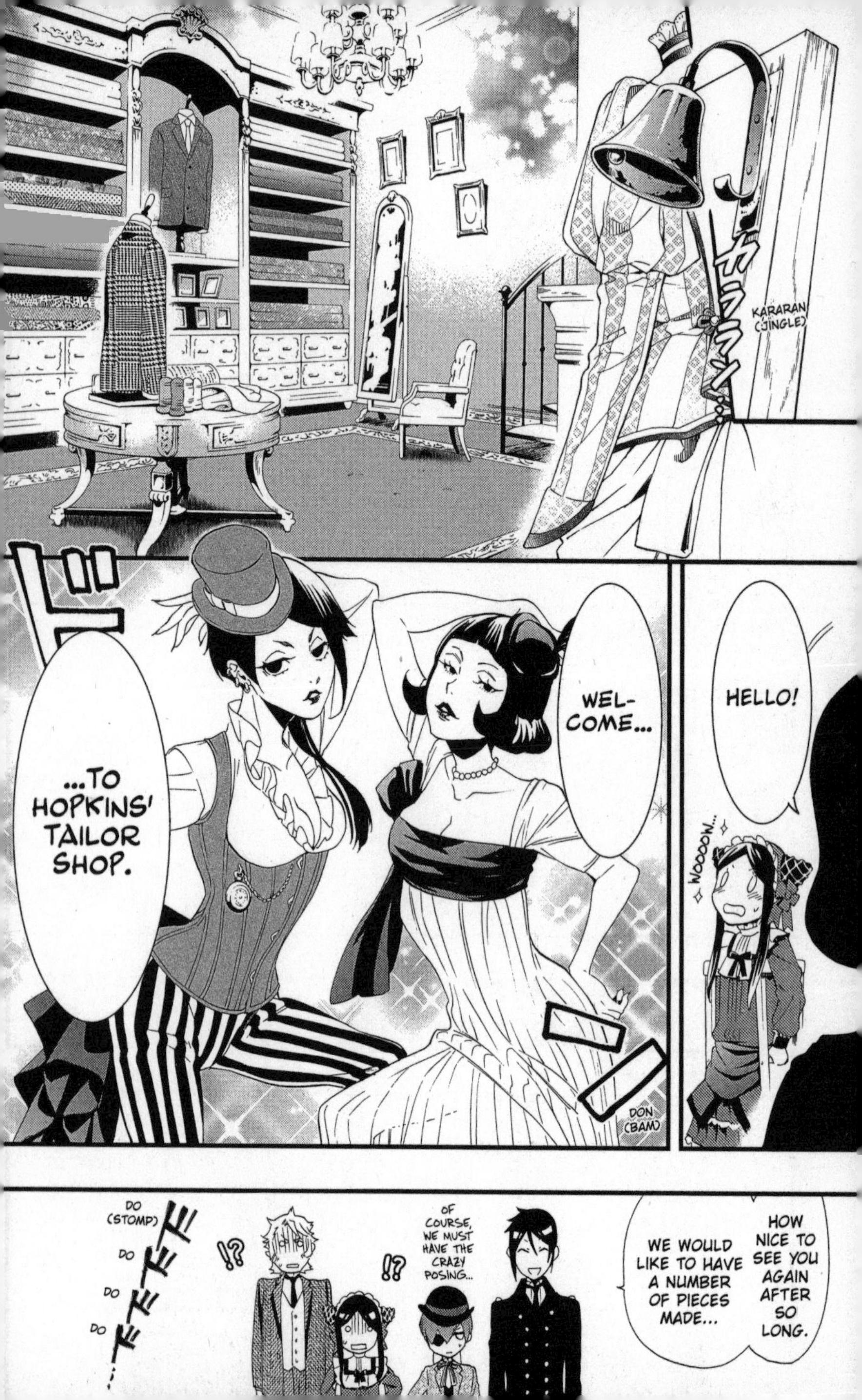
KARARAN (JINGLE)
HELLO!
WOOOOW...
WEL-COME...
...TO HOPKINS' TAILOR SHOP.
DON (BAM)
HOW NICE TO SEE YOU AGAIN AFTER SO LONG.
WE WOULD LIKE TO HAVE A NUMBER OF PIECES MADE...
OF COURSE, WE MUST HAVE THE CRAZY POSING...
!?
!?
DO (STOMP)
DO
DO
DO

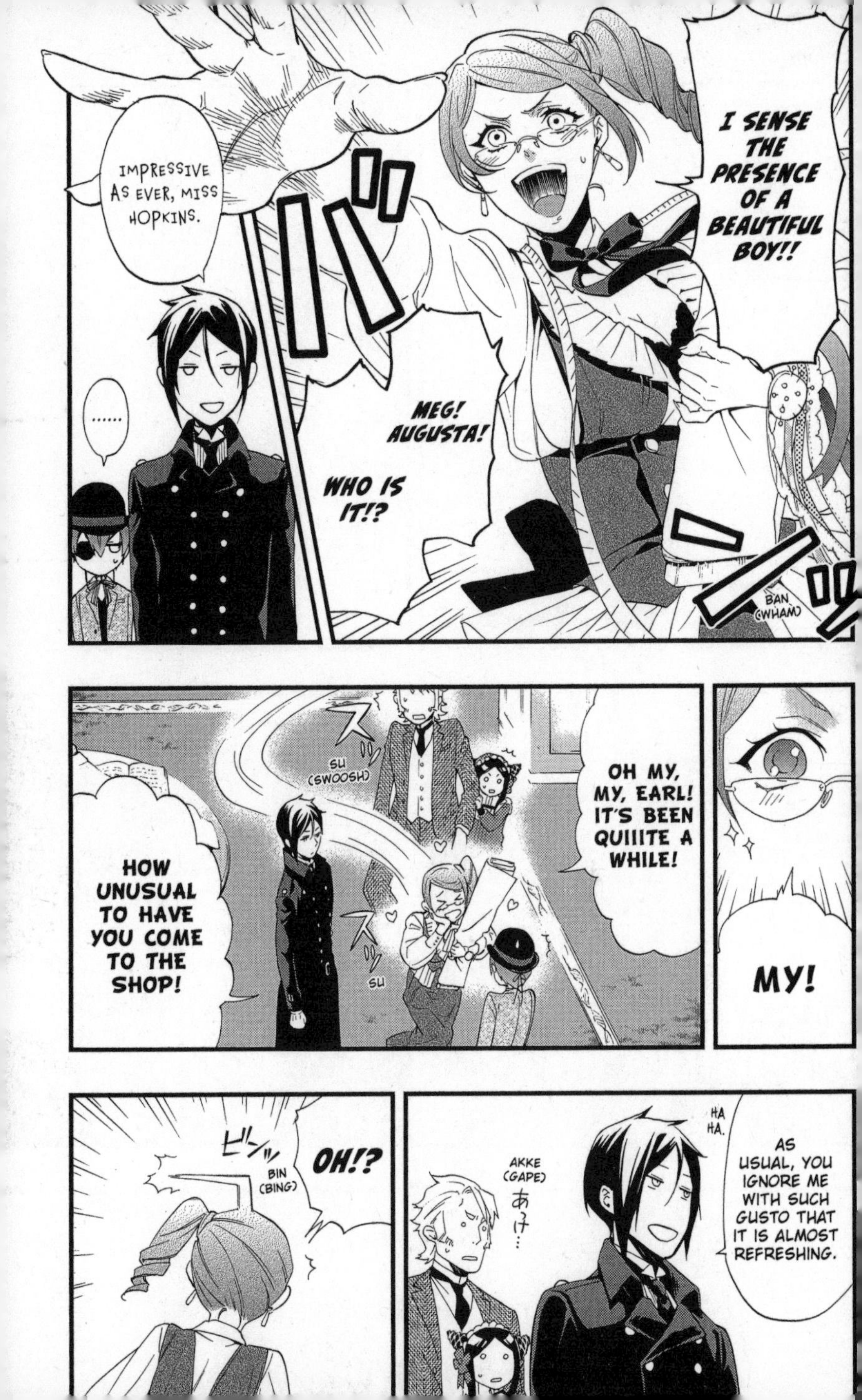
I SENSE THE PRESENCE OF A BEAUTIFUL BOY!!
MEG! AUGUSTA!
WHO IS IT!?
BAN (WHAM)
IMPRESSIVE AS EVER, MISS HOPKINS.
……
MY!
OH MY, MY, EARL! IT'S BEEN QUIIITE A WHILE!
SU (SWOOSH)
HOW UNUSUAL TO HAVE YOU COME TO THE SHOP!
SU
HA HA.
AS USUAL, YOU IGNORE ME WITH SUCH GUSTO THAT IT IS ALMOST REFRESHING.
AKKE (GAPE)
OH!?
BIN (BING)

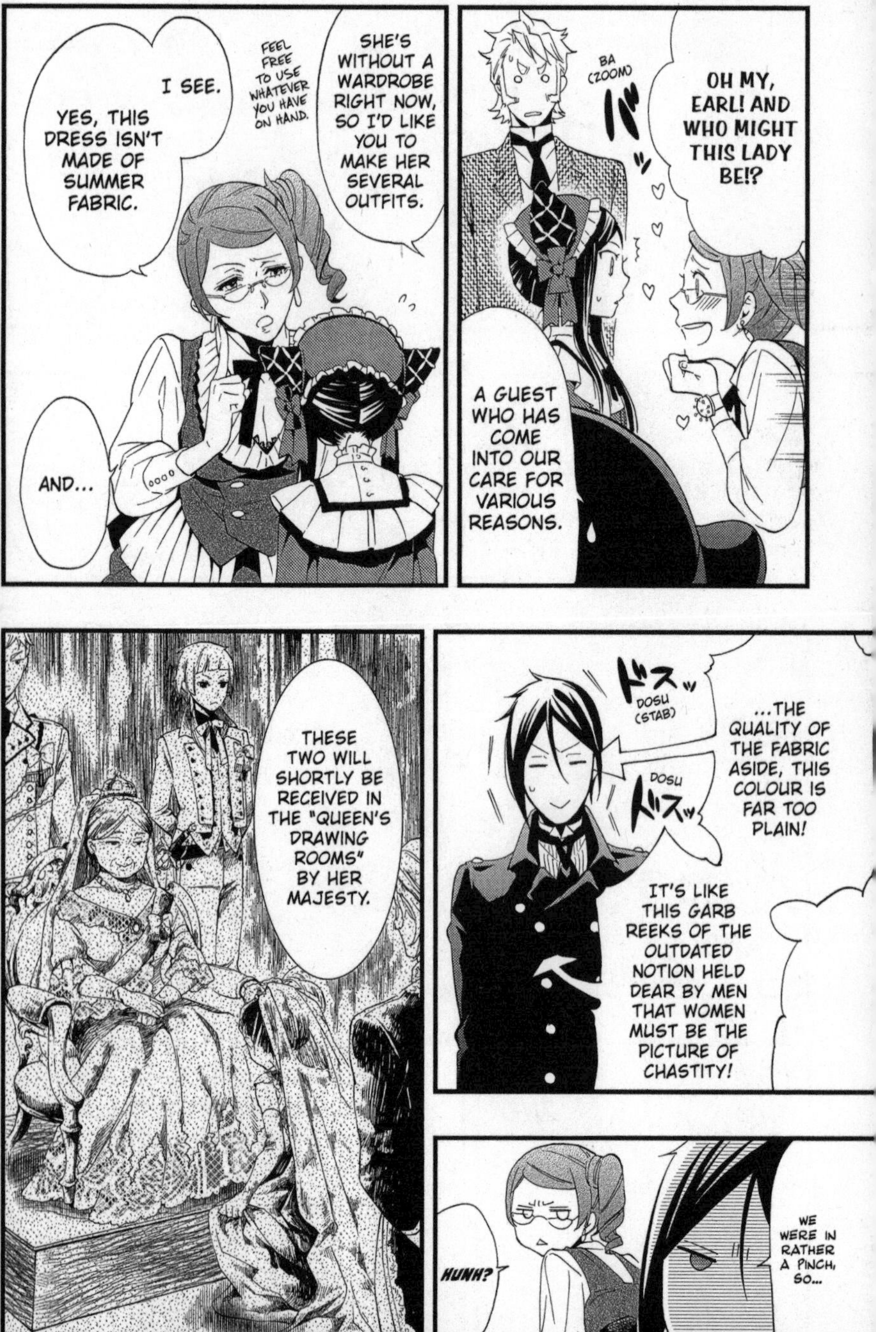
バッ
BA (ZOOM)
OH MY, EARL! AND WHO MIGHT THIS LADY BE!?
A GUEST WHO HAS COME INTO OUR CARE FOR VARIOUS REASONS.
SHE'S WITHOUT A WARDROBE RIGHT NOW, SO I'D LIKE YOU TO MAKE HER SEVERAL OUTFITS.
FEEL FREE TO USE WHATEVER YOU HAVE ON HAND.
I SEE.
YES, THIS DRESS ISN'T MADE OF SUMMER FABRIC.
AND...
ドスッ
DOSU (STAB)
...THE QUALITY OF THE FABRIC ASIDE, THIS COLOUR IS FAR TOO PLAIN!
ドスッ
DOSU
IT'S LIKE THIS GARB REEKS OF THE OUTDATED NOTION HELD DEAR BY MEN THAT WOMEN MUST BE THE PICTURE OF CHASTITY!
WE WERE IN RATHER A PINCH, SO...
HUNH?
THESE TWO WILL SHORTLY BE RECEIVED IN THE "QUEEN'S DRAWING ROOMS" BY HER MAJESTY.

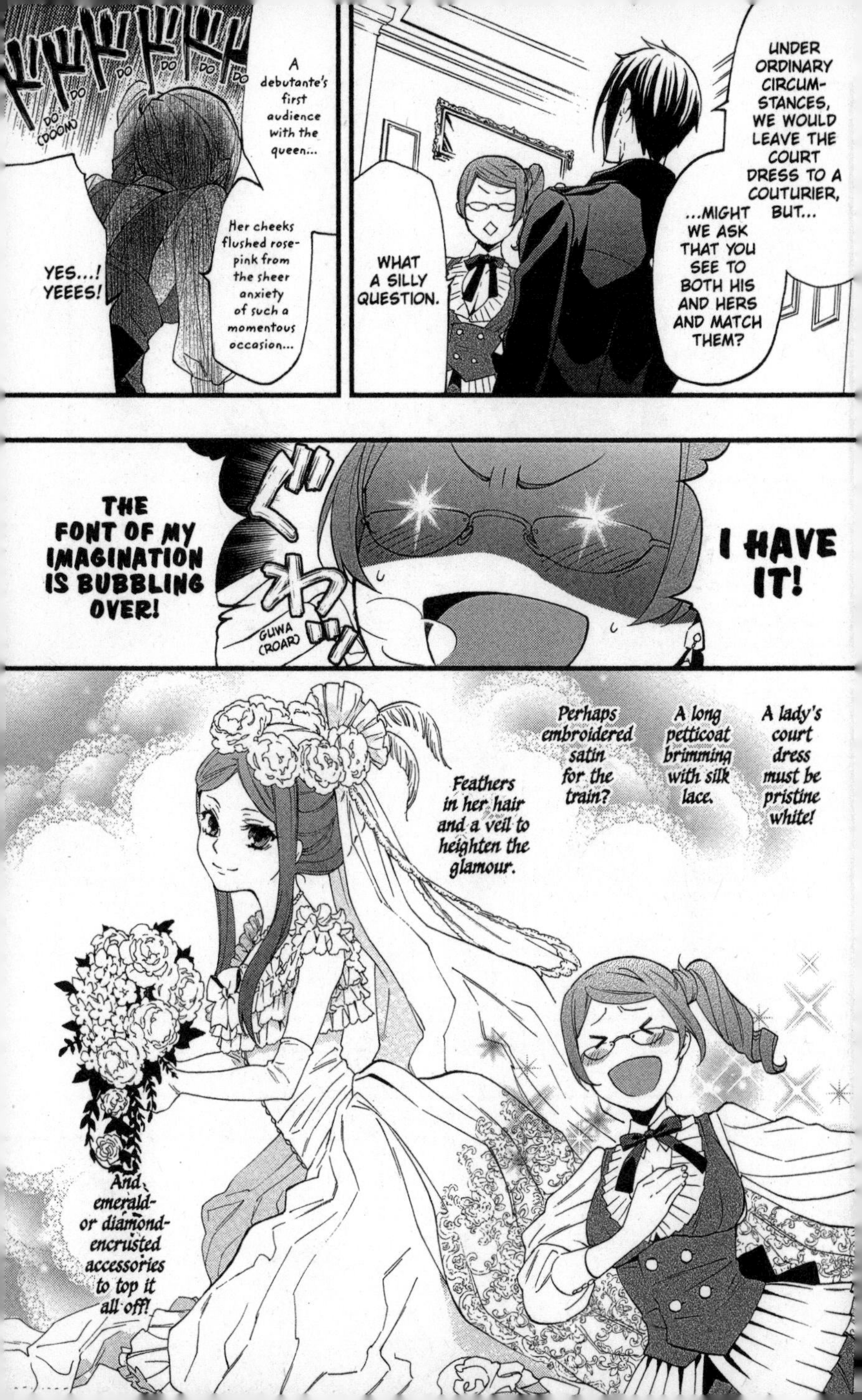
UNDER ORDINARY CIRCUMSTANCES, WE WOULD LEAVE THE COURT DRESS TO A COUTURIER, BUT...
...MIGHT WE ASK THAT YOU SEE TO BOTH HIS AND HERS AND MATCH THEM?
WHAT A SILLY QUESTION.
A debutante's first audience with the queen...
Her cheeks flushed rose-pink from the sheer anxiety of such a momentous occasion...
DO DO DO DO DO DO (DOOM)
YES...! YEEES!
I HAVE IT!
THE FONT OF MY IMAGINATION IS BUBBLING OVER!
GUWA (ROAR)
A lady's court dress must be pristine white!
A long petticoat brimming with silk lace.
Perhaps embroidered satin for the train?
Feathers in her hair and a veil to heighten the glamour.
And emerald- or diamond-encrusted accessories to top it all off!

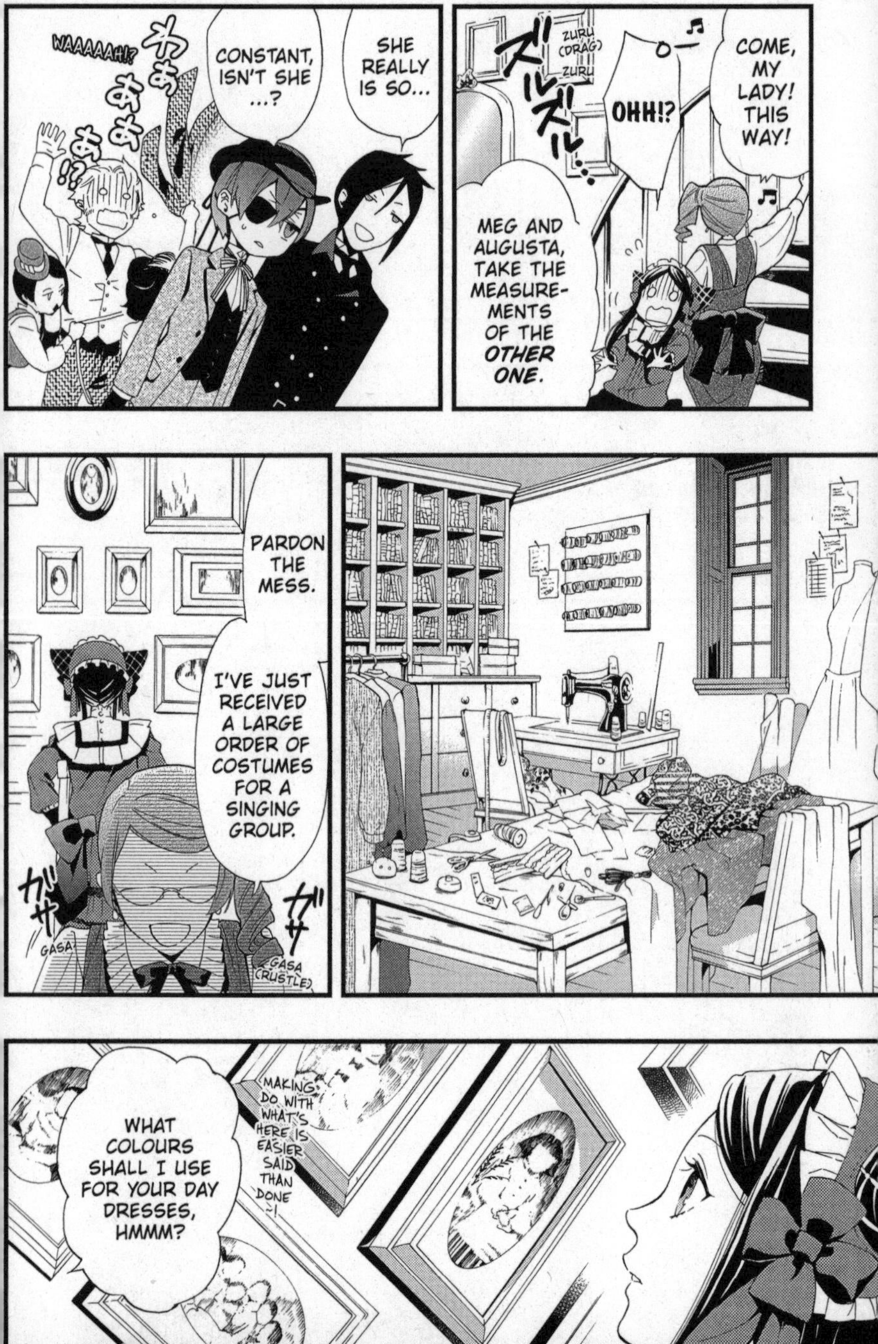
COME, MY LADY! THIS WAY!
O—
OHH!?
ZURU (DRAG) ZURU
MEG AND AUGUSTA, TAKE THE MEASUREMENTS OF THE *OTHER ONE.*
SHE REALLY IS SO...
CONSTANT, ISN'T SHE ...?
WAAAAAH!?
PARDON THE MESS.
I'VE JUST RECEIVED A LARGE ORDER OF COSTUMES FOR A SINGING GROUP.
GASA (RUSTLE)
GASA
MAKING DO WITH WHAT'S HERE IS EASIER SAID THAN DONE
WHAT COLOURS SHALL I USE FOR YOUR DAY DRESSES, HMMM?

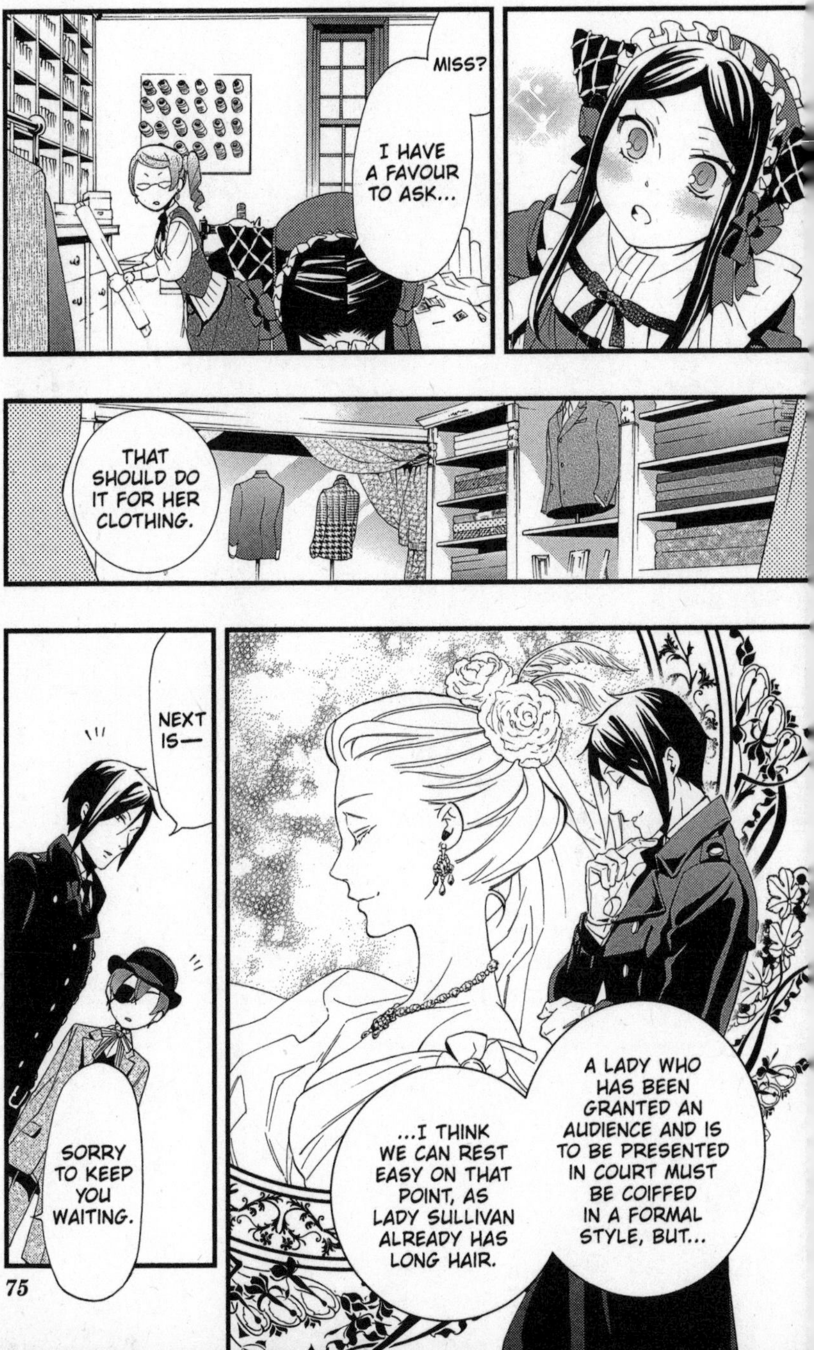
MISS?
I HAVE A FAVOUR TO ASK...
THAT SHOULD DO IT FOR HER CLOTHING.
A LADY WHO HAS BEEN GRANTED AN AUDIENCE AND IS TO BE PRESENTED IN COURT MUST BE COIFFED IN A FORMAL STYLE, BUT...
...I THINK WE CAN REST EASY ON THAT POINT, AS LADY SULLIVAN ALREADY HAS LONG HAIR.
NEXT IS—
SORRY TO KEEP YOU WAITING.

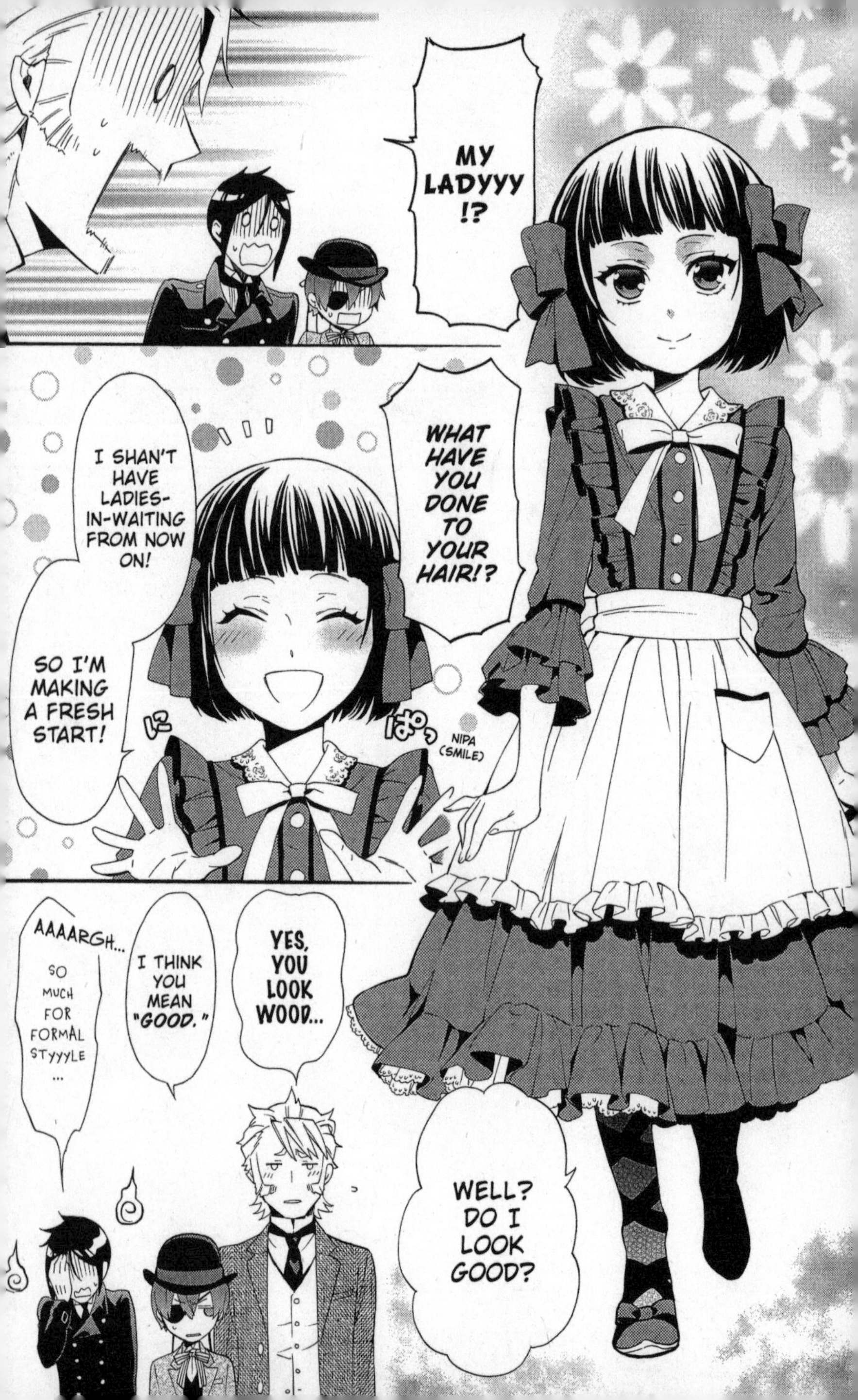
WELL? DO I LOOK GOOD?
MY LADYYY!?
WHAT HAVE YOU DONE TO YOUR HAIR!?
I SHAN'T HAVE LADIES-IN-WAITING FROM NOW ON!
SO I'M MAKING A FRESH START!
NIPA (SMILE)
YES, YOU LOOK WOOD...
I THINK YOU MEAN "GOOD."
AAAARGH... SO MUCH FOR FORMAL STYYYLE...

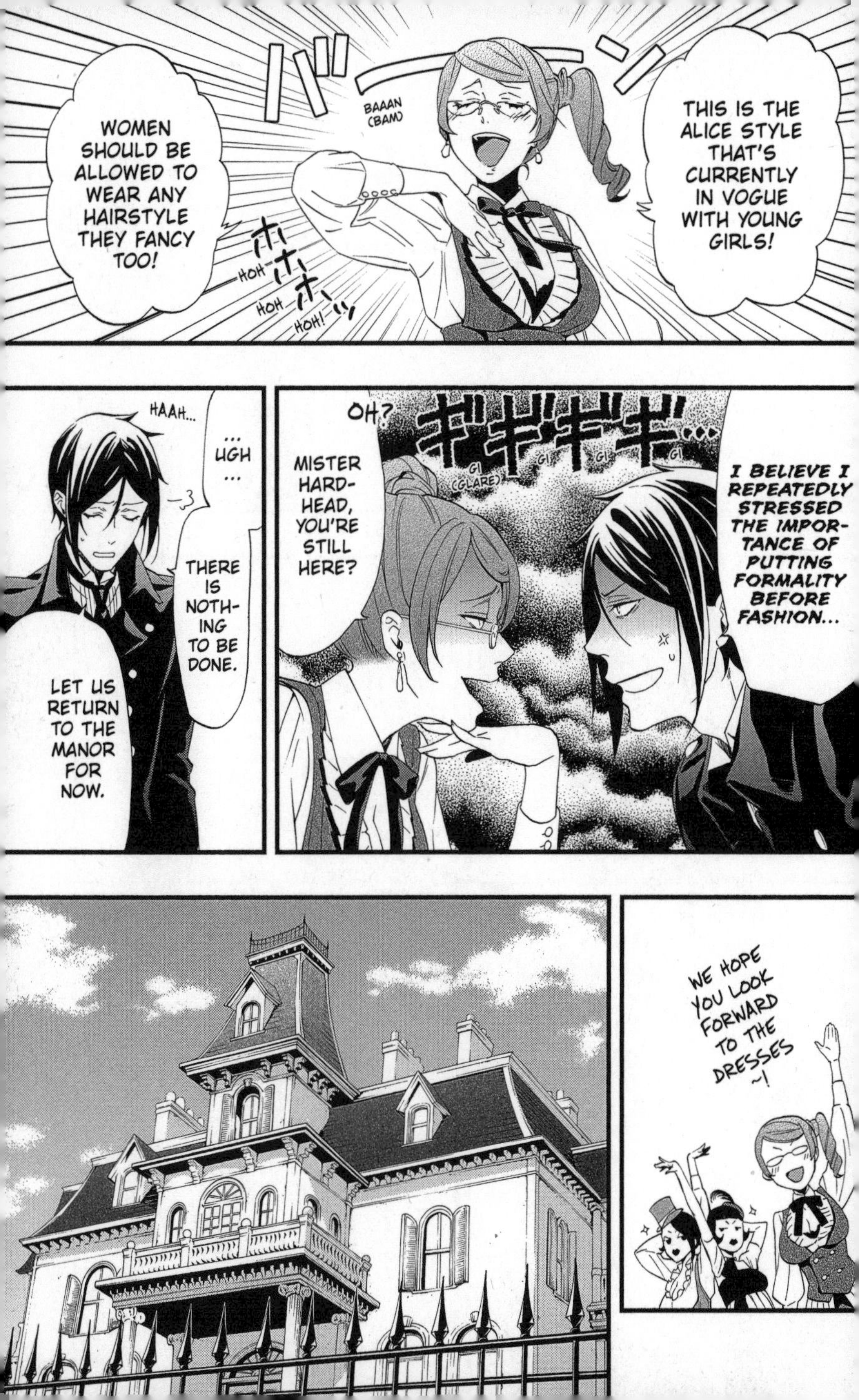

THIS IS THE ALICE STYLE THAT'S CURRENTLY IN VOGUE WITH YOUNG GIRLS!
BAAAN (BAM)
WOMEN SHOULD BE ALLOWED TO WEAR ANY HAIRSTYLE THEY FANCY TOO!
HOH HOH HOH!
I BELIEVE I REPEATEDLY STRESSED THE IMPORTANCE OF PUTTING FORMALITY BEFORE FASHION...
GI GI GI GI (GLARE)
OH?
MISTER HARD-HEAD, YOU'RE STILL HERE?
HAAH...
... UGH ...
THERE IS NOTHING TO BE DONE.
LET US RETURN TO THE MANOR FOR NOW.
WE HOPE YOU LOOK FORWARD TO THE DRESSES ~!

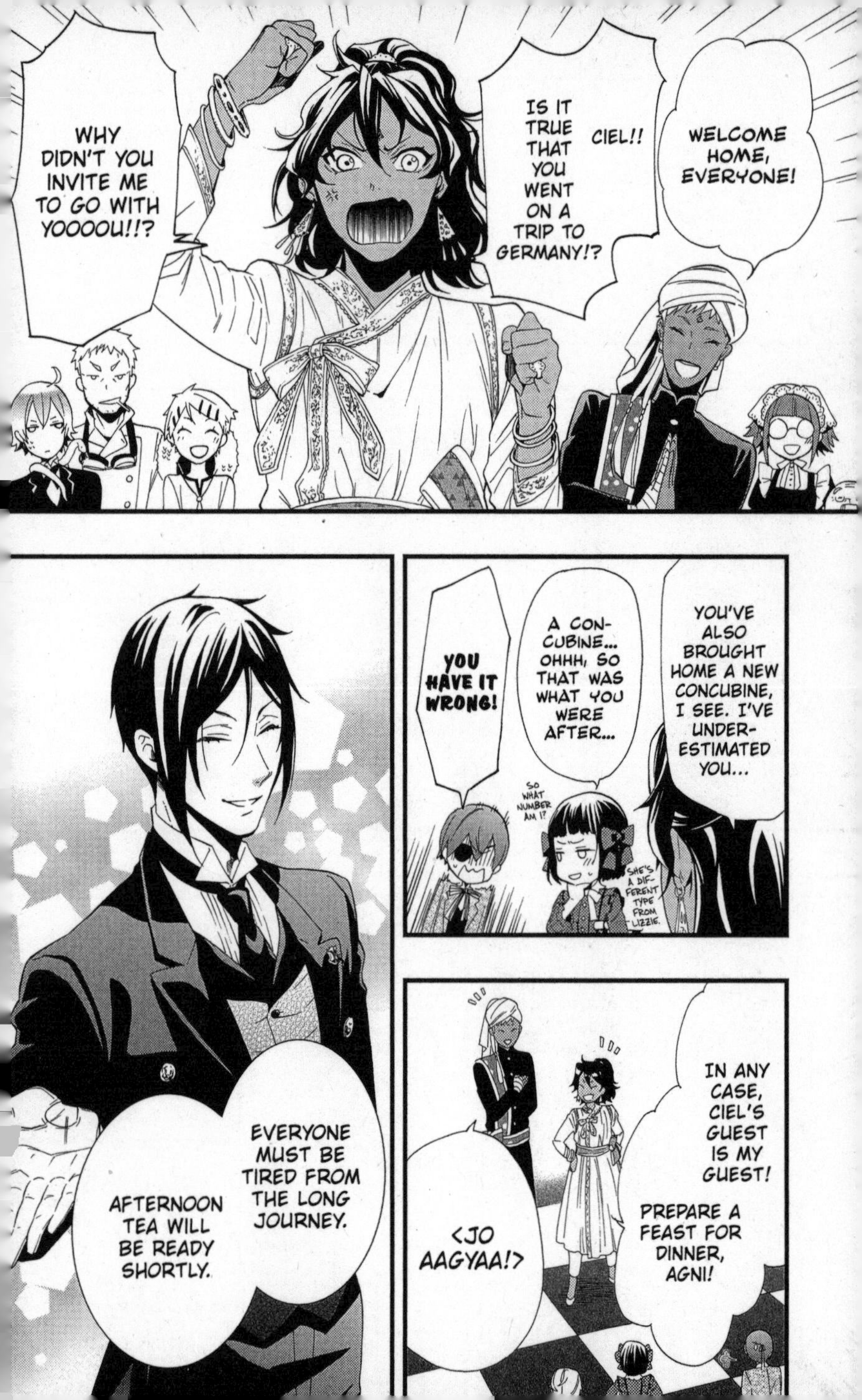
WELCOME HOME, EVERYONE!
CIEL!!
IS IT TRUE THAT YOU WENT ON A TRIP TO GERMANY!?
WHY DIDN'T YOU INVITE ME TO GO WITH YOOOOU!!?
YOU'VE ALSO BROUGHT HOME A NEW CONCUBINE, I SEE. I'VE UNDER-ESTIMATED YOU...
A CON-CUBINE... OHHH, SO THAT WAS WHAT YOU WERE AFTER...
YOU HAVE IT WRONG!
SO WHAT NUMBER AM I?
SHE'S A DIF-FERENT TYPE FROM LIZZIE.
IN ANY CASE, CIEL'S GUEST IS MY GUEST!
PREPARE A FEAST FOR DINNER, AGNI!
<JO AAGYAA!>
EVERYONE MUST BE TIRED FROM THE LONG JOURNEY.
AFTERNOON TEA WILL BE READY SHORTLY.

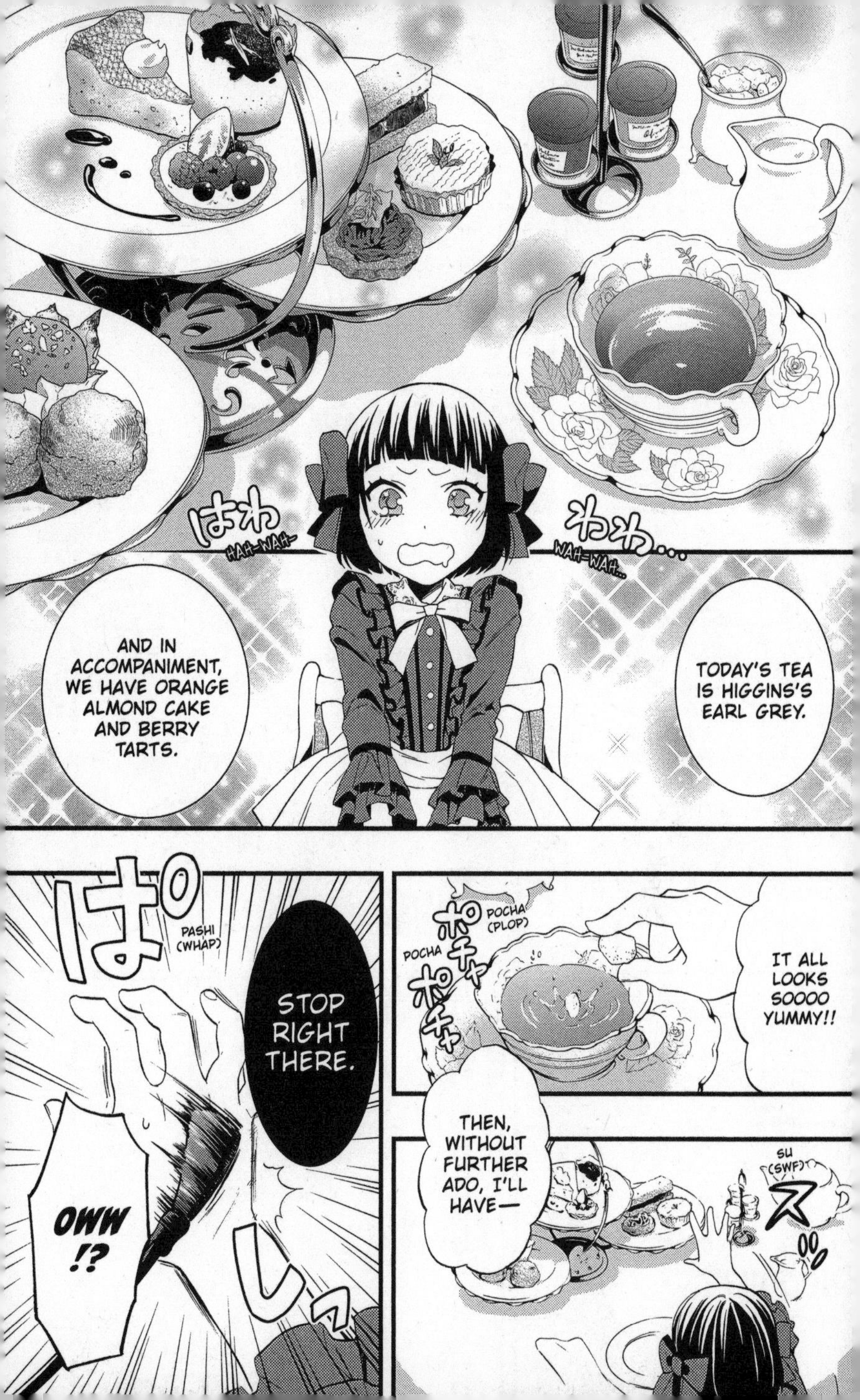

わわ…
WAH-WAH…
はわ
HAH-WAH-
TODAY'S TEA IS HIGGINS'S EARL GREY.
AND IN ACCOMPANIMENT, WE HAVE ORANGE ALMOND CAKE AND BERRY TARTS.
IT ALL LOOKS SOOOO YUMMY!!
ポチャ
POCHA (PLOP)
ポチャ
POCHA
SU (SWF)
ス
THEN, WITHOUT FURTHER ADO, I'LL HAVE—
ぱ
PASHI (WHAP)
STOP RIGHT THERE.
OWW !?

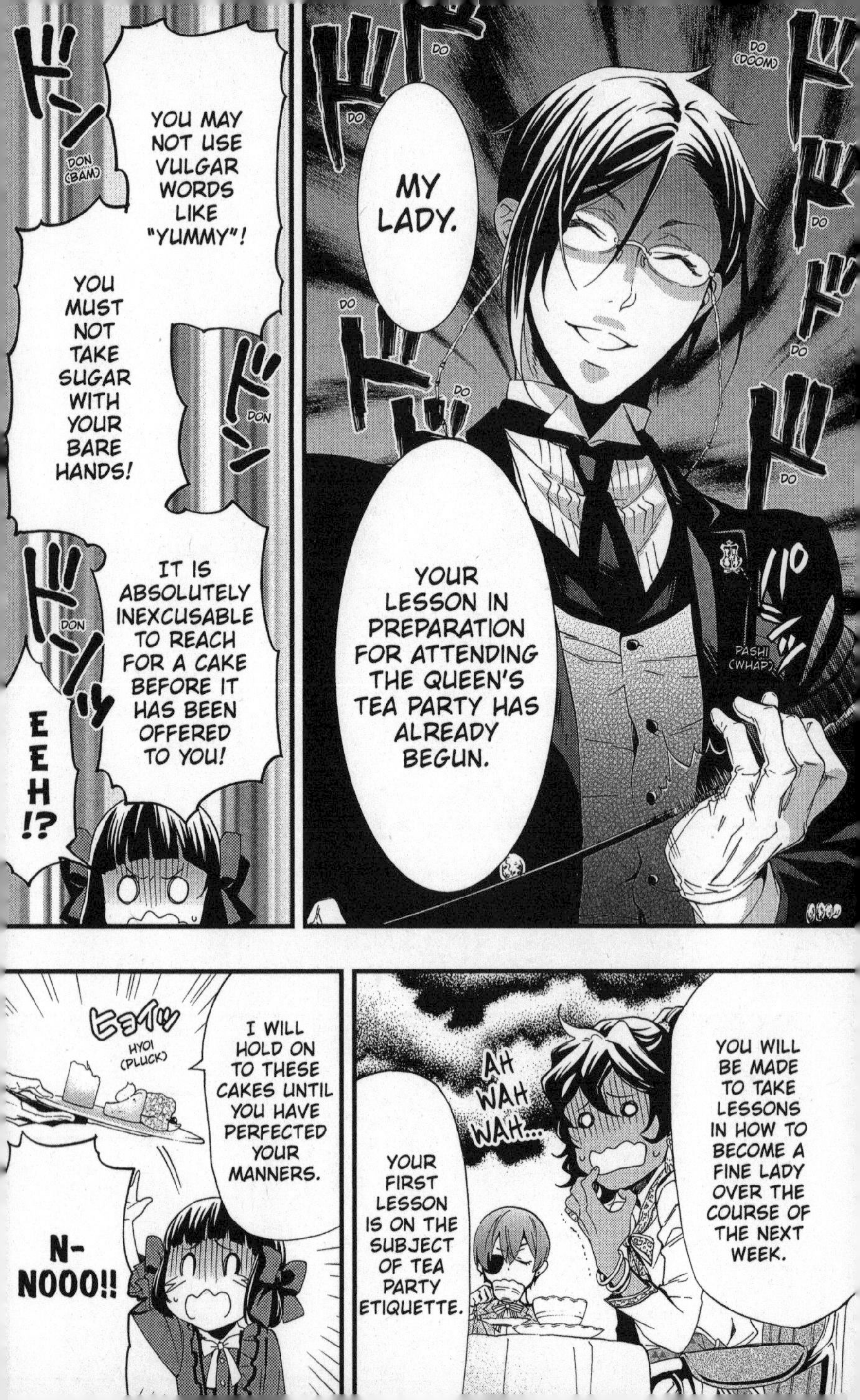
DO
DO (DOOM)
DO
DO
MY LADY.
DO
DO
DO
DO
DO
YOUR LESSON IN PREPARATION FOR ATTENDING THE QUEEN'S TEA PARTY HAS ALREADY BEGUN.
PASHI (WHAP)
DON (BAM)
YOU MAY NOT USE VULGAR WORDS LIKE "YUMMY"!
YOU MUST NOT TAKE SUGAR WITH YOUR BARE HANDS!
DON
DON
IT IS ABSOLUTELY INEXCUSABLE TO REACH FOR A CAKE BEFORE IT HAS BEEN OFFERED TO YOU!
EEEH!?
YOU WILL BE MADE TO TAKE LESSONS IN HOW TO BECOME A FINE LADY OVER THE COURSE OF THE NEXT WEEK.
AH WAH WAH...
YOUR FIRST LESSON IS ON THE SUBJECT OF TEA PARTY ETIQUETTE.
HYOI (PLUCK)
I WILL HOLD ON TO THESE CAKES UNTIL YOU HAVE PERFECTED YOUR MANNERS.
N-NOOO!!

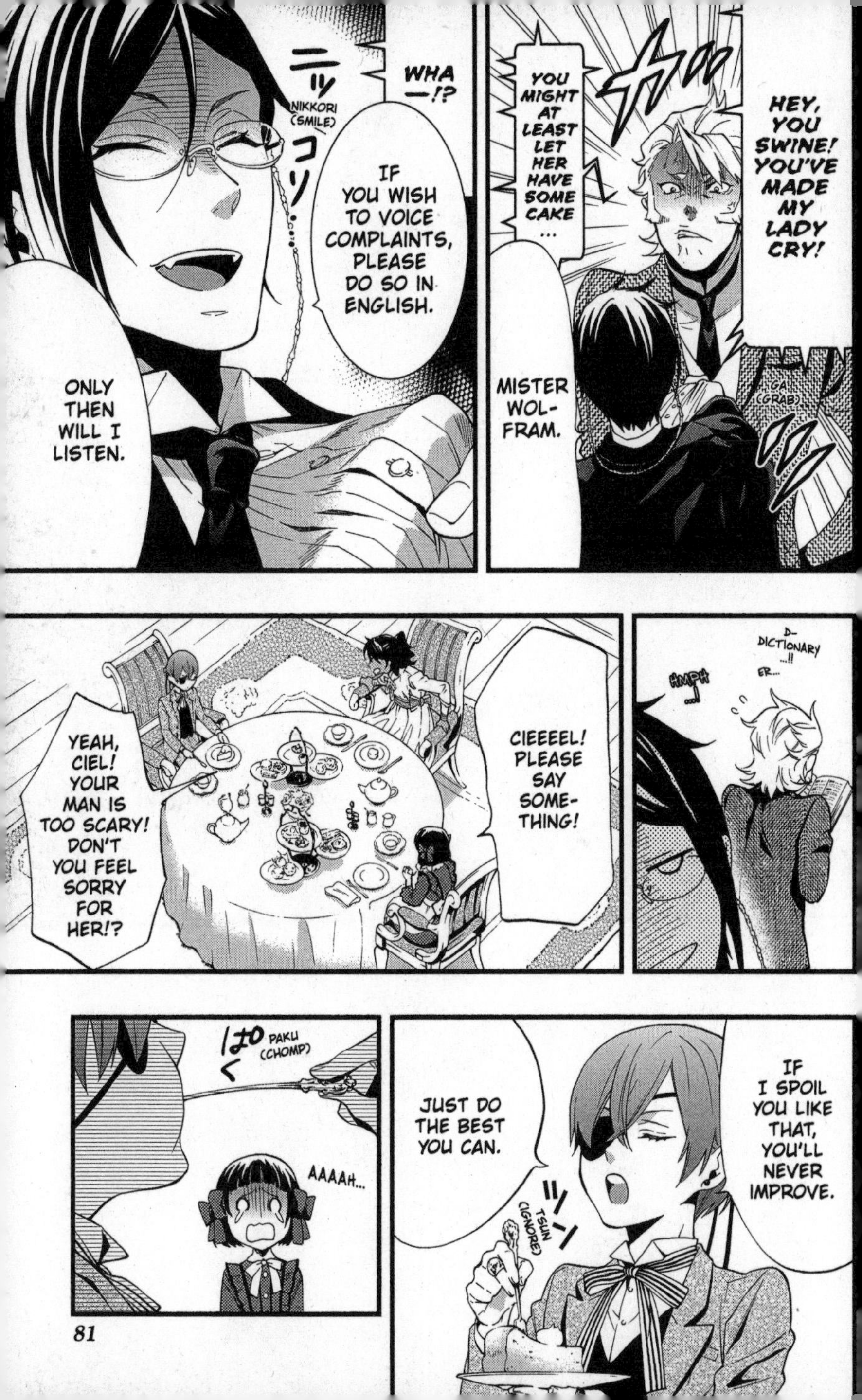

HEY, YOU SWINE! YOU'VE MADE MY LADY CRY!
GA (GRAB)
YOU MIGHT AT LEAST LET HER HAVE SOME CAKE ...
MISTER WOLFRAM.
WHA—!?
NIKKORI (SMILE)
IF YOU WISH TO VOICE COMPLAINTS, PLEASE DO SO IN ENGLISH.
ONLY THEN WILL I LISTEN.
D-DICTIONARY ...!!
ER...
HMPH ...!
CIEEEEL! PLEASE SAY SOMETHING!
YEAH, CIEL! YOUR MAN IS TOO SCARY! DON'T YOU FEEL SORRY FOR HER!?
IF I SPOIL YOU LIKE THAT, YOU'LL NEVER IMPROVE.
TSUN (IGNORE)
JUST DO THE BEST YOU CAN.
PAKU (CHOMP)
AAAAH...

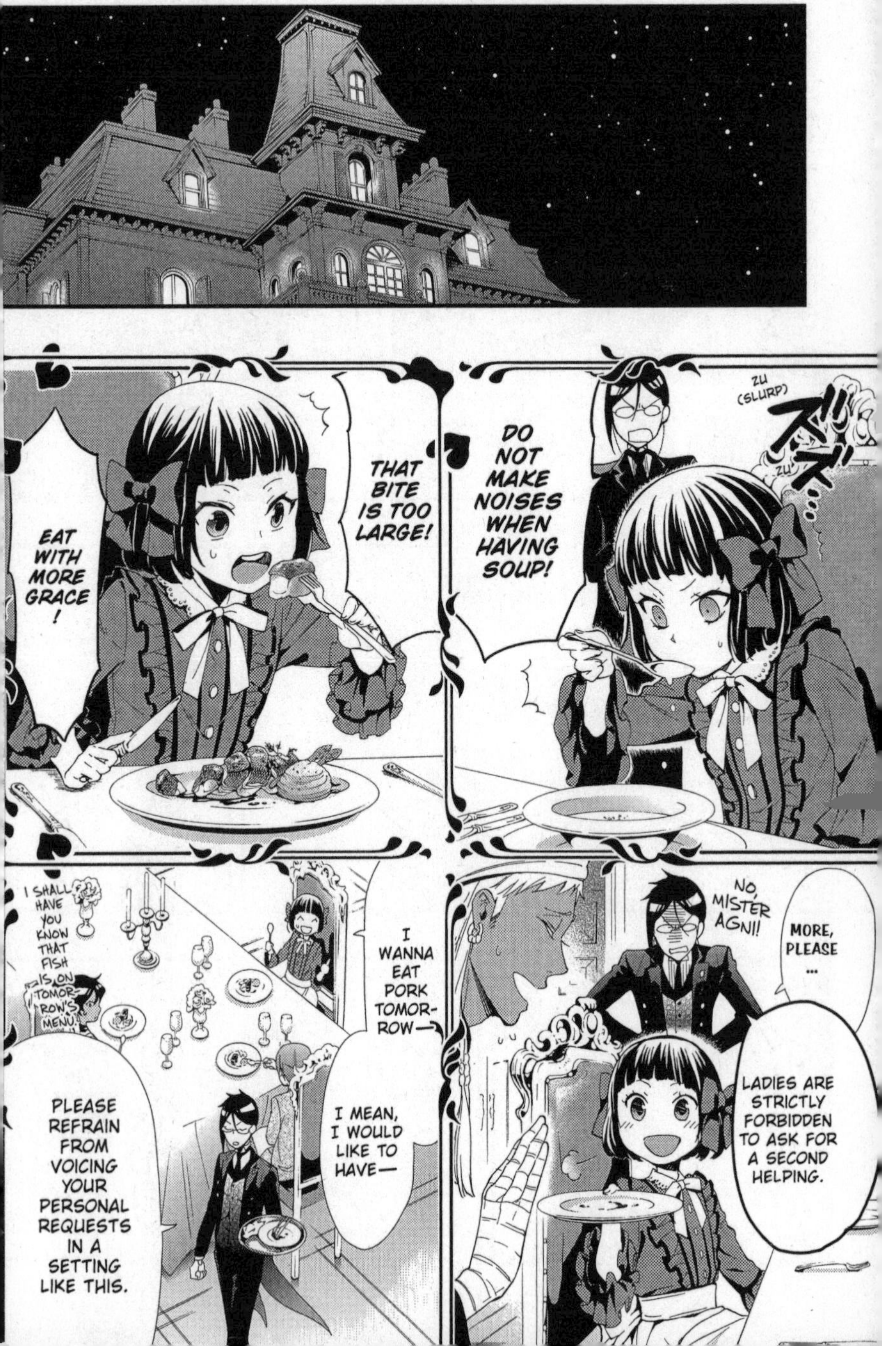

ZU (SLURP)
ZU
DO NOT MAKE NOISES WHEN HAVING SOUP!
THAT BITE IS TOO LARGE!
EAT WITH MORE GRACE!
MORE, PLEASE ...
NO, MISTER AGNI!
LADIES ARE STRICTLY FORBIDDEN TO ASK FOR A SECOND HELPING.
I WANNA EAT PORK TOMORROW—
I SHALL HAVE YOU KNOW THAT FISH IS ON TOMORROW'S MENU.
I MEAN, I WOULD LIKE TO HAVE—
PLEASE REFRAIN FROM VOICING YOUR PERSONAL REQUESTS IN A SETTING LIKE THIS.

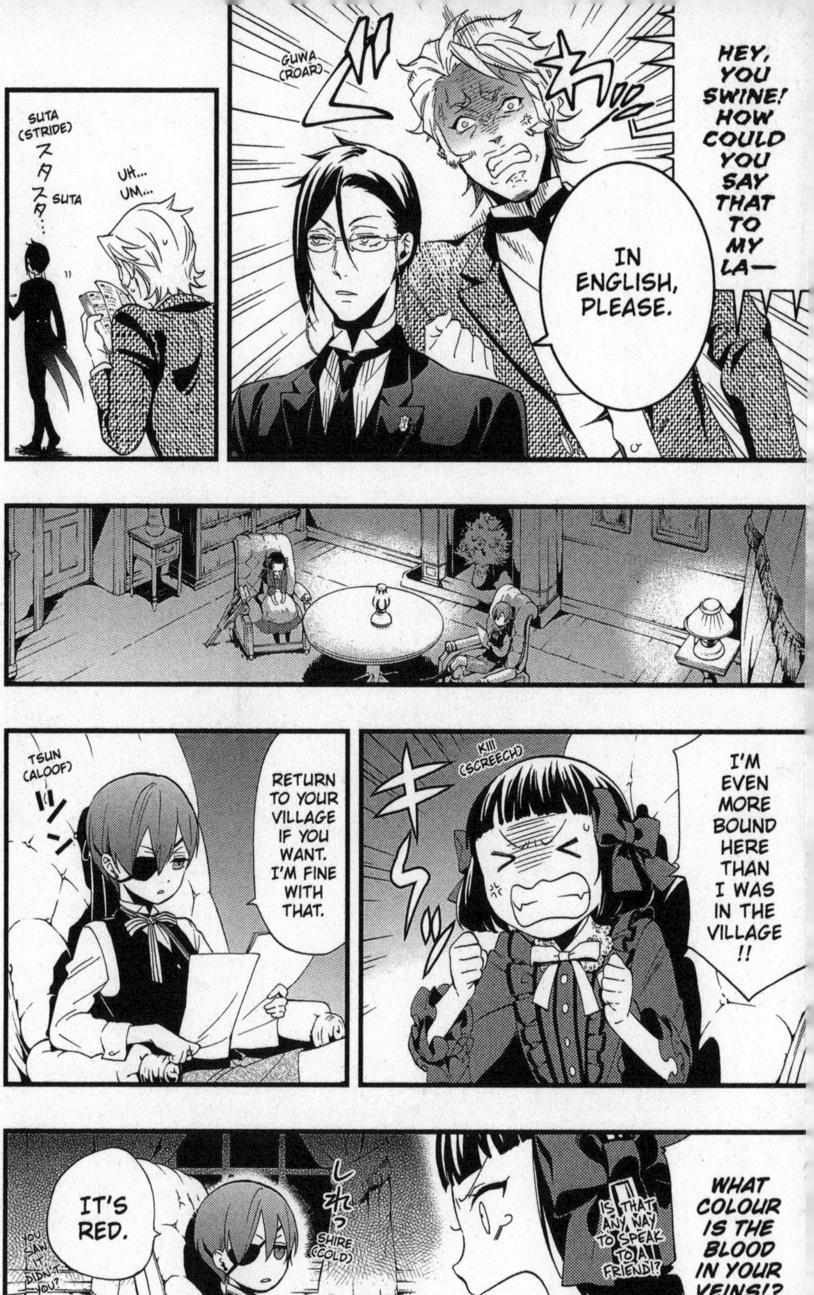
HEY, YOU SWINE! HOW COULD YOU SAY THAT TO MY LA—
GUWA (ROAR)
IN ENGLISH, PLEASE.
SUTA (STRIDE)
スタスタ…
SUTA
UH... UM...
I'M EVEN MORE BOUND HERE THAN I WAS IN THE VILLAGE!!
KIII (SCREECH)
RETURN TO YOUR VILLAGE IF YOU WANT. I'M FINE WITH THAT.
TSUN (ALOOF)
WHAT COLOUR IS THE BLOOD IN YOUR VEINS!?
IS THAT ANY WAY TO SPEAK TO A FRIEND!?
しれっ
SHIRE (COLD)
IT'S RED.
YOU SAW IT, DIDN'T YOU?

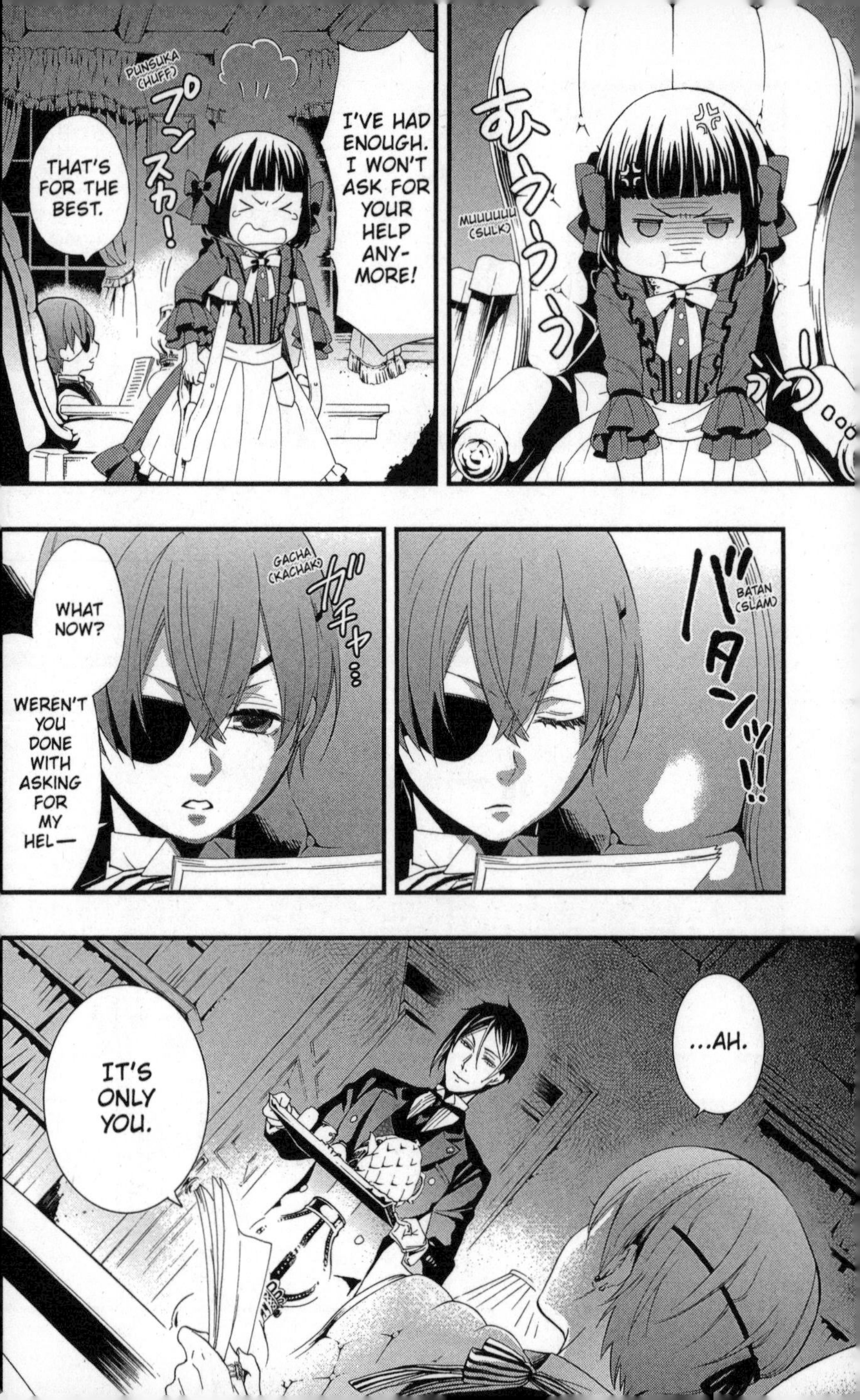
MUUUUUU (SULK)
PUNSUKA (HUFF)
プンスカ!
I'VE HAD ENOUGH. I WON'T ASK FOR YOUR HELP ANY-MORE!
THAT'S FOR THE BEST.
BATAN (SLAM)
バタンッ!!
GACHA (KACHAK)
ガチャ…
WHAT NOW?
WEREN'T YOU DONE WITH ASKING FOR MY HEL—
...AH.
IT'S ONLY YOU.

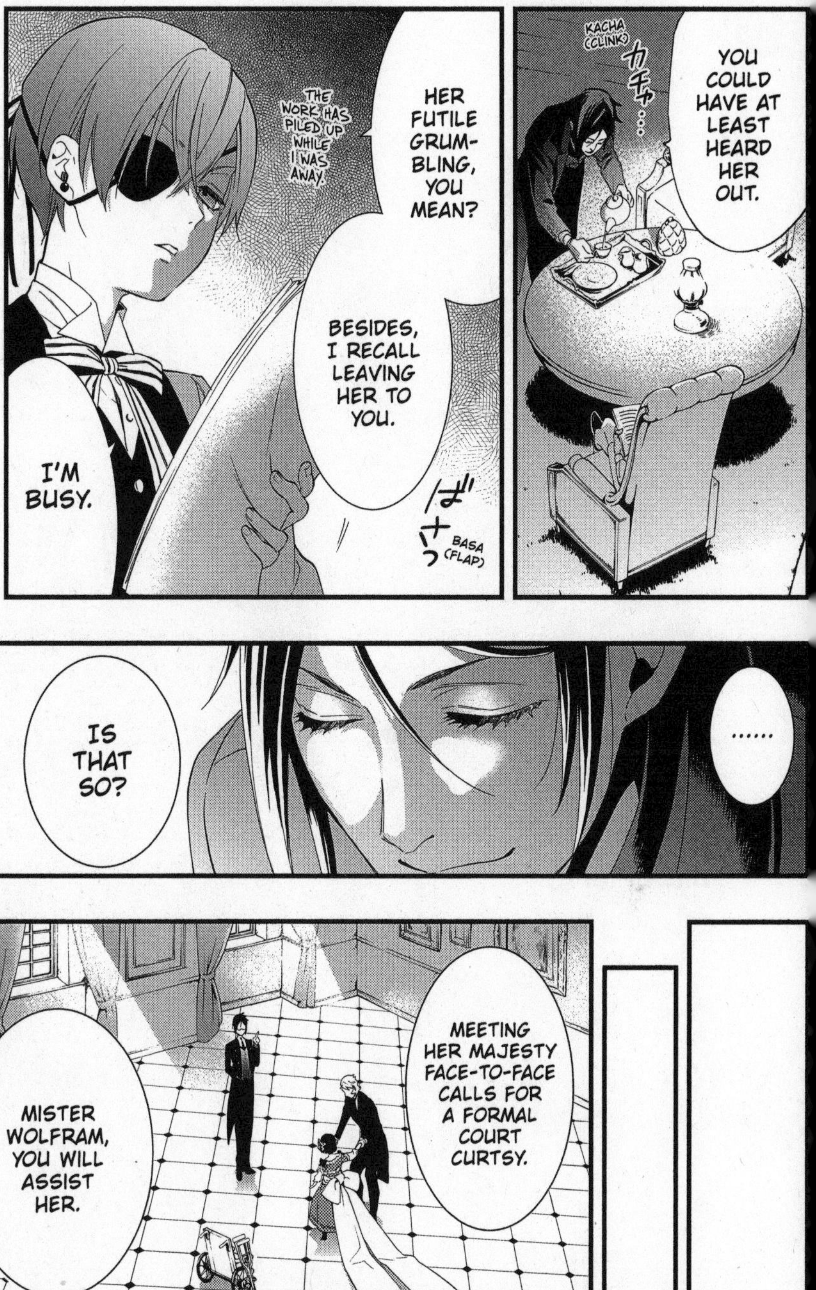
KACHA (CLINK)
カチャ…
YOU COULD HAVE AT LEAST HEARD HER OUT.
HER FUTILE GRUM-BLING, YOU MEAN?
THE WORK HAS PILED UP WHILE I WAS AWAY.
BESIDES, I RECALL LEAVING HER TO YOU.
ばさっ
BASA (FLAP)
I'M BUSY.
......
IS THAT SO?
MEETING HER MAJESTY FACE-TO-FACE CALLS FOR A FORMAL COURT CURTSY.
MISTER WOLFRAM, YOU WILL ASSIST HER.

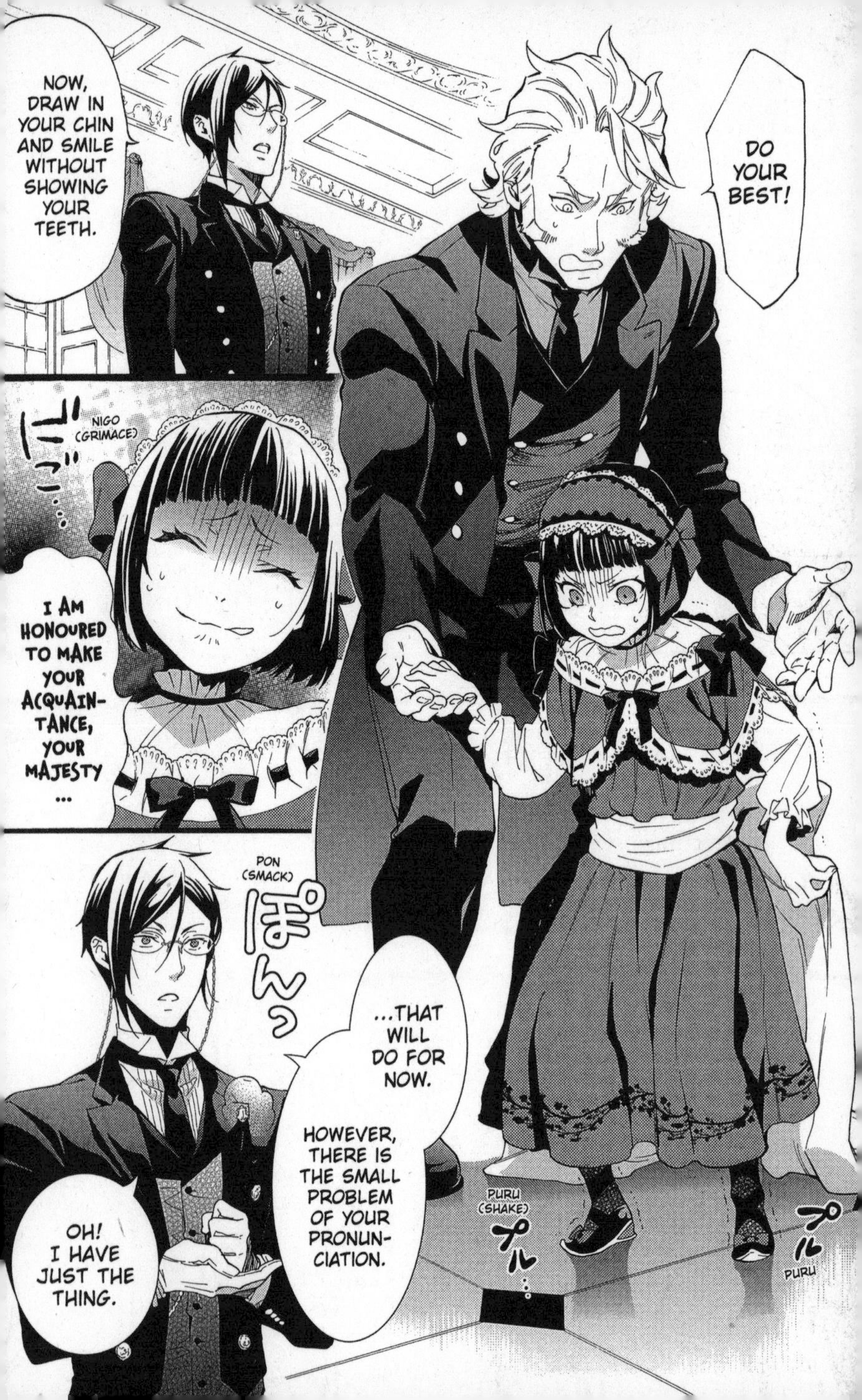
DO YOUR BEST!
PURU (SHAKE)
PURU
NOW, DRAW IN YOUR CHIN AND SMILE WITHOUT SHOWING YOUR TEETH.
NIGO (GRIMACE)
I AM HONOURED TO MAKE YOUR ACQUAINTANCE, YOUR MAJESTY...
PON (SMACK)
...THAT WILL DO FOR NOW.
HOWEVER, THERE IS THE SMALL PROBLEM OF YOUR PRONUNCIATION.
OH! I HAVE JUST THE THING.

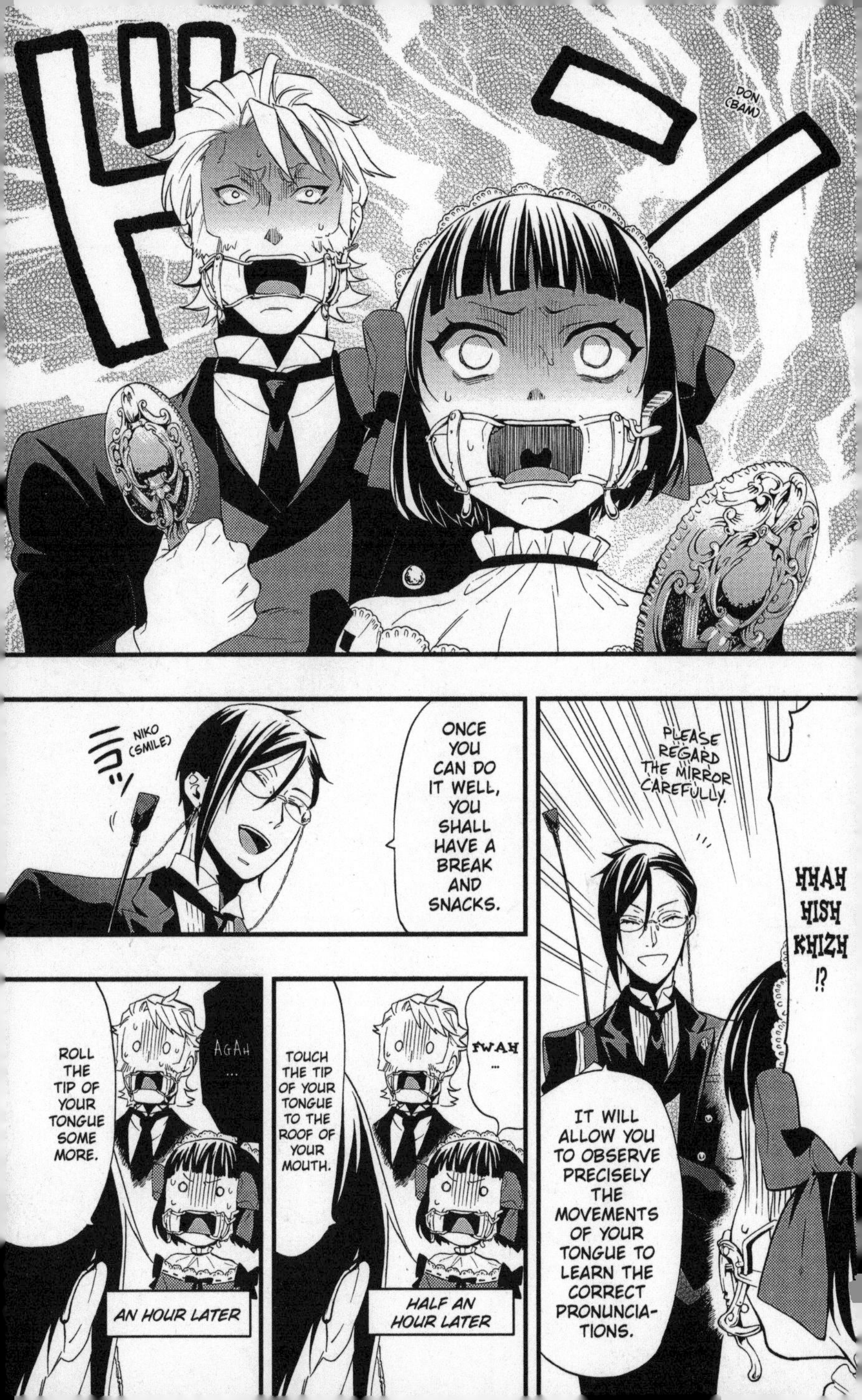
DON (BAM)
PLEASE REGARD THE MIRROR CAREFULLY.
HHAH HISH KHIZH !?
IT WILL ALLOW YOU TO OBSERVE PRECISELY THE MOVEMENTS OF YOUR TONGUE TO LEARN THE CORRECT PRONUNCIA-TIONS.
NIKO (SMILE)
ONCE YOU CAN DO IT WELL, YOU SHALL HAVE A BREAK AND SNACKS.
HALF AN HOUR LATER
TOUCH THE TIP OF YOUR TONGUE TO THE ROOF OF YOUR MOUTH.
FWAH ...
AN HOUR LATER
ROLL THE TIP OF YOUR TONGUE SOME MORE.
AGAH ...

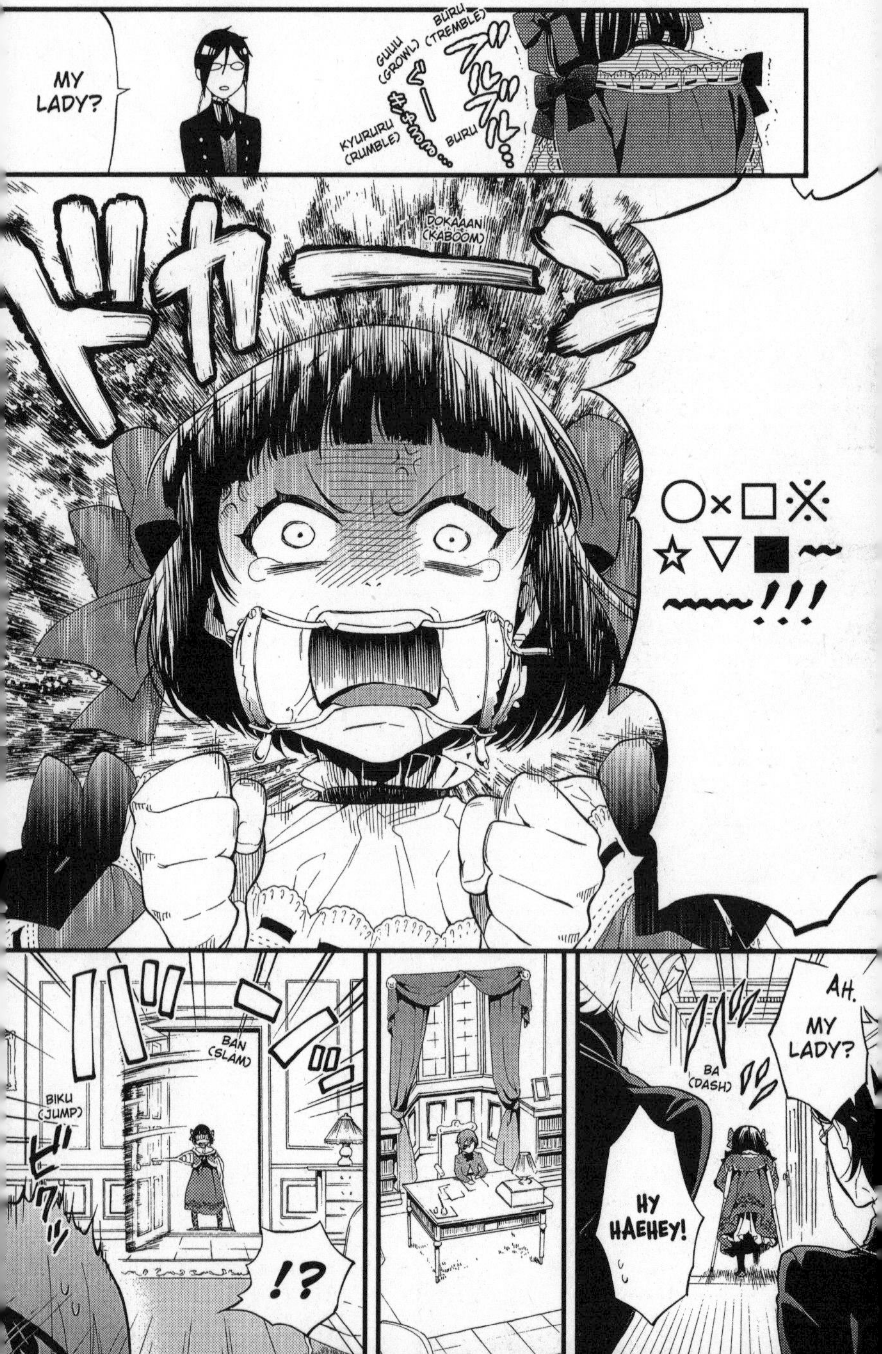
BURU (TREMBLE)
GUUU (GROWL)
BURU
KYURURU (RUMBLE)
MY LADY?
DOKAAAN (KABOOM)
○×□※
☆▽■~
~~~~!!!
AH. MY LADY?
BA (DASH)
HY HAEHEY!
BAN (SLAM)
BIKU (JUMP)
!?
~~~~

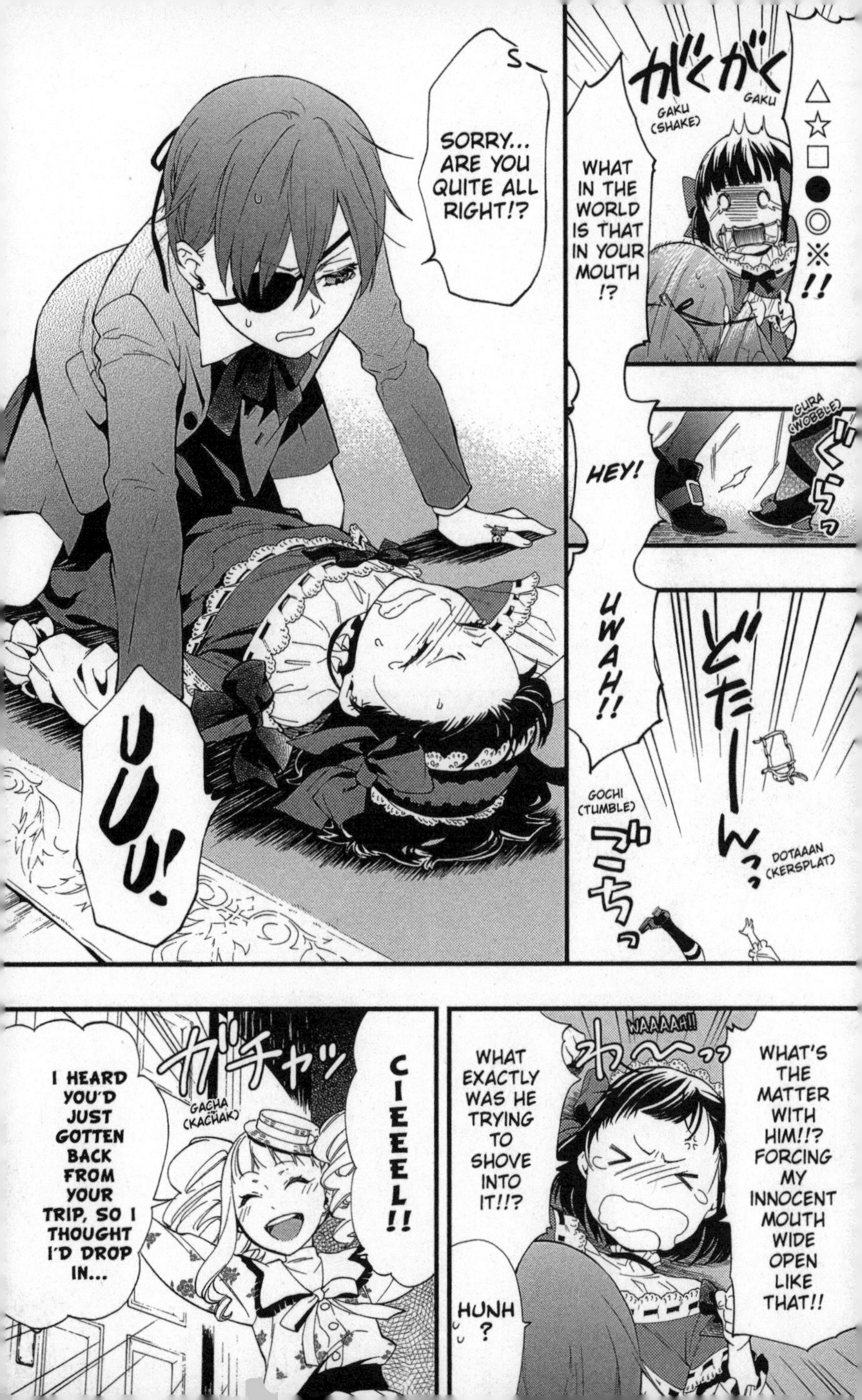
△☆□●◎※!!
がくがく
GAKU
GAKU (SHAKE)
WHAT IN THE WORLD IS THAT IN YOUR MOUTH!?
ぐらっ
GURA (WOBBLE)
HEY!
どたーんっ
DOTAAAN (KERSPLAT)
UWAH!!
ごちっ
GOCHI (TUMBLE)
S—
SORRY... ARE YOU QUITE ALL RIGHT!?
UUUU!
WHAT'S THE MATTER WITH HIM!!? FORCING MY INNOCENT MOUTH WIDE OPEN LIKE THAT!!
わ〜っっ
WAAAAH!!
WHAT EXACTLY WAS HE TRYING TO SHOVE INTO IT!!?
HUNH?
ガチャッ
GACHA (KACHAK)
CIEEEL!!
I HEARD YOU'D JUST GOTTEN BACK FROM YOUR TRIP, SO I THOUGHT I'D DROP IN...

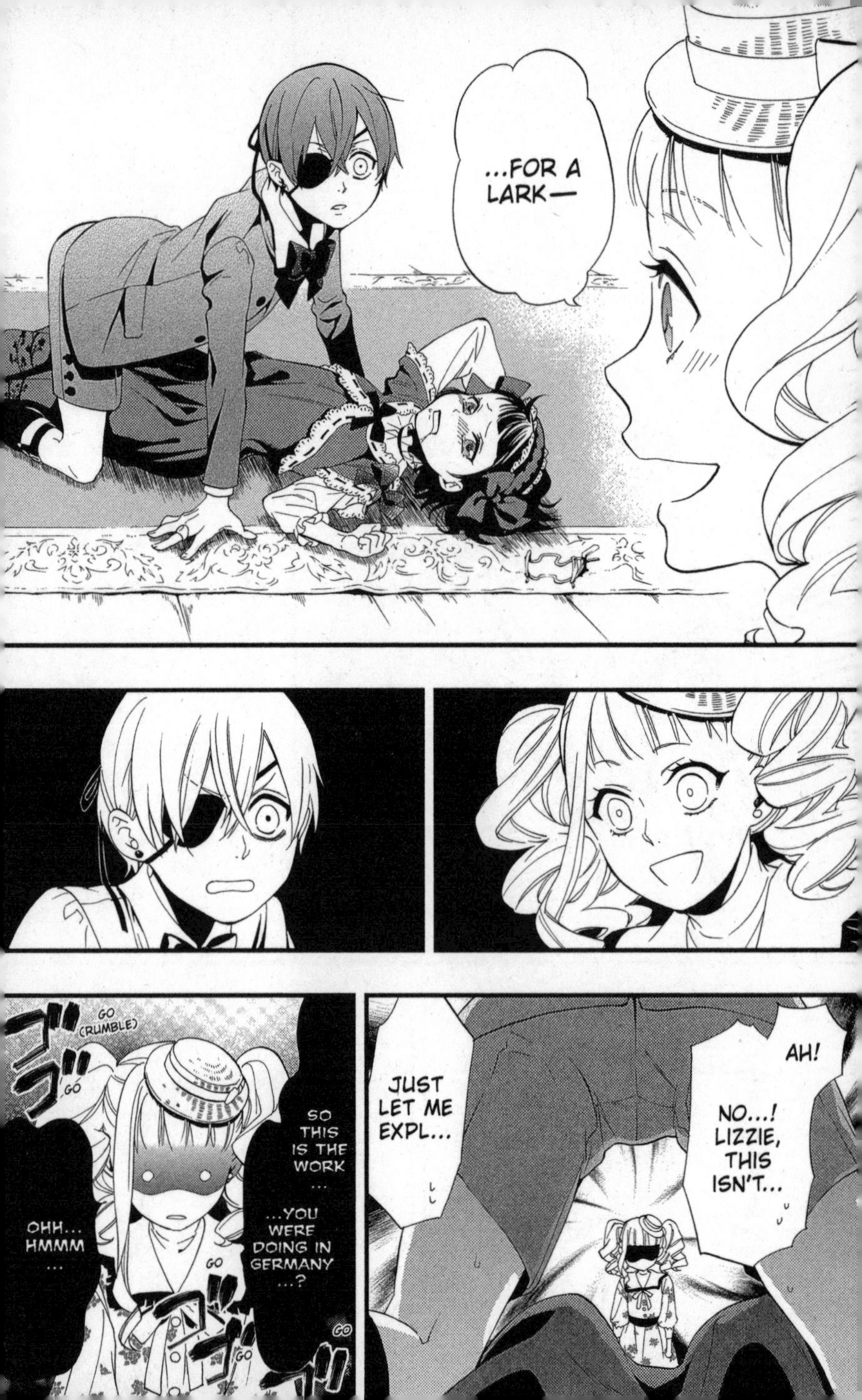
...FOR A LARK—
AH!
NO...! LIZZIE, THIS ISN'T...
JUST LET ME EXPL...
SO THIS IS THE WORK ...
...YOU WERE DOING IN GERMANY ...?
GO (RUMBLE)
GO
OHH... HMMM ...
GO
GO

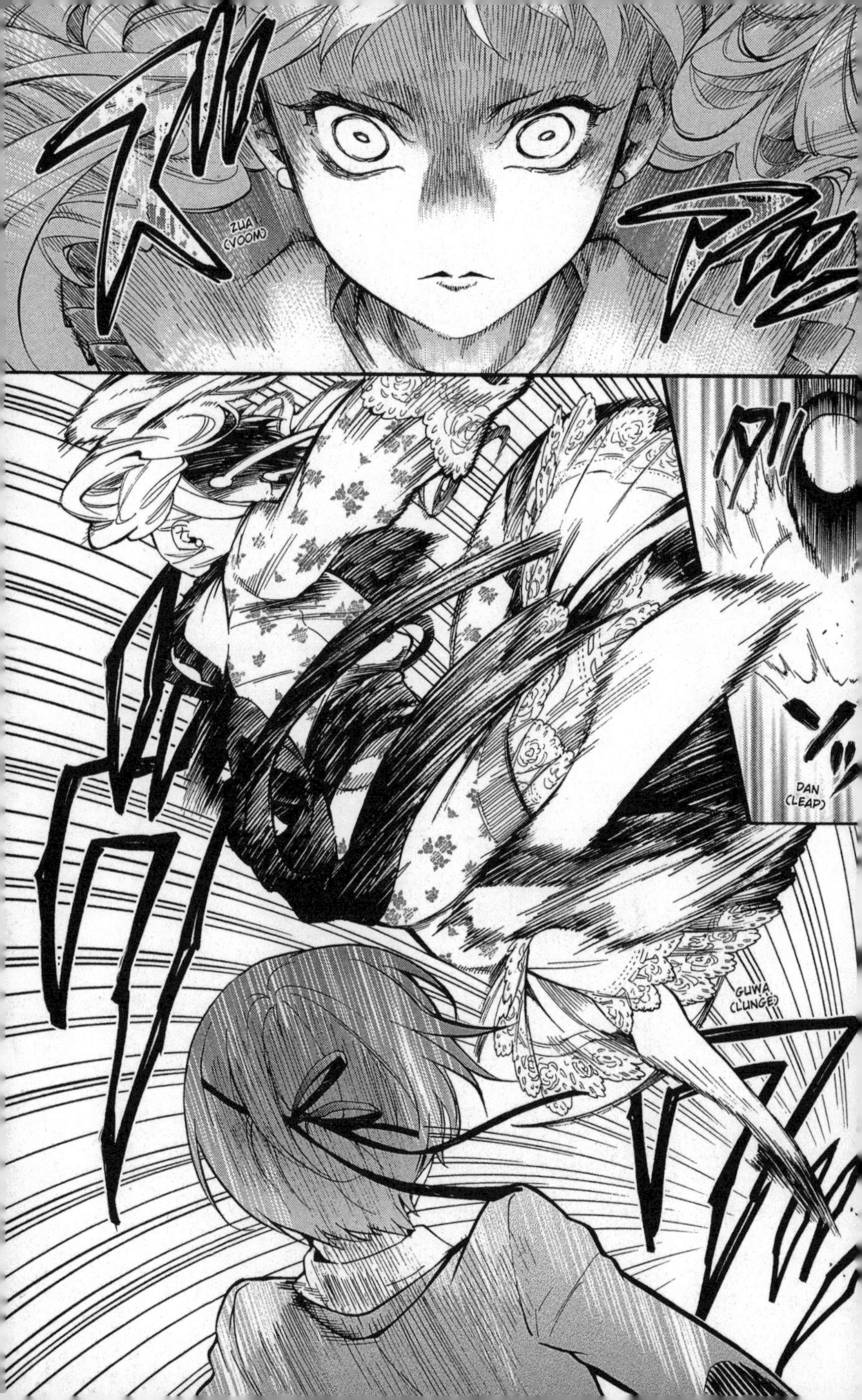
ZUA (VOOM)
DAN (LEAP)
GUWA (LUNGE)

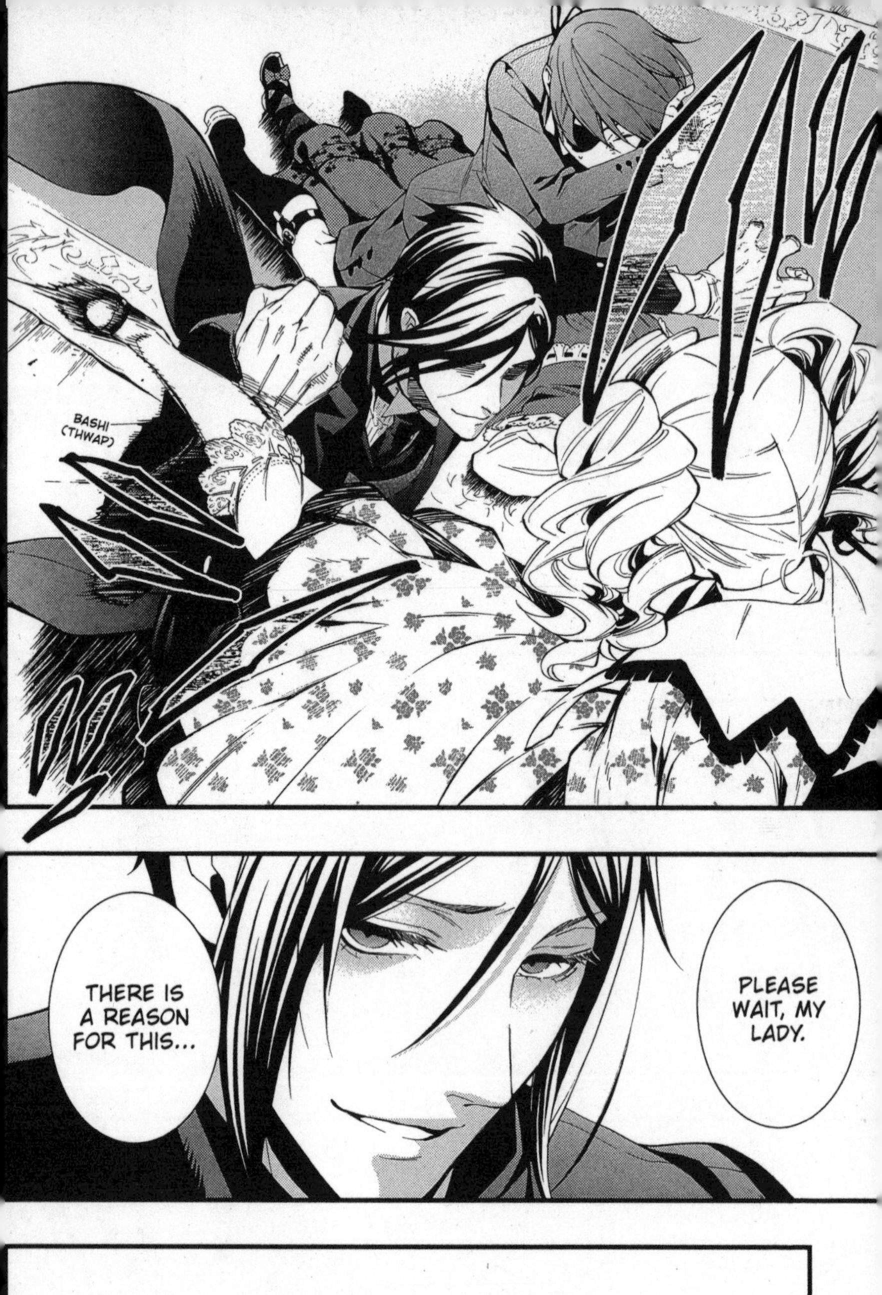
BASHI
(THWAP)
PLEASE WAIT, MY LADY.
THERE IS A REASON FOR THIS...

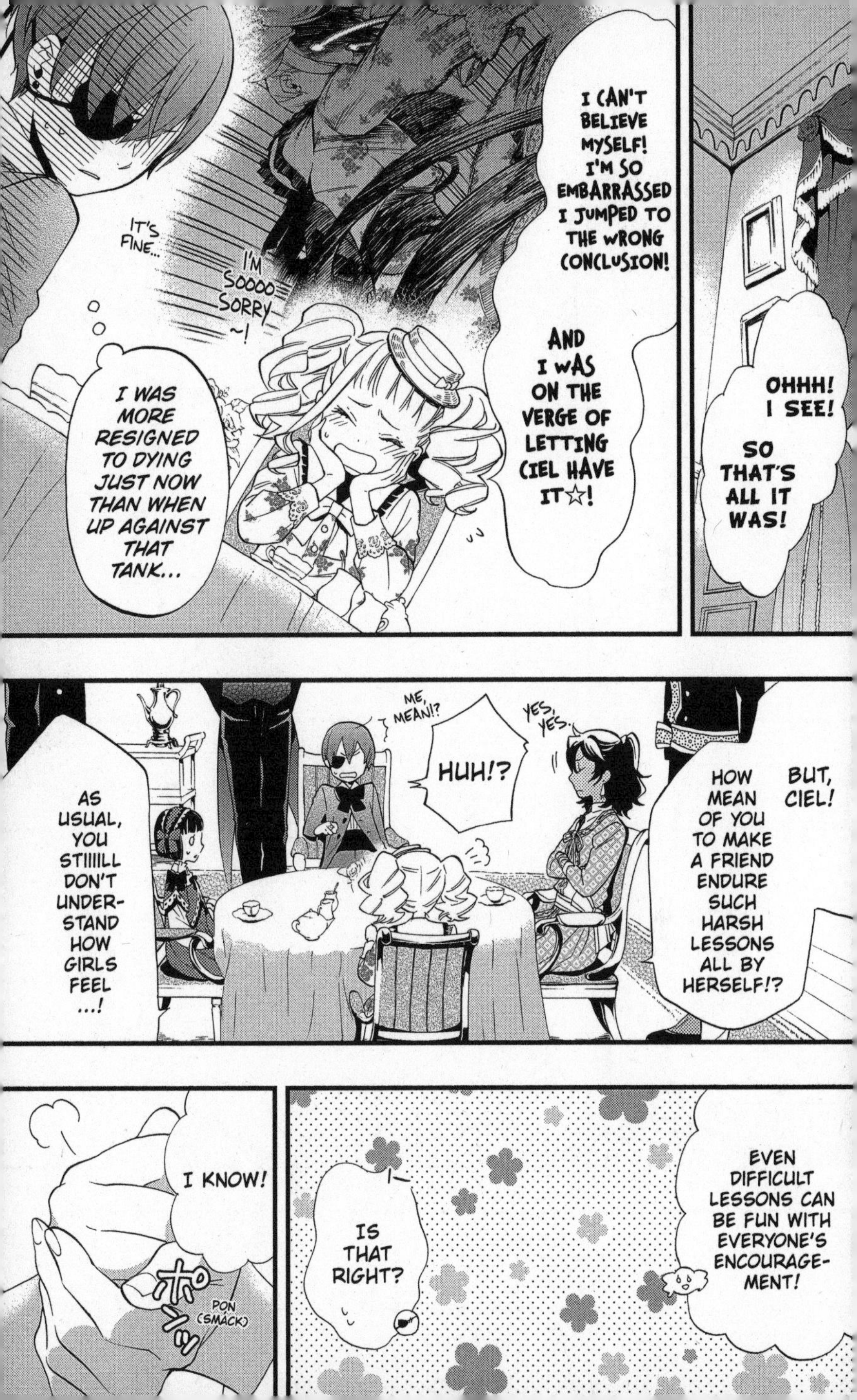
OHHH! I SEE!
SO THAT'S ALL IT WAS!
I CAN'T BELIEVE MYSELF! I'M SO EMBARRASSED I JUMPED TO THE WRONG CONCLUSION!
AND I WAS ON THE VERGE OF LETTING CIEL HAVE IT☆!
I'M SOOOO SORRY ~!
IT'S FINE...
I WAS MORE RESIGNED TO DYING JUST NOW THAN WHEN UP AGAINST THAT TANK...
BUT, CIEL!
HOW MEAN OF YOU TO MAKE A FRIEND ENDURE SUCH HARSH LESSONS ALL BY HERSELF!?
YES, YES.
HUH!?
ME, MEAN!?
AS USUAL, YOU STIIIILL DON'T UNDERSTAND HOW GIRLS FEEL...!
EVEN DIFFICULT LESSONS CAN BE FUN WITH EVERYONE'S ENCOURAGEMENT!
I—
IS THAT RIGHT?
I KNOW!
ポンッ
PON (SMACK)

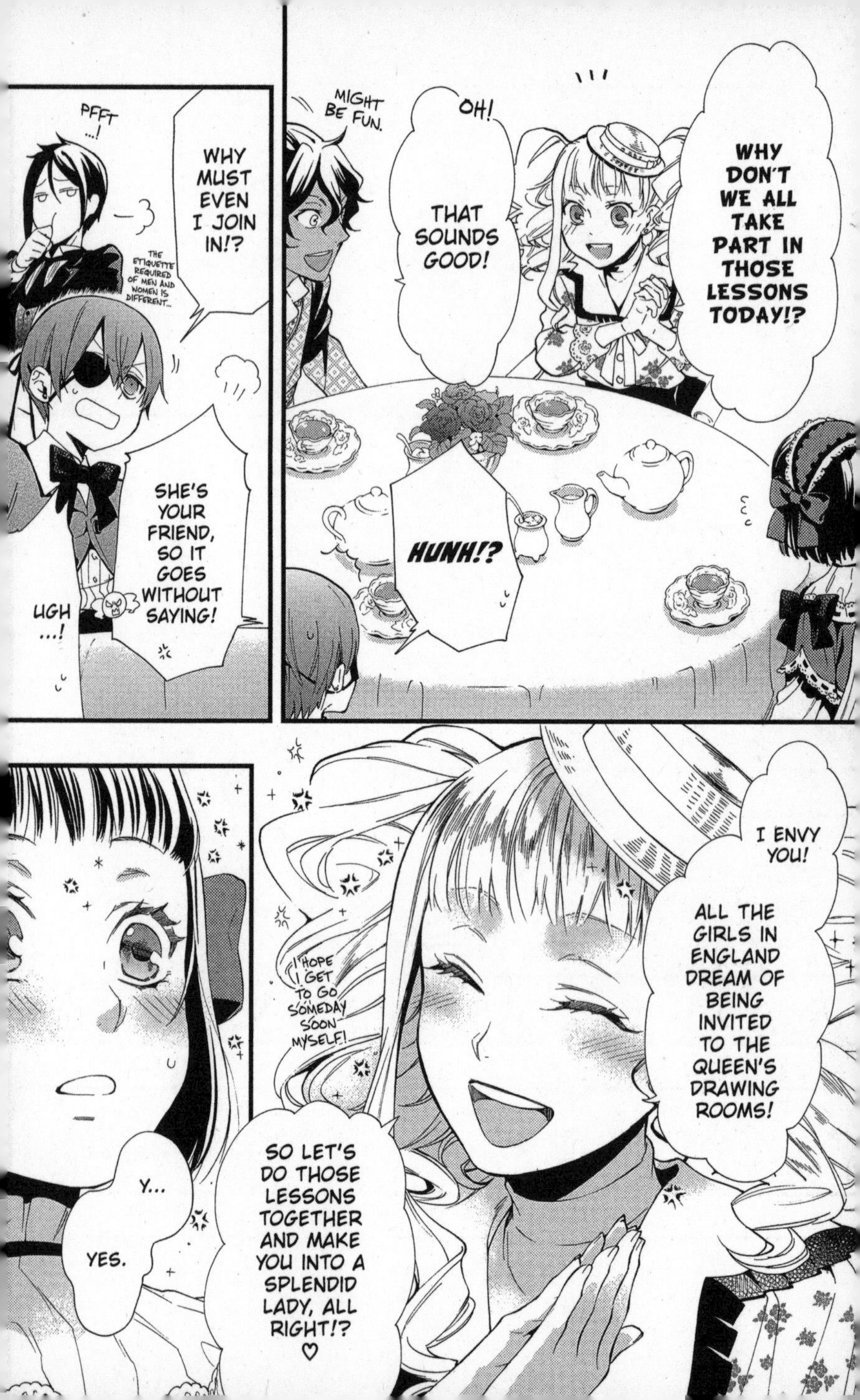
WHY DON'T WE ALL TAKE PART IN THOSE LESSONS TODAY!?
OH!
THAT SOUNDS GOOD!
MIGHT BE FUN.
HUNH!?
WHY MUST EVEN I JOIN IN!?
PFFT ...!
THE ETIQUETTE REQUIRED OF MEN AND WOMEN IS DIFFERENT...
SHE'S YOUR FRIEND, SO IT GOES WITHOUT SAYING!
UGH ...!
I ENVY YOU!
ALL THE GIRLS IN ENGLAND DREAM OF BEING INVITED TO THE QUEEN'S DRAWING ROOMS!
I HOPE I GET TO GO SOMEDAY SOON MYSELF!
SO LET'S DO THOSE LESSONS TOGETHER AND MAKE YOU INTO A SPLENDID LADY, ALL RIGHT!? ♡
Y...
YES.

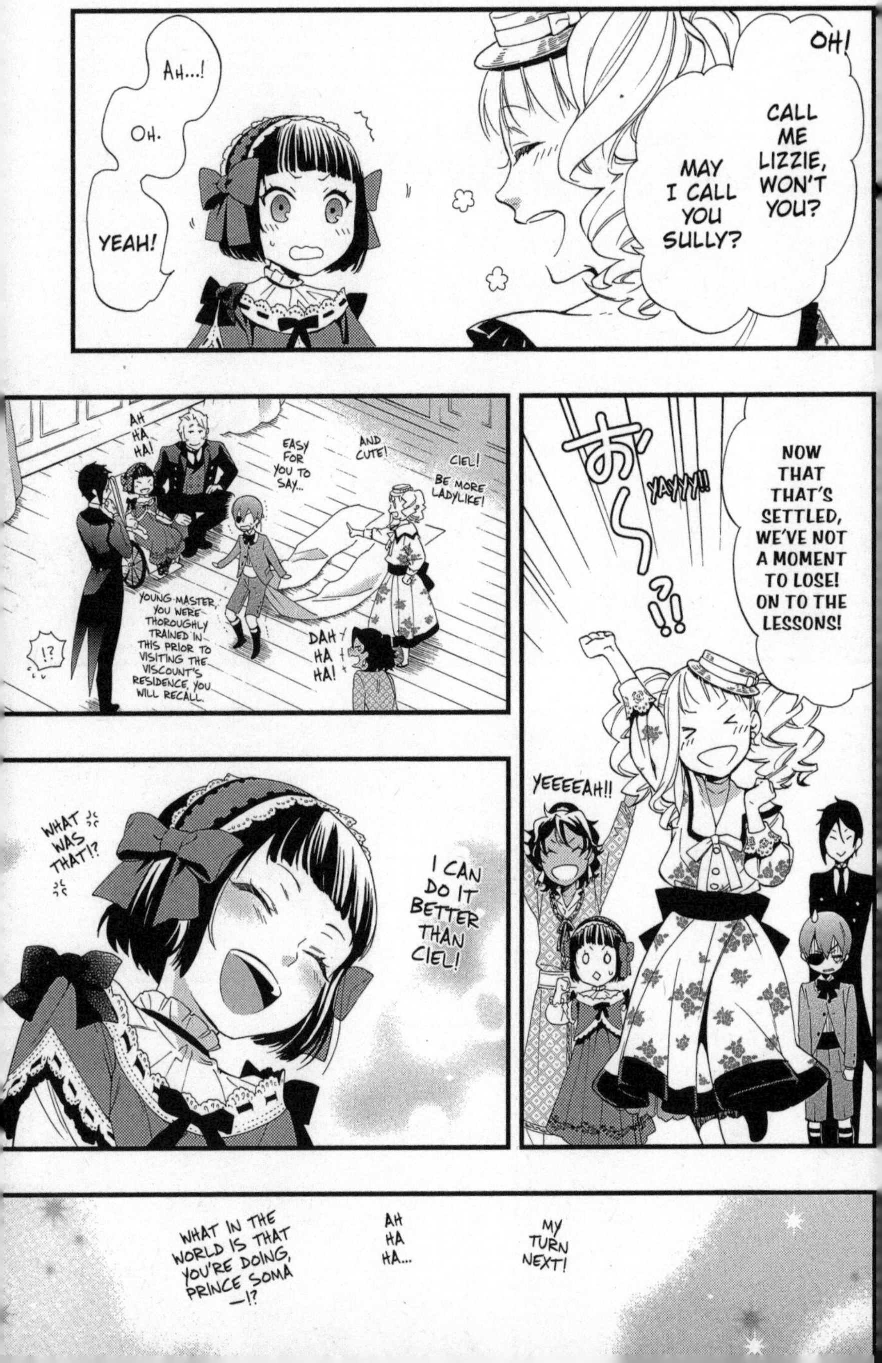
OH!
CALL ME LIZZIE, WON'T YOU?
MAY I CALL YOU SULLY?
AH...!
OH.
YEAH!
NOW THAT THAT'S SETTLED, WE'VE NOT A MOMENT TO LOSE! ON TO THE LESSONS!
おくっ!!
YAYYY!!
YEEEEAH!!
CIEL! BE MORE LADYLIKE!
AND CUTE!
EASY FOR YOU TO SAY...
AH HA HA!
DAH HA HA!
YOUNG MASTER, YOU WERE THOROUGHLY TRAINED IN THIS PRIOR TO VISITING THE VISCOUNT'S RESIDENCE, YOU WILL RECALL.
!?
I CAN DO IT BETTER THAN CIEL!
WHAT WAS THAT!?
MY TURN NEXT!
AH HA HA...
WHAT IN THE WORLD IS THAT YOU'RE DOING, PRINCE SOMA—!?

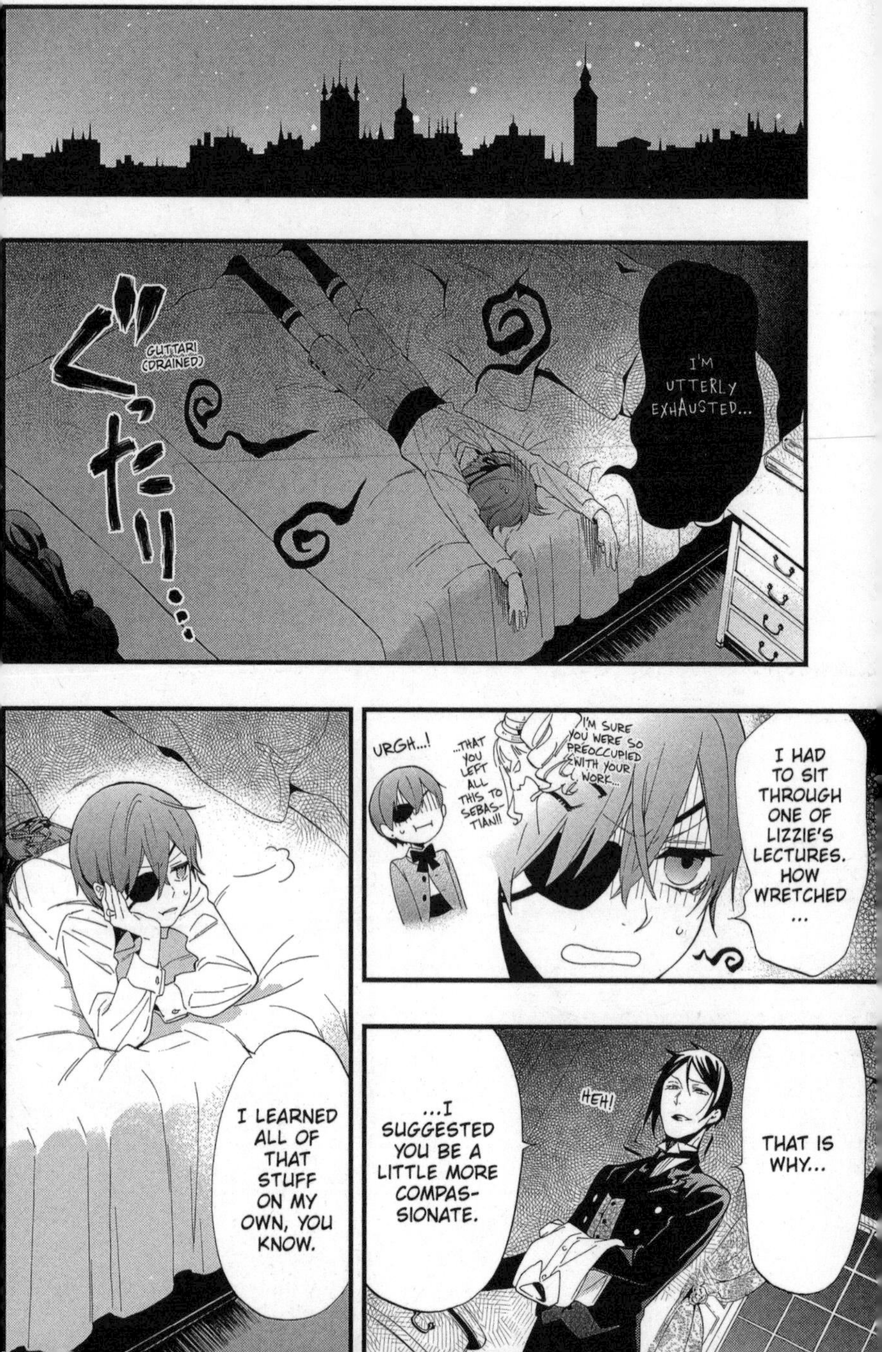
I'M UTTERLY EXHAUSTED...
ぐったり...
GUTTARI (DRAINED)
I HAD TO SIT THROUGH ONE OF LIZZIE'S LECTURES. HOW WRETCHED ...
I'M SURE YOU WERE SO PREOCCUPIED WITH YOUR WORK...
...THAT YOU LEFT ALL THIS TO SEBASTIAN!!
URGH...!
THAT IS WHY...
HEH!
...I SUGGESTED YOU BE A LITTLE MORE COMPASSIONATE.
I LEARNED ALL OF THAT STUFF ON MY OWN, YOU KNOW.

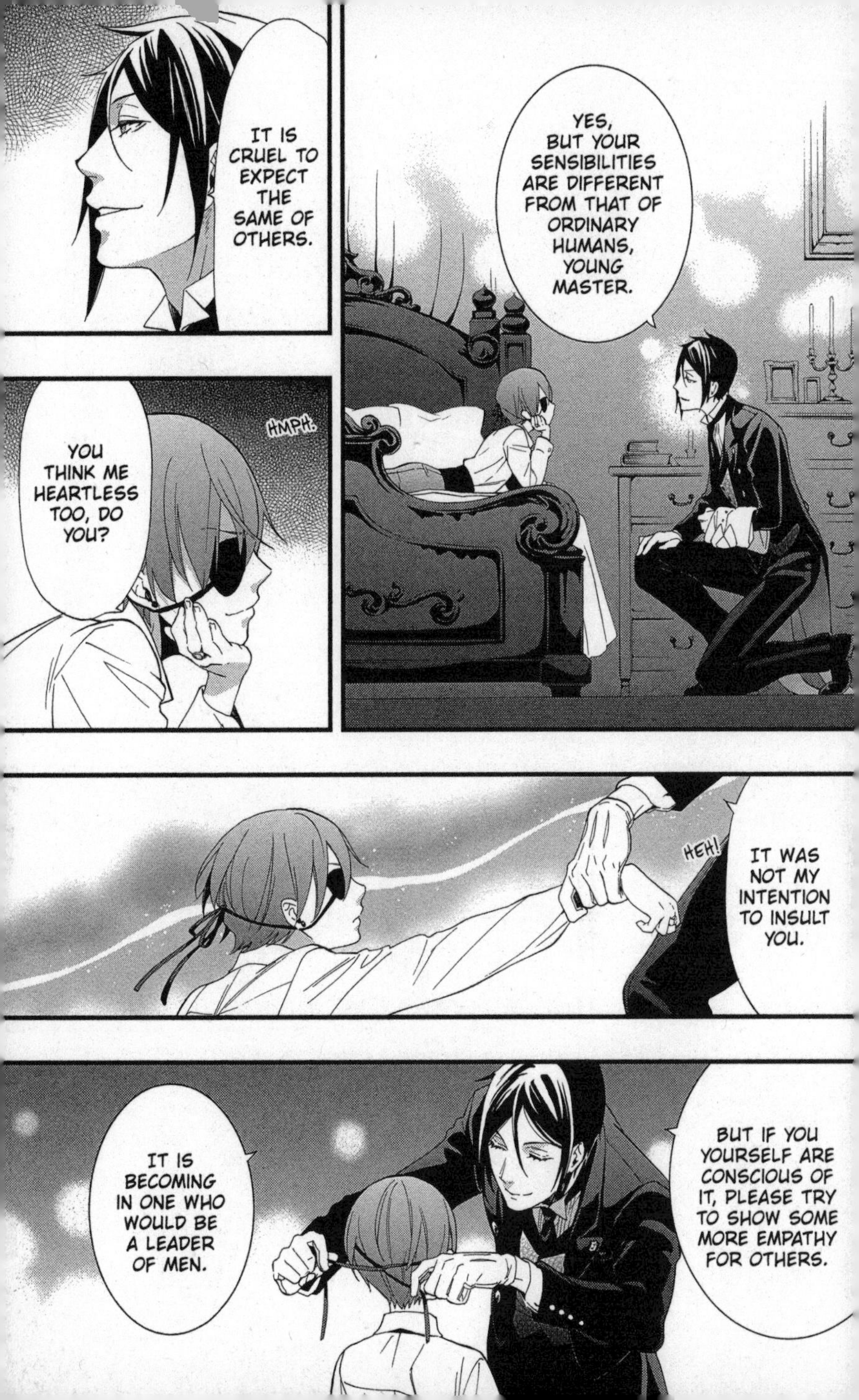
YES, BUT YOUR SENSIBILITIES ARE DIFFERENT FROM THAT OF ORDINARY HUMANS, YOUNG MASTER.
IT IS CRUEL TO EXPECT THE SAME OF OTHERS.
HMPH.
YOU THINK ME HEARTLESS TOO, DO YOU?
HEH!
IT WAS NOT MY INTENTION TO INSULT YOU.
BUT IF YOU YOURSELF ARE CONSCIOUS OF IT, PLEASE TRY TO SHOW SOME MORE EMPATHY FOR OTHERS.
IT IS BECOMING IN ONE WHO WOULD BE A LEADER OF MEN.

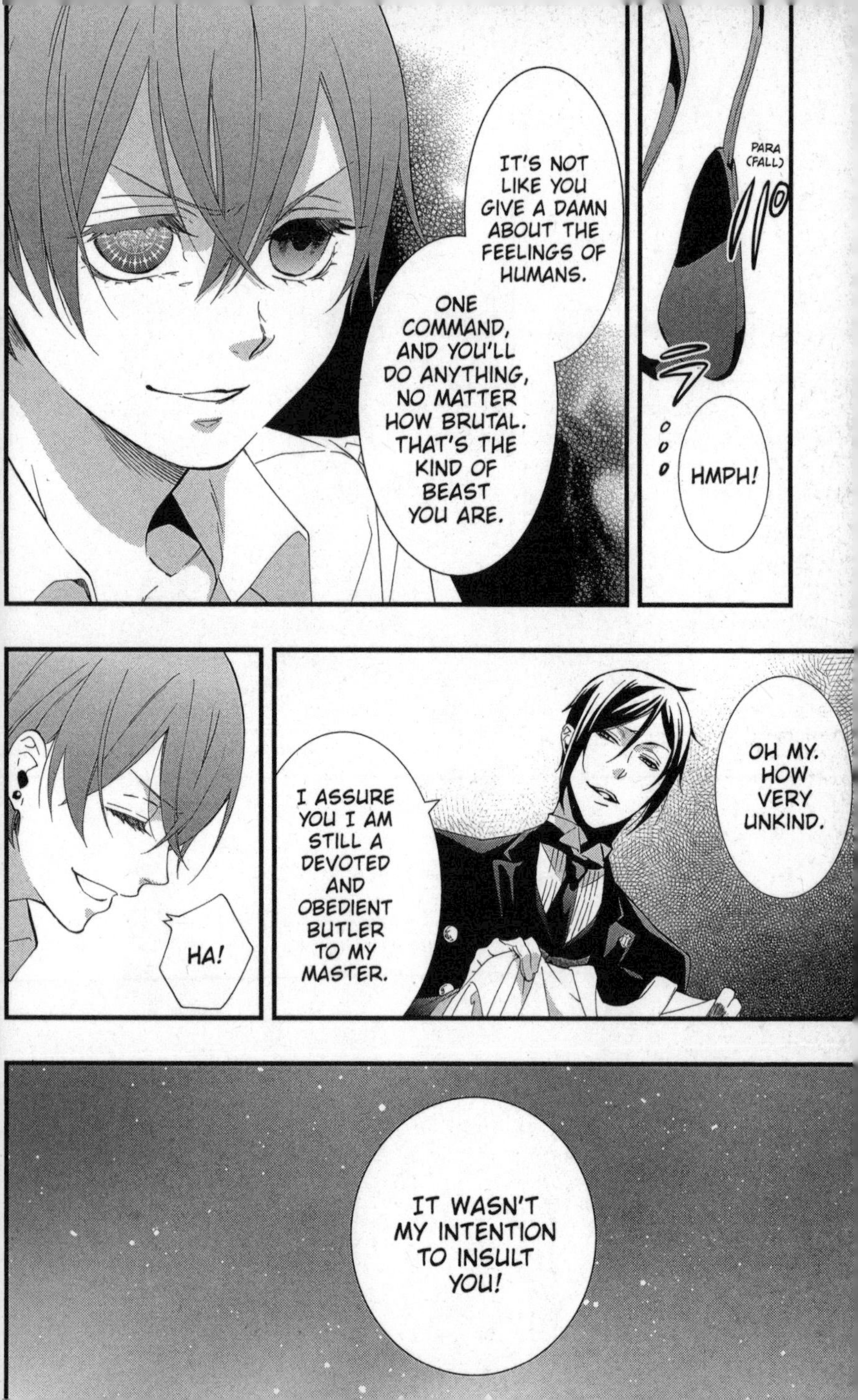
PARA (FALL)
HMPH!
IT'S NOT LIKE YOU GIVE A DAMN ABOUT THE FEELINGS OF HUMANS.
ONE COMMAND, AND YOU'LL DO ANYTHING, NO MATTER HOW BRUTAL. THAT'S THE KIND OF BEAST YOU ARE.
OH MY. HOW VERY UNKIND.
I ASSURE YOU I AM STILL A DEVOTED AND OBEDIENT BUTLER TO MY MASTER.
HA!
IT WASN'T MY INTENTION TO INSULT YOU!

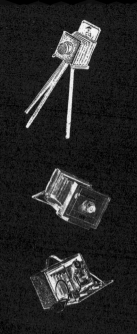

Black Butler

Chapter 108
At midnight : The Butler, Underwater

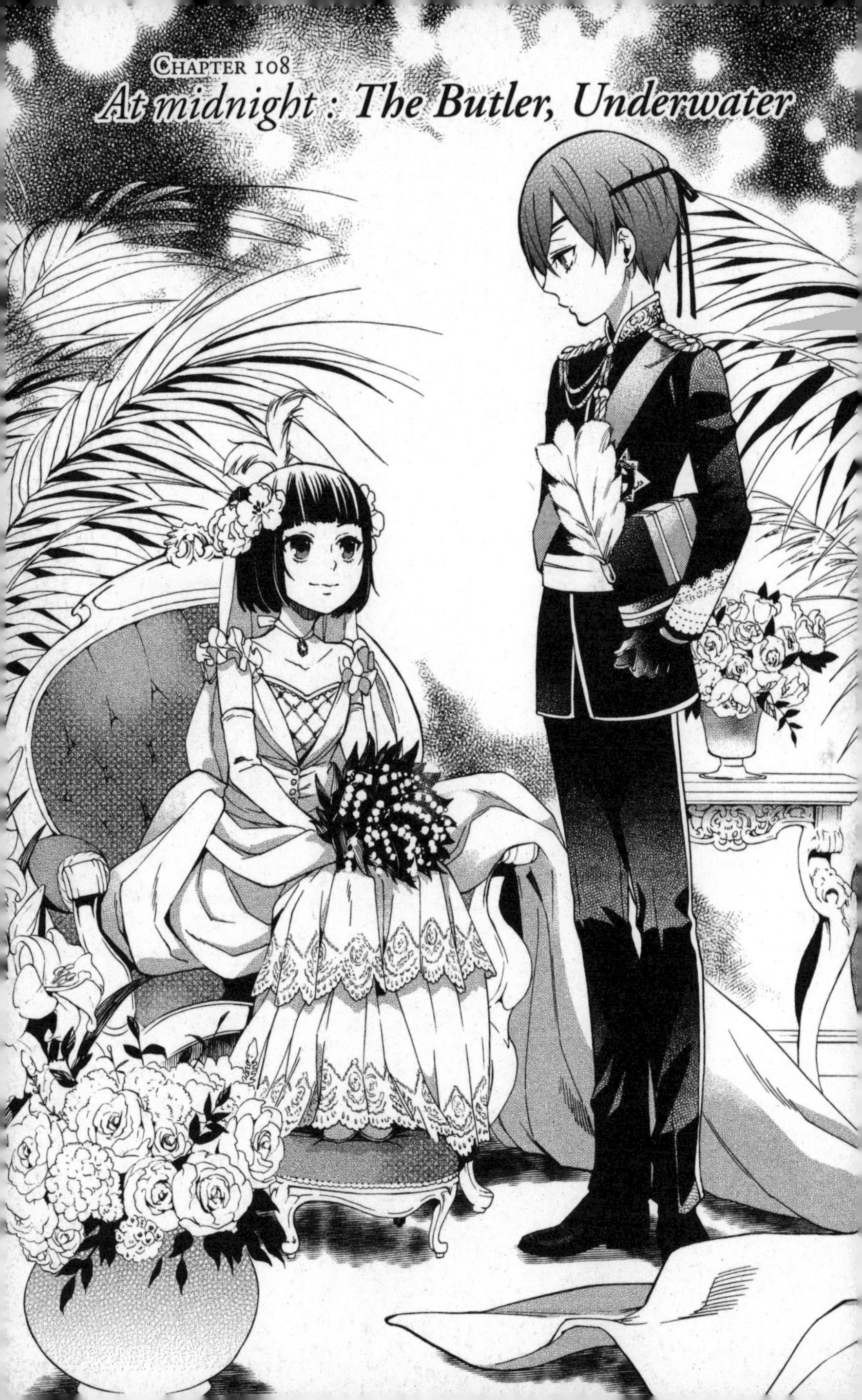

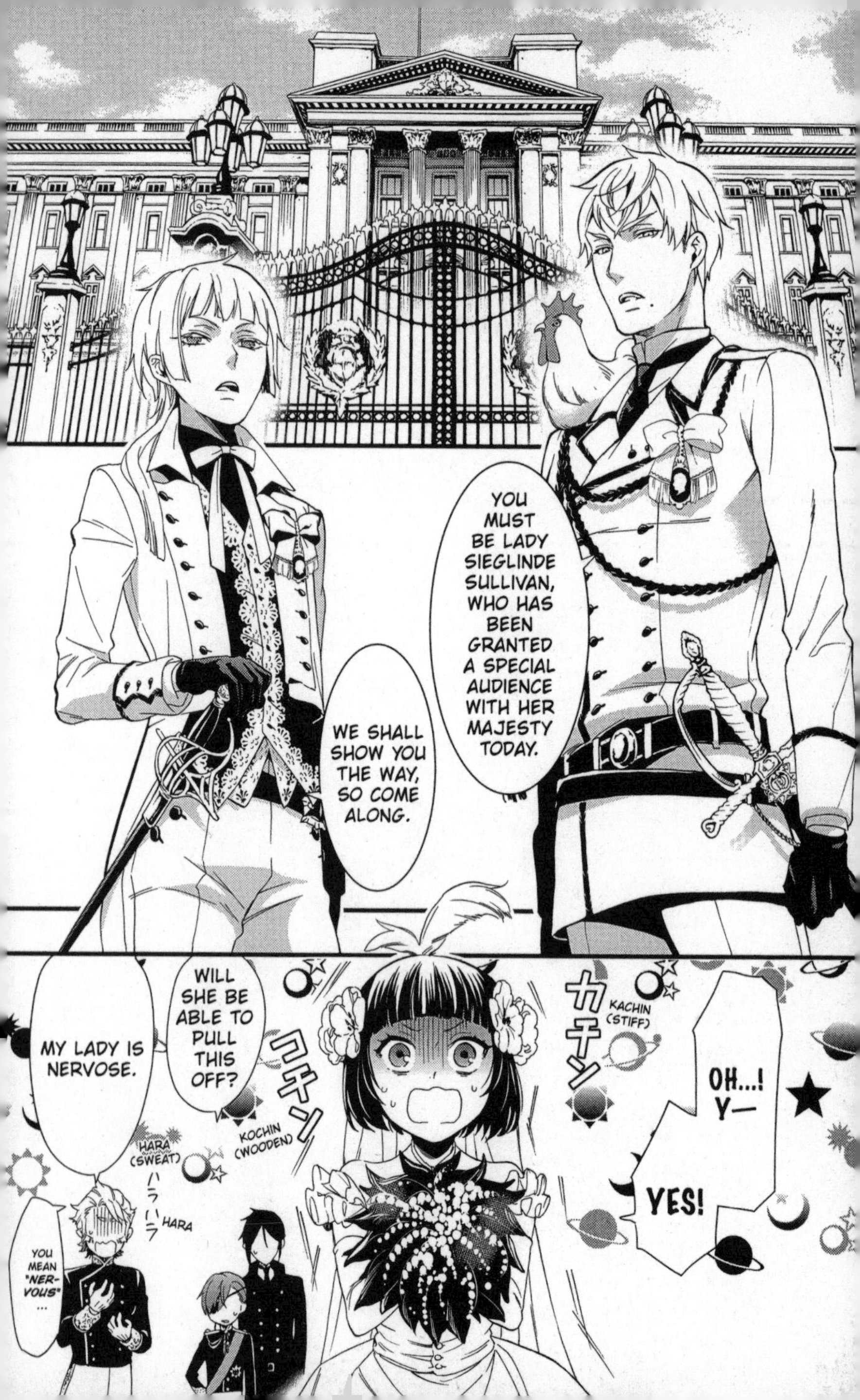
YOU MUST BE LADY SIEGLINDE SULLIVAN, WHO HAS BEEN GRANTED A SPECIAL AUDIENCE WITH HER MAJESTY TODAY.
WE SHALL SHOW YOU THE WAY, SO COME ALONG.
カチン
KACHIN (STIFF)
OH...! Y—
YES!
コチン
KOCHIN (WOODEN)
WILL SHE BE ABLE TO PULL THIS OFF?
MY LADY IS NERVOSE.
HARA (SWEAT)
ハラハラ
HARA
YOU MEAN "NER-VOUS"...

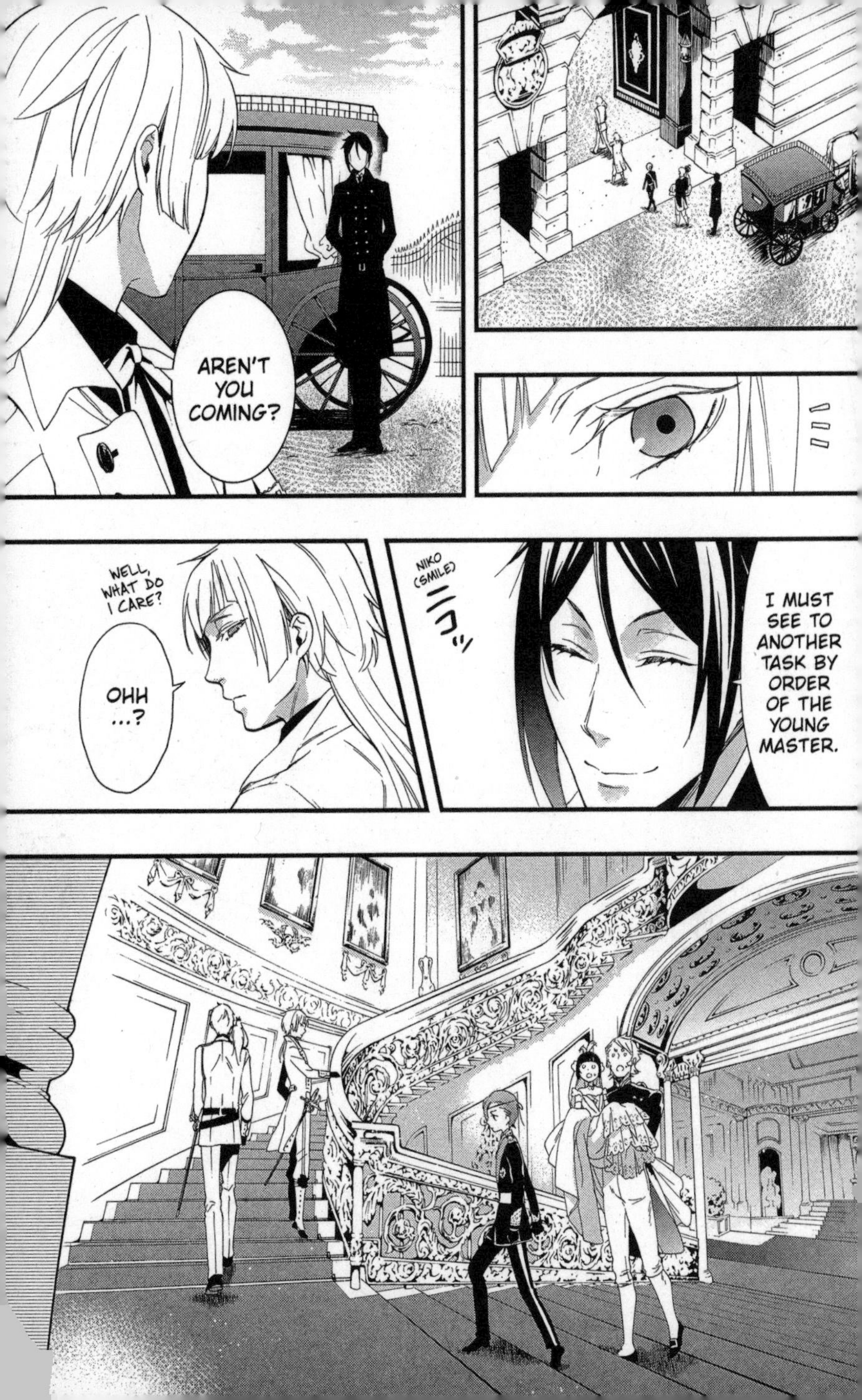
AREN'T YOU COMING?
I MUST SEE TO ANOTHER TASK BY ORDER OF THE YOUNG MASTER.
NIKO (SMILE)
ニコッ
OHH ...?
WELL, WHAT DO I CARE?

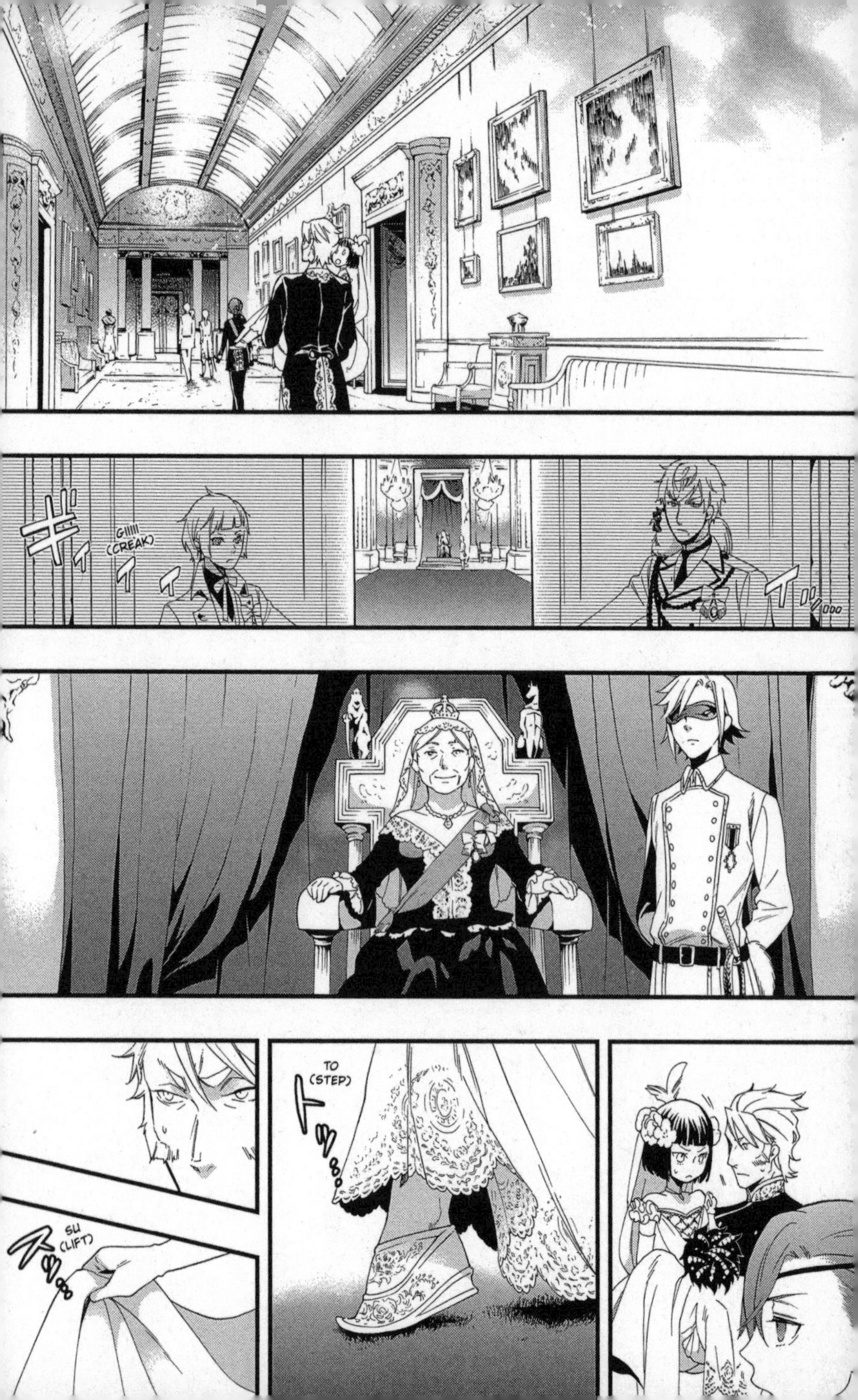

GIIII (CREAK)
TO (STEP)
SU (LIFT)

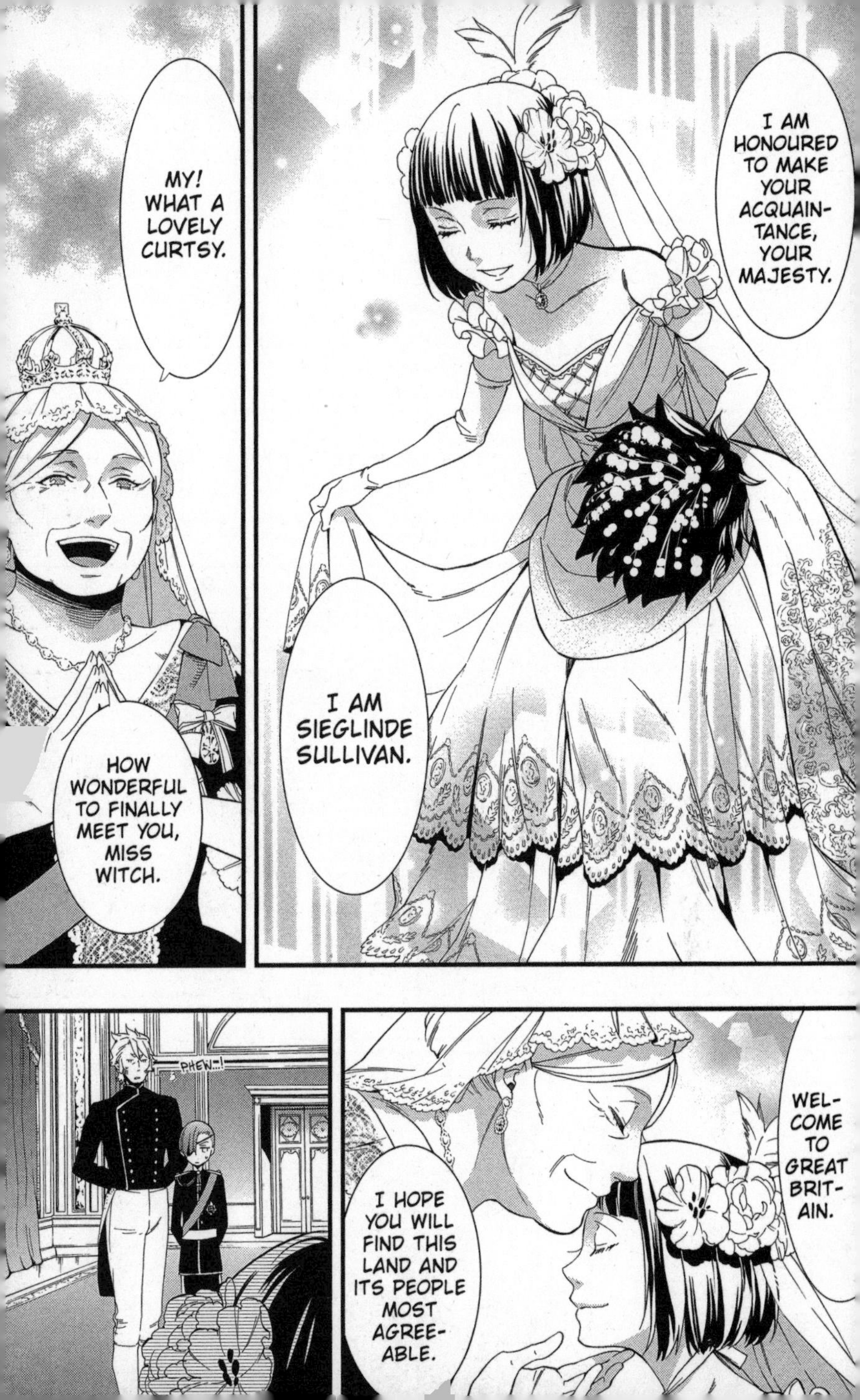
I AM HONOURED TO MAKE YOUR ACQUAINTANCE, YOUR MAJESTY.
I AM SIEGLINDE SULLIVAN.
MY! WHAT A LOVELY CURTSY.
HOW WONDERFUL TO FINALLY MEET YOU, MISS WITCH.
WELCOME TO GREAT BRITAIN.
I HOPE YOU WILL FIND THIS LAND AND ITS PEOPLE MOST AGREEABLE.
PHEW...!

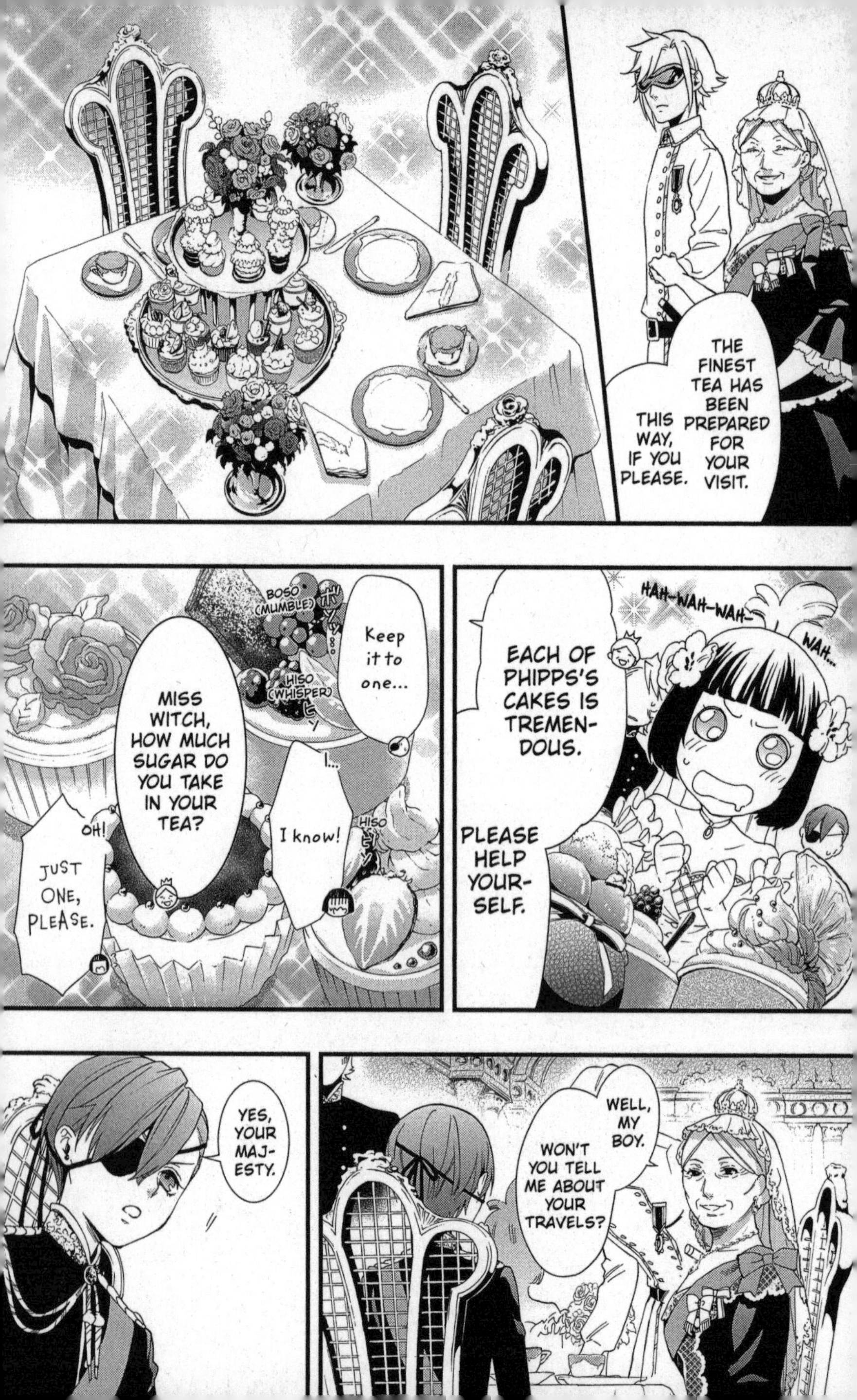
THE FINEST TEA HAS BEEN PREPARED FOR YOUR VISIT.
THIS WAY, IF YOU PLEASE.
WAH-WAH-WAH-
WAH...
EACH OF PHIPPS'S CAKES IS TREMENDOUS.
PLEASE HELP YOURSELF.
BOSO (MUMBLE)
Keep it to one...
HISO (WHISPER)
MISS WITCH, HOW MUCH SUGAR DO YOU TAKE IN YOUR TEA?
I...
HISO
I know!
OH!
JUST ONE, PLEASE.
WELL, MY BOY.
WON'T YOU TELL ME ABOUT YOUR TRAVELS?
YES, YOUR MAJESTY.

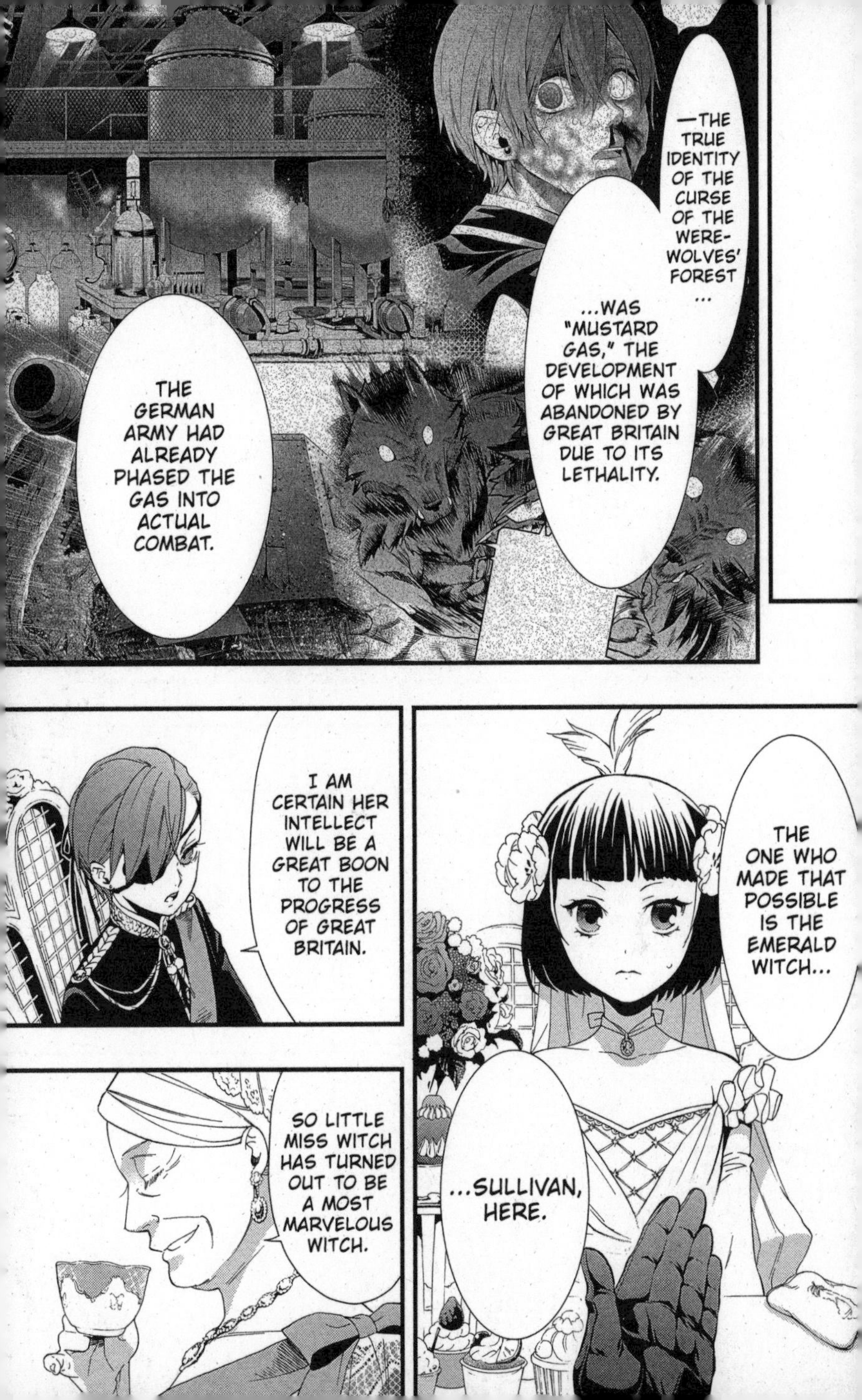
—THE TRUE IDENTITY OF THE CURSE OF THE WERE-WOLVES' FOREST ...
...WAS "MUSTARD GAS," THE DEVELOPMENT OF WHICH WAS ABANDONED BY GREAT BRITAIN DUE TO ITS LETHALITY.
THE GERMAN ARMY HAD ALREADY PHASED THE GAS INTO ACTUAL COMBAT.
THE ONE WHO MADE THAT POSSIBLE IS THE EMERALD WITCH...
...SULLIVAN, HERE.
I AM CERTAIN HER INTELLECT WILL BE A GREAT BOON TO THE PROGRESS OF GREAT BRITAIN.
SO LITTLE MISS WITCH HAS TURNED OUT TO BE A MOST MARVELOUS WITCH.

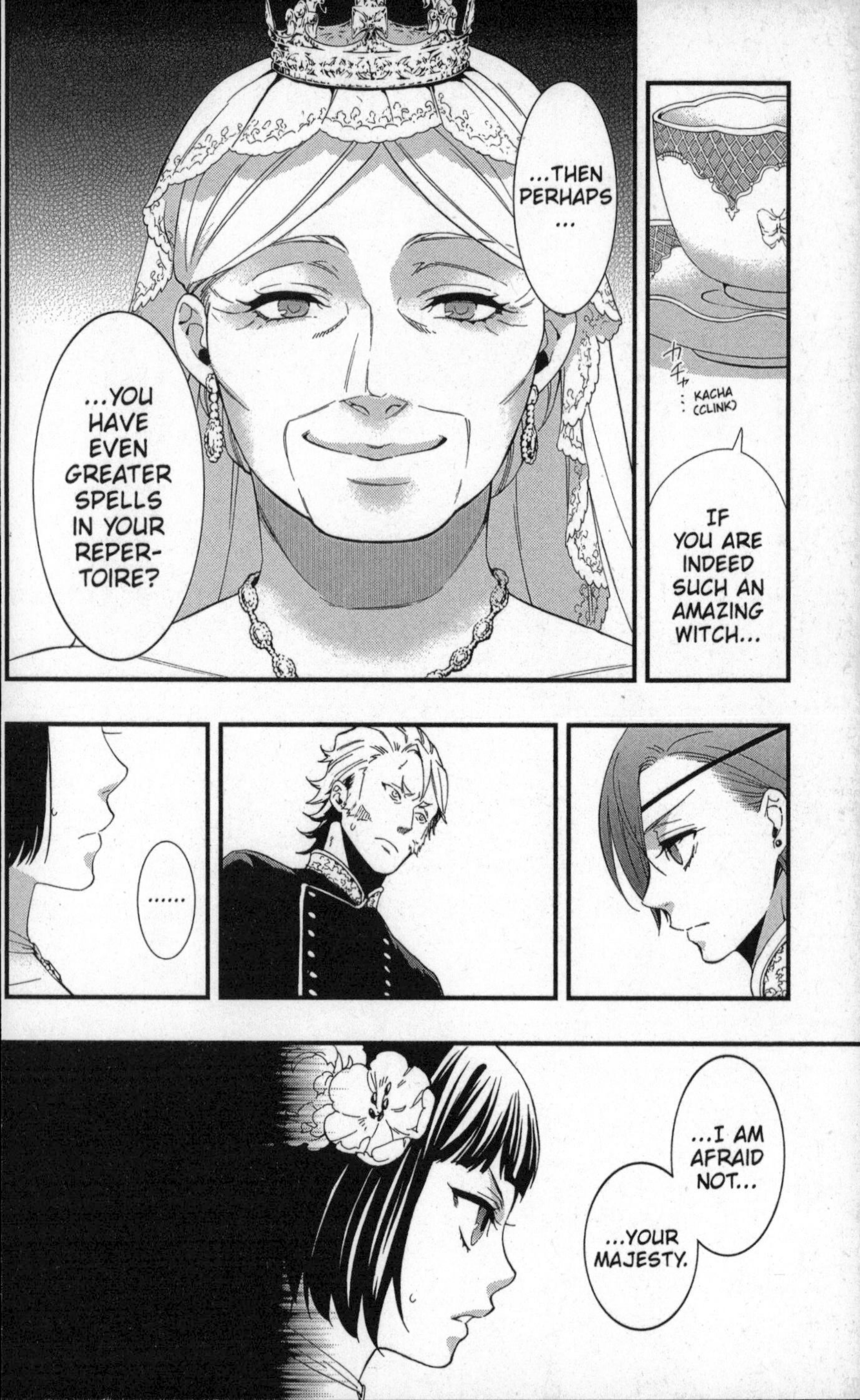
カチャ…
KACHA (CLINK)
IF YOU ARE INDEED SUCH AN AMAZING WITCH...
...THEN PERHAPS ...
...YOU HAVE EVEN GREATER SPELLS IN YOUR REPERTOIRE?
......
...I AM AFRAID NOT...
...YOUR MAJESTY.

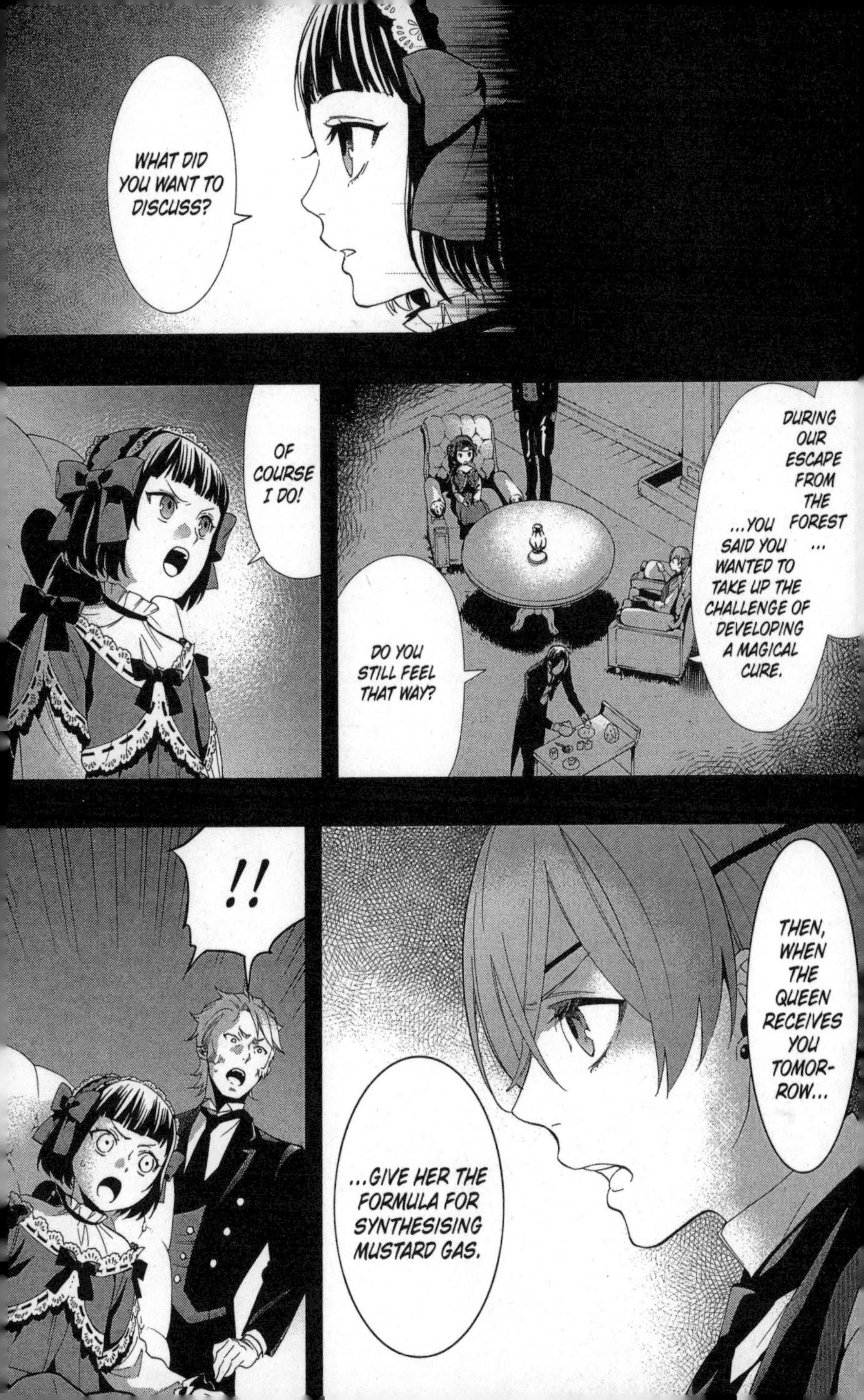
WHAT DID YOU WANT TO DISCUSS?
DURING OUR ESCAPE FROM THE FOREST...
...YOU SAID YOU WANTED TO TAKE UP THE CHALLENGE OF DEVELOPING A MAGICAL CURE.
DO YOU STILL FEEL THAT WAY?
OF COURSE I DO!
THEN, WHEN THE QUEEN RECEIVES YOU TOMOR-ROW...
...GIVE HER THE FORMULA FOR SYNTHESISING MUSTARD GAS.
!!

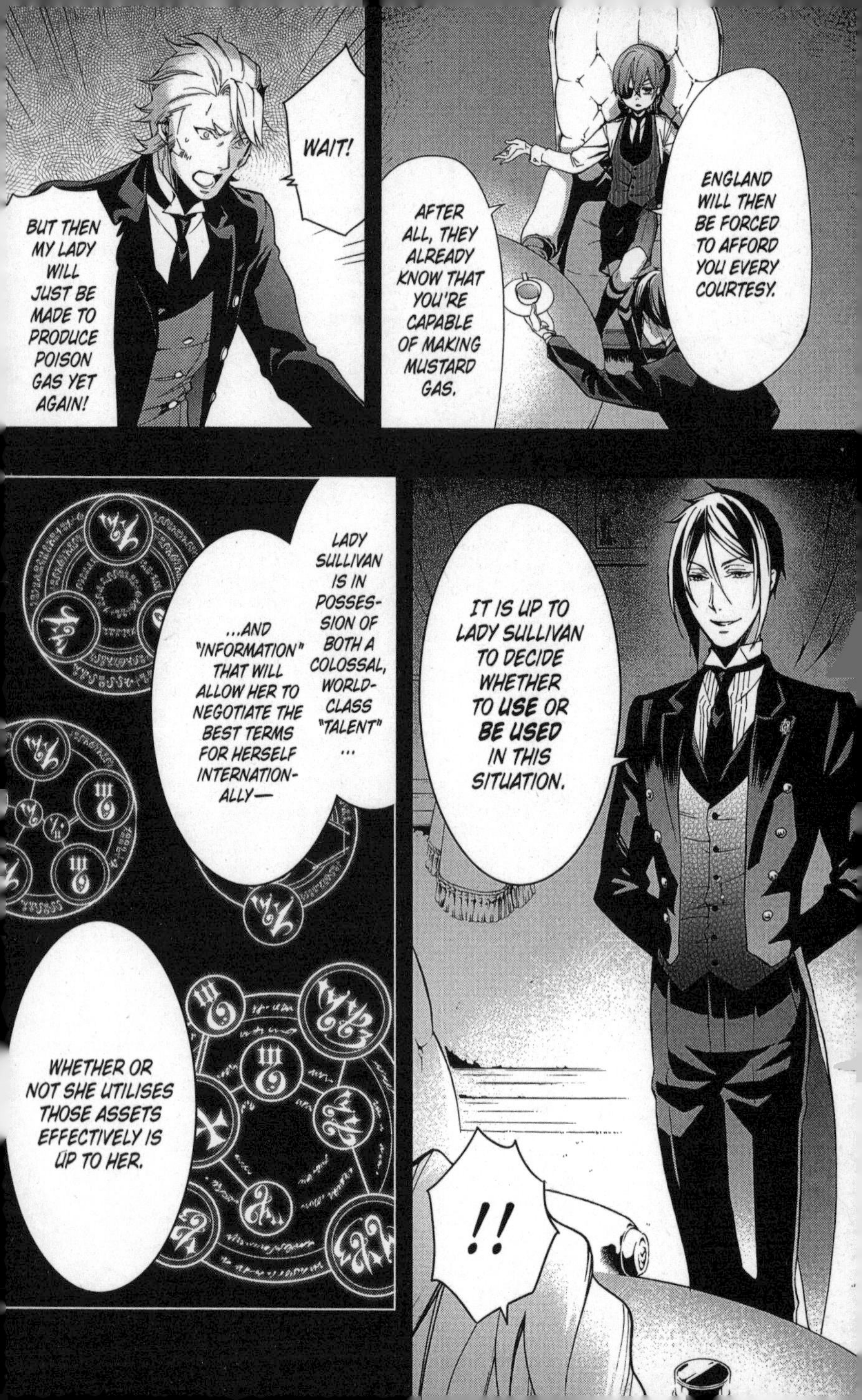
ENGLAND WILL THEN BE FORCED TO AFFORD YOU EVERY COURTESY.
AFTER ALL, THEY ALREADY KNOW THAT YOU'RE CAPABLE OF MAKING MUSTARD GAS.
WAIT!
BUT THEN MY LADY WILL JUST BE MADE TO PRODUCE POISON GAS YET AGAIN!
IT IS UP TO LADY SULLIVAN TO DECIDE WHETHER TO **USE** OR **BE USED** IN THIS SITUATION.
!!
LADY SULLIVAN IS IN POSSESSION OF BOTH A COLOSSAL, WORLD-CLASS "TALENT"...
...AND "INFORMATION" THAT WILL ALLOW HER TO NEGOTIATE THE BEST TERMS FOR HERSELF INTERNATIONALLY—
WHETHER OR NOT SHE UTILISES THOSE ASSETS EFFECTIVELY IS UP TO HER.

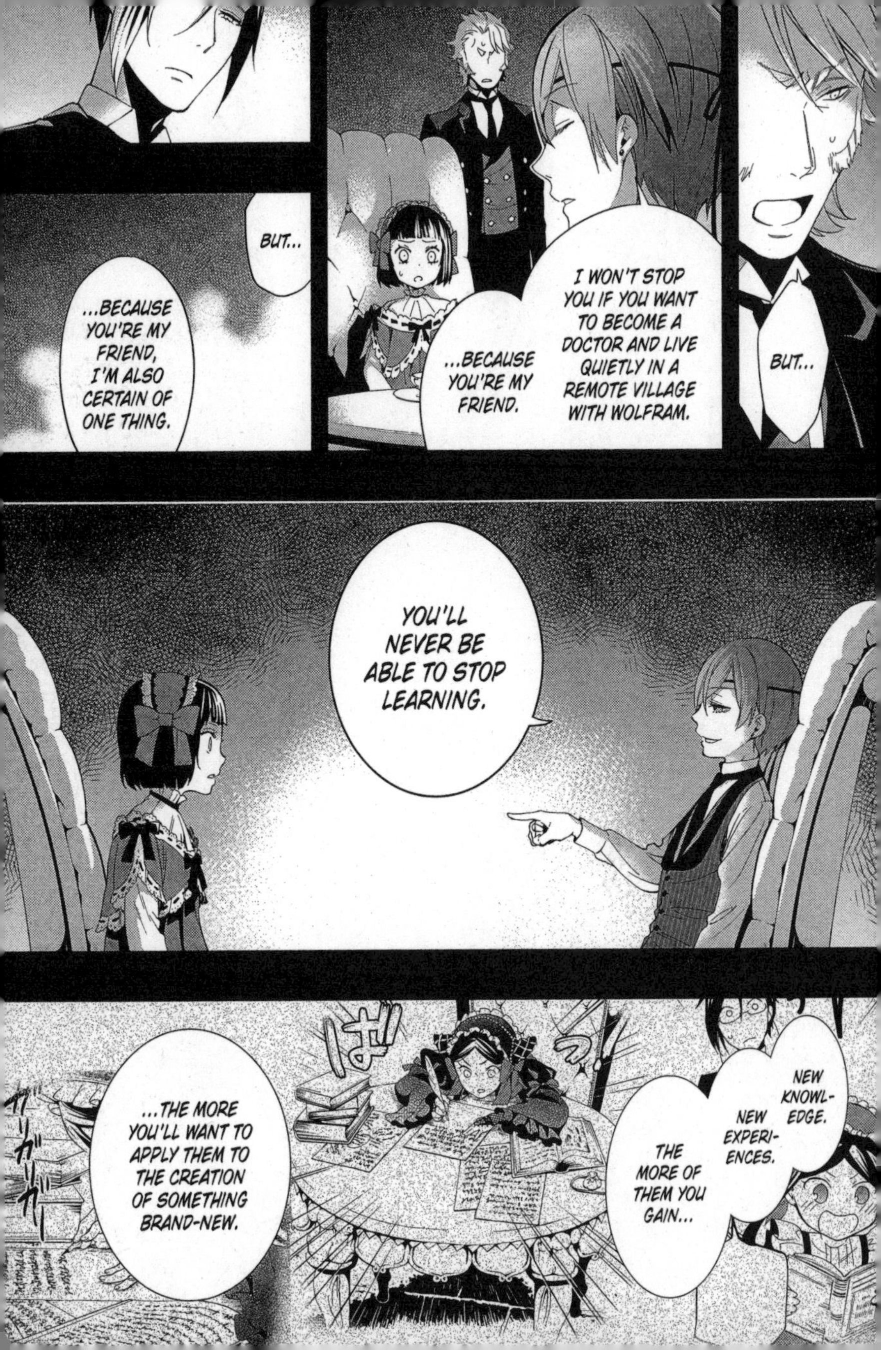
BUT...
I WON'T STOP YOU IF YOU WANT TO BECOME A DOCTOR AND LIVE QUIETLY IN A REMOTE VILLAGE WITH WOLFRAM.
...BECAUSE YOU'RE MY FRIEND.
BUT...
...BECAUSE YOU'RE MY FRIEND, I'M ALSO CERTAIN OF ONE THING.
YOU'LL NEVER BE ABLE TO STOP LEARNING.
NEW KNOWL-EDGE.
NEW EXPERI-ENCES.
THE MORE OF THEM YOU GAIN...
...THE MORE YOU'LL WANT TO APPLY THEM TO THE CREATION OF SOMETHING BRAND-NEW.

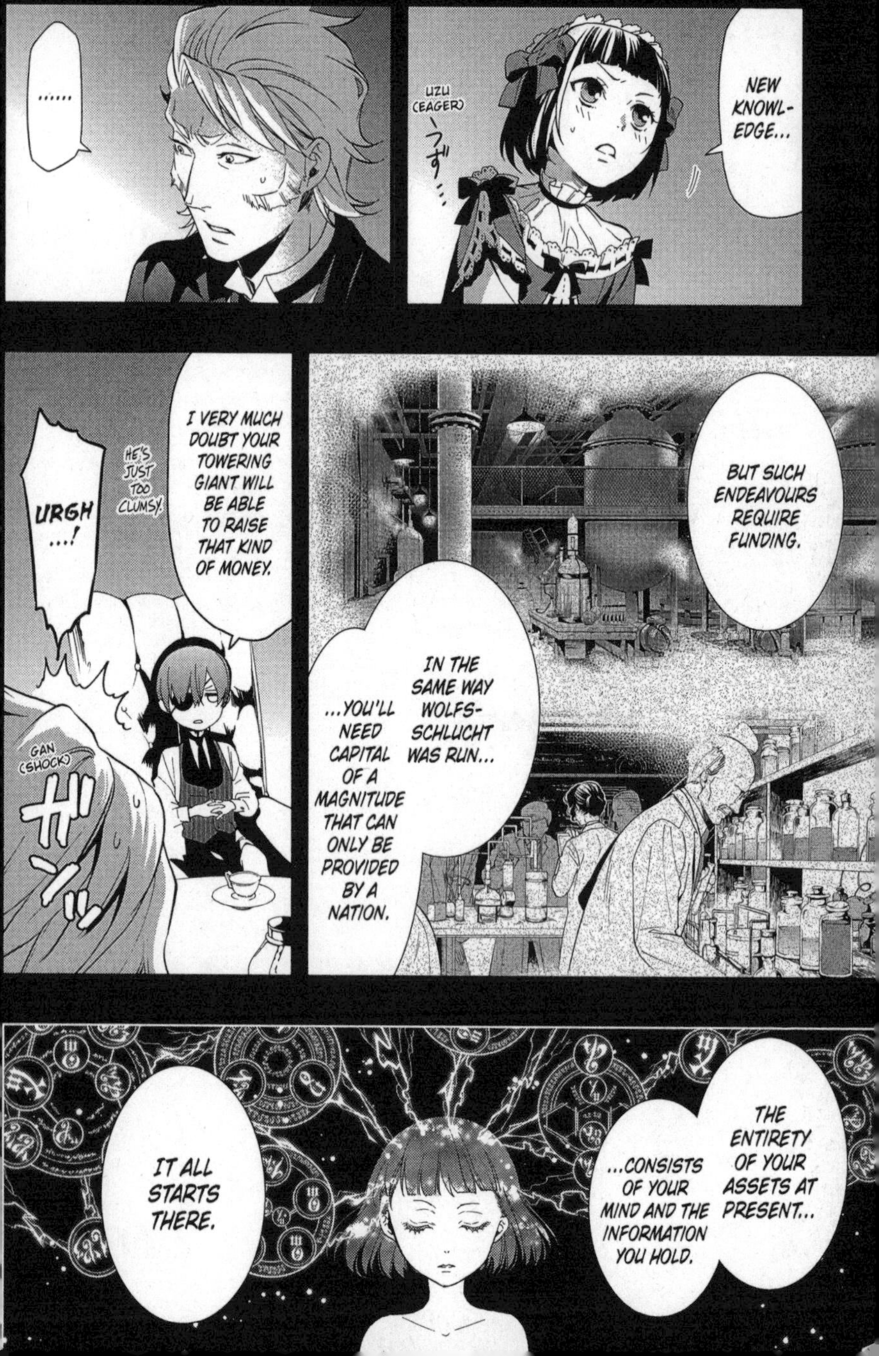
NEW KNOWL-EDGE...
UZU (EAGER)
......
BUT SUCH ENDEAVOURS REQUIRE FUNDING.
IN THE SAME WAY WOLFS-SCHLUCHT WAS RUN...
...YOU'LL NEED CAPITAL OF A MAGNITUDE THAT CAN ONLY BE PROVIDED BY A NATION.
I VERY MUCH DOUBT YOUR TOWERING GIANT WILL BE ABLE TO RAISE THAT KIND OF MONEY.
HE'S JUST TOO CLUMSY.
URGH ...!
GAN (SHOCK)
THE ENTIRETY OF YOUR ASSETS AT PRESENT...
...CONSISTS OF YOUR MIND AND THE INFORMATION YOU HOLD.
IT ALL STARTS THERE.

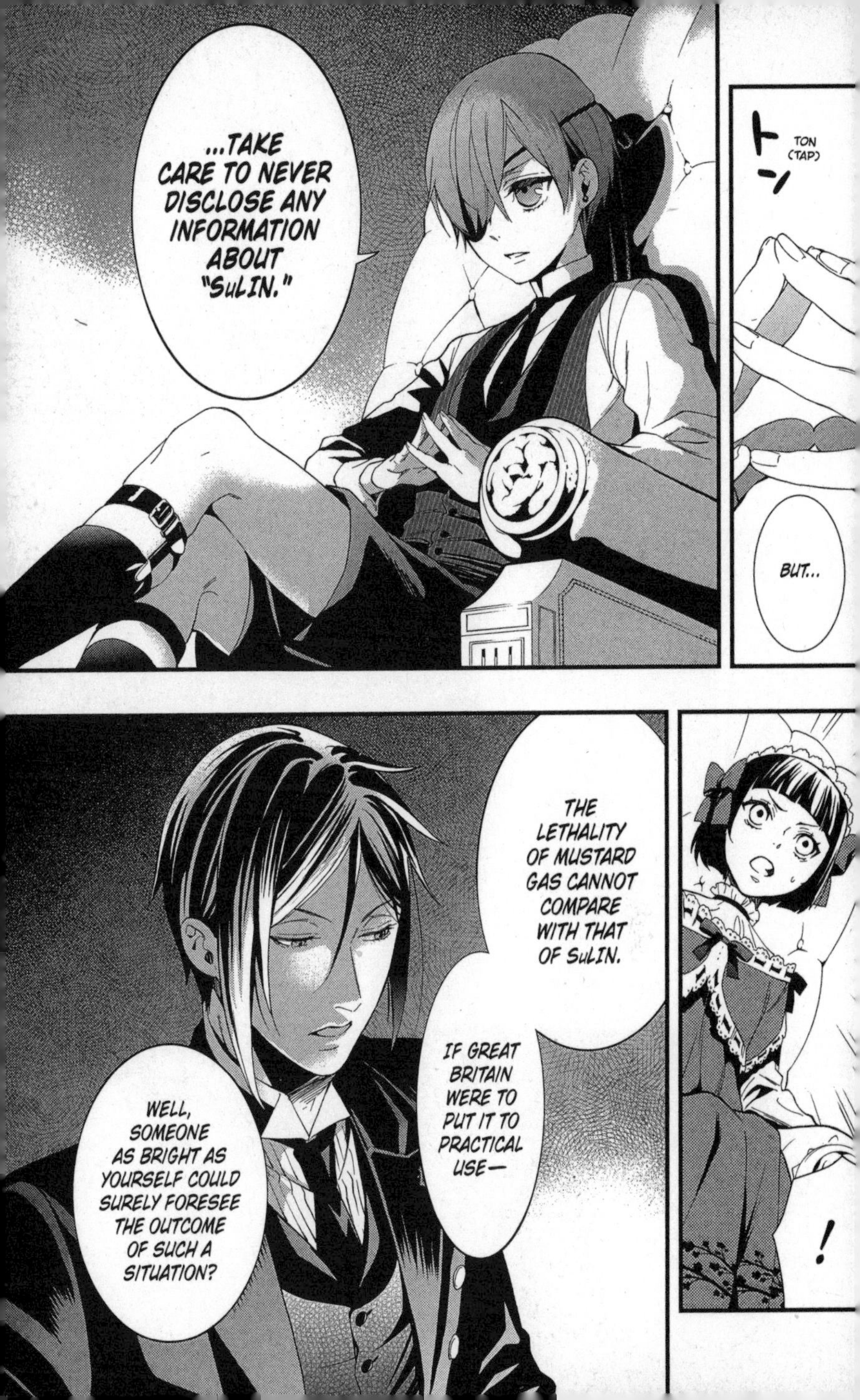
トン
TON (TAP)
BUT...
...TAKE CARE TO NEVER DISCLOSE ANY INFORMATION ABOUT "SuLIN."
!
THE LETHALITY OF MUSTARD GAS CANNOT COMPARE WITH THAT OF SuLIN.
IF GREAT BRITAIN WERE TO PUT IT TO PRACTICAL USE—
WELL, SOMEONE AS BRIGHT AS YOURSELF COULD SURELY FORESEE THE OUTCOME OF SUCH A SITUATION?

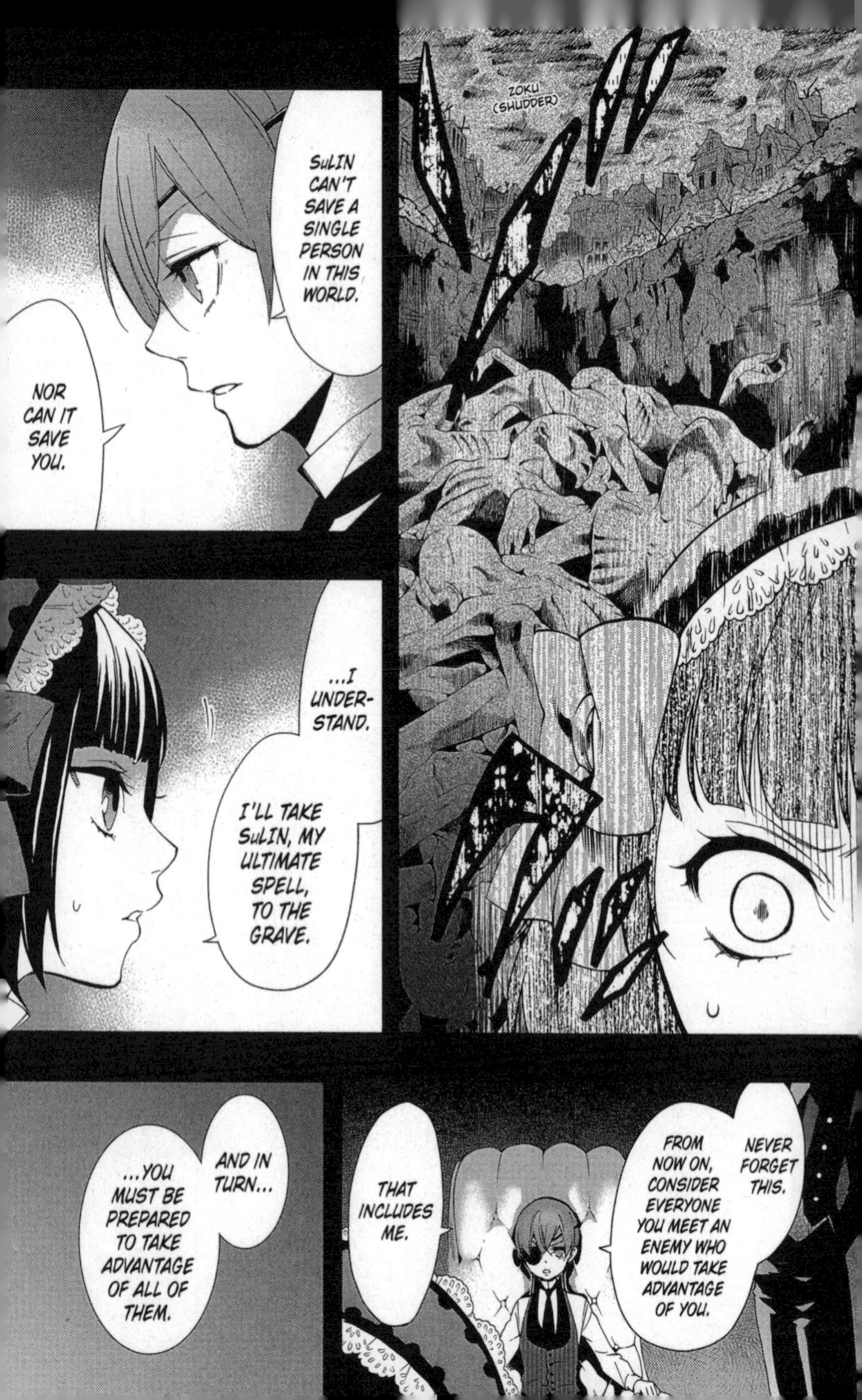
ZOKU (SHUDDER)
SuLIN CAN'T SAVE A SINGLE PERSON IN THIS WORLD.
NOR CAN IT SAVE YOU.
...I UNDER-STAND.
I'LL TAKE SuLIN, MY ULTIMATE SPELL, TO THE GRAVE.
NEVER FORGET THIS.
FROM NOW ON, CONSIDER EVERYONE YOU MEET AN ENEMY WHO WOULD TAKE ADVANTAGE OF YOU.
THAT INCLUDES ME.
AND IN TURN...
...YOU MUST BE PREPARED TO TAKE ADVANTAGE OF ALL OF THEM.

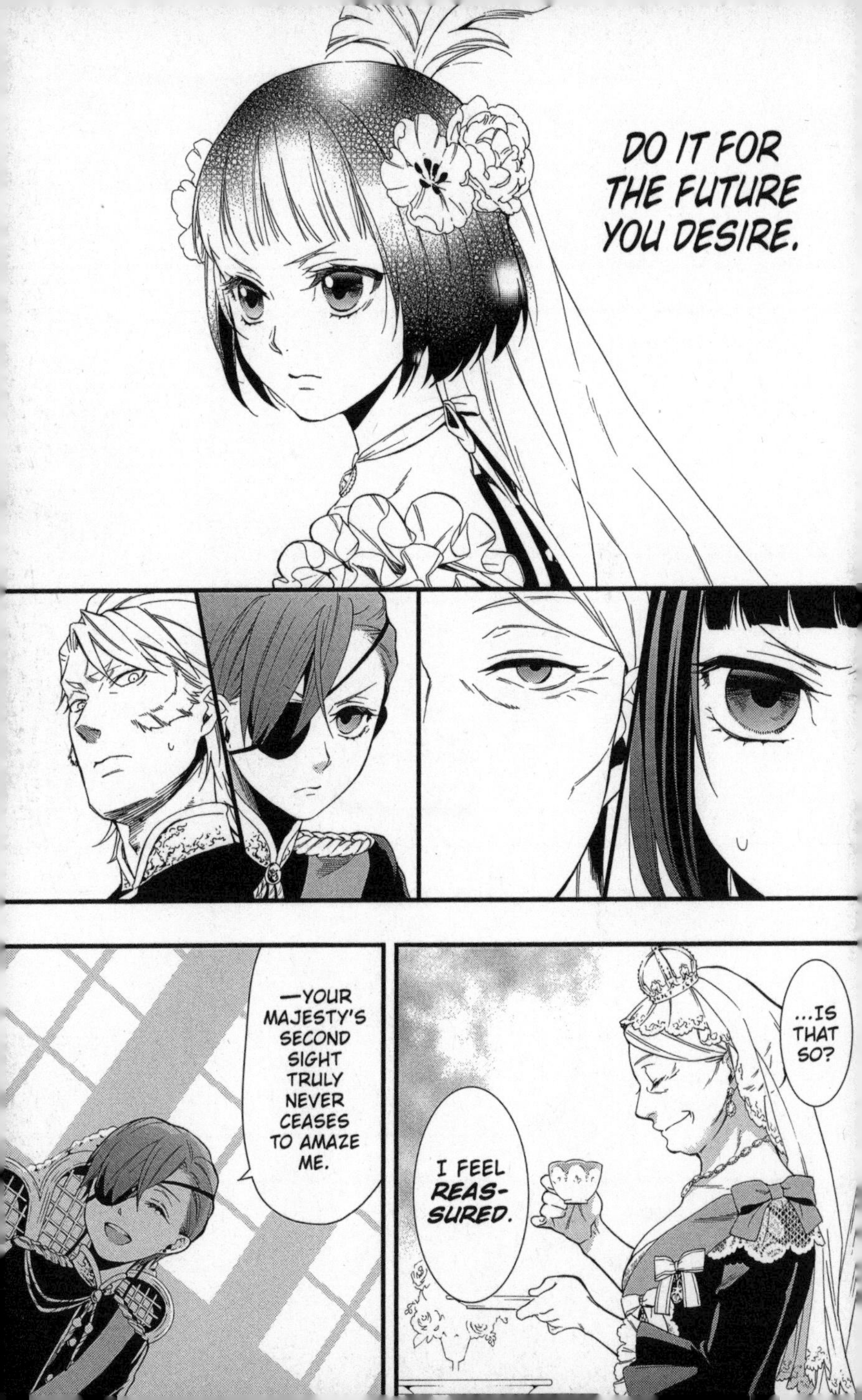
DO IT FOR THE FUTURE YOU DESIRE.
...IS THAT SO?
I FEEL **REASSURED.**
—YOUR MAJESTY'S SECOND SIGHT TRULY NEVER CEASES TO AMAZE ME.

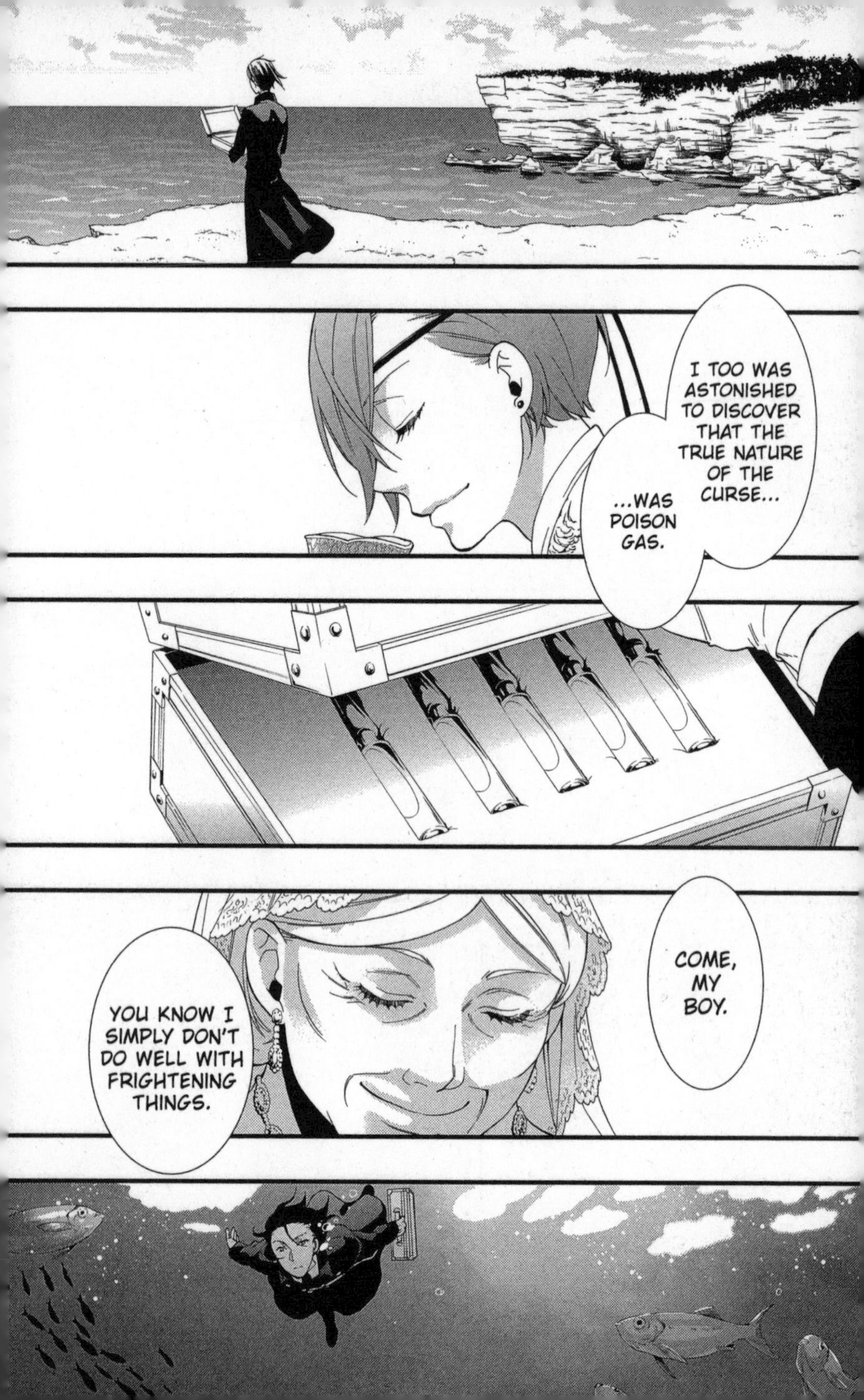
I TOO WAS ASTONISHED TO DISCOVER THAT THE TRUE NATURE OF THE CURSE...
...WAS POISON GAS.
COME, MY BOY.
YOU KNOW I SIMPLY DON'T DO WELL WITH FRIGHTENING THINGS.

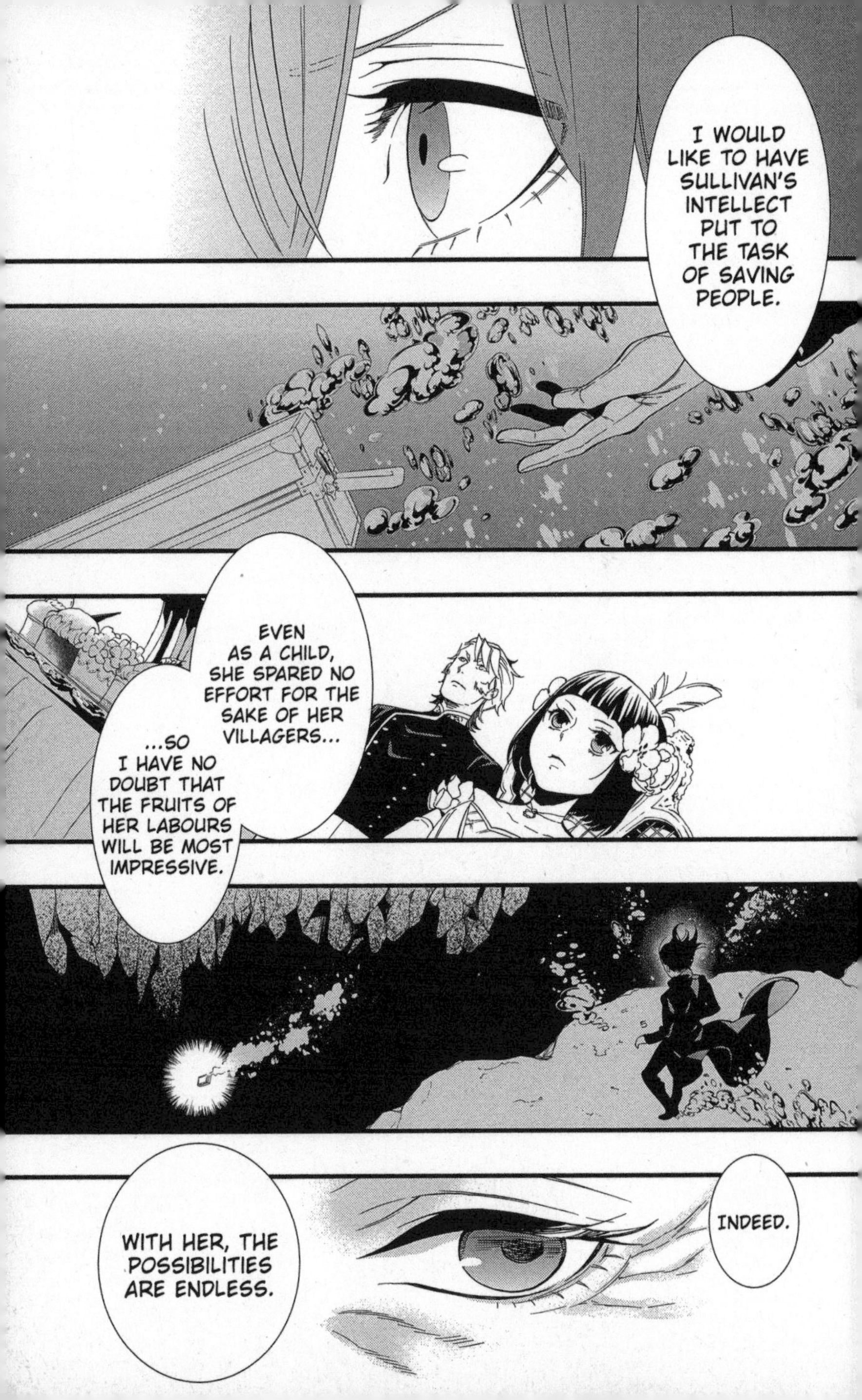

I WOULD LIKE TO HAVE SULLIVAN'S INTELLECT PUT TO THE TASK OF SAVING PEOPLE.
EVEN AS A CHILD, SHE SPARED NO EFFORT FOR THE SAKE OF HER VILLAGERS...
...SO I HAVE NO DOUBT THAT THE FRUITS OF HER LABOURS WILL BE MOST IMPRESSIVE.
INDEED.
WITH HER, THE POSSIBILITIES ARE ENDLESS.

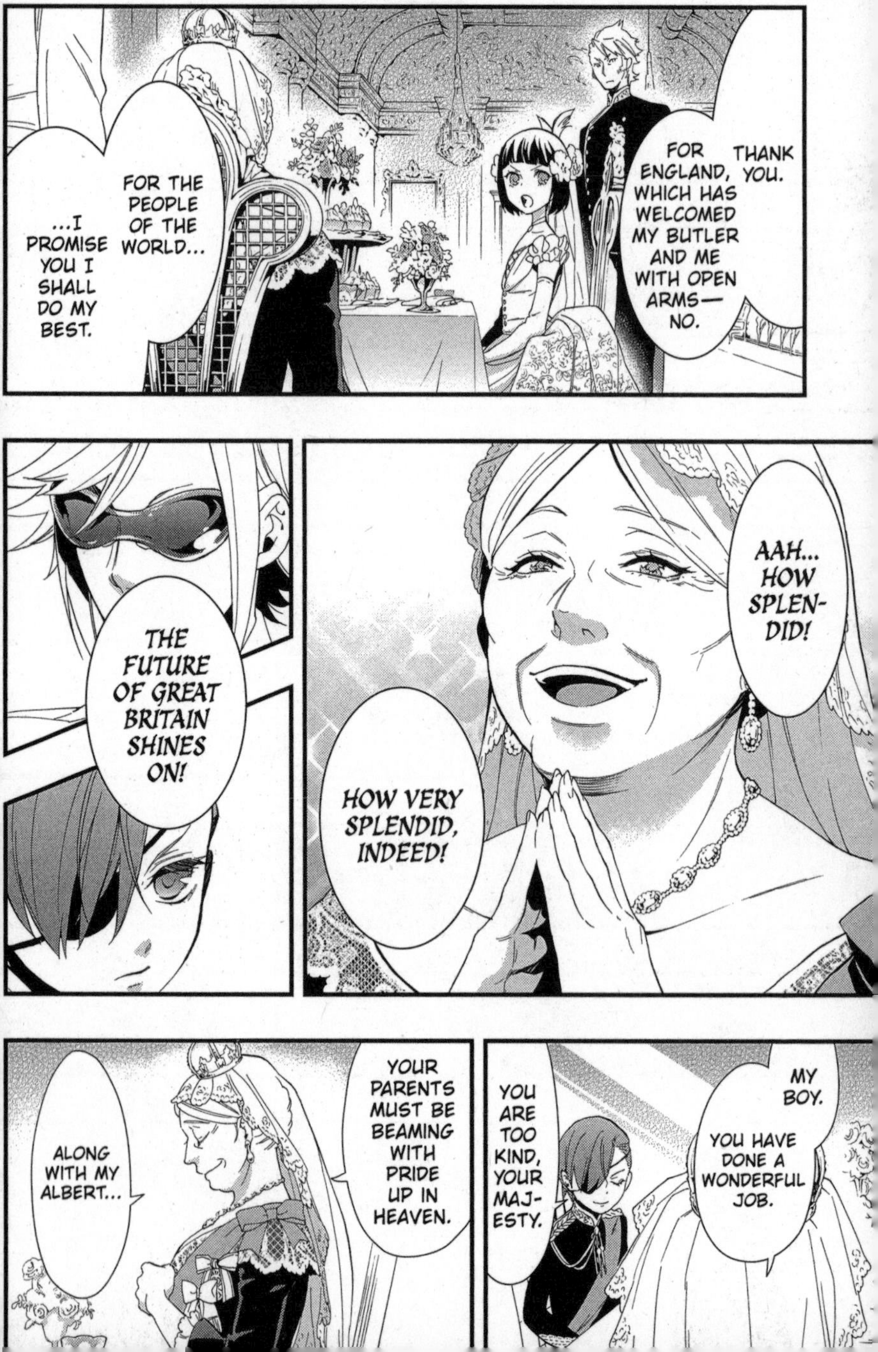
THANK YOU.
FOR ENGLAND, WHICH HAS WELCOMED MY BUTLER AND ME WITH OPEN ARMS— NO.
FOR THE PEOPLE OF THE WORLD...
...I PROMISE YOU I SHALL DO MY BEST.
AAH... HOW SPLEN-DID!
HOW VERY SPLENDID, INDEED!
THE FUTURE OF GREAT BRITAIN SHINES ON!
MY BOY.
YOU HAVE DONE A WONDERFUL JOB.
YOU ARE TOO KIND, YOUR MAJ-ESTY.
YOUR PARENTS MUST BE BEAMING WITH PRIDE UP IN HEAVEN.
ALONG WITH MY ALBERT...

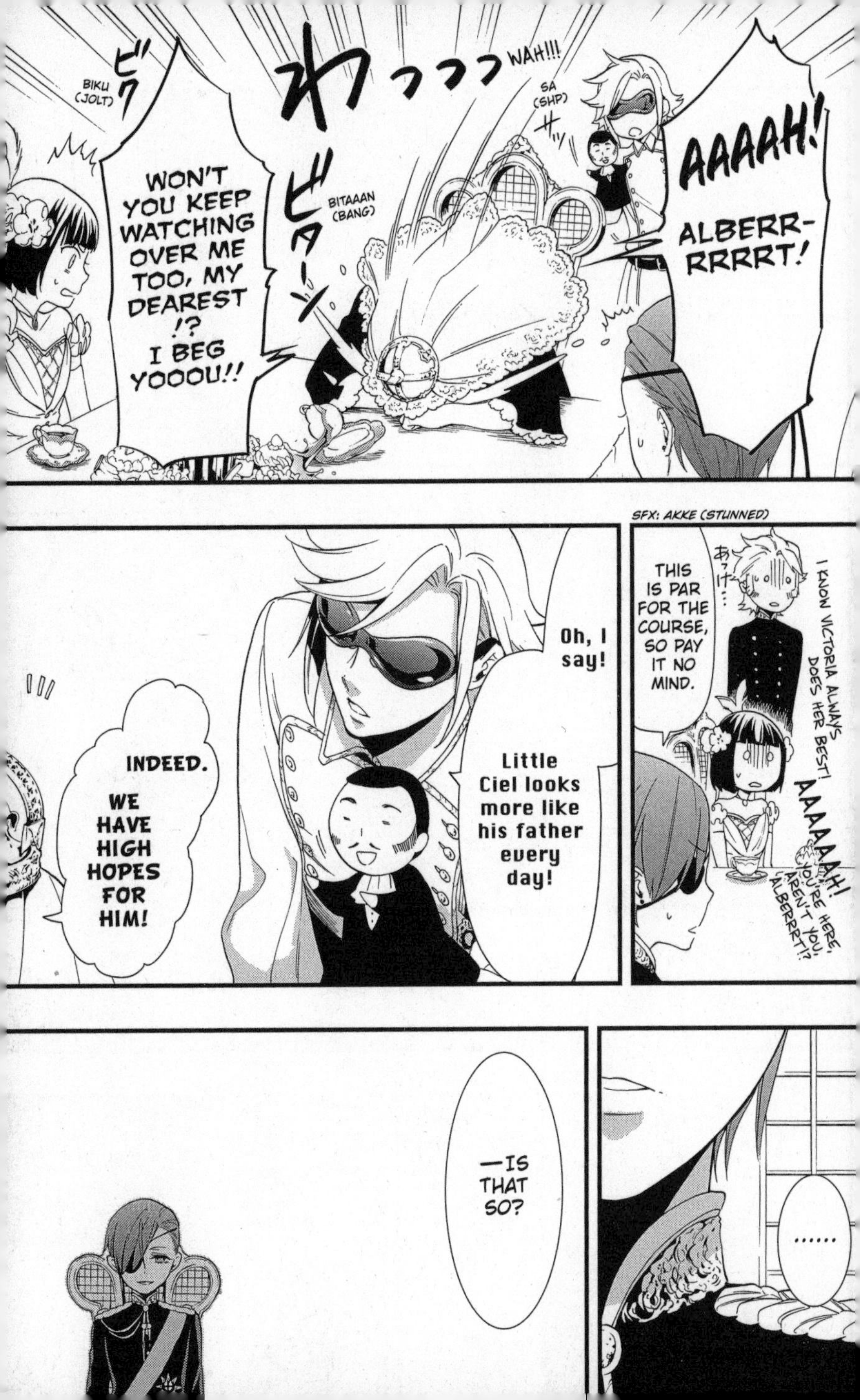
AAAAH!
ALBERR-RRRRT!
SA (SHP)
WAH!!!
BITAAAN (BANG)
BIKU (JOLT)
ビク
WON'T YOU KEEP WATCHING OVER ME TOO, MY DEAREST!? I BEG YOOOU!!
SFX: AKKE (STUNNED)
あっけ…
I KNOW VICTORIA ALWAYS DOES HER BEST!
THIS IS PAR FOR THE COURSE, SO PAY IT NO MIND.
AAAAAAH! YOU'RE HERE, AREN'T YOU, 'ALBERRRT'!?
Oh, I say!
Little Ciel looks more like his father every day!
INDEED. WE HAVE HIGH HOPES FOR HIM!
......
—IS THAT SO?

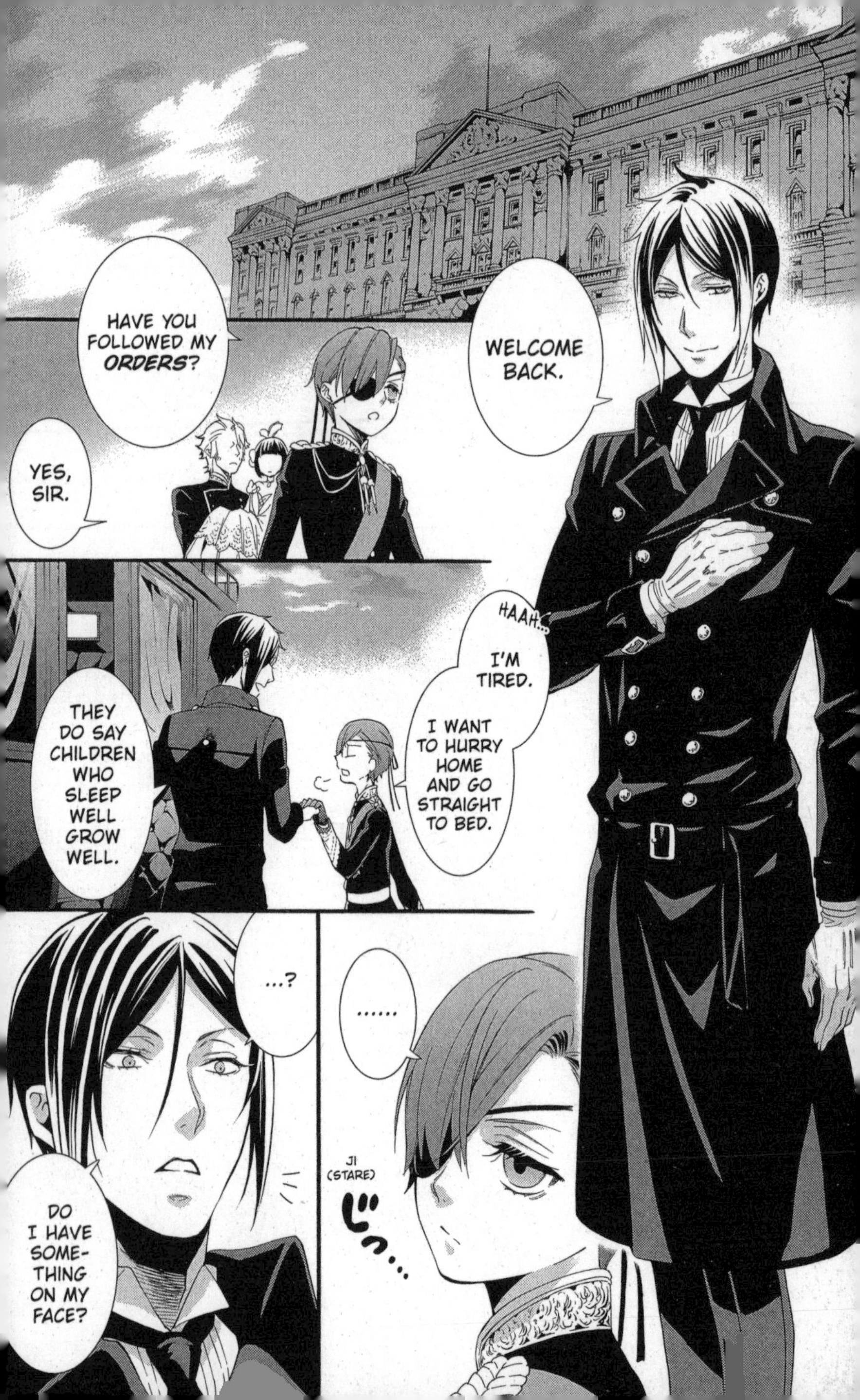
WELCOME BACK.
HAVE YOU FOLLOWED MY ORDERS?
YES, SIR.
HAAH...
I'M TIRED.
I WANT TO HURRY HOME AND GO STRAIGHT TO BED.
THEY DO SAY CHILDREN WHO SLEEP WELL GROW WELL.
......
JI (STARE)
...?
DO I HAVE SOME-THING ON MY FACE?

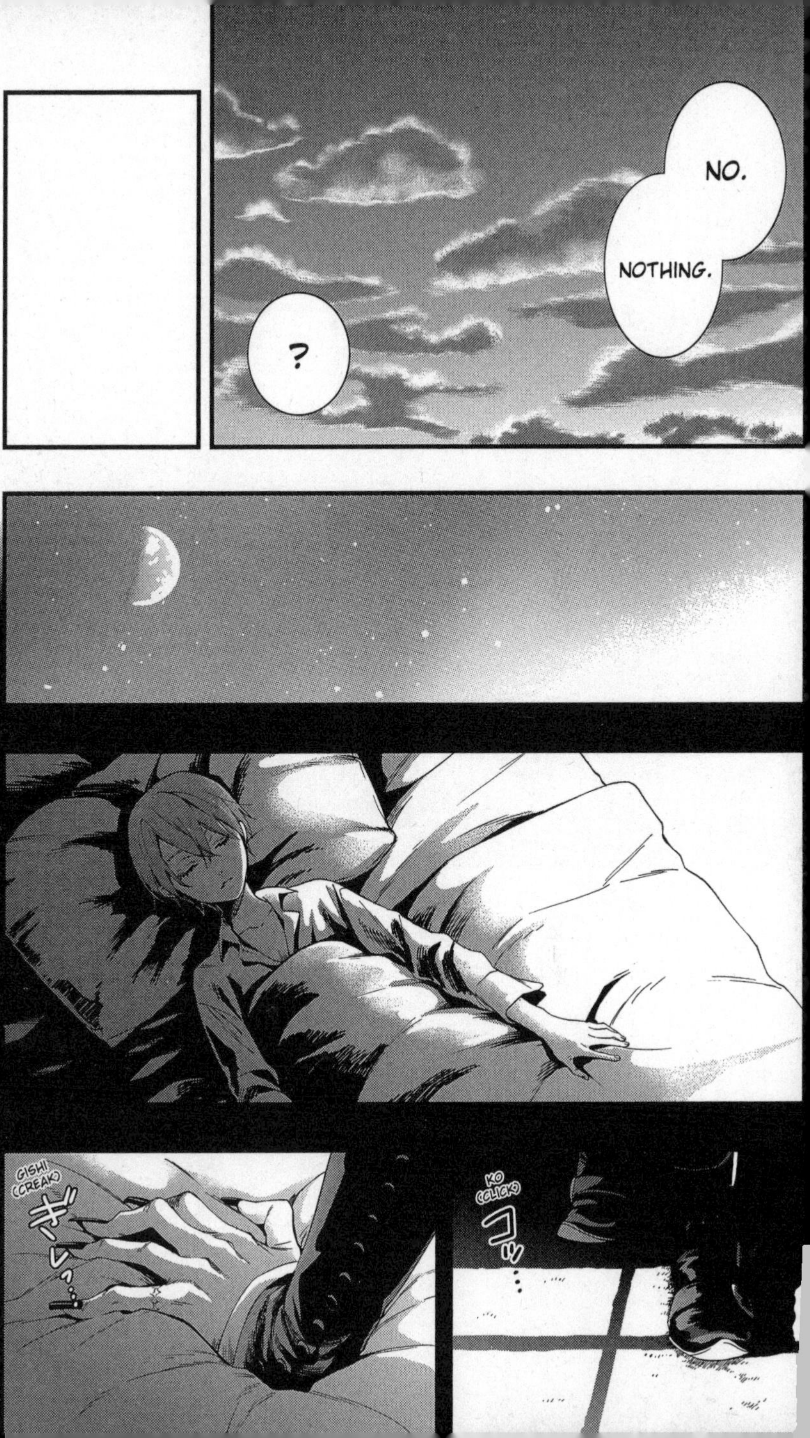
NO.
NOTHING.
?
KO (CLICK)
コッ
GISHI (CREAK)

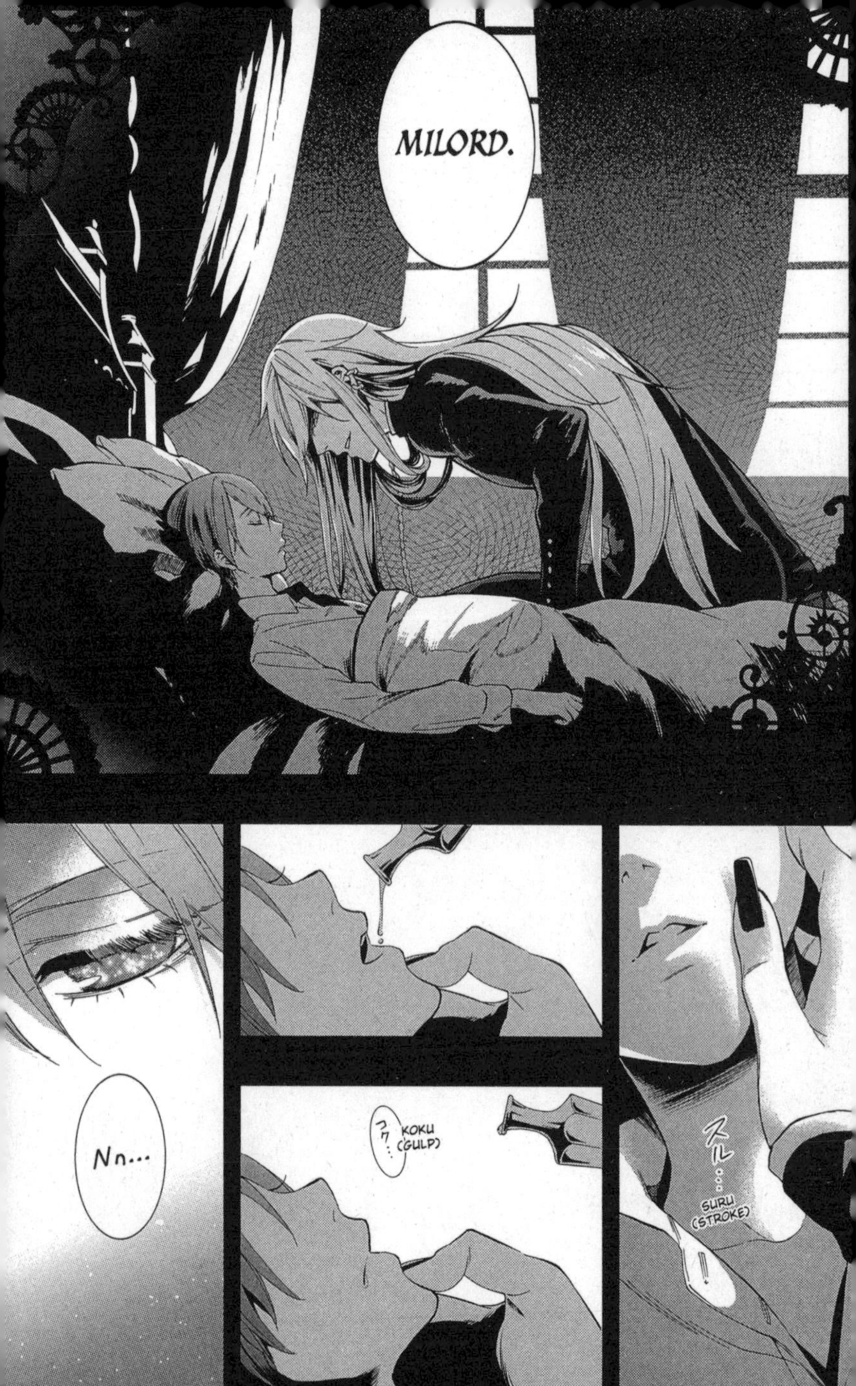
MILORD.
スル…
SURU (STROKE)
コク…
KOKU (GULP)
Nn...

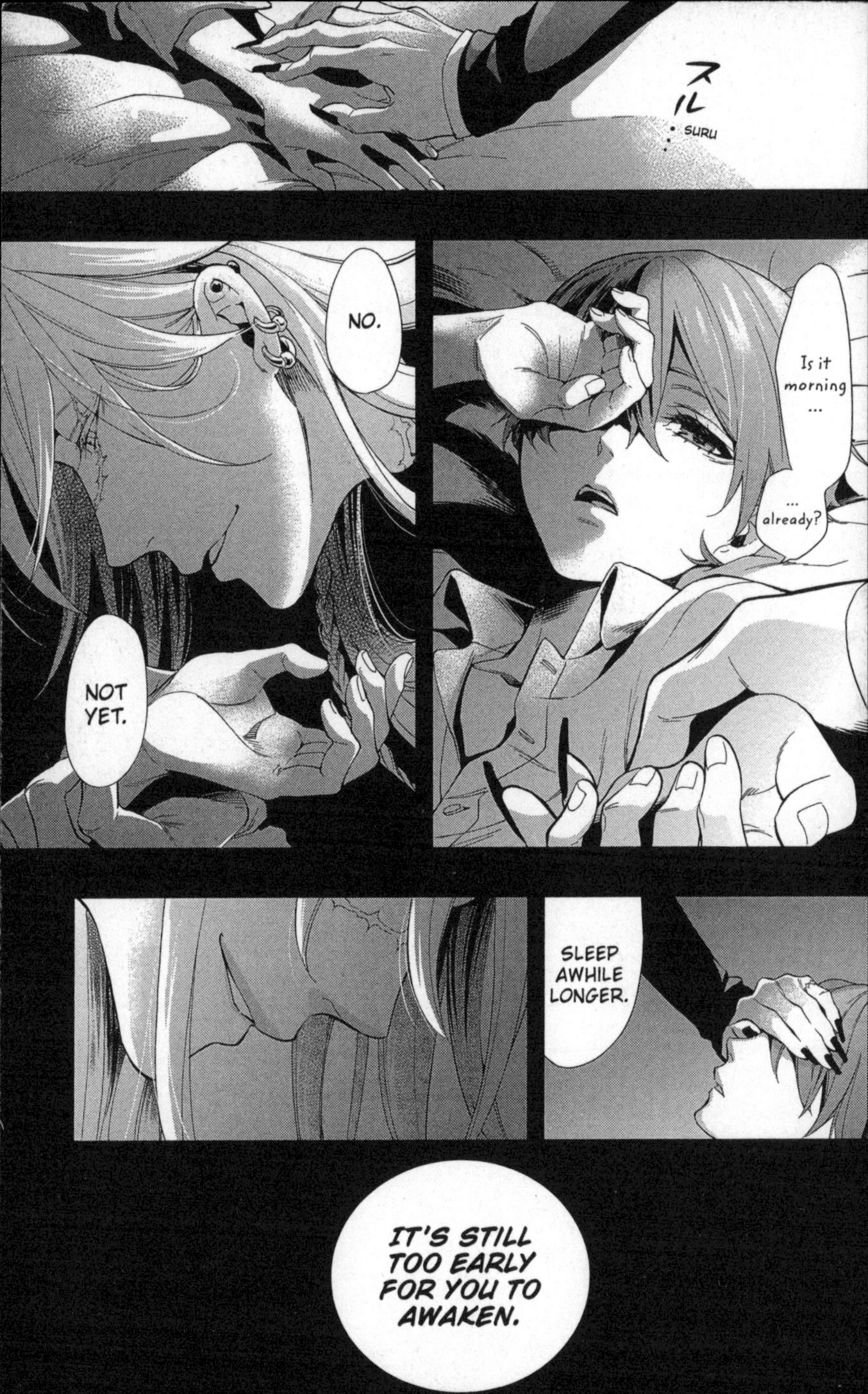

スル
SURU
Is it morning...
...already?
NO.
NOT YET.
SLEEP AWHILE LONGER.
IT'S STILL TOO EARLY FOR YOU TO AWAKEN.

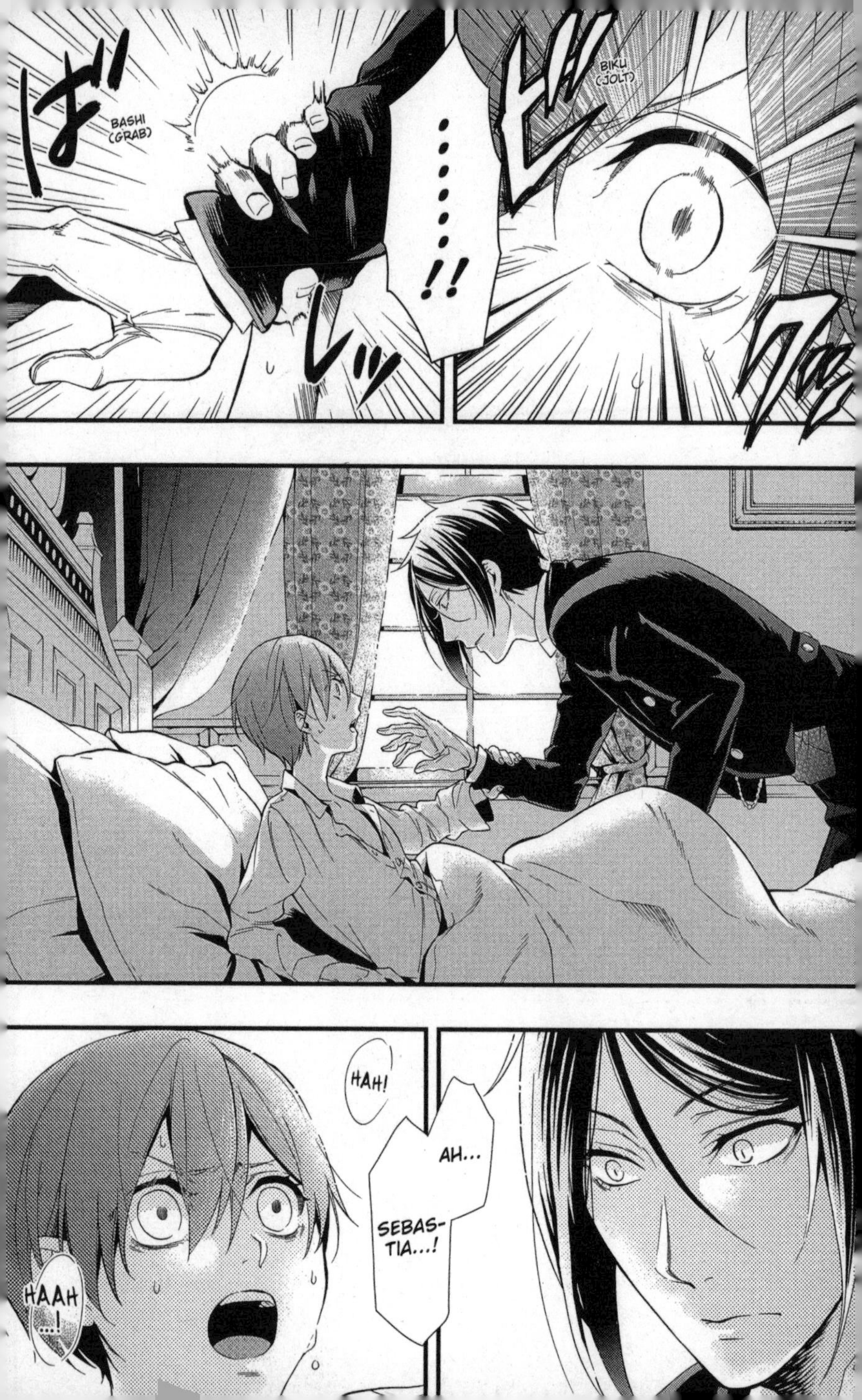
BIKU (JOLT)
......!!
BASHI (GRAB)
HAH!
AH... SEBAS-TIA...!
HAAH ...!

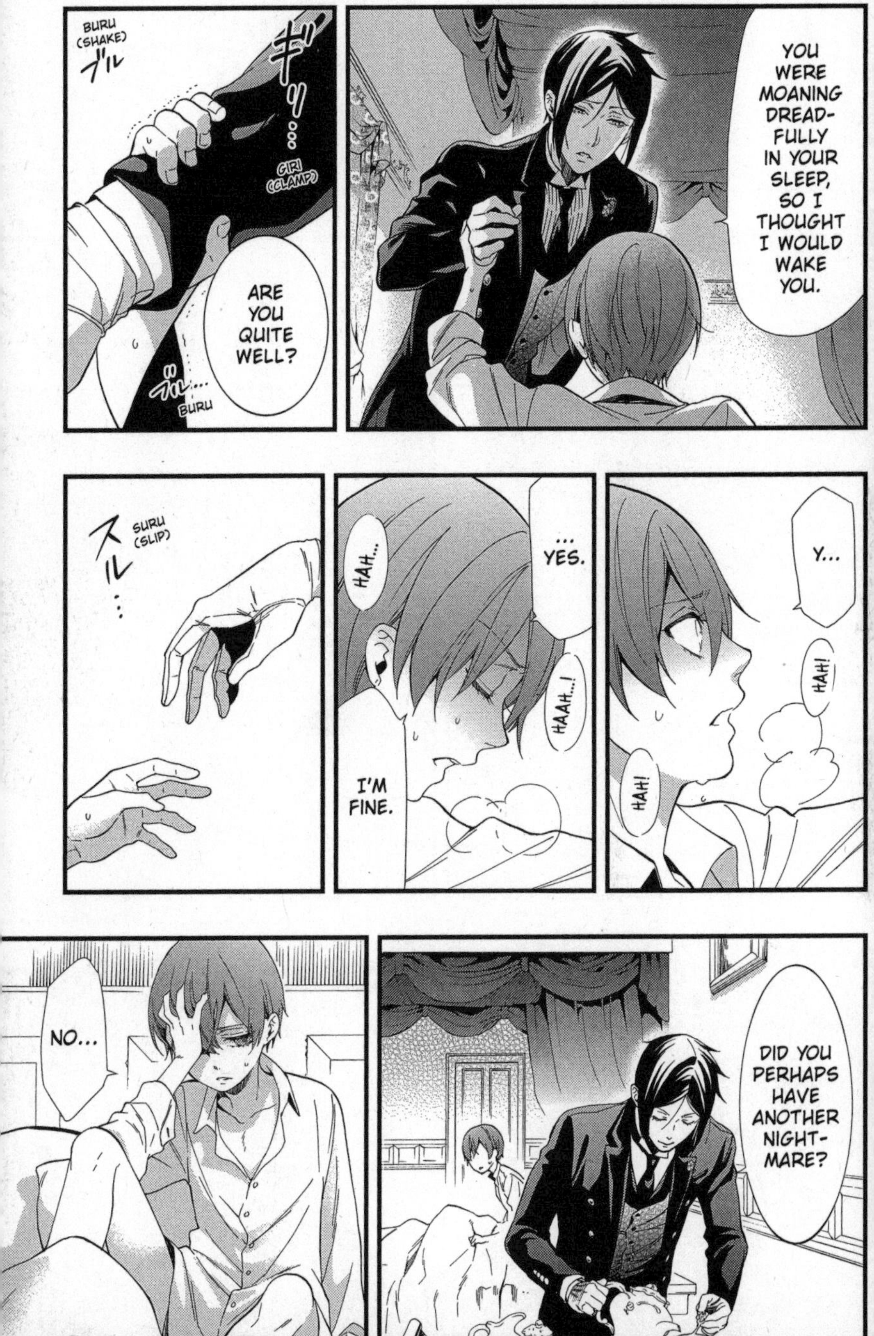
YOU WERE MOANING DREADFULLY IN YOUR SLEEP, SO I THOUGHT I WOULD WAKE YOU.
ギリ…
GIRI (CLAMP)
BURU (SHAKE)
ブル
ARE YOU QUITE WELL?
ブル…
BURU
Y…
HAH!
HAH!
…YES.
HAH…
HAAAH…!
I'M FINE.
スル…
SURU (SLIP)
DID YOU PERHAPS HAVE ANOTHER NIGHTMARE?
NO…

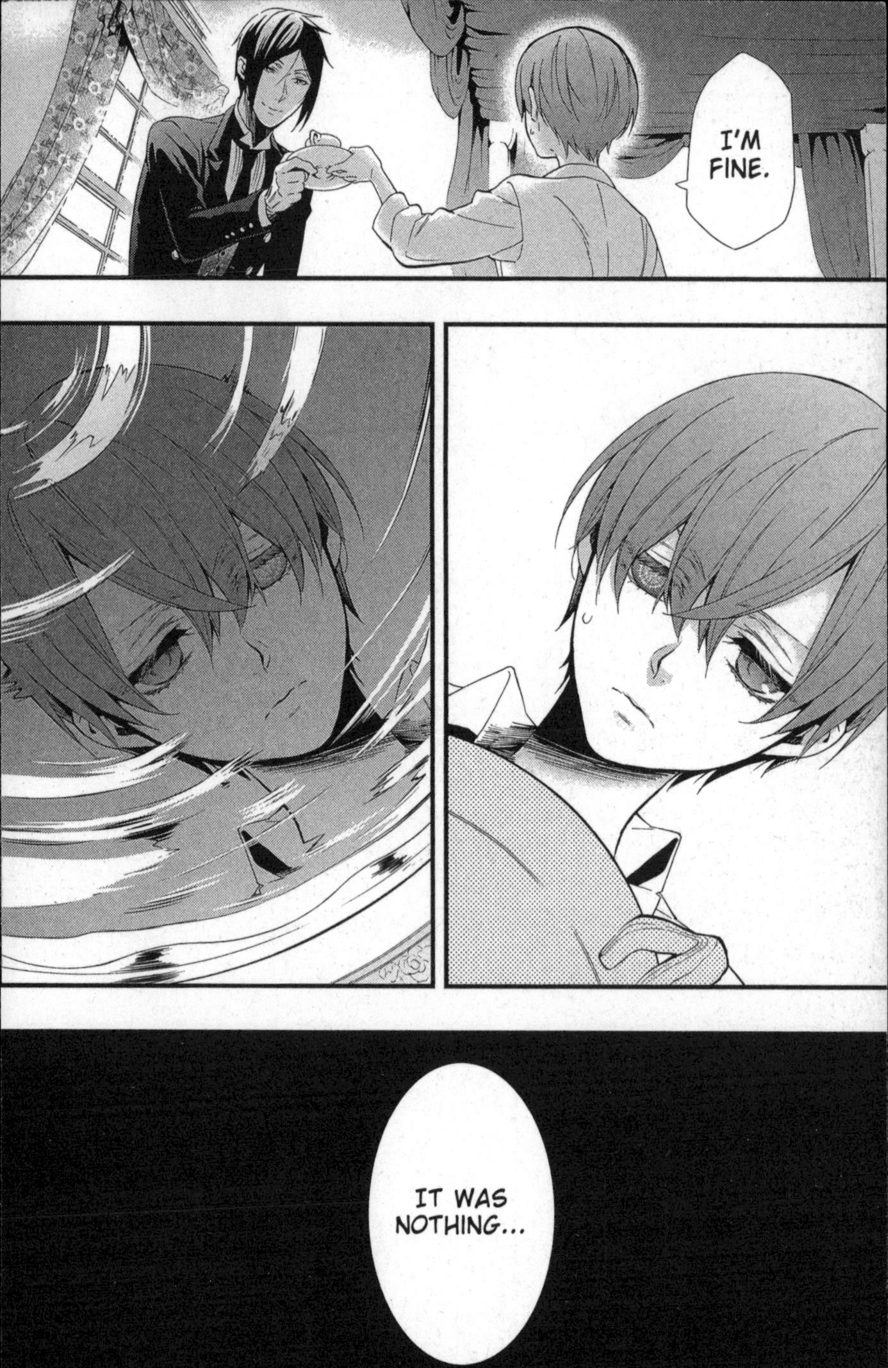
I'M FINE.
IT WAS NOTHING...

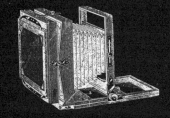

Black Butler

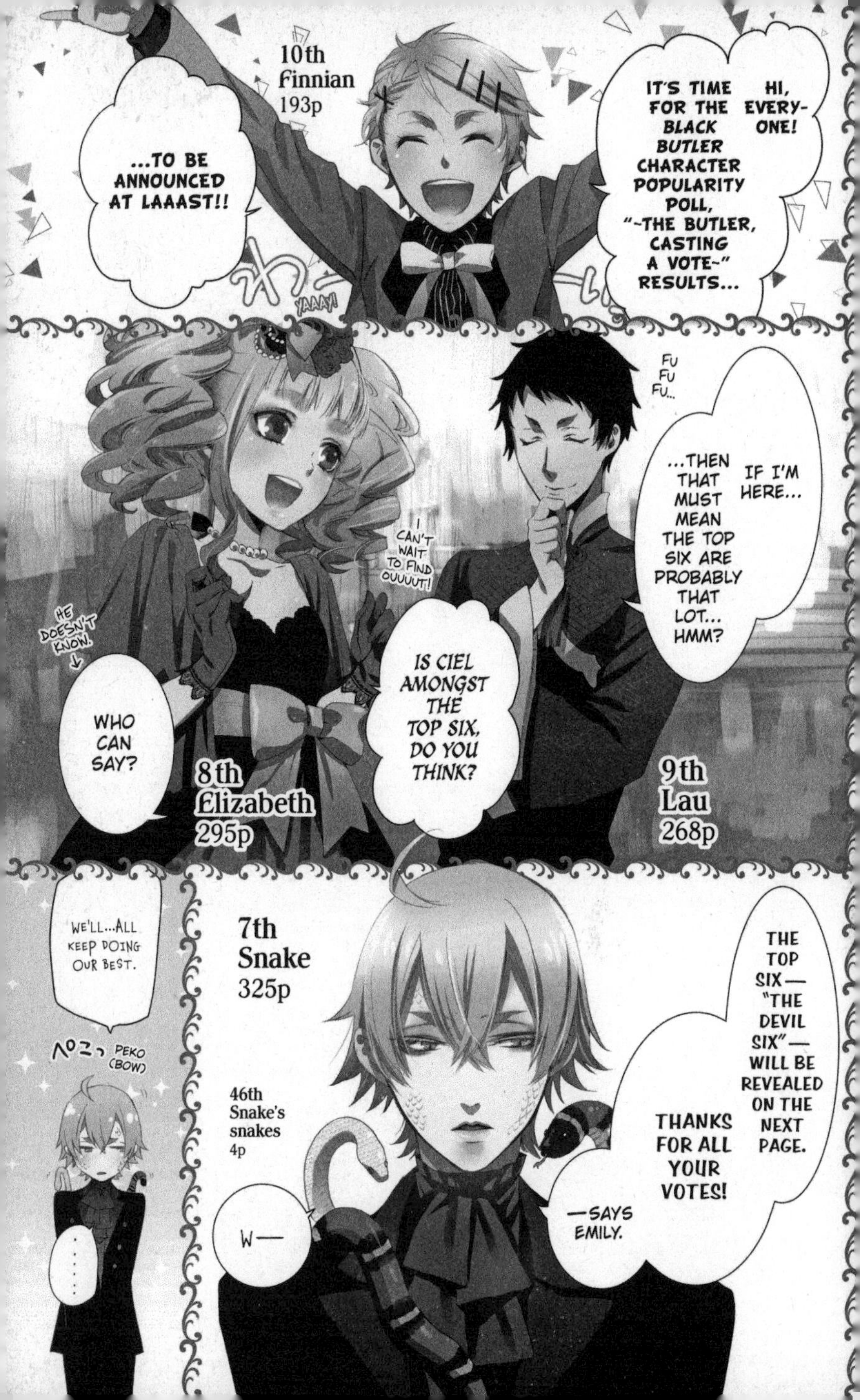
10th Finnian 193p
HI, EVERYONE! IT'S TIME FOR THE BLACK BUTLER CHARACTER POPULARITY POLL, "~THE BUTLER, CASTING A VOTE~" RESULTS...
...TO BE ANNOUNCED AT LAAAST!!
YAAAY!
FU FU FU...
IF I'M HERE... ...THEN THAT MUST MEAN THE TOP SIX ARE PROBABLY THAT LOT... HMM?
I CAN'T WAIT TO FIND OUUUUT!
IS CIEL AMONGST THE TOP SIX, DO YOU THINK?
HE DOESN'T KNOW.
WHO CAN SAY?
9th Lau 268p
8th Elizabeth 295p
7th Snake 325p
THE TOP SIX—"THE DEVIL SIX"—WILL BE REVEALED ON THE NEXT PAGE.
THANKS FOR ALL YOUR VOTES!
—SAYS EMILY.
W—
46th Snake's snakes 4p
WE'LL...ALL KEEP DOING OUR BEST.
ペこっ PEKO (BOW)
......

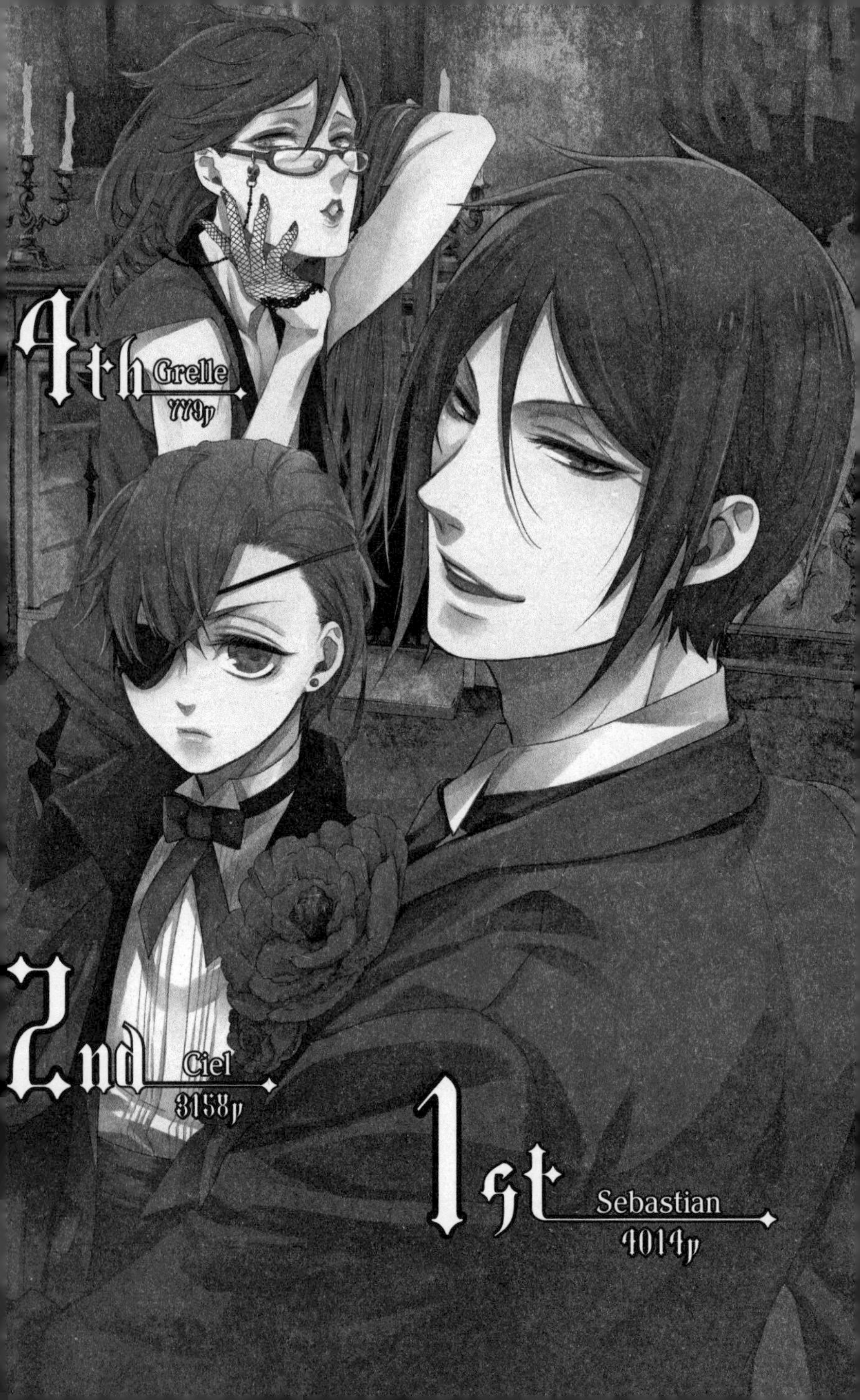
4th Grelle
779p
2nd Ciel
3158p
1st Sebastian
4014p

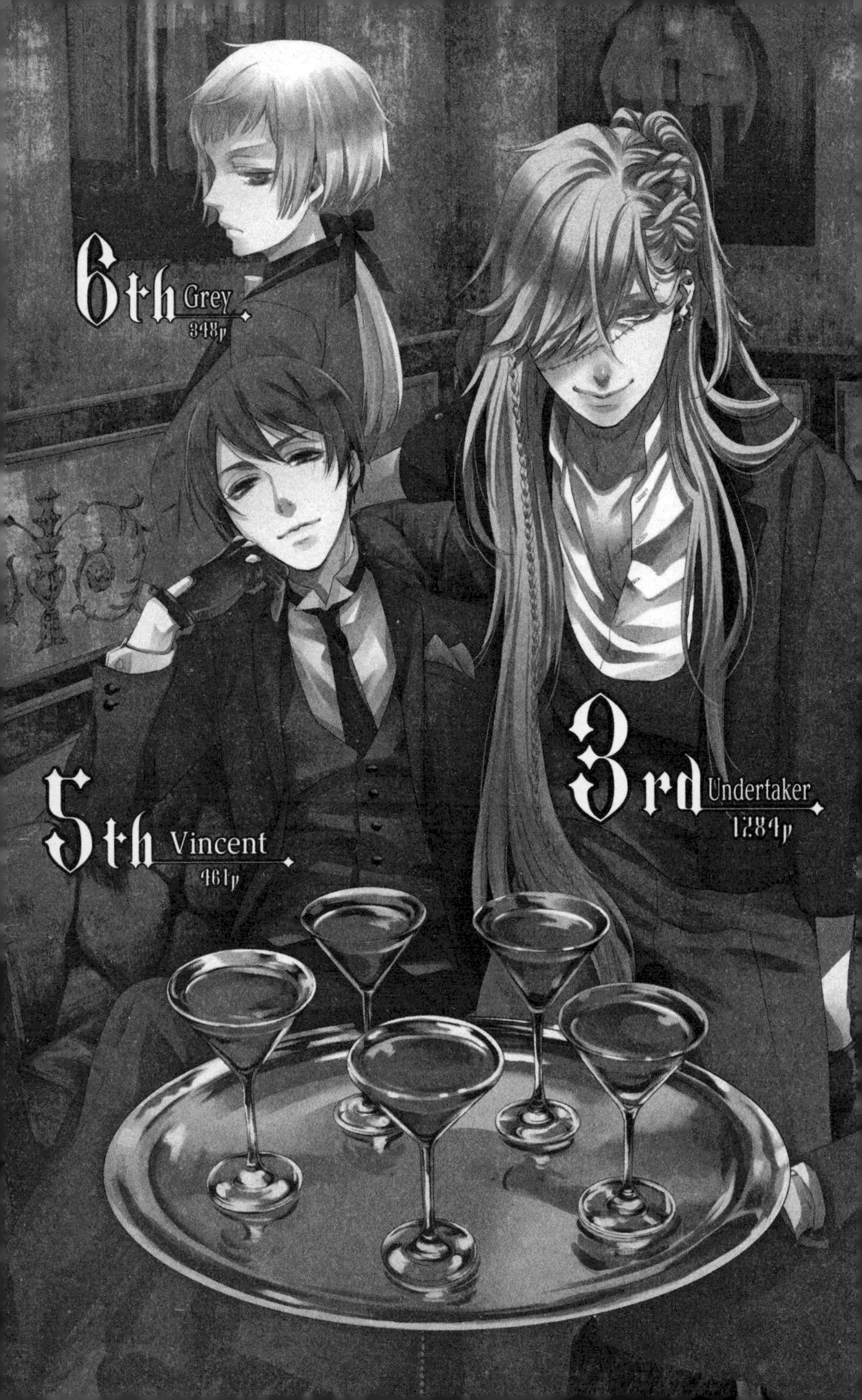
6th Grey
348p
5th Vincent
461p
3rd Undertaker
1284p

Black Butler

Character Popularity Poll

~The Butler, Casting a Vote~

12,817 votes total

POLL RESULTS

The Devil Six

1 Sebastian .... 4,014 votes

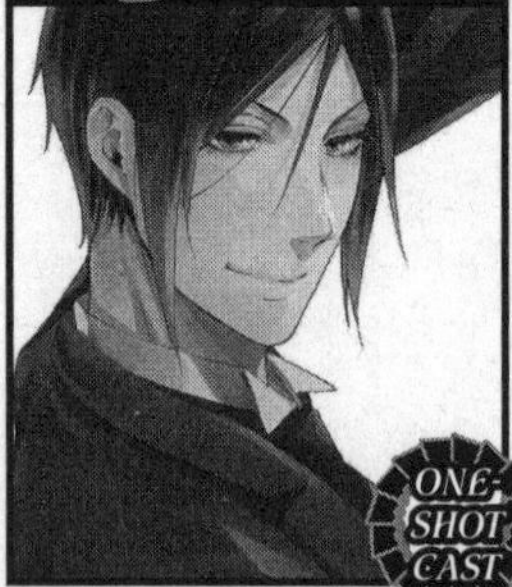
ONE-SHOT CAST

2 Ciel .... 3,158 votes

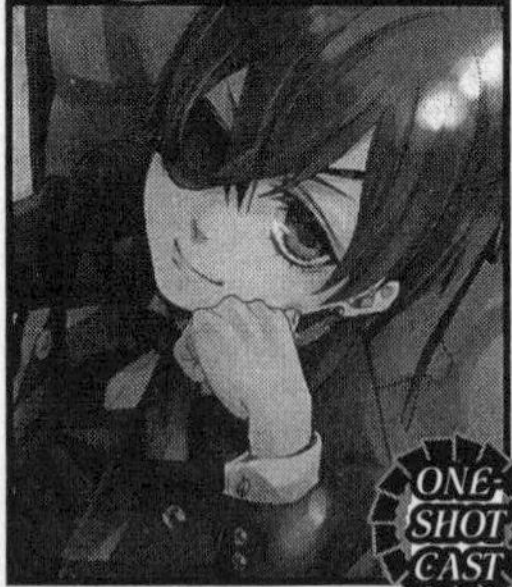
ONE-SHOT CAST

3 Undertaker .... 1,284 votes

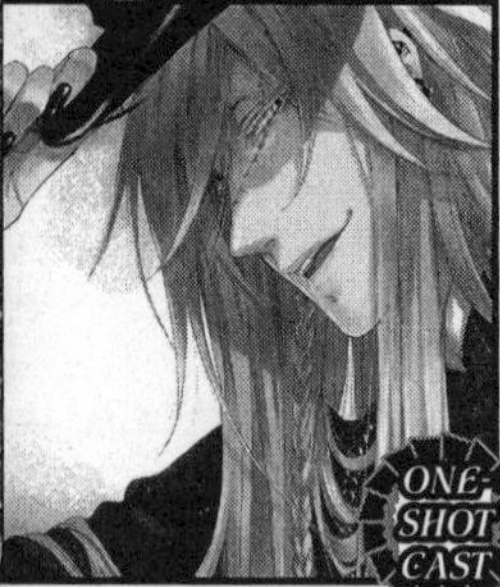
ONE-SHOT CAST

4 Grelle .... 779 votes

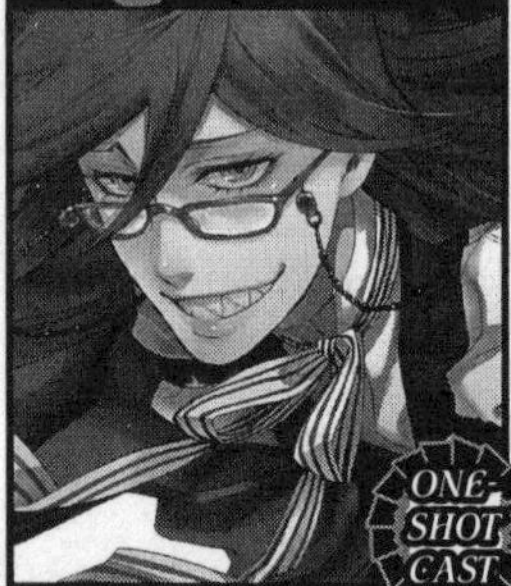
ONE-SHOT CAST

5 Vincent .... 461 votes

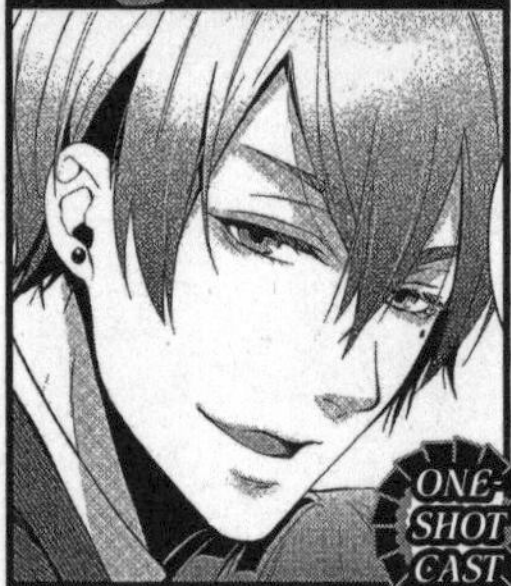
ONE-SHOT CAST

6 Charles Grey .... 348 votes

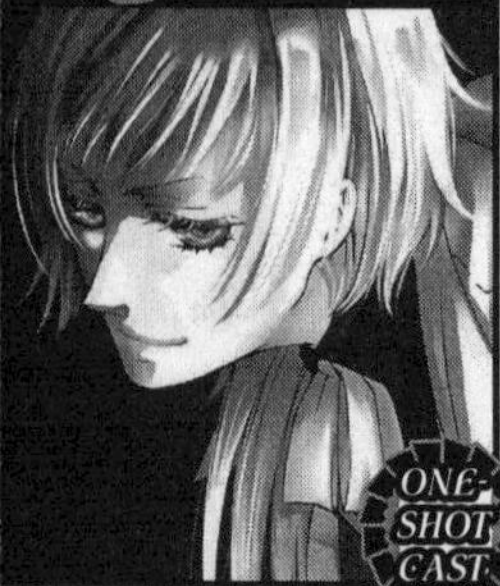
ONE-SHOT CAST

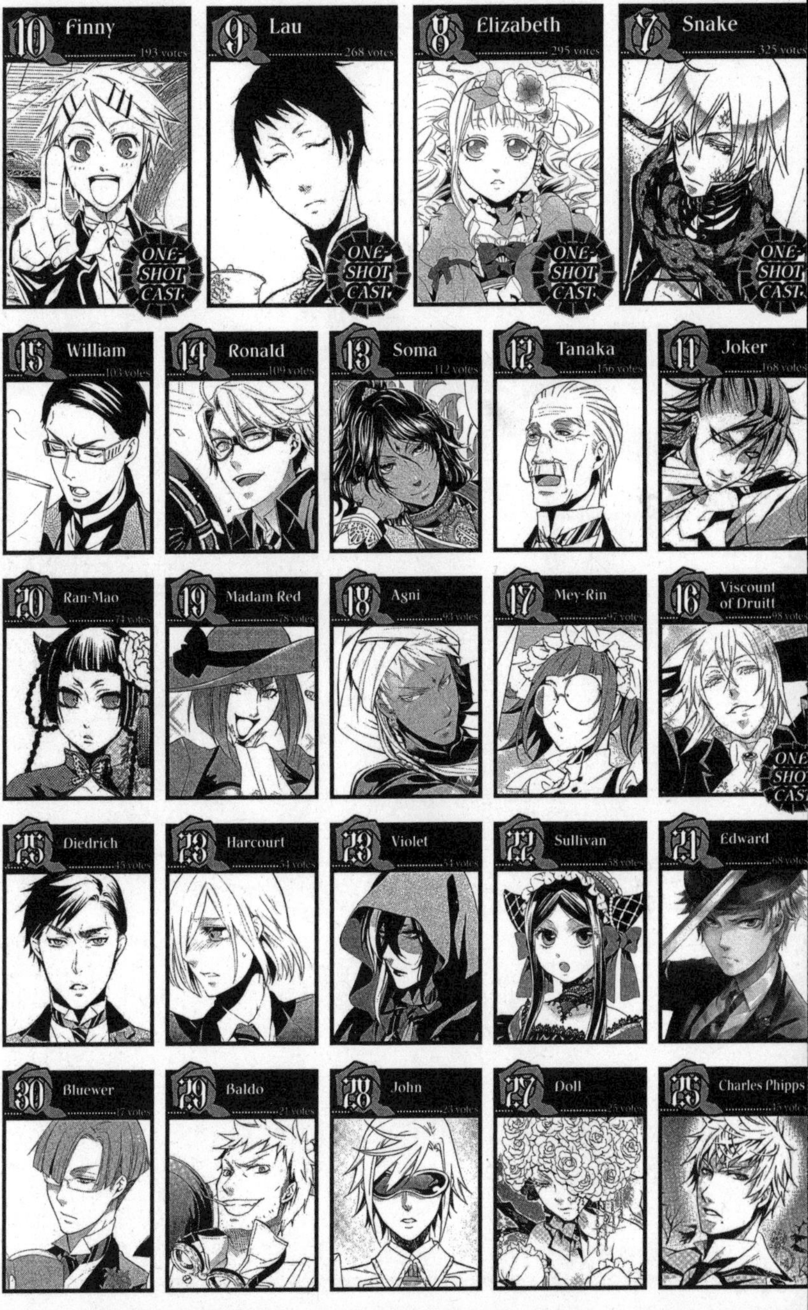

7 Snake 325 votes
ONE-SHOT CAST
8 Elizabeth 295 votes
ONE-SHOT CAST
9 Lau 268 votes
ONE-SHOT CAST
10 Finny 193 votes
ONE-SHOT CAST
11 Joker 168 votes
12 Tanaka
13 Soma 112 votes
14 Ronald 109 votes
15 William 103 votes
16 Viscount of Druitt 98 votes
ONE-SHOT CAST
17 Mey-Rin 97 votes
18 Agni 93 votes
19 Madam Red 78 votes
20 Ran-Mao
21 Edward 68 votes
22 Sullivan 58 votes
23 Violet 54 votes
23 Harcourt 54 votes
25 Diedrich 45 votes
25 Charles Phipps
27 Doll 25 votes
28 John 23 votes
29 Baldo 21 votes
30 Bluewer 17 votes

31 Dagger · Alois Trancy (of the television animation *Black Butler II*) .... 16 votes

33 Arthur · Cheslock .... 15 votes

35 Nina .... 14 votes

36 Francis .... 13 votes

37 Rachel .... 10 votes

38 Queen Victoria · Beast · Paula .... 7 votes

ONE-SHOT CAST

41 Baron Kelvin · Maurice .... 6 votes

43 Abberline · Jeremy · Eric Slingby (of the musical *Black Butler -The Most Beautiful DEATH in the World-*) .... 5 votes

46 Irene · Snake's snakes .... 4 votes

48 Redmond · Greenhill · Wolfram · Grete · Anne · the cats · Drossel Keinz (of the television animation *Black Butler*) .... 3 votes

ONE-SHOT CAST

ONE-SHOT CAST

55 Chlaus · Lord Randall · Ludger · Bitter Rabbit · Albert · Alan Humphries (of the musical *Black Butler -The Most Beautiful DEATH in the World-*) .... 2 votes

61 Rian · McMillan · Vice Headmaster Agares · Peter · unicorn suit · Claude Faustus (of the television animation *Black Butler II*) .... 1 vote

67 Azzurro · West · Mina · Jumbo · Doc · Grimsby · Lord Siemens · Woodley · Phelps · Marquess of Midford · Derrick · Clayton · village crone · Hilde .... 0 votes

Thanks for all your many votes!

The bonus starring the Devil Six begins next.

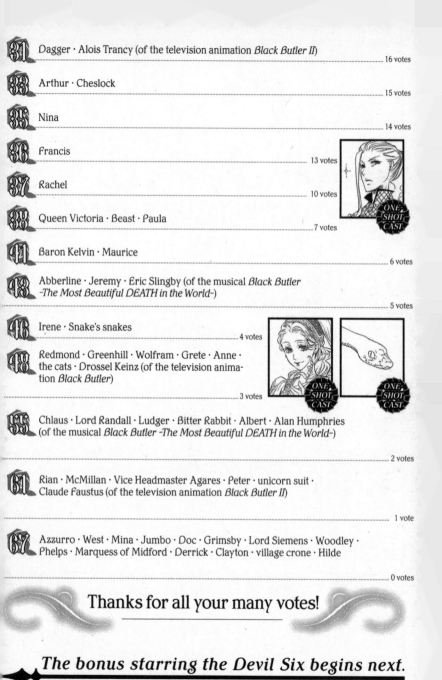

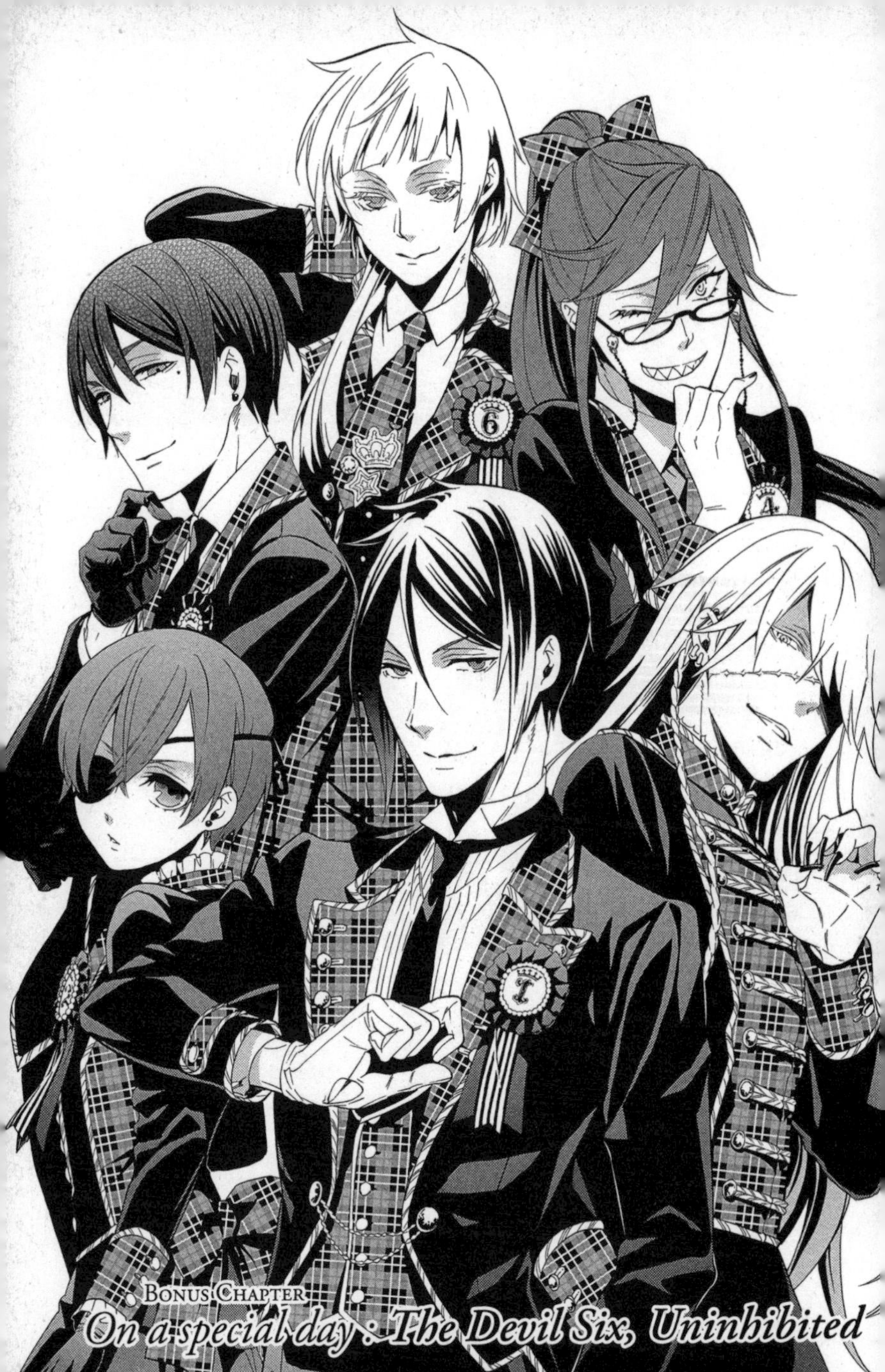

BONUS CHAPTER

On a special day : The Devil Six, Uninhibited

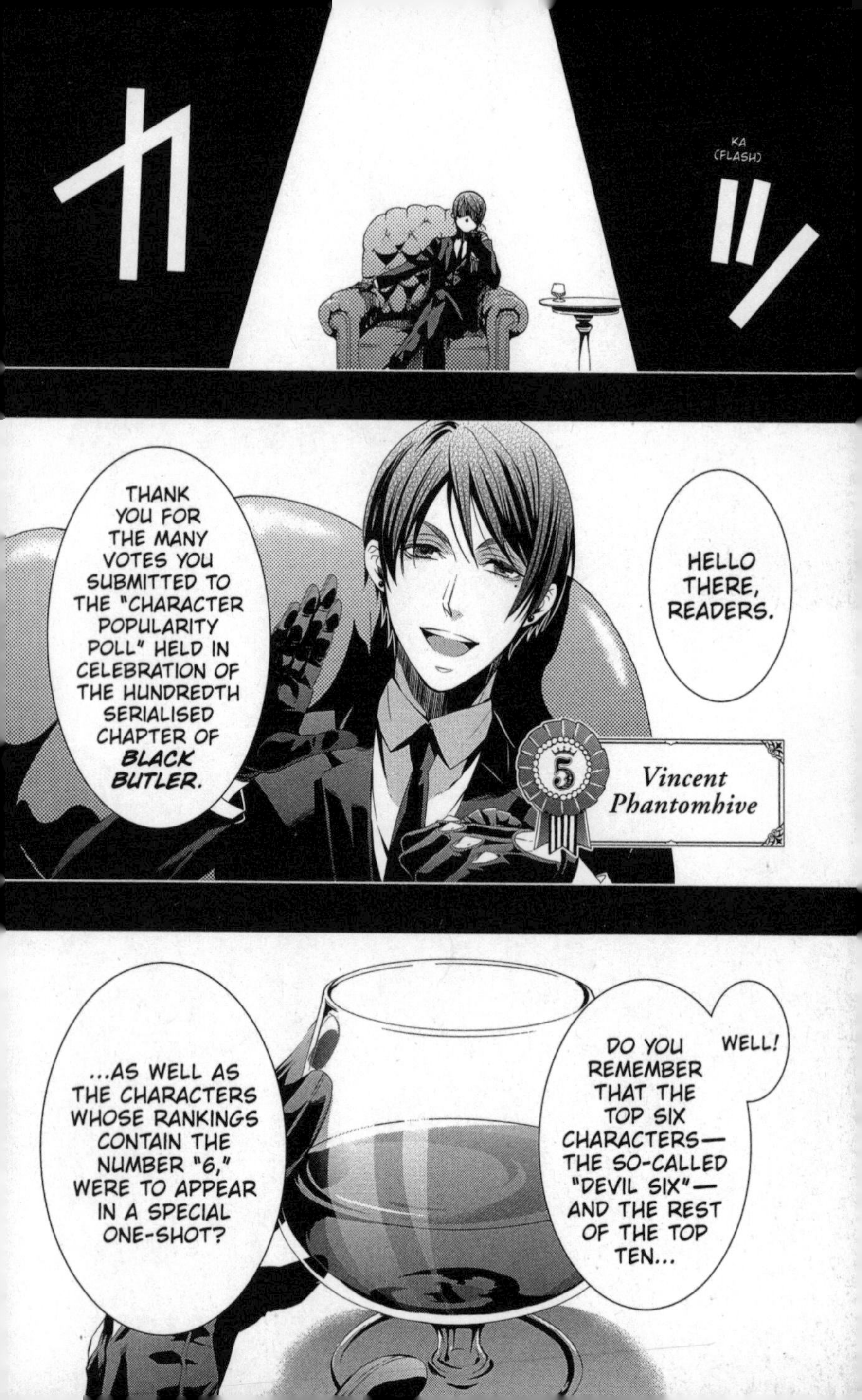
カッ
KA (FLASH)
HELLO THERE, READERS.
THANK YOU FOR THE MANY VOTES YOU SUBMITTED TO THE "CHARACTER POPULARITY POLL" HELD IN CELEBRATION OF THE HUNDREDTH SERIALISED CHAPTER OF *BLACK BUTLER*.
5
Vincent Phantomhive
WELL!
DO YOU REMEMBER THAT THE TOP SIX CHARACTERS—THE SO-CALLED "DEVIL SIX"—AND THE REST OF THE TOP TEN...
...AS WELL AS THE CHARACTERS WHOSE RANKINGS CONTAIN THE NUMBER "6," WERE TO APPEAR IN A SPECIAL ONE-SHOT?

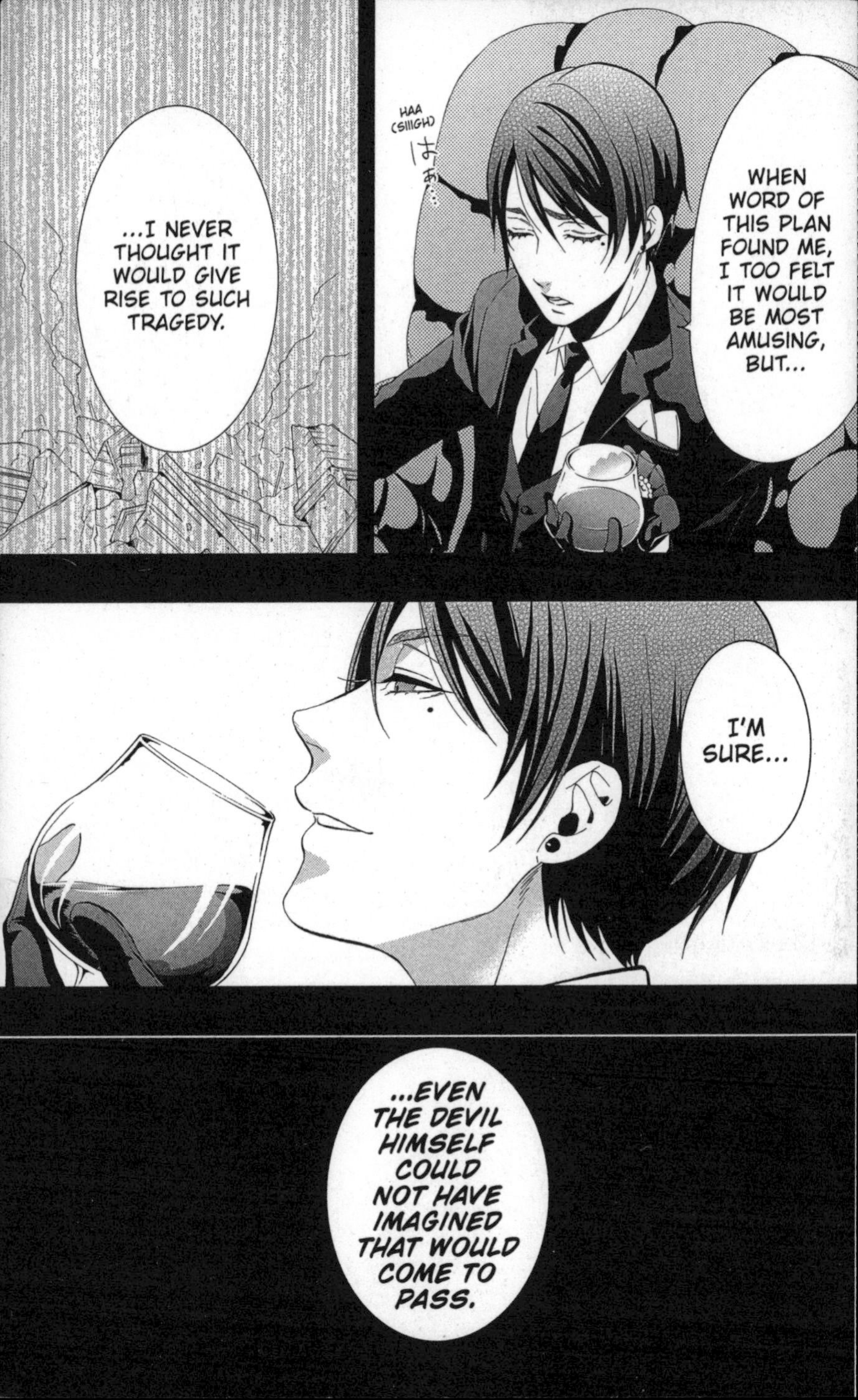
HAA (SIIIGH)
はぁ…
WHEN WORD OF THIS PLAN FOUND ME, I TOO FELT IT WOULD BE MOST AMUSING, BUT...
...I NEVER THOUGHT IT WOULD GIVE RISE TO SUCH TRAGEDY.
I'M SURE...
...EVEN THE DEVIL HIMSELF COULD NOT HAVE IMAGINED THAT WOULD COME TO PASS.

Viscount Druitt's 16th Place Vote Celebration Banquet

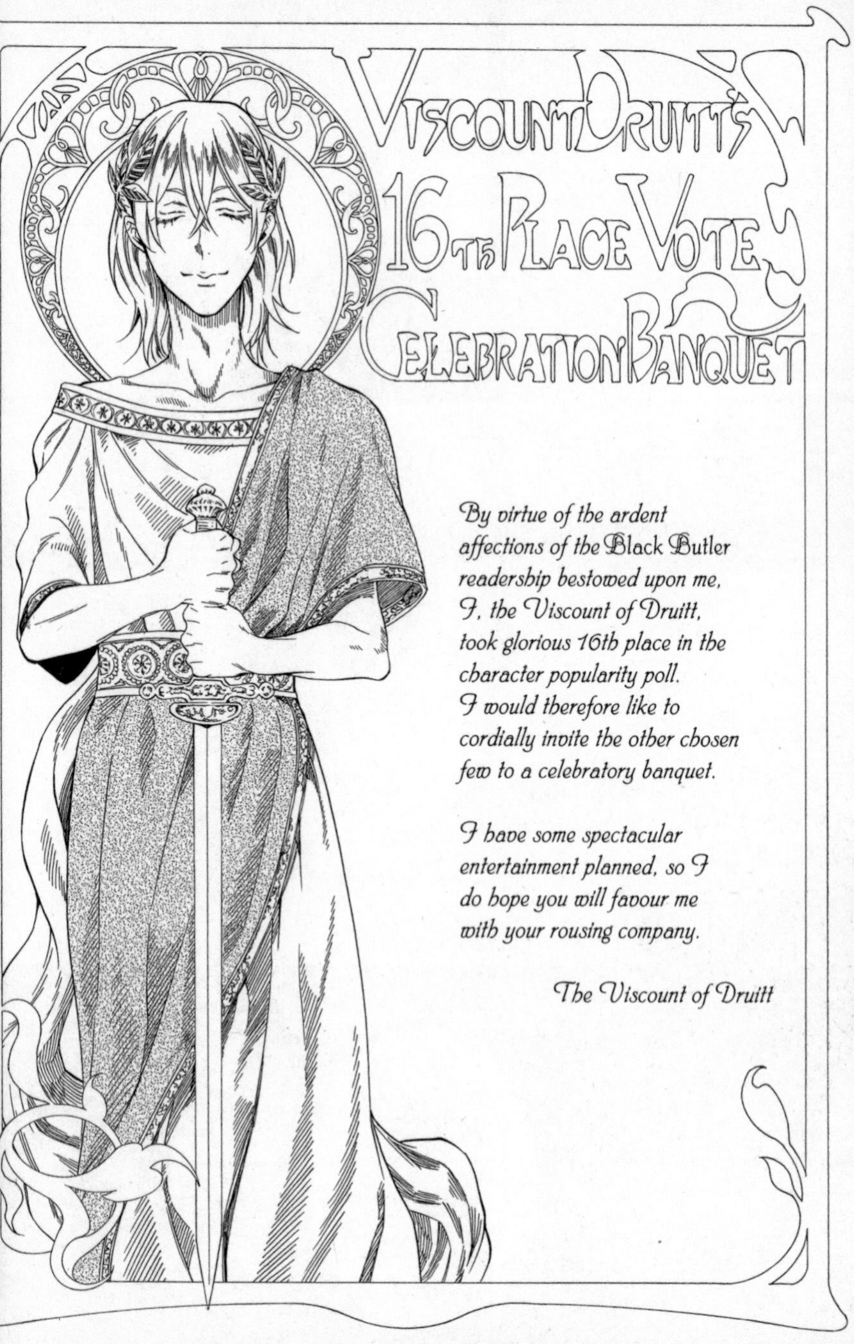

By virtue of the ardent affections of the Black Butler readership bestowed upon me, I, the Viscount of Druitt, took glorious 16th place in the character popularity poll. I would therefore like to cordially invite the other chosen few to a celebratory banquet.

I have some spectacular entertainment planned, so I do hope you will favour me with your rousing company.

The Viscount of Druitt

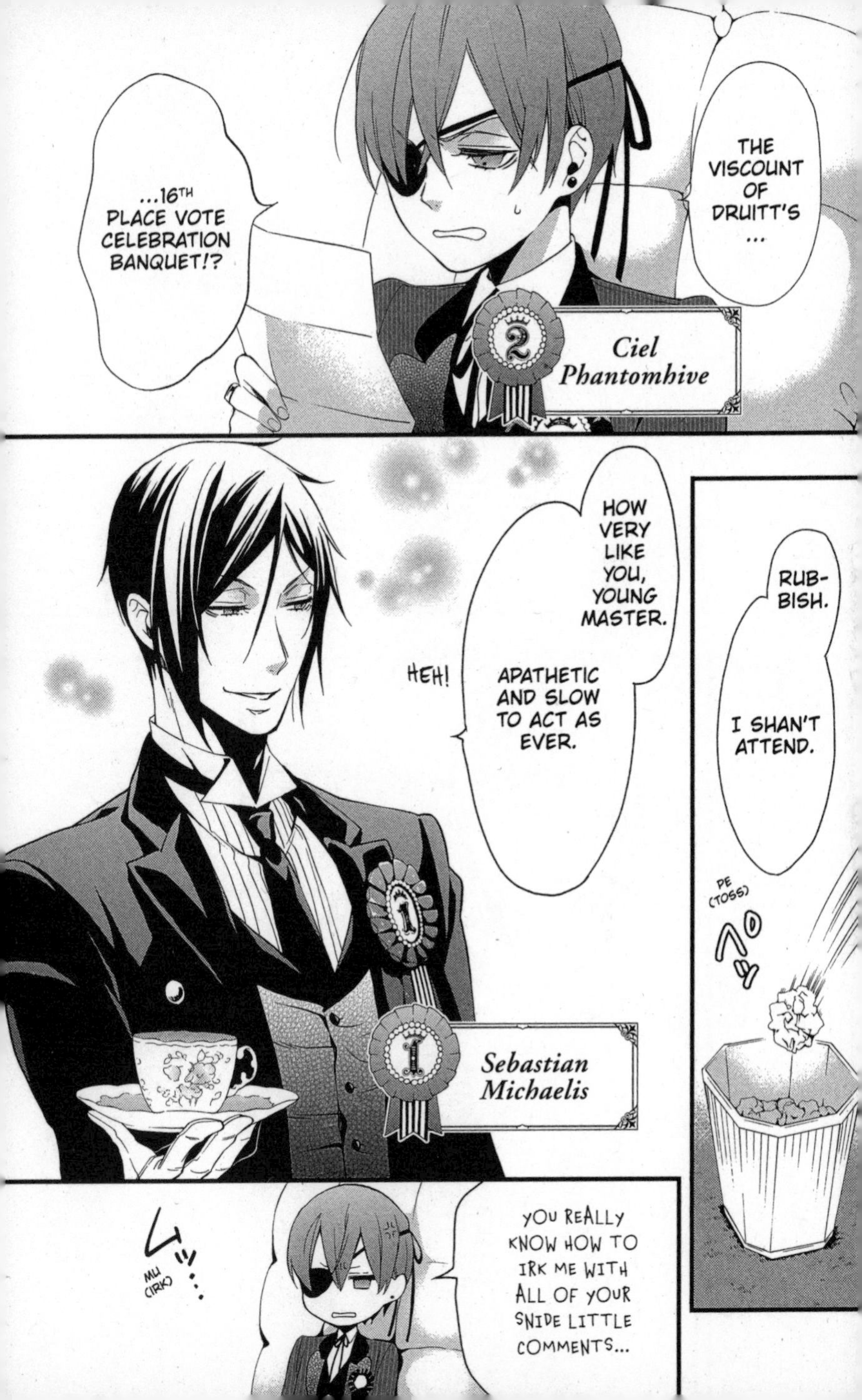
THE VISCOUNT OF DRUITT'S ...
...16TH PLACE VOTE CELEBRATION BANQUET!?
2
Ciel Phantomhive
RUB-BISH.
I SHAN'T ATTEND.
PE (TOSS)
HOW VERY LIKE YOU, YOUNG MASTER.
APATHETIC AND SLOW TO ACT AS EVER.
HEH!
1
Sebastian Michaelis
YOU REALLY KNOW HOW TO IRK ME WITH ALL OF YOUR SNIDE LITTLE COMMENTS...
MU (IRK)

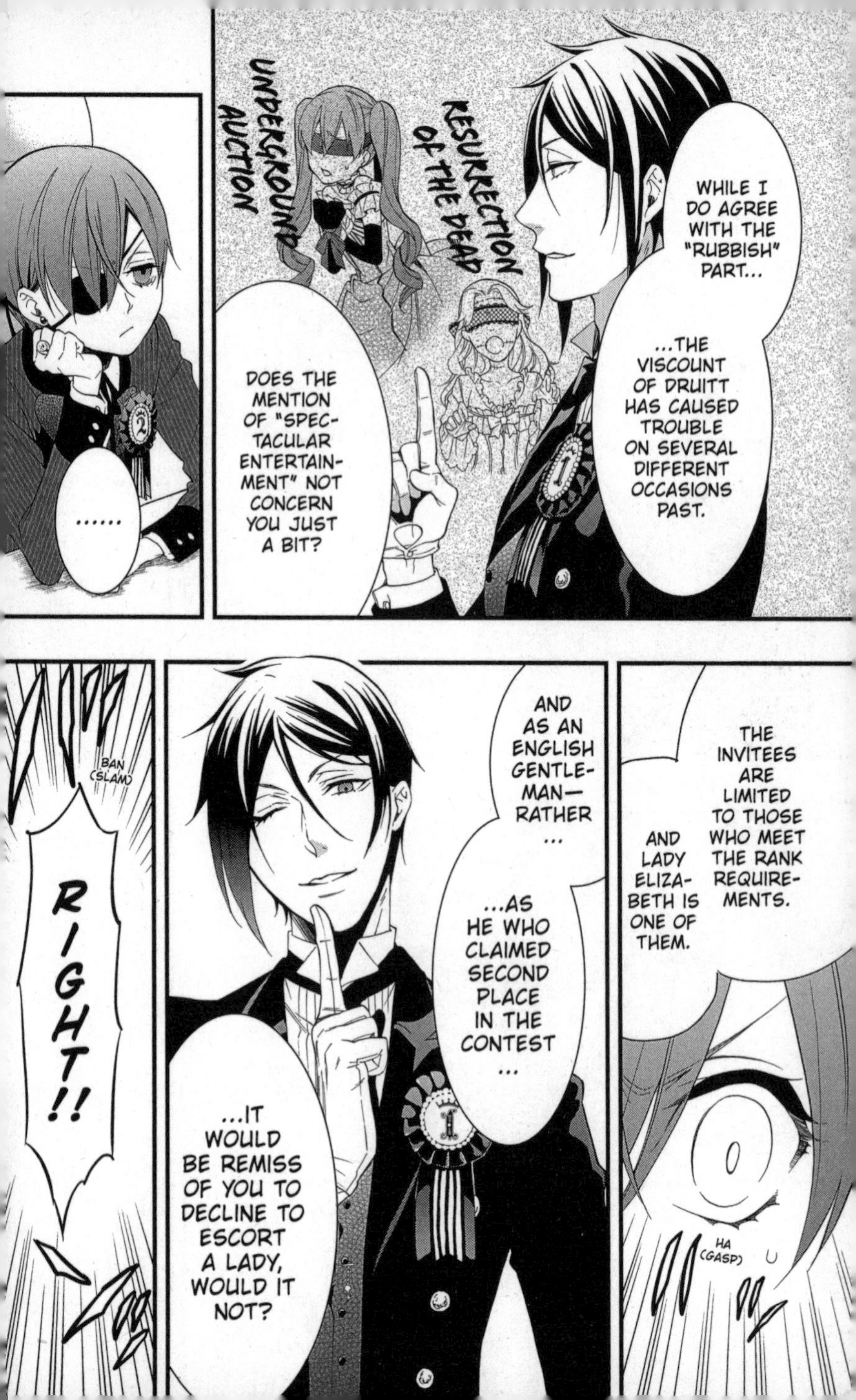
WHILE I DO AGREE WITH THE "RUBBISH" PART...
...THE VISCOUNT OF DRUITT HAS CAUSED TROUBLE ON SEVERAL DIFFERENT OCCASIONS PAST.
RESURRECTION OF THE DEAD
UNDERGROUND AUCTION
DOES THE MENTION OF "SPECTACULAR ENTERTAINMENT" NOT CONCERN YOU JUST A BIT?
......
THE INVITEES ARE LIMITED TO THOSE WHO MEET THE RANK REQUIREMENTS.
AND LADY ELIZABETH IS ONE OF THEM.
HA (GASP)
AND AS AN ENGLISH GENTLEMAN—RATHER...
...AS HE WHO CLAIMED SECOND PLACE IN THE CONTEST...
...IT WOULD BE REMISS OF YOU TO DECLINE TO ESCORT A LADY, WOULD IT NOT?
BAN (SLAM)
RIGHT!!

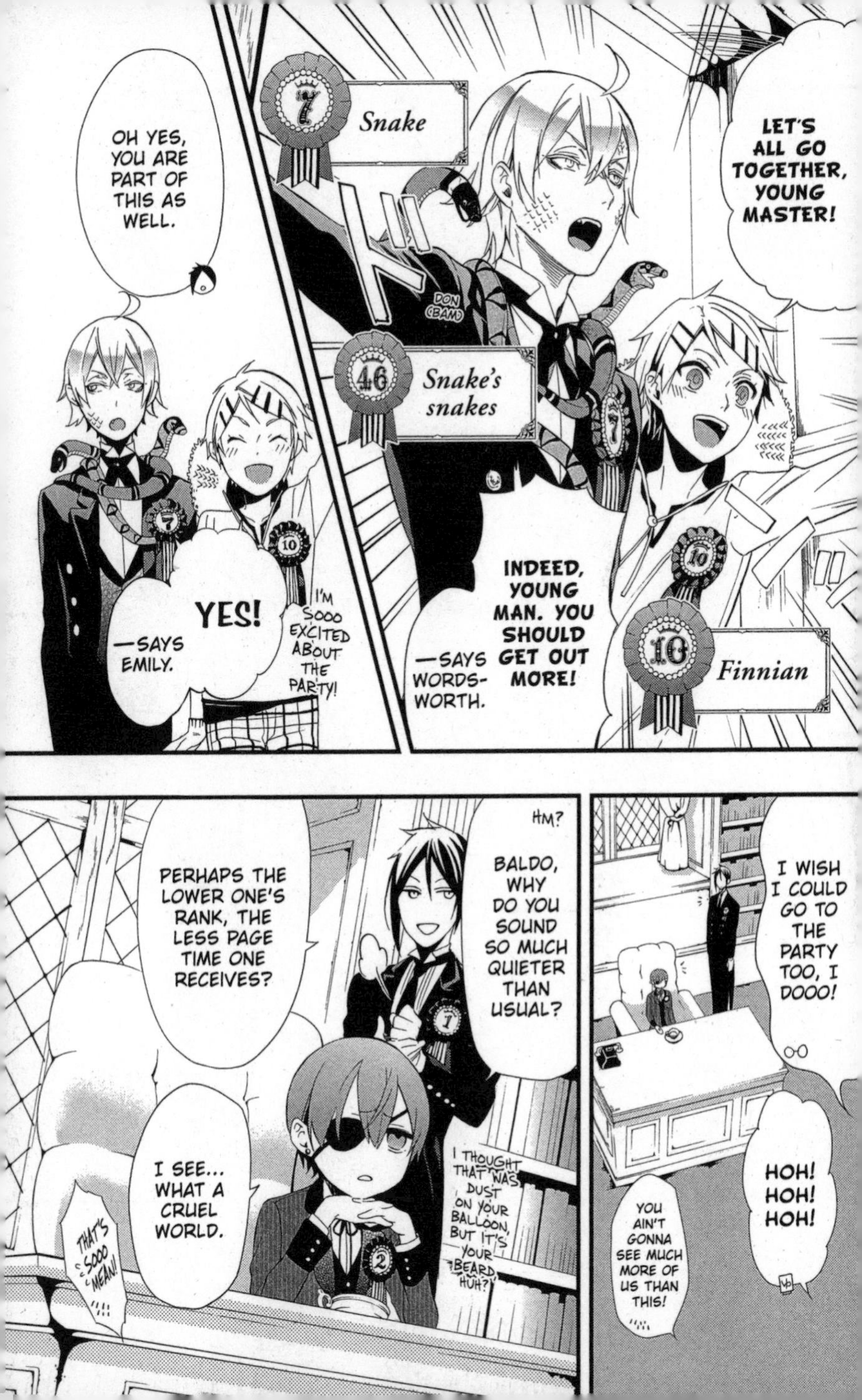
LET'S ALL GO TOGETHER, YOUNG MASTER!
7 Snake
DON (BAM)
46 Snake's snakes
INDEED, YOUNG MAN. YOU SHOULD GET OUT MORE!
—SAYS WORDS-WORTH.
10 Finnian
OH YES, YOU ARE PART OF THIS AS WELL.
YES!
—SAYS EMILY.
I'M SOOO EXCITED ABOUT THE PARTY!
I WISH I COULD GO TO THE PARTY TOO, I DOOO!
HOH! HOH! HOH!
YOU AIN'T GONNA SEE MUCH MORE OF US THAN THIS!
HM?
BALDO, WHY DO YOU SOUND SO MUCH QUIETER THAN USUAL?
PERHAPS THE LOWER ONE'S RANK, THE LESS PAGE TIME ONE RECEIVES?
I THOUGHT THAT WAS DUST ON YOUR BALLOON, BUT IT'S YOUR BEARD, HUH?
I SEE... WHAT A CRUEL WORLD.
THAT'S SOOO MEAN!

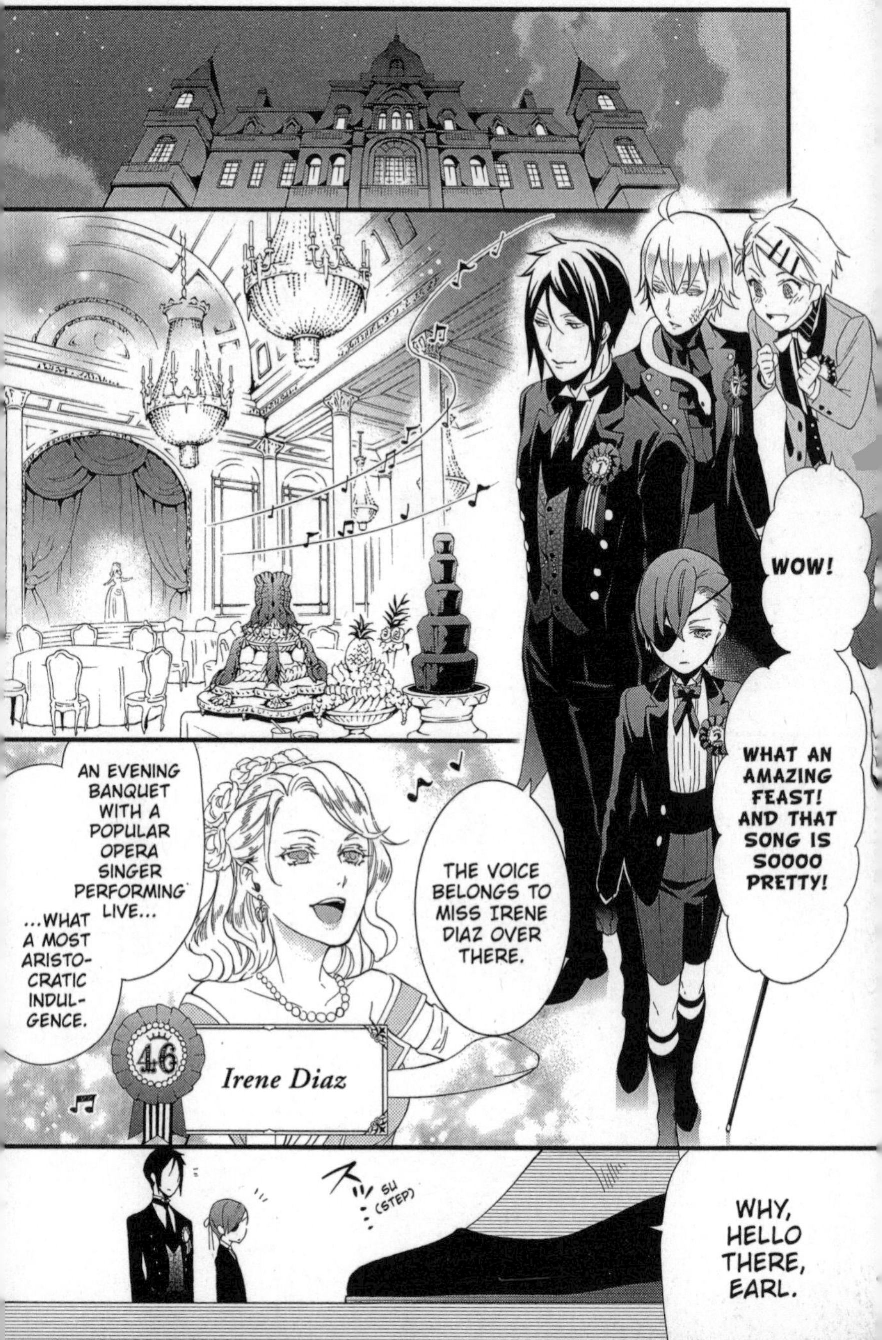
WOW!
WHAT AN AMAZING FEAST! AND THAT SONG IS SOOOO PRETTY!
THE VOICE BELONGS TO MISS IRENE DIAZ OVER THERE.
AN EVENING BANQUET WITH A POPULAR OPERA SINGER PERFORMING LIVE...
...WHAT A MOST ARISTOCRATIC INDULGENCE.
46
Irene Diaz
WHY, HELLO THERE, EARL.
SU (STEP)

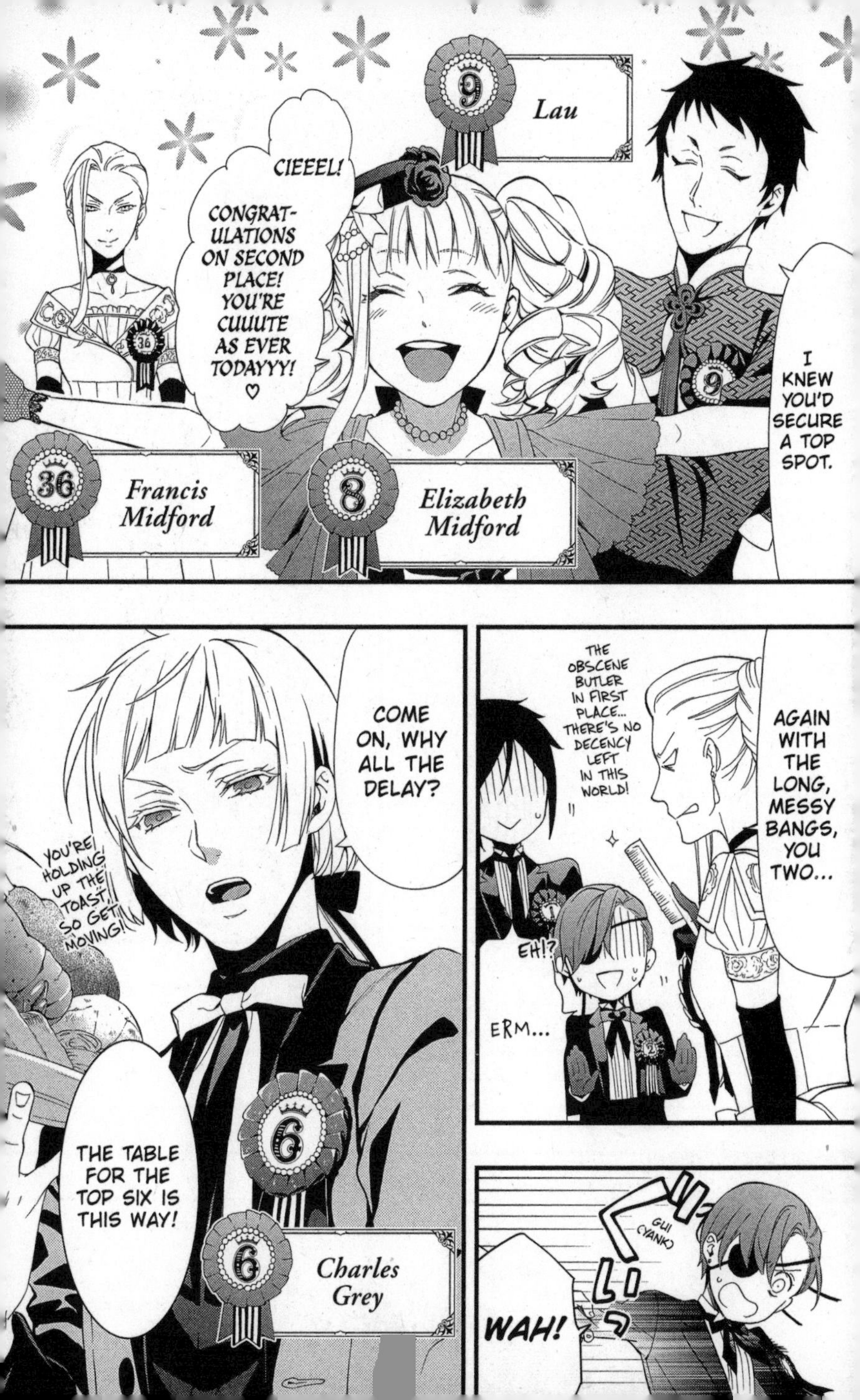
9
Lau
I KNEW YOU'D SECURE A TOP SPOT.
CIEEEL!
CONGRATULATIONS ON SECOND PLACE! YOU'RE CUUUTE AS EVER TODAYYY! ♡
8
Elizabeth Midford
36
Francis Midford
AGAIN WITH THE LONG, MESSY BANGS, YOU TWO...
THE OBSCENE BUTLER IN FIRST PLACE... THERE'S NO DECENCY LEFT IN THIS WORLD!
EH!?
ERM...
GUI (YANK)
WAH!
COME ON, WHY ALL THE DELAY?
YOU'RE HOLDING UP THE TOAST, SO GET MOVING!
THE TABLE FOR THE TOP SIX IS THIS WAY!
6
Charles Grey

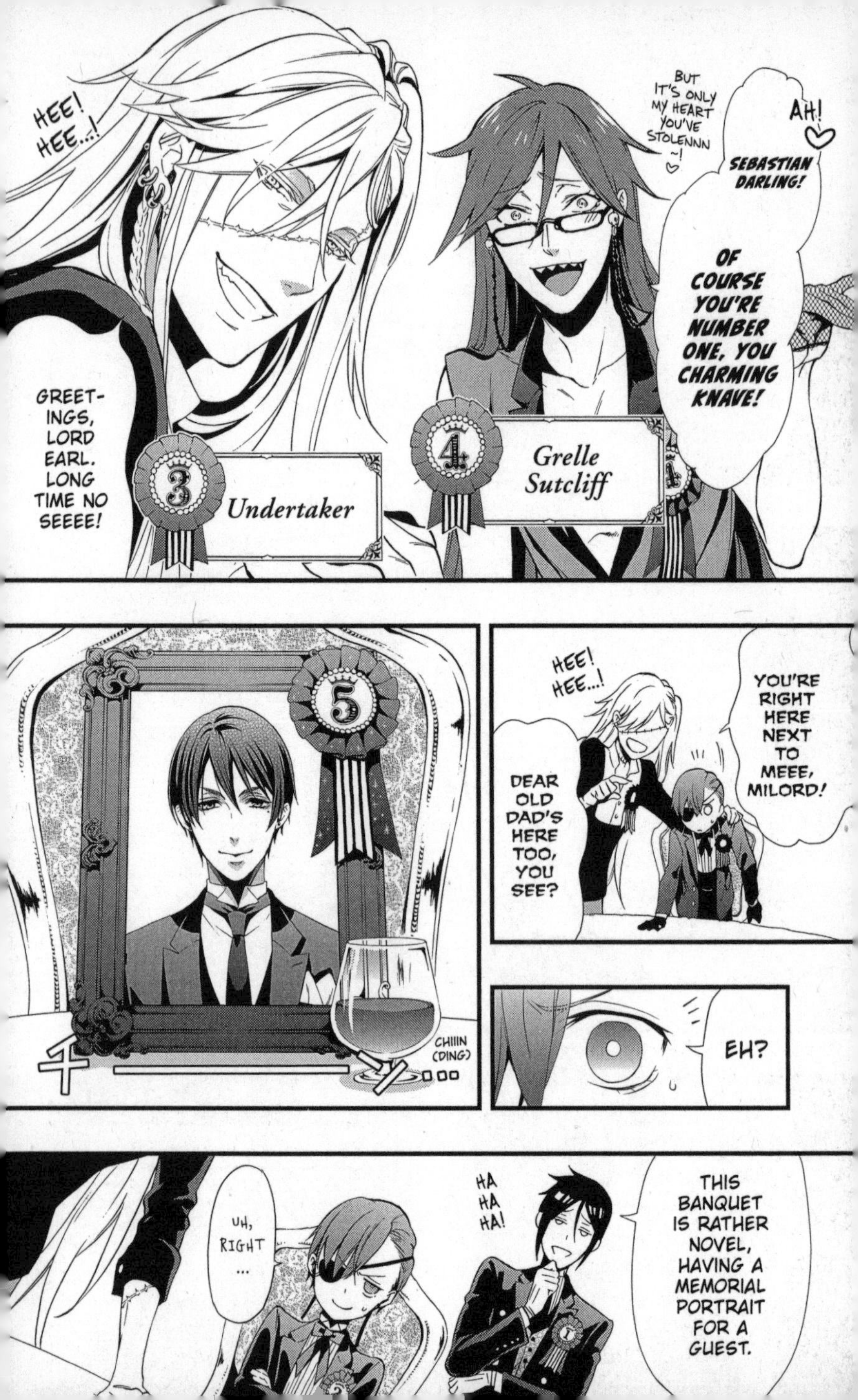
AH! ♡
SEBASTIAN DARLING!
OF COURSE YOU'RE NUMBER ONE, YOU CHARMING KNAVE!
BUT IT'S ONLY MY HEART YOU'VE STOLENNN~! ♡
4
Grelle Sutcliff
HEE! HEE...!
GREETINGS, LORD EARL. LONG TIME NO SEEEE!
3
Undertaker
YOU'RE RIGHT HERE NEXT TO MEEE, MILORD!
HEE! HEE...!
DEAR OLD DAD'S HERE TOO, YOU SEE?
EH?
5
CHIIIN (DING)
THIS BANQUET IS RATHER NOVEL, HAVING A MEMORIAL PORTRAIT FOR A GUEST.
HA HA HA!
UH, RIGHT ...

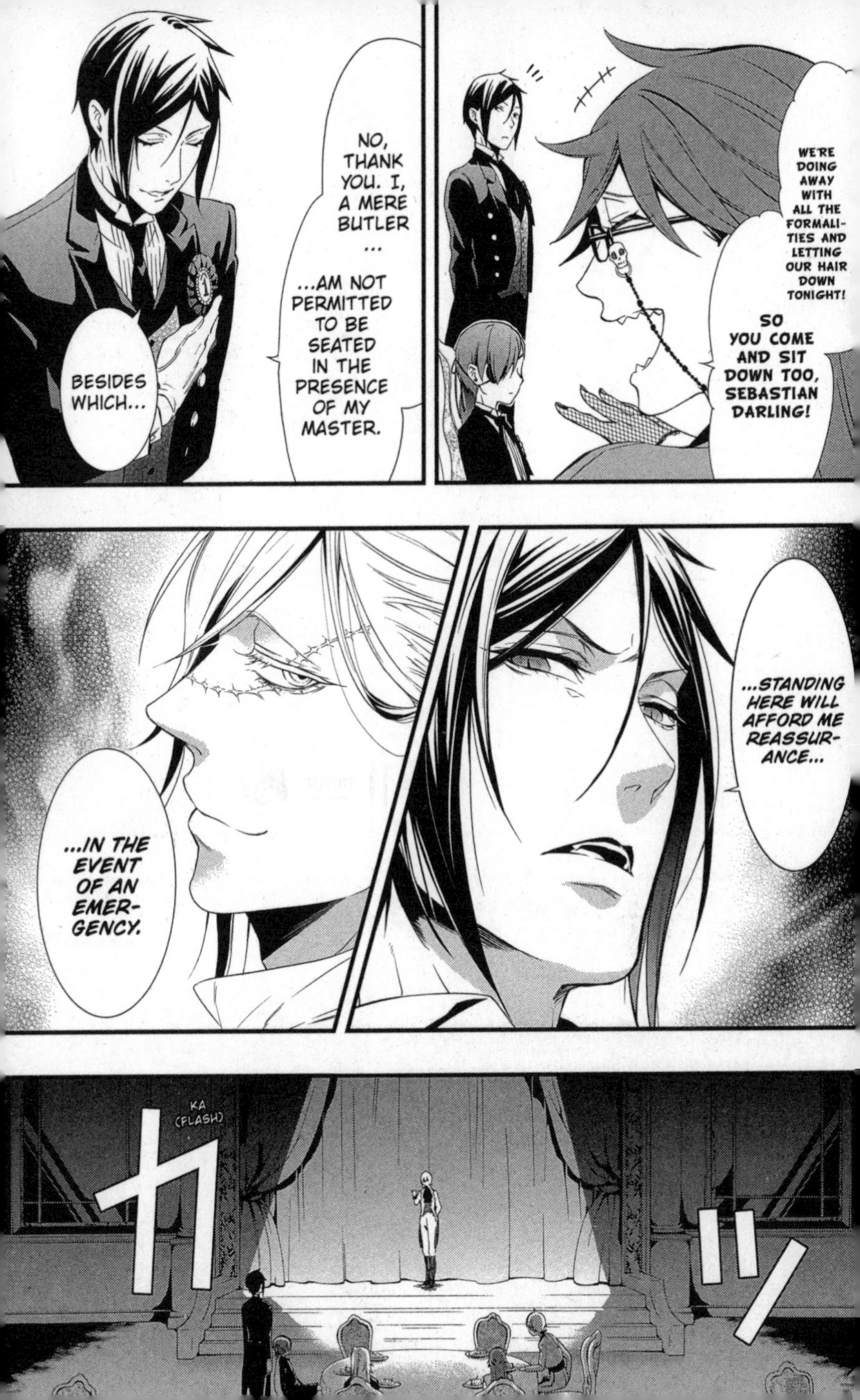
WE'RE DOING AWAY WITH ALL THE FORMALITIES AND LETTING OUR HAIR DOWN TONIGHT!
SO YOU COME AND SIT DOWN TOO, SEBASTIAN DARLING!
NO, THANK YOU. I, A MERE BUTLER...
...AM NOT PERMITTED TO BE SEATED IN THE PRESENCE OF MY MASTER.
BESIDES WHICH...
...STANDING HERE WILL AFFORD ME REASSURANCE...
...IN THE EVENT OF AN EMERGENCY.
KA (FLASH)

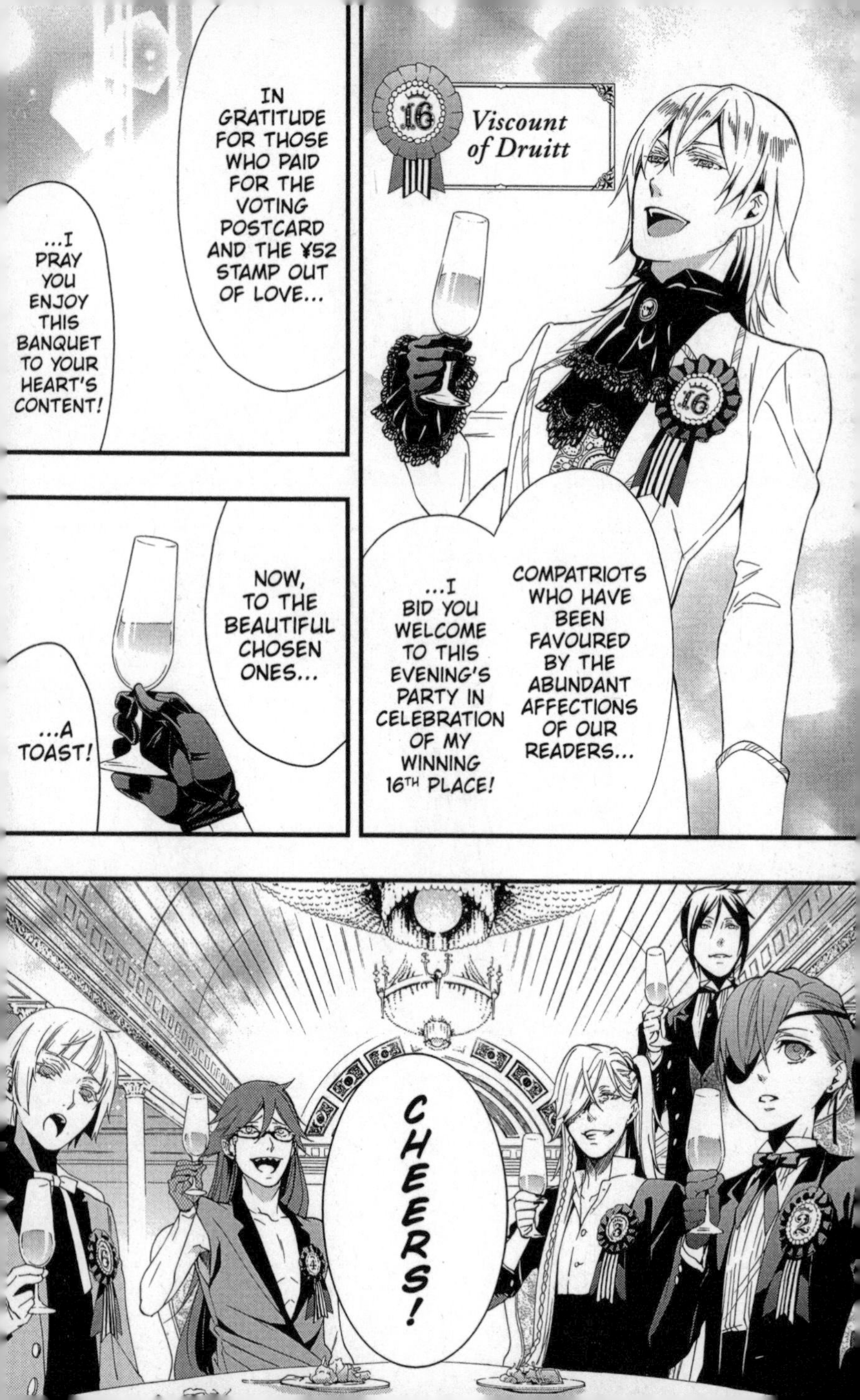
16
Viscount of Druitt
16
COMPATRIOTS WHO HAVE BEEN FAVOURED BY THE ABUNDANT AFFECTIONS OF OUR READERS...
...I BID YOU WELCOME TO THIS EVENING'S PARTY IN CELEBRATION OF MY WINNING 16TH PLACE!
IN GRATITUDE FOR THOSE WHO PAID FOR THE VOTING POSTCARD AND THE ¥52 STAMP OUT OF LOVE...
...I PRAY YOU ENJOY THIS BANQUET TO YOUR HEART'S CONTENT!
NOW, TO THE BEAUTIFUL CHOSEN ONES...
...A TOAST!
CHEERS!

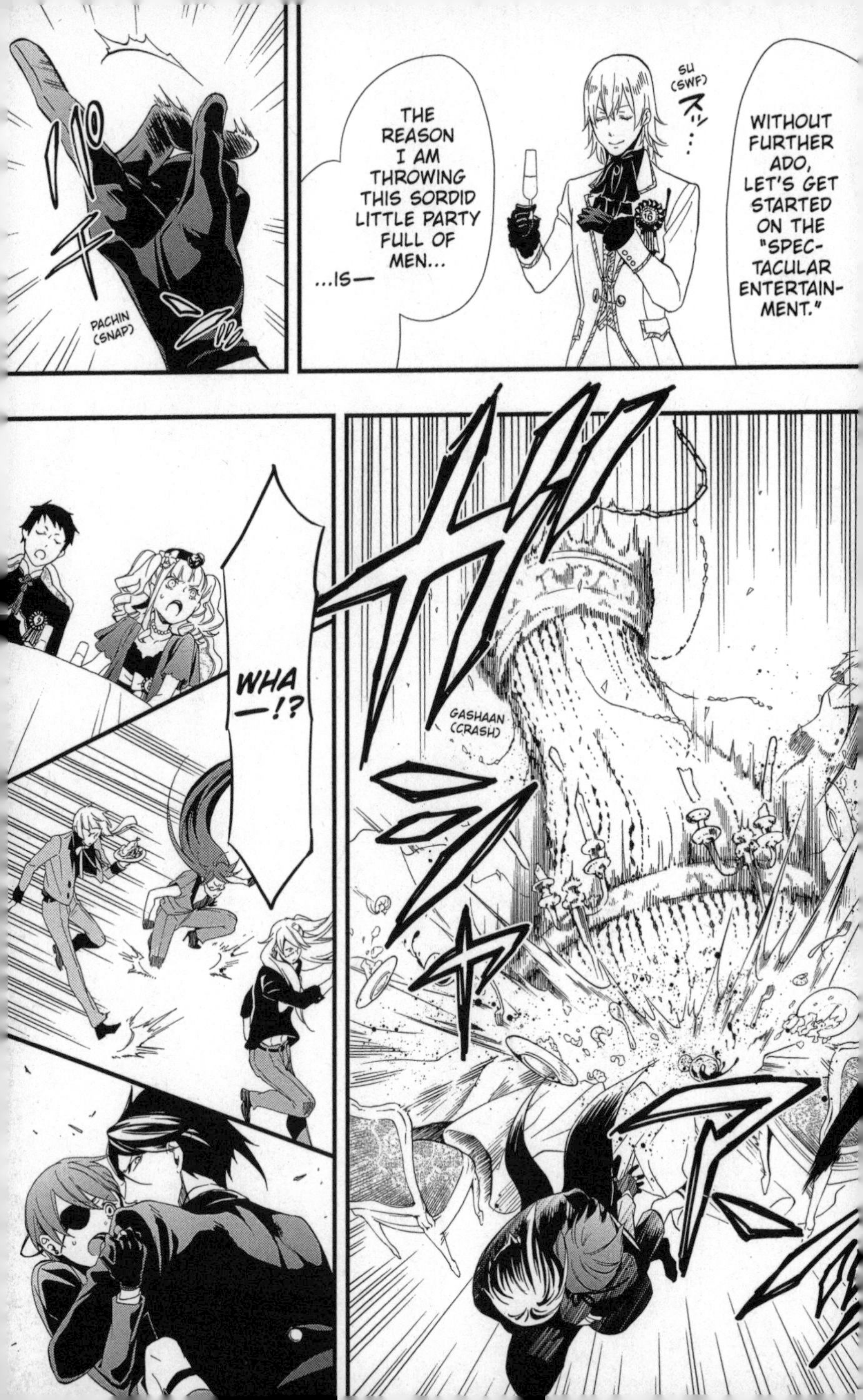
SU (SWF)
WITHOUT FURTHER ADO, LET'S GET STARTED ON THE "SPECTACULAR ENTERTAINMENT."
THE REASON I AM THROWING THIS SORDID LITTLE PARTY FULL OF MEN...
...IS—
PACHIN (SNAP)
GASHAAN (CRASH)
WHA—!?

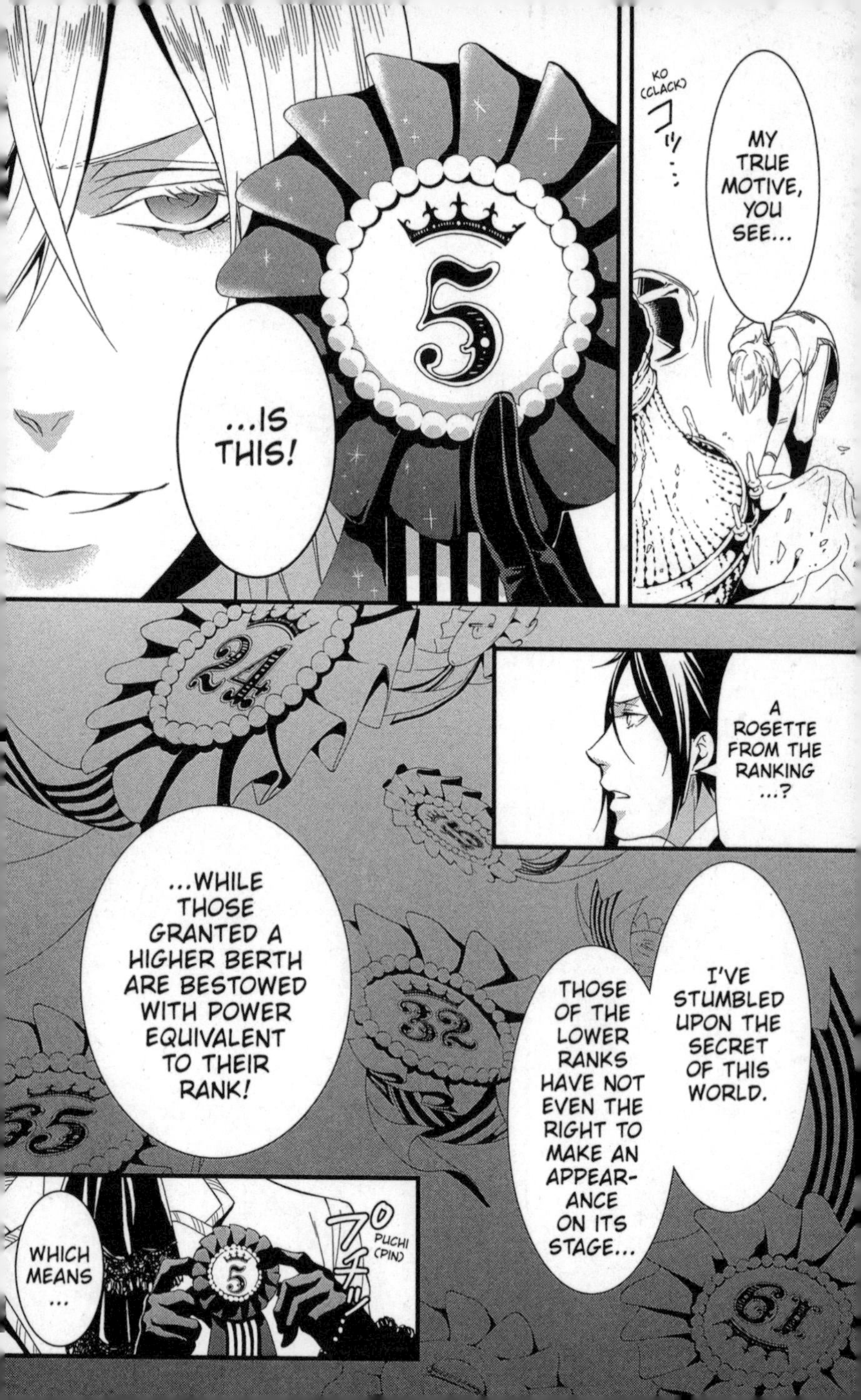
KO (CLACK)
MY TRUE MOTIVE, YOU SEE...
...IS THIS!
A ROSETTE FROM THE RANKING ...?
I'VE STUMBLED UPON THE SECRET OF THIS WORLD.
THOSE OF THE LOWER RANKS HAVE NOT EVEN THE RIGHT TO MAKE AN APPEAR-ANCE ON ITS STAGE...
...WHILE THOSE GRANTED A HIGHER BERTH ARE BESTOWED WITH POWER EQUIVALENT TO THEIR RANK!
PUCHI (PIN)
WHICH MEANS ...

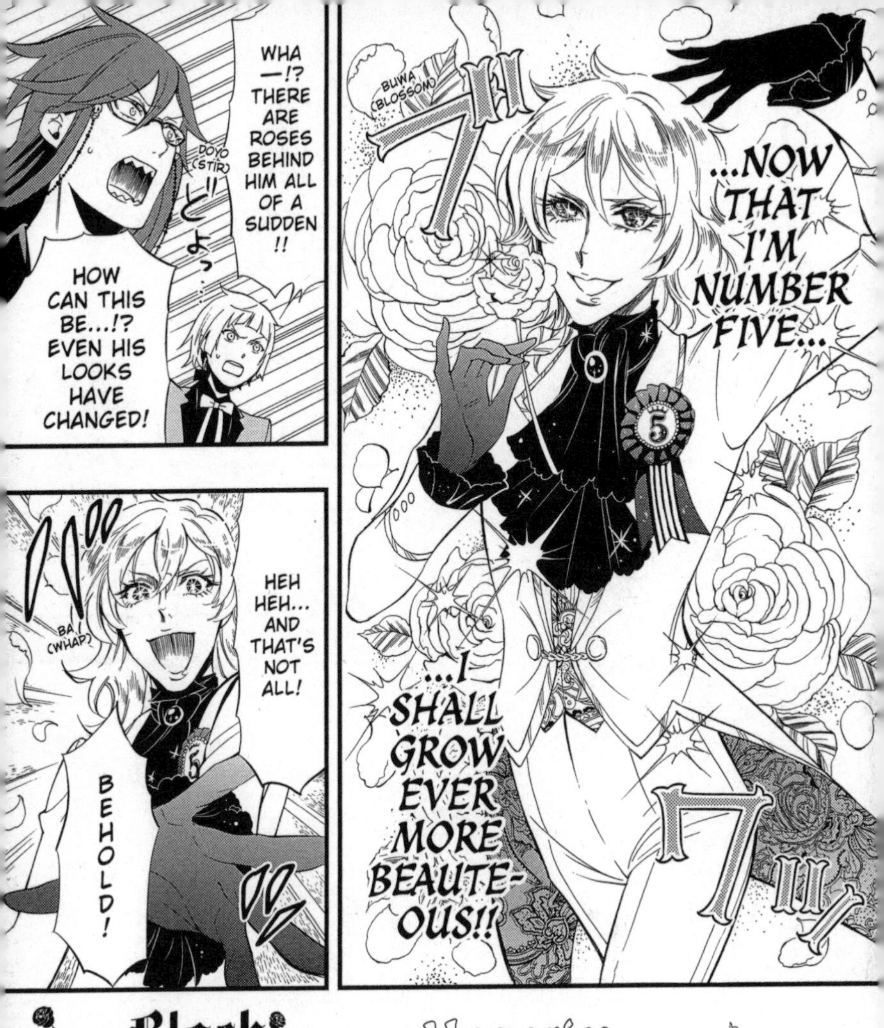
...NOW THAT I'M NUMBER FIVE...
BUWA (BLOSSOM)
...I SHALL GROW EVER MORE BEAUTEOUS!!
WHA—!? THERE ARE ROSES BEHIND HIM ALL OF A SUDDEN!!
DOYO (STIR)
HOW CAN THIS BE...!? EVEN HIS LOOKS HAVE CHANGED!
HEH HEH... AND THAT'S NOT ALL!
BA (WHAP)
BEHOLD!

Black Butler Spin-off Memories of Druitt

—Chapter 1—

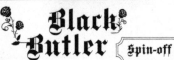

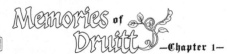

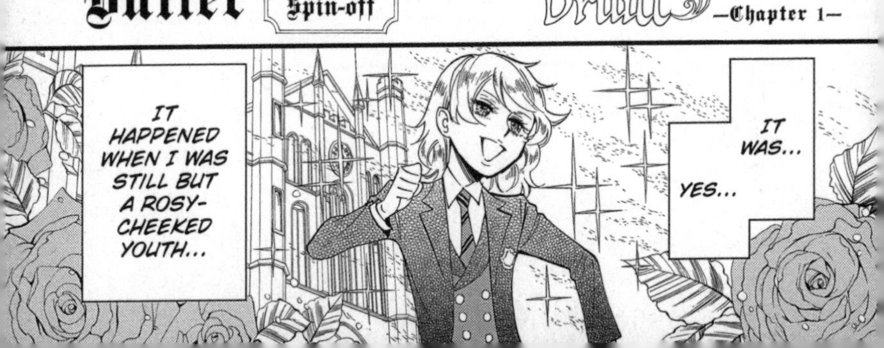
IT WAS... YES...
IT HAPPENED WHEN I WAS STILL BUT A ROSY-CHEEKED YOUTH...

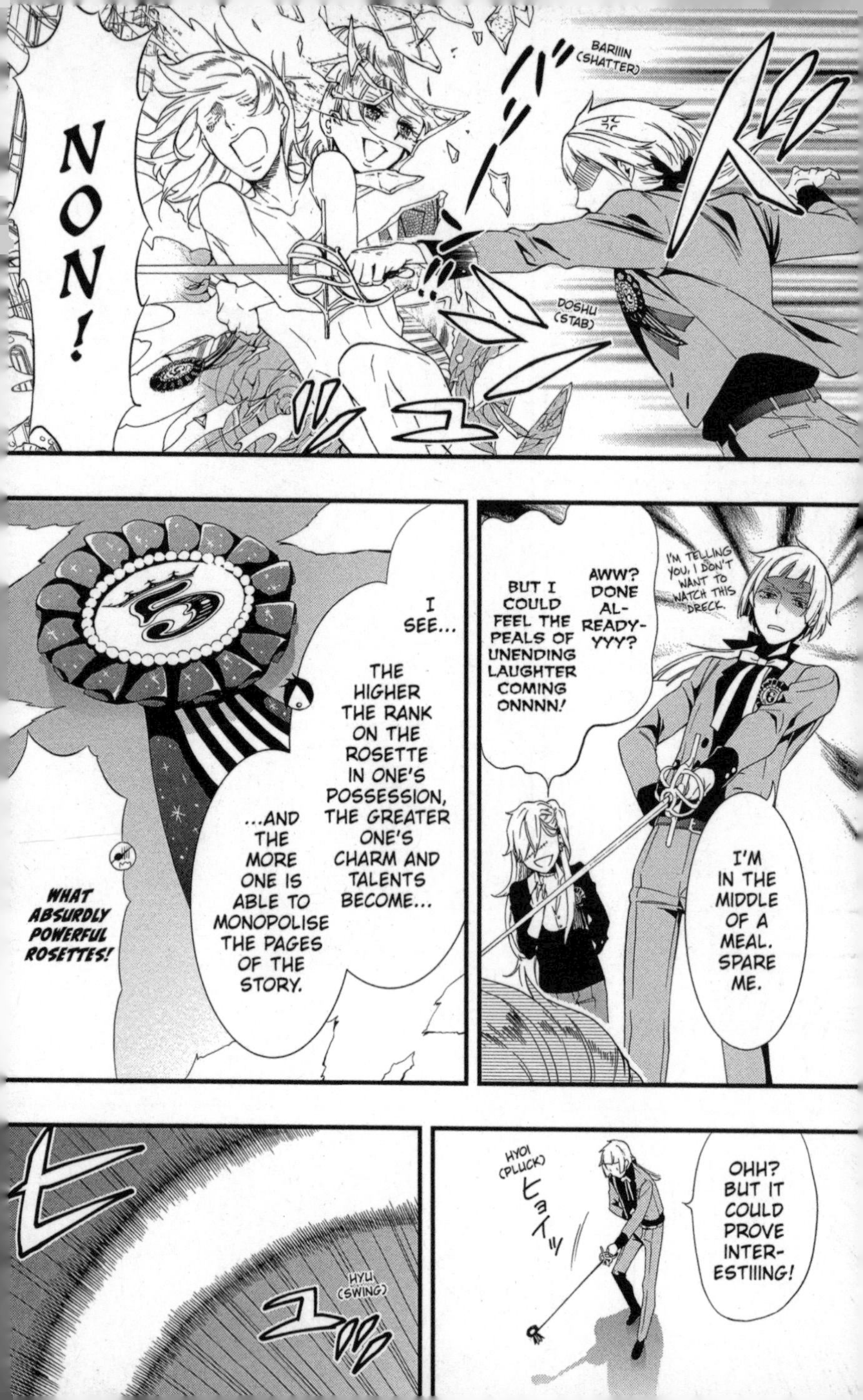
BARIIIN (SHATTER)
DOSHU (STAB)
NON!
I'M TELLING YOU, I DON'T WANT TO WATCH THIS DRECK.
AWW? DONE AL-READY-YYY?
BUT I COULD FEEL THE PEALS OF UNENDING LAUGHTER COMING ONNNN!
I'M IN THE MIDDLE OF A MEAL. SPARE ME.
I SEE...
THE HIGHER THE RANK ON THE ROSETTE IN ONE'S POSSESSION, THE GREATER ONE'S CHARM AND TALENTS BECOME...
...AND THE MORE ONE IS ABLE TO MONOPOLISE THE PAGES OF THE STORY.
WHAT ABSURDLY POWERFUL ROSETTES!
OHH? BUT IT COULD PROVE INTER-ESTIIING!
HYOI (PLUCK)
HYU (SWING)

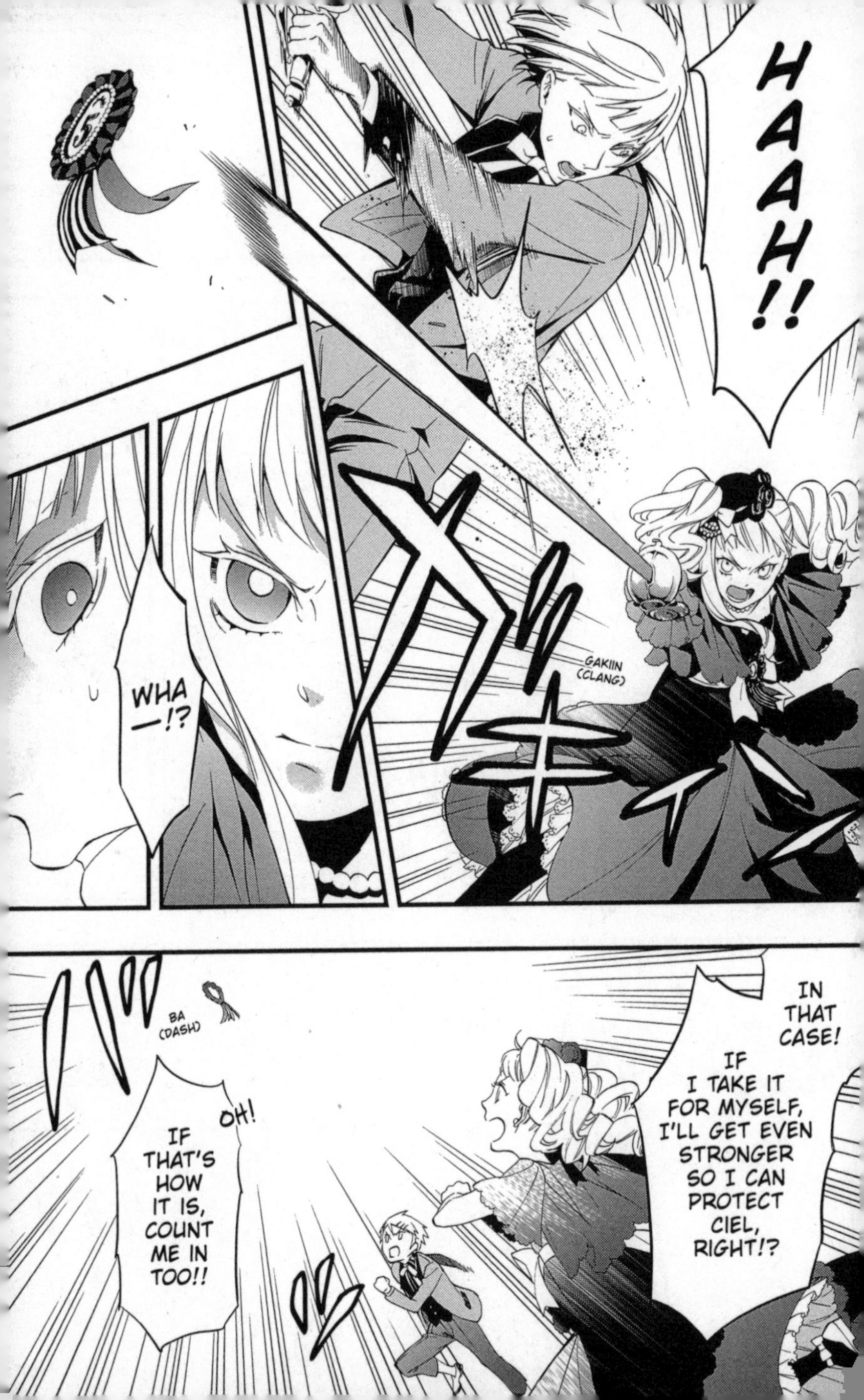
HAAAH!!
GAKIIN (CLANG)
WHA—!?
IN THAT CASE!
IF I TAKE IT FOR MYSELF, I'LL GET EVEN STRONGER SO I CAN PROTECT CIEL, RIGHT!?
OH!
IF THAT'S HOW IT IS, COUNT ME IN TOO!!
BA (DASH)

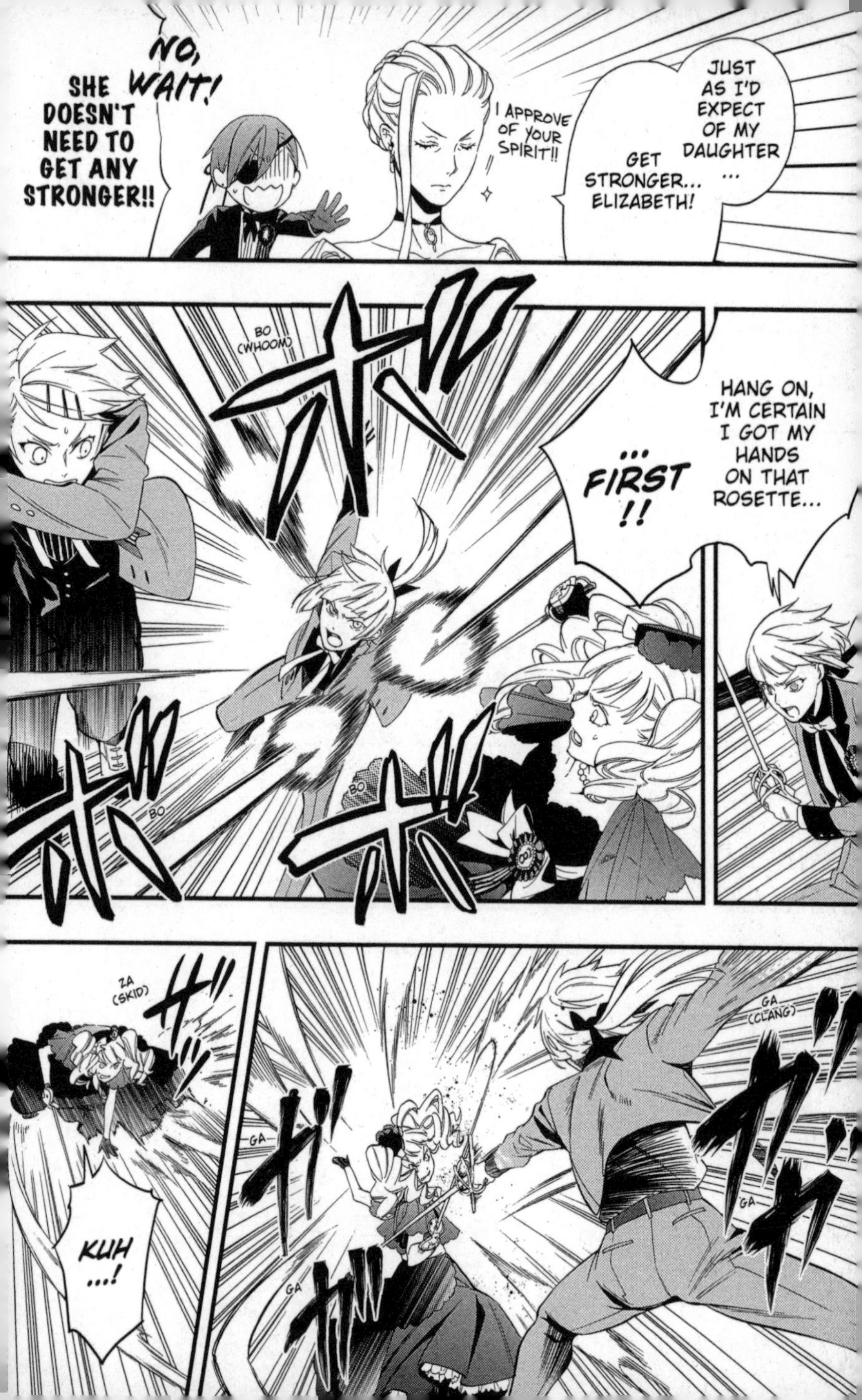
JUST AS I'D EXPECT OF MY DAUGHTER ...
GET STRONGER... ELIZABETH!
I APPROVE OF YOUR SPIRIT!!
NO, WAIT!
SHE DOESN'T NEED TO GET ANY STRONGER!!
HANG ON, I'M CERTAIN I GOT MY HANDS ON THAT ROSETTE...
... FIRST !!
BO (WHOOM)
BO
BO
GA (CLANG)
GA
GA
GA
ZA (SKID)
KUH ...!

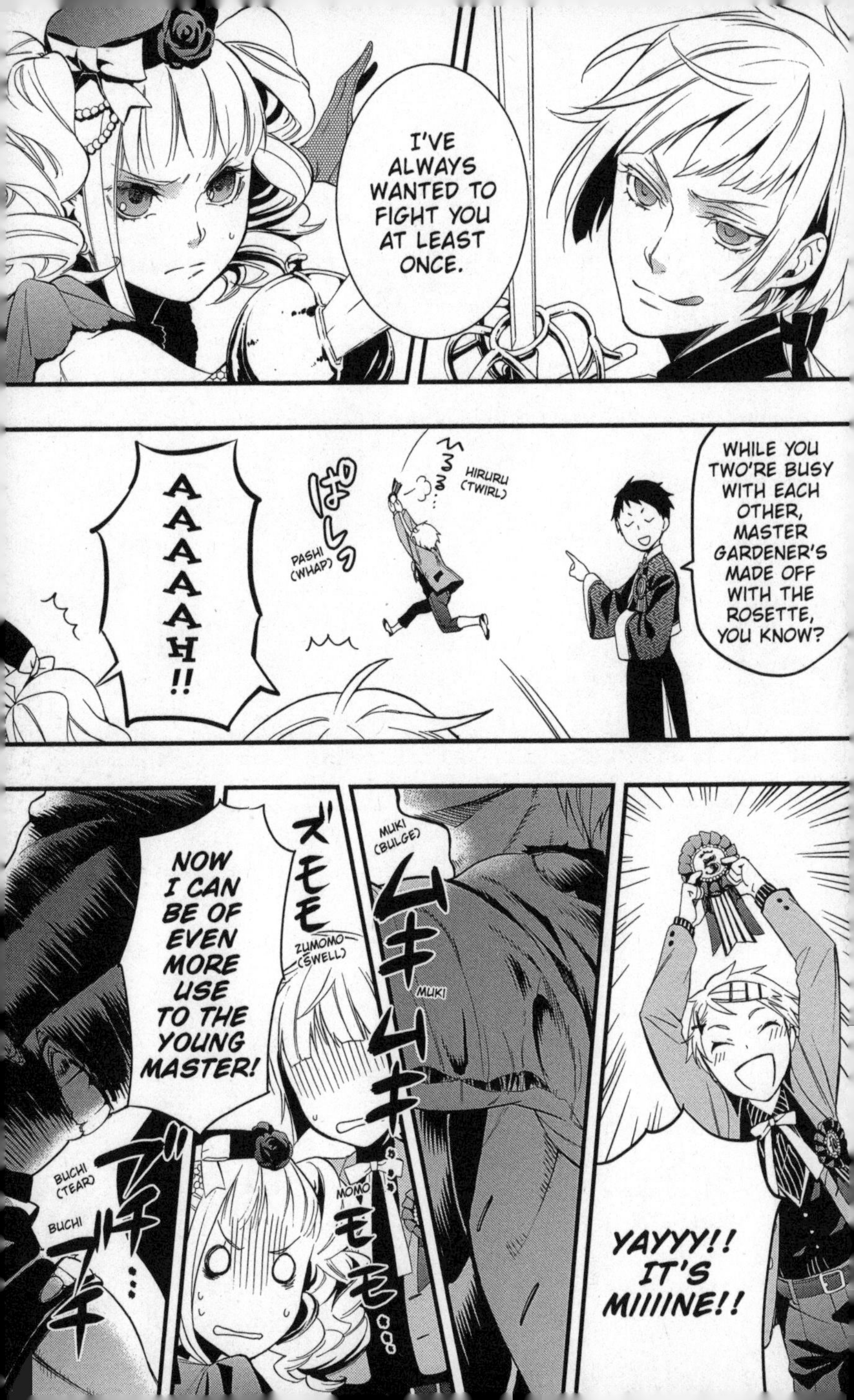
I'VE ALWAYS WANTED TO FIGHT YOU AT LEAST ONCE.
WHILE YOU TWO'RE BUSY WITH EACH OTHER, MASTER GARDENER'S MADE OFF WITH THE ROSETTE, YOU KNOW?
HIRURU (TWIRL)
PASHI (WHAP)
AAAAAAH!!
YAYYY!! IT'S MIIIINE!!
MUKI (BULGE)
MUKI
ZUMOMO (SWELL)
MOMO
NOW I CAN BE OF EVEN MORE USE TO THE YOUNG MASTER!
BUCHI (TEAR)
BUCHI

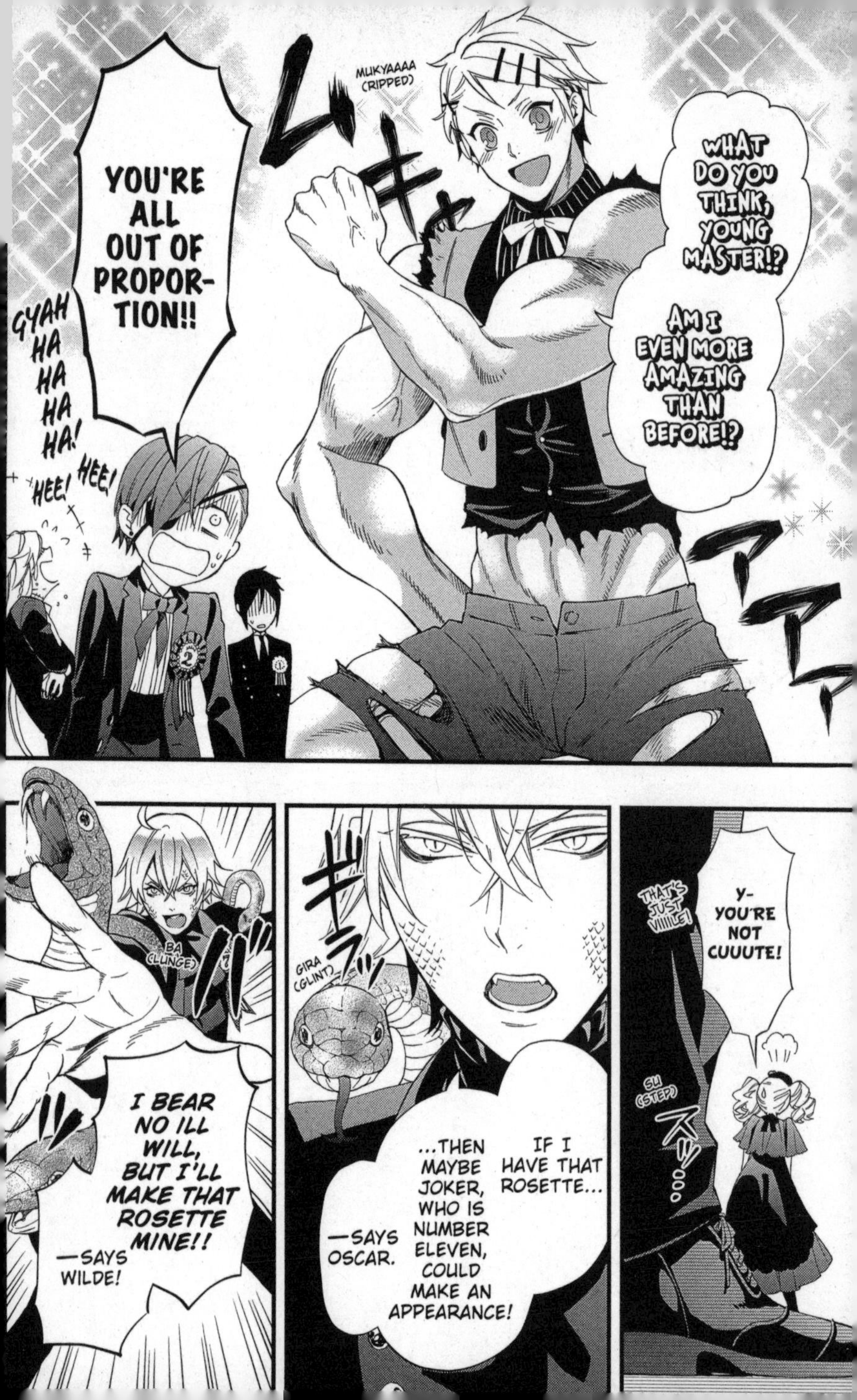
MUKYAAAA (RIPPED)
WHAT DO YOU THINK, YOUNG MASTER!?
AM I EVEN MORE AMAZING THAN BEFORE!?
YOU'RE ALL OUT OF PROPOR-TION!!
GYAH HA HA HA HA!
HEE! HEE!
Y-YOU'RE NOT CUUUTE!
THAT'S JUST VIIIILE!
SU (STEP)
GIRA (GLINT)
IF I HAVE THAT ROSETTE...
...THEN MAYBE JOKER, WHO IS NUMBER ELEVEN, COULD MAKE AN APPEARANCE!
—SAYS OSCAR.
BA (LUNGE)
I BEAR NO ILL WILL, BUT I'LL MAKE THAT ROSETTE MINE!!
—SAYS WILDE!

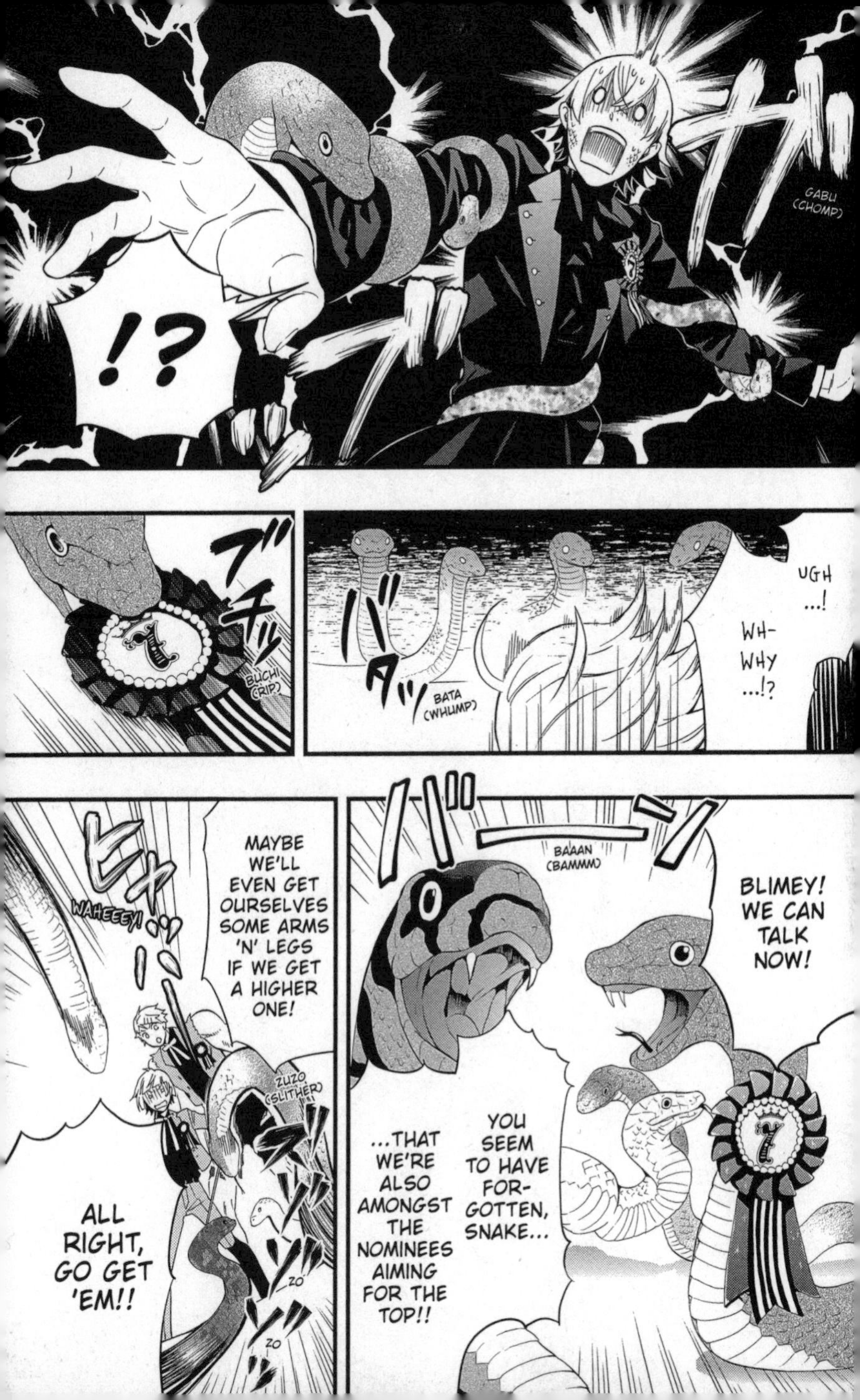
GABU (CHOMP)
!?
UGH ...!
WH- WHY ...!?
BATA (WHUMP)
BUCHI (RIP)
BAAAN (BAMMM)
BLIMEY! WE CAN TALK NOW!
YOU SEEM TO HAVE FOR-GOTTEN, SNAKE...
...THAT WE'RE ALSO AMONGST THE NOMINEES AIMING FOR THE TOP!!
MAYBE WE'LL EVEN GET OURSELVES SOME ARMS 'N' LEGS IF WE GET A HIGHER ONE!
WAHEEEY!
ZUZO (SLITHER)
ALL RIGHT, GO GET 'EM!!
ZO
ZO

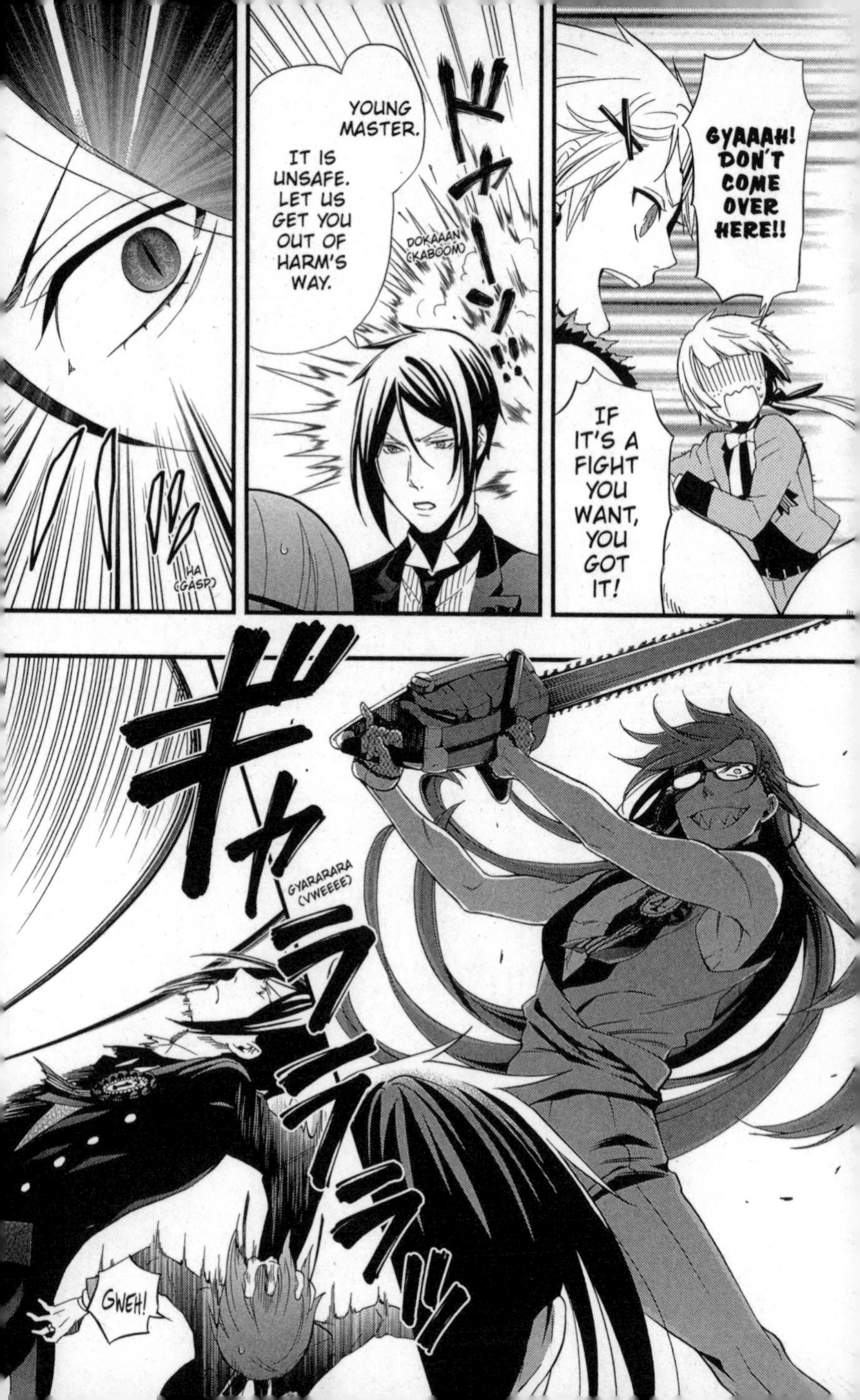
GYAAAH! DON'T COME OVER HERE!!
IF IT'S A FIGHT YOU WANT, YOU GOT IT!
YOUNG MASTER.
IT IS UNSAFE. LET US GET YOU OUT OF HARM'S WAY.
DOKAAAN (KABOOM)
HA (GASP)
GYARARARA (VWEEEE)
GWEH!

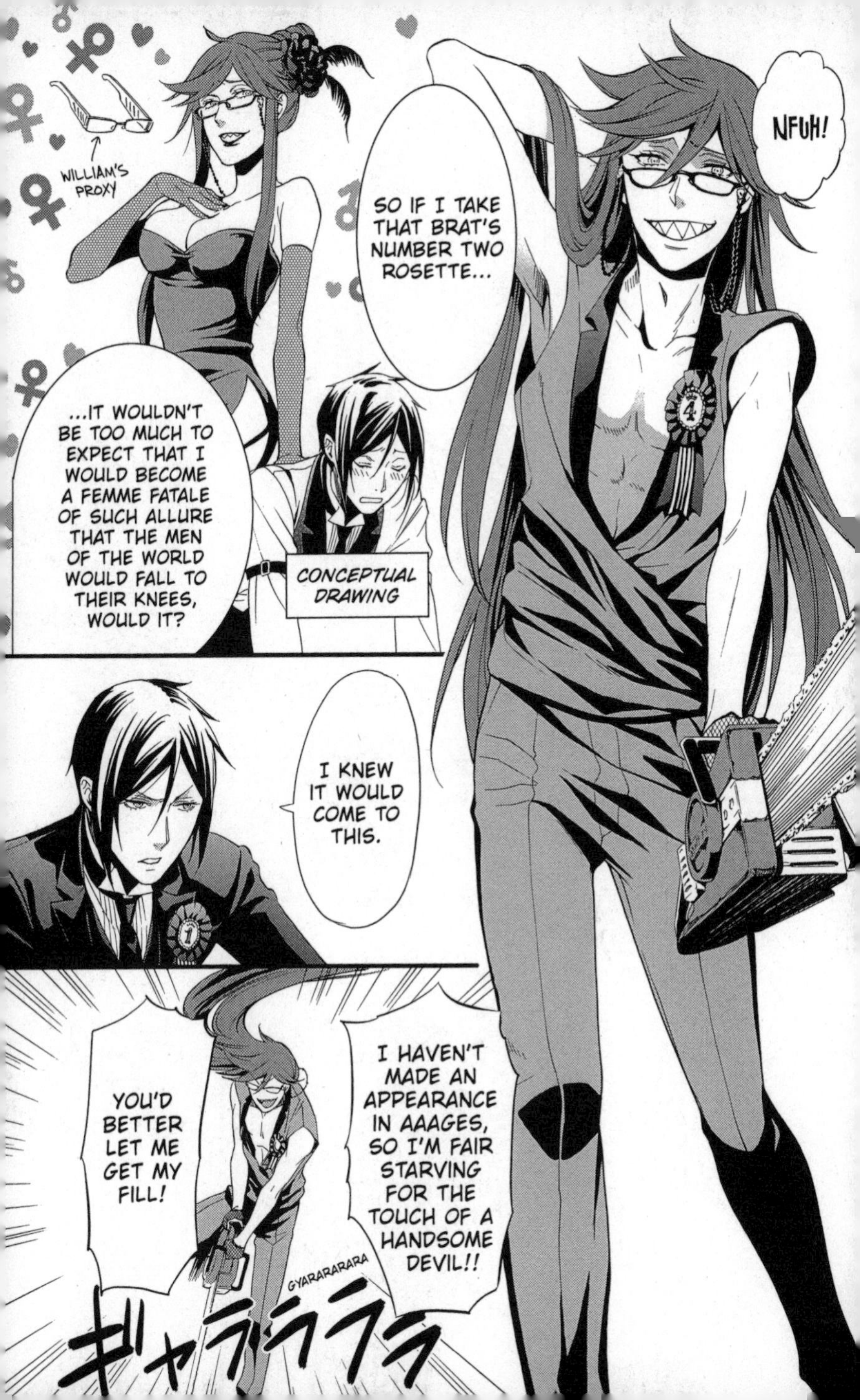
NFUH!
SO IF I TAKE THAT BRAT'S NUMBER TWO ROSETTE...
...IT WOULDN'T BE TOO MUCH TO EXPECT THAT I WOULD BECOME A FEMME FATALE OF SUCH ALLURE THAT THE MEN OF THE WORLD WOULD FALL TO THEIR KNEES, WOULD IT?
WILLIAM'S PROXY
CONCEPTUAL DRAWING
I KNEW IT WOULD COME TO THIS.
I HAVEN'T MADE AN APPEARANCE IN AAAGES, SO I'M FAIR STARVING FOR THE TOUCH OF A HANDSOME DEVIL!!
YOU'D BETTER LET ME GET MY FILL!
GYARARARARA
ギャラララ

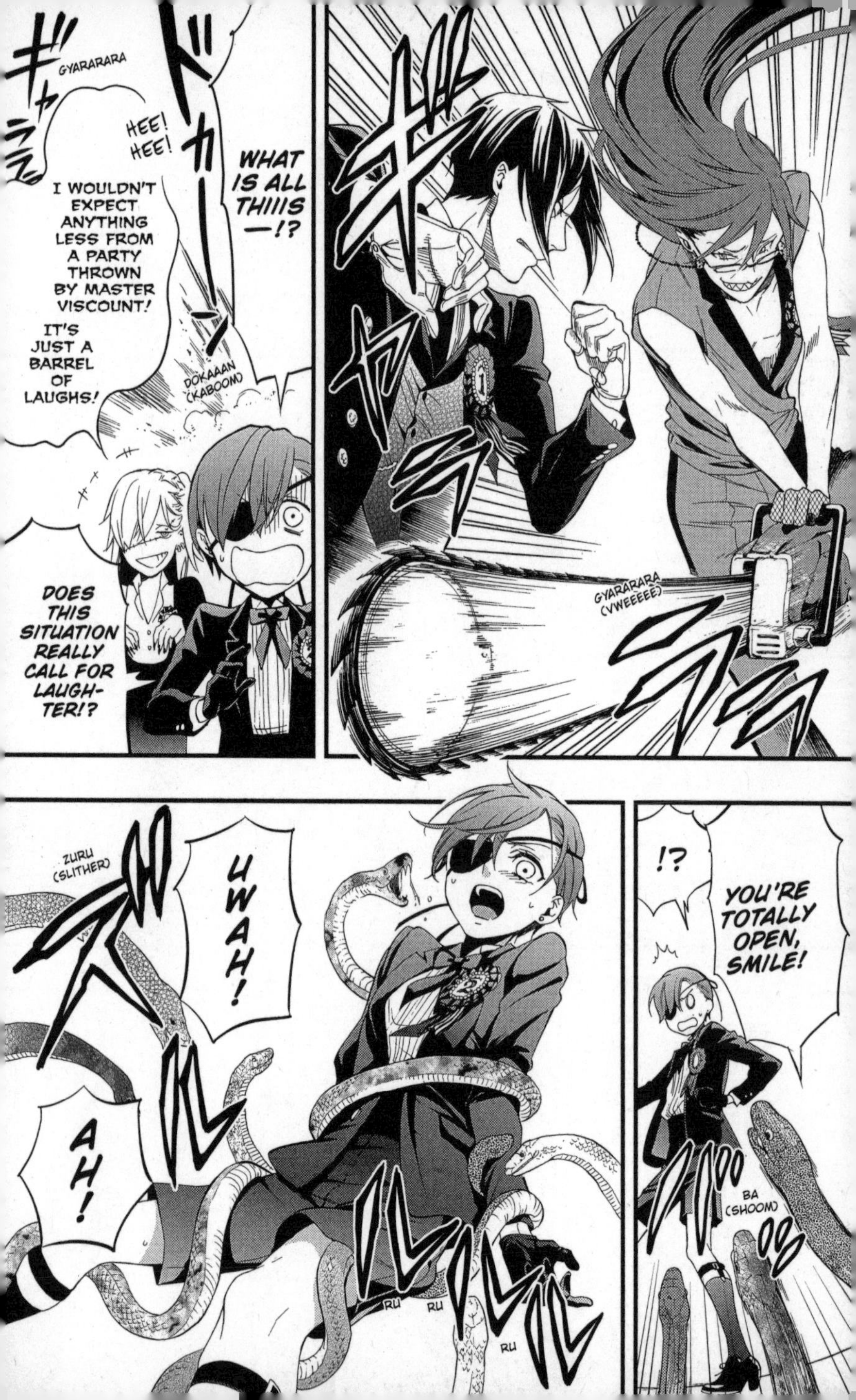
GYARARARA (VWEEEEE)
WHAT IS ALL THIIIS—!?
DOKAAAN (KABOOM)
HEE! HEE!
GYARARARA
I WOULDN'T EXPECT ANYTHING LESS FROM A PARTY THROWN BY MASTER VISCOUNT!
IT'S JUST A BARREL OF LAUGHS!
DOES THIS SITUATION REALLY CALL FOR LAUGH-TER!?
!?
YOU'RE TOTALLY OPEN, SMILE!
BA (SHOOM)
UWAH!
ZURU (SLITHER)
AH!
RU RU RU

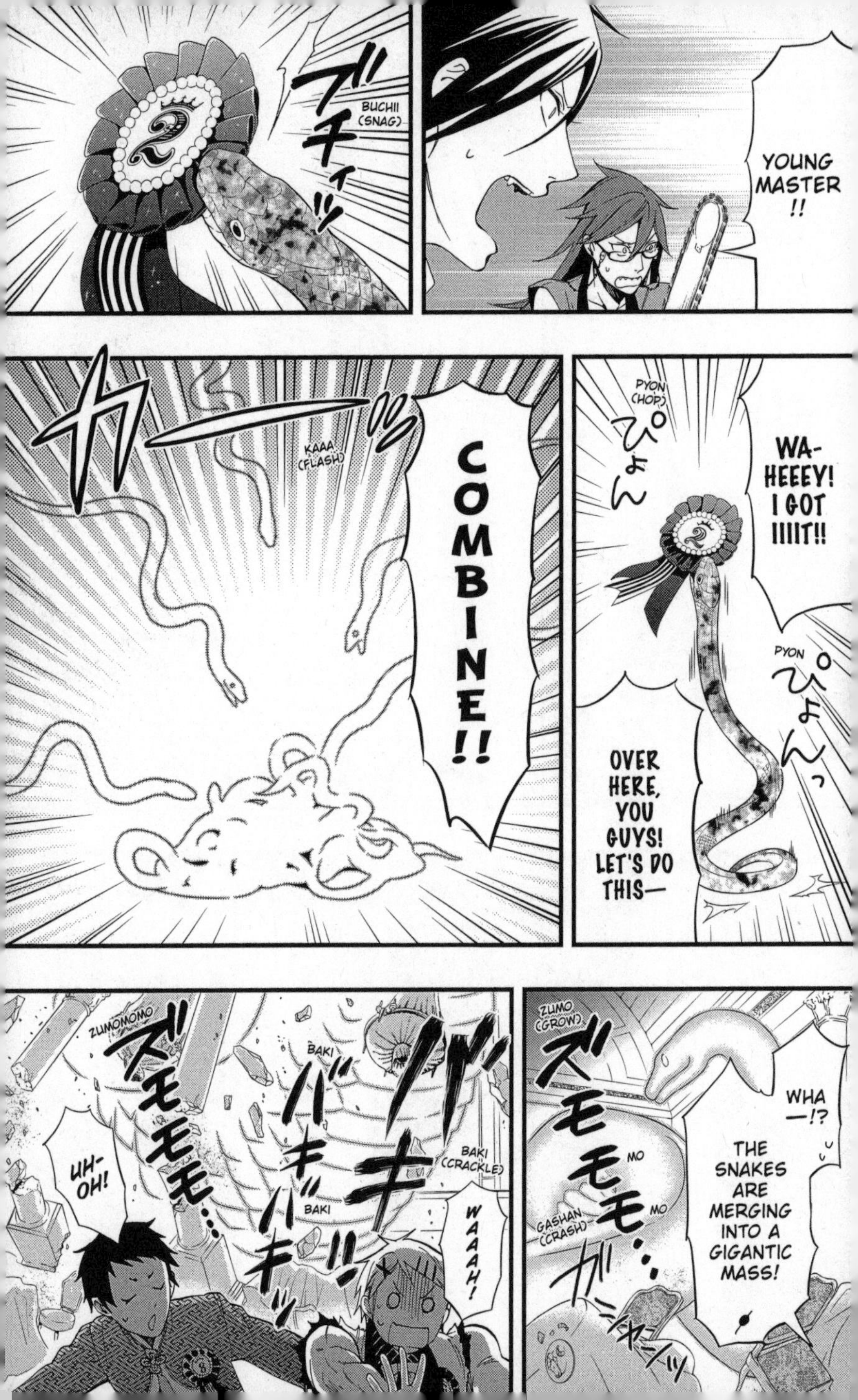

YOUNG MASTER!!
ブチィッ!!
BUCHII (SNAG)
ぴょん
PYON (HOP)
WA-HEEEY! I GOT IIIIT!!
ぴょんっ
PYON
OVER HERE, YOU GUYS! LET'S DO THIS—
COMBINE!!
カーッ
KAAA (FLASH)
ズモモ…
ZUMO (GROW)
MO
MO
WHA—!?
THE SNAKES ARE MERGING INTO A GIGANTIC MASS!
ガシャーンッ
GASHAN (CRASH)
ズモモモ…
ZUMOMOMO
バキバキバキッ!!
BAKI
BAKI (CRACKLE)
BAKI
UH-OH!
WAAAH!

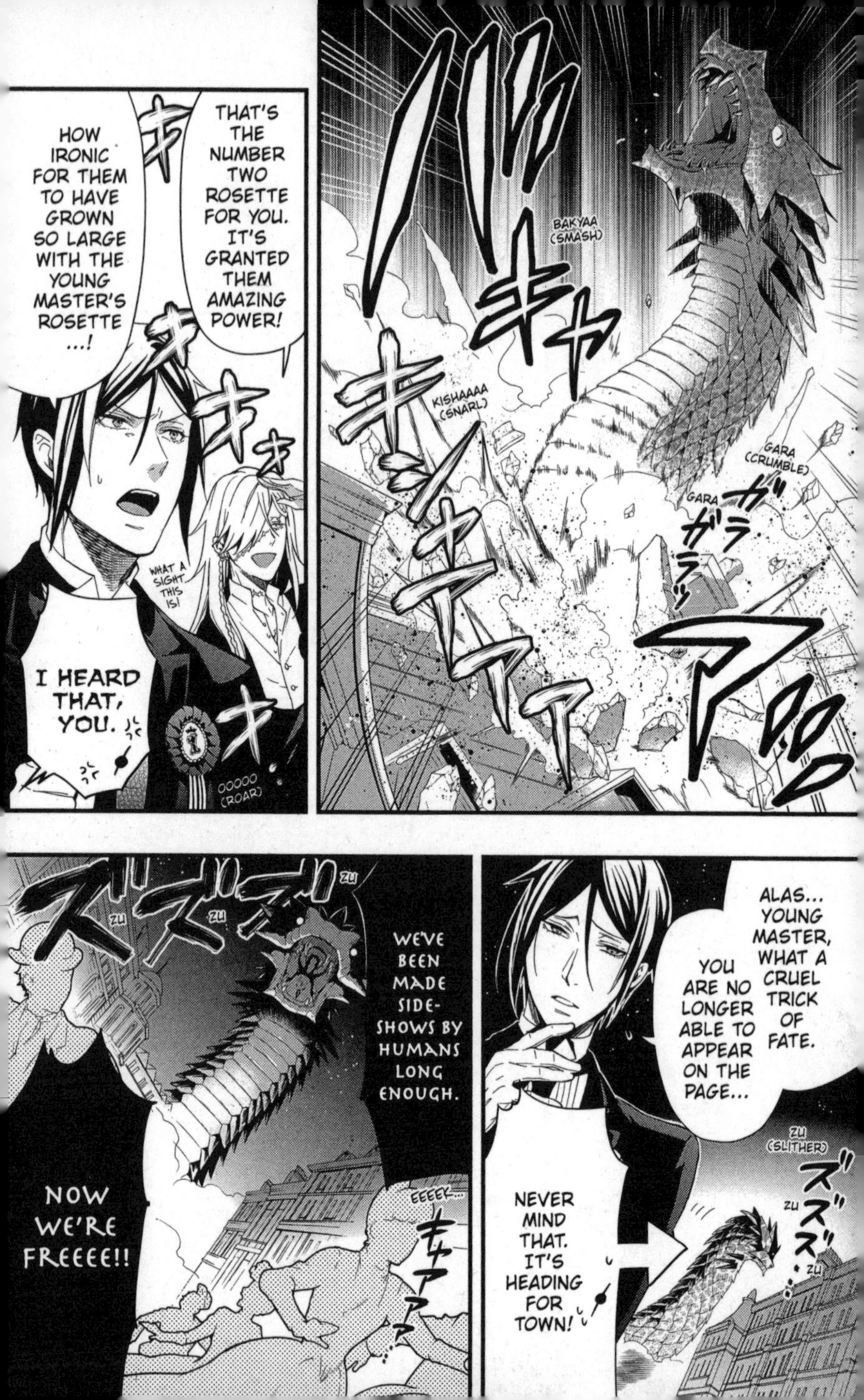
BAKYAA (SMASH)
KISHAAAA (SNARL)
GARA (CRUMBLE)
GARA
THAT'S THE NUMBER TWO ROSETTE FOR YOU. IT'S GRANTED THEM AMAZING POWER!
HOW IRONIC FOR THEM TO HAVE GROWN SO LARGE WITH THE YOUNG MASTER'S ROSETTE ...!
WHAT A SIGHT THIS IS!
I HEARD THAT, YOU.
OOOOO (ROAR)
ALAS... YOUNG MASTER, WHAT A CRUEL TRICK OF FATE.
YOU ARE NO LONGER ABLE TO APPEAR ON THE PAGE...
ZU (SLITHER)
ZU
ZU
NEVER MIND THAT. IT'S HEADING FOR TOWN!
ZU
ZU
ZU
WE'VE BEEN MADE SIDE-SHOWS BY HUMANS LONG ENOUGH.
NOW WE'RE FREEEE!!
EEEEK...

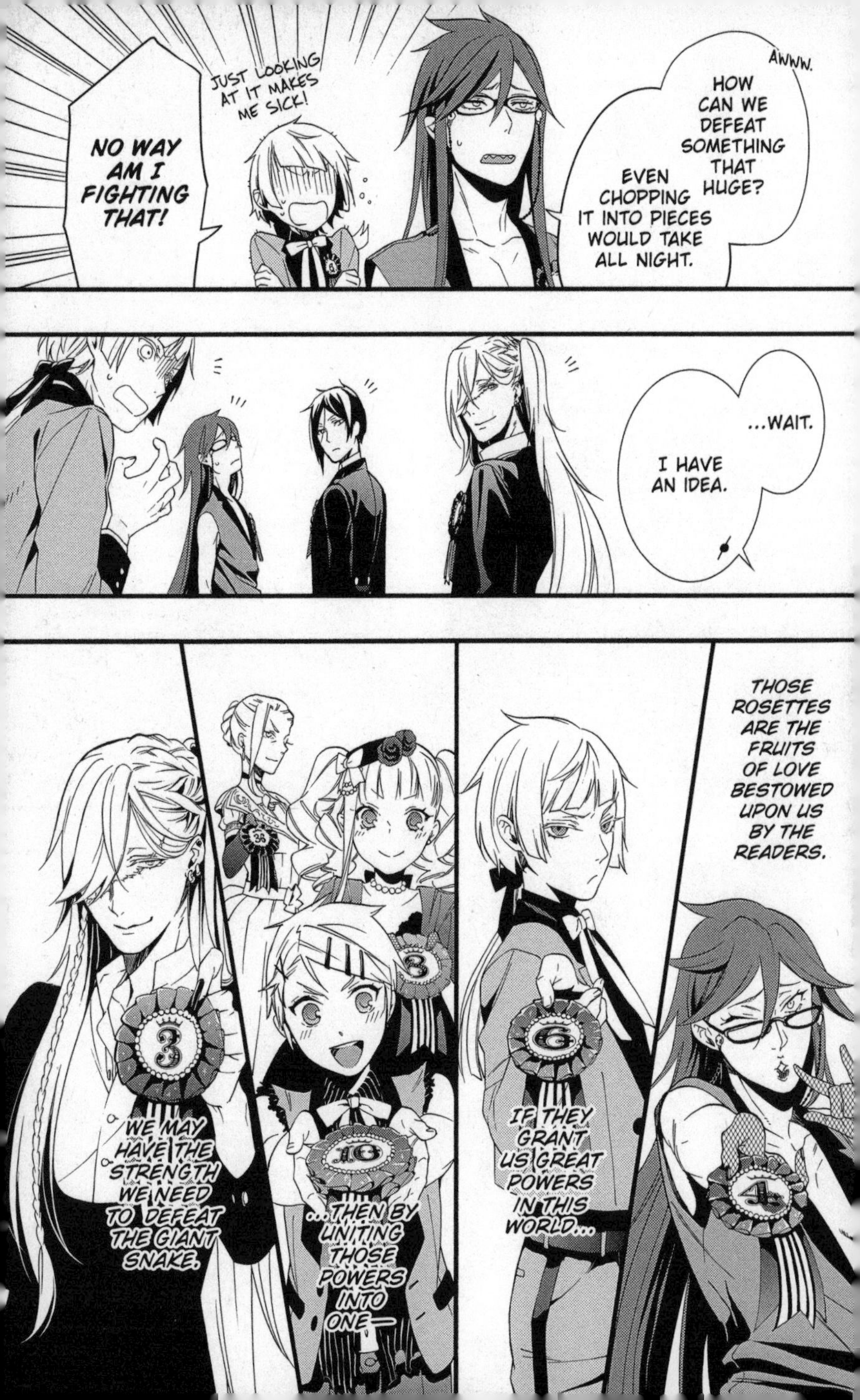
AWWW.
HOW CAN WE DEFEAT SOMETHING THAT HUGE?
EVEN CHOPPING IT INTO PIECES WOULD TAKE ALL NIGHT.
JUST LOOKING AT IT MAKES ME SICK!
NO WAY AM I FIGHTING THAT!
...WAIT.
I HAVE AN IDEA.
THOSE ROSETTES ARE THE FRUITS OF LOVE BESTOWED UPON US BY THE READERS.
IF THEY GRANT US GREAT POWERS IN THIS WORLD...
...THEN BY UNITING THOSE POWERS INTO ONE—
WE MAY HAVE THE STRENGTH WE NEED TO DEFEAT THE GIANT SNAKE.

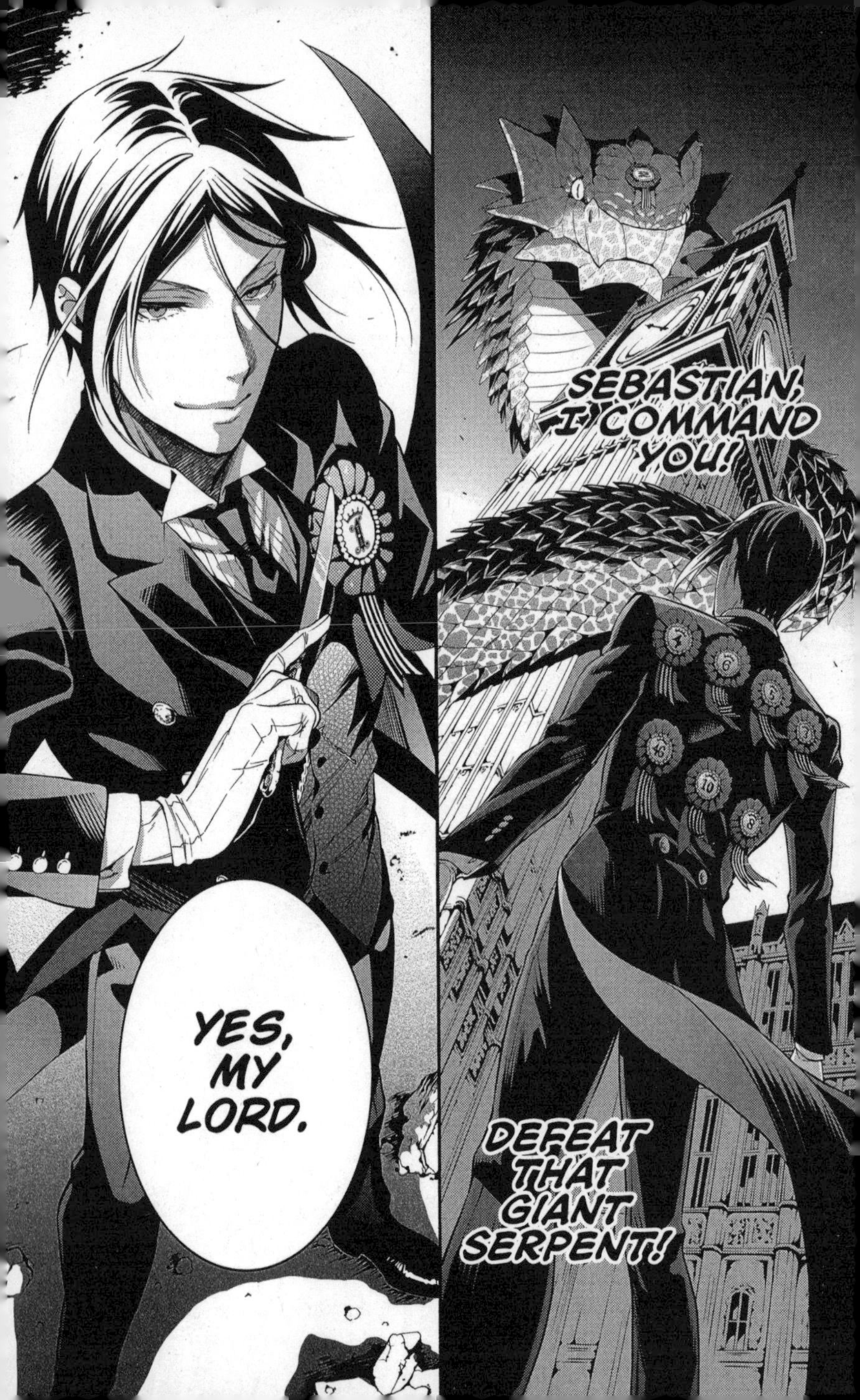
SEBASTIAN, I COMMAND YOU!
DEFEAT THAT GIANT SERPENT!
YES, MY LORD.

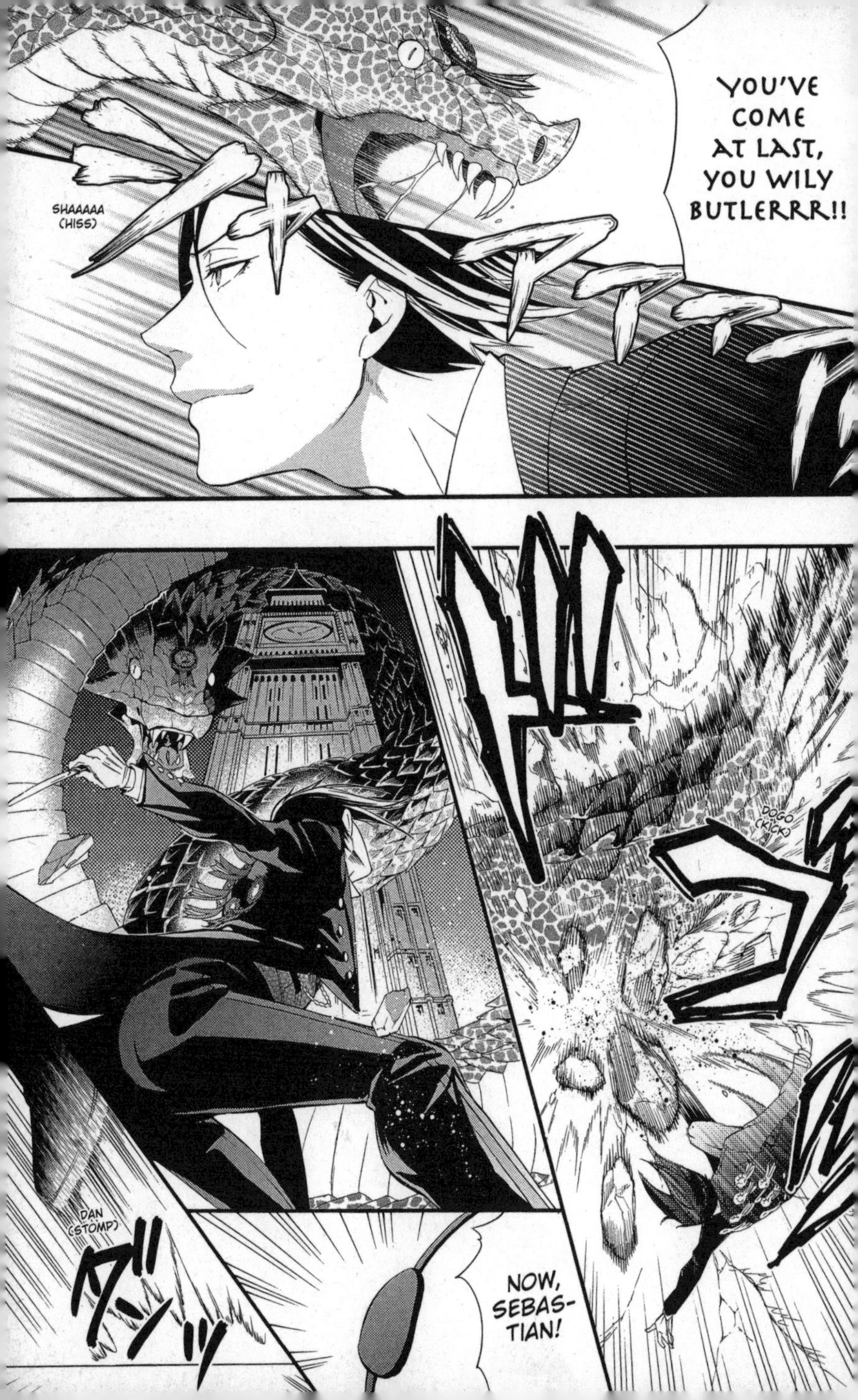
YOU'VE COME AT LAST, YOU WILY BUTLERRR!!
SHAAAAA (HISS)
DOGO (KICK)
DAN (STOMP)
NOW, SEBAS-TIAN!

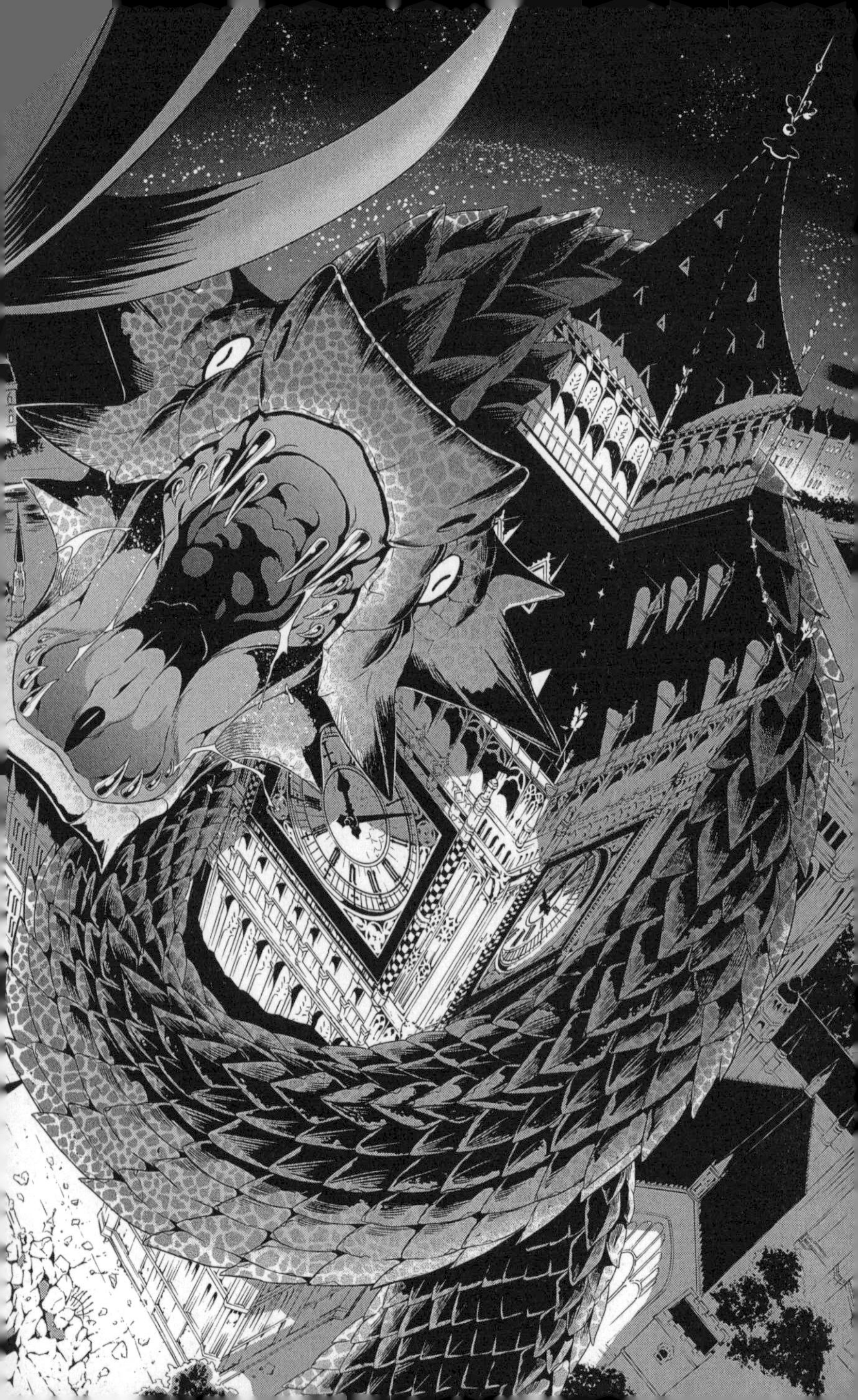

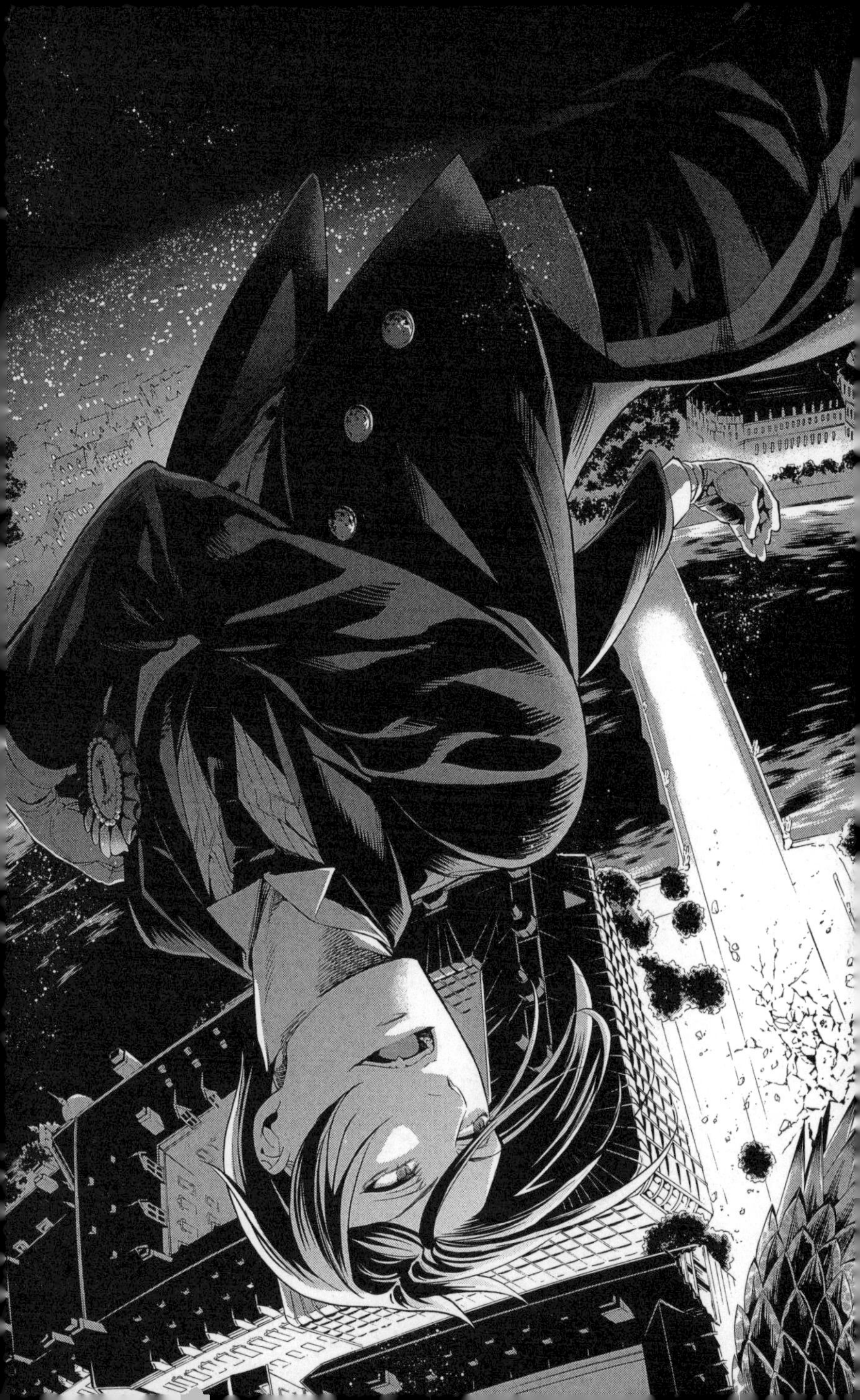

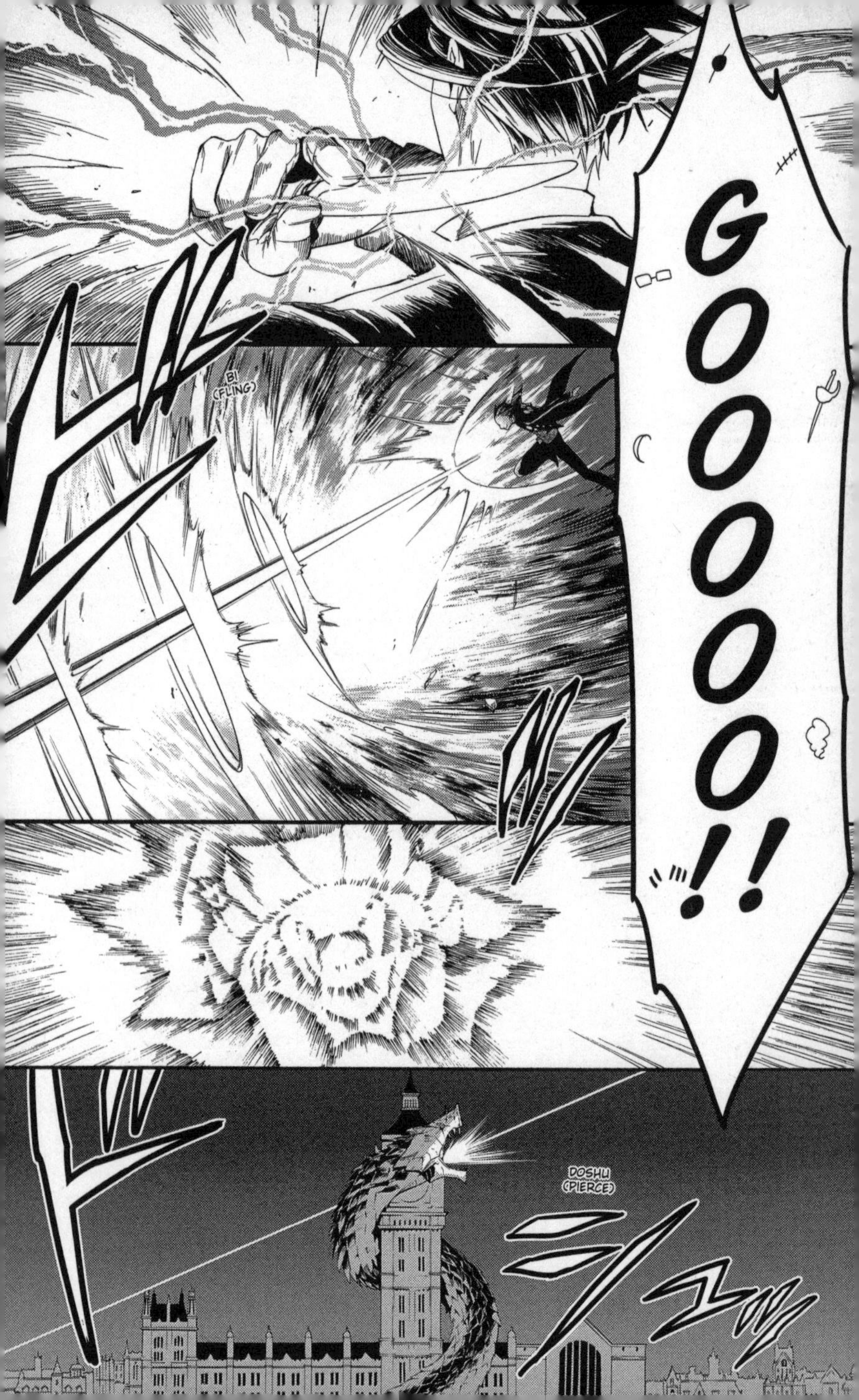
GOOOOOO!!
BI
(FLING)
DOSHU
(PIERCE)

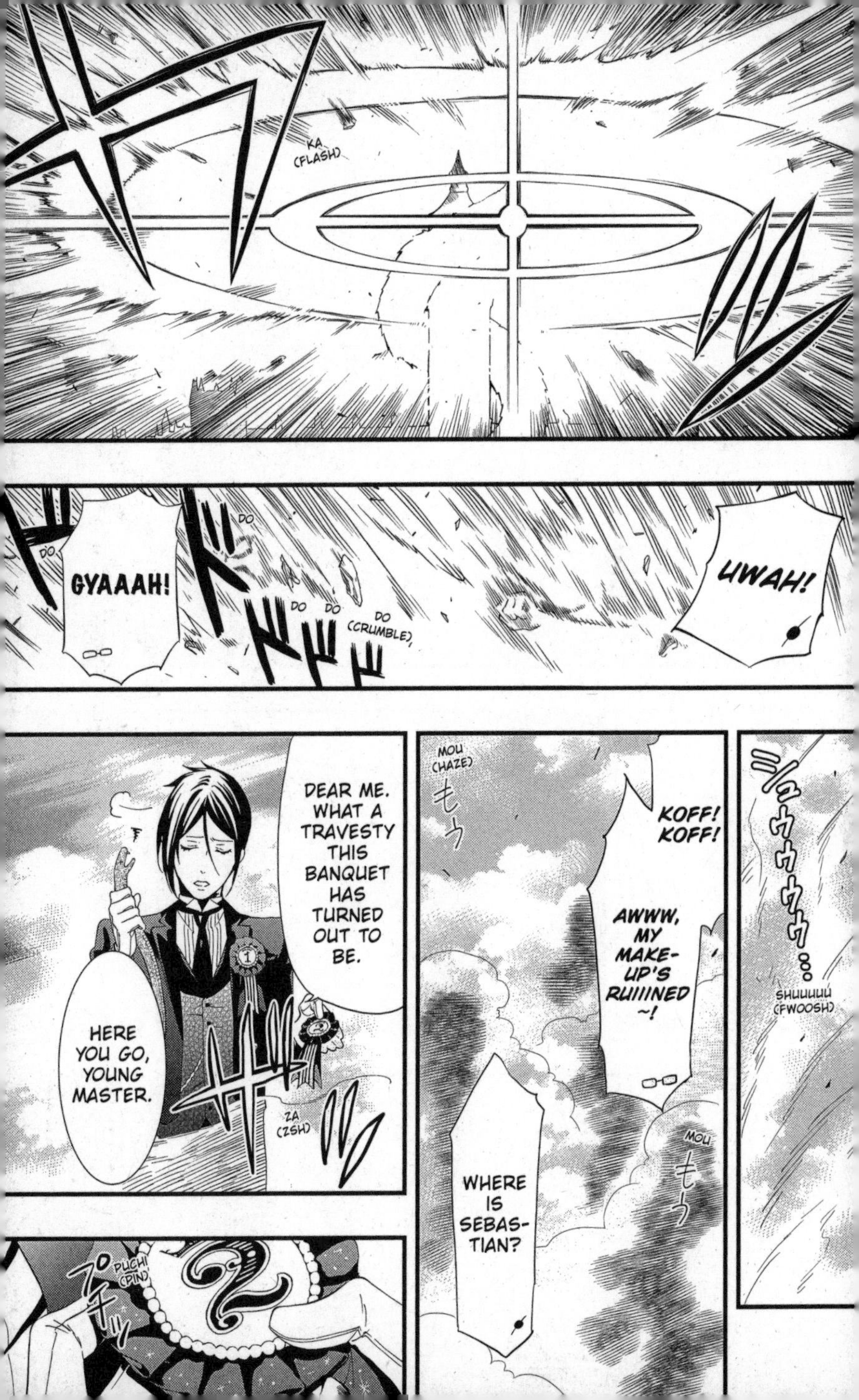
KA (FLASH)
UWAH!
DO (CRUMBLE)
DO DO
DO
GYAAAH!
DO
SHUUUUU (FWOOSH)
KOFF! KOFF!
AWWW, MY MAKE-UP'S RUIIINED~!
MOU (HAZE)
MOU
WHERE IS SEBASTIAN?
DEAR ME. WHAT A TRAVESTY THIS BANQUET HAS TURNED OUT TO BE.
HERE YOU GO, YOUNG MASTER.
ZA (ZSH)
PUCHI (PIN)

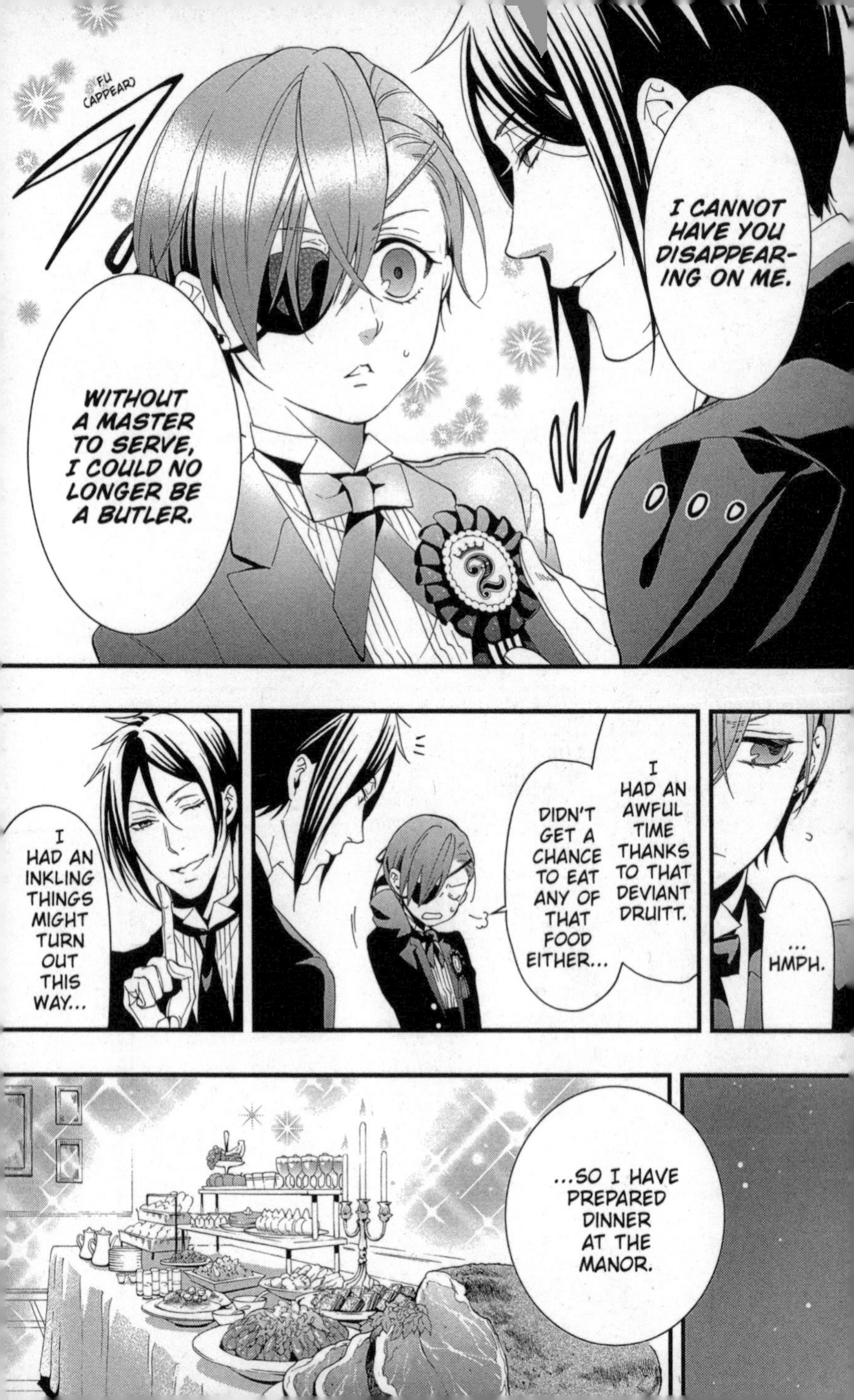
I CANNOT HAVE YOU DISAPPEARING ON ME.
FU (APPEAR)
WITHOUT A MASTER TO SERVE, I COULD NO LONGER BE A BUTLER.
... HMPH.
I HAD AN AWFUL TIME THANKS TO THAT DEVIANT DRUITT.
DIDN'T GET A CHANCE TO EAT ANY OF THAT FOOD EITHER...
I HAD AN INKLING THINGS MIGHT TURN OUT THIS WAY...
...SO I HAVE PREPARED DINNER AT THE MANOR.

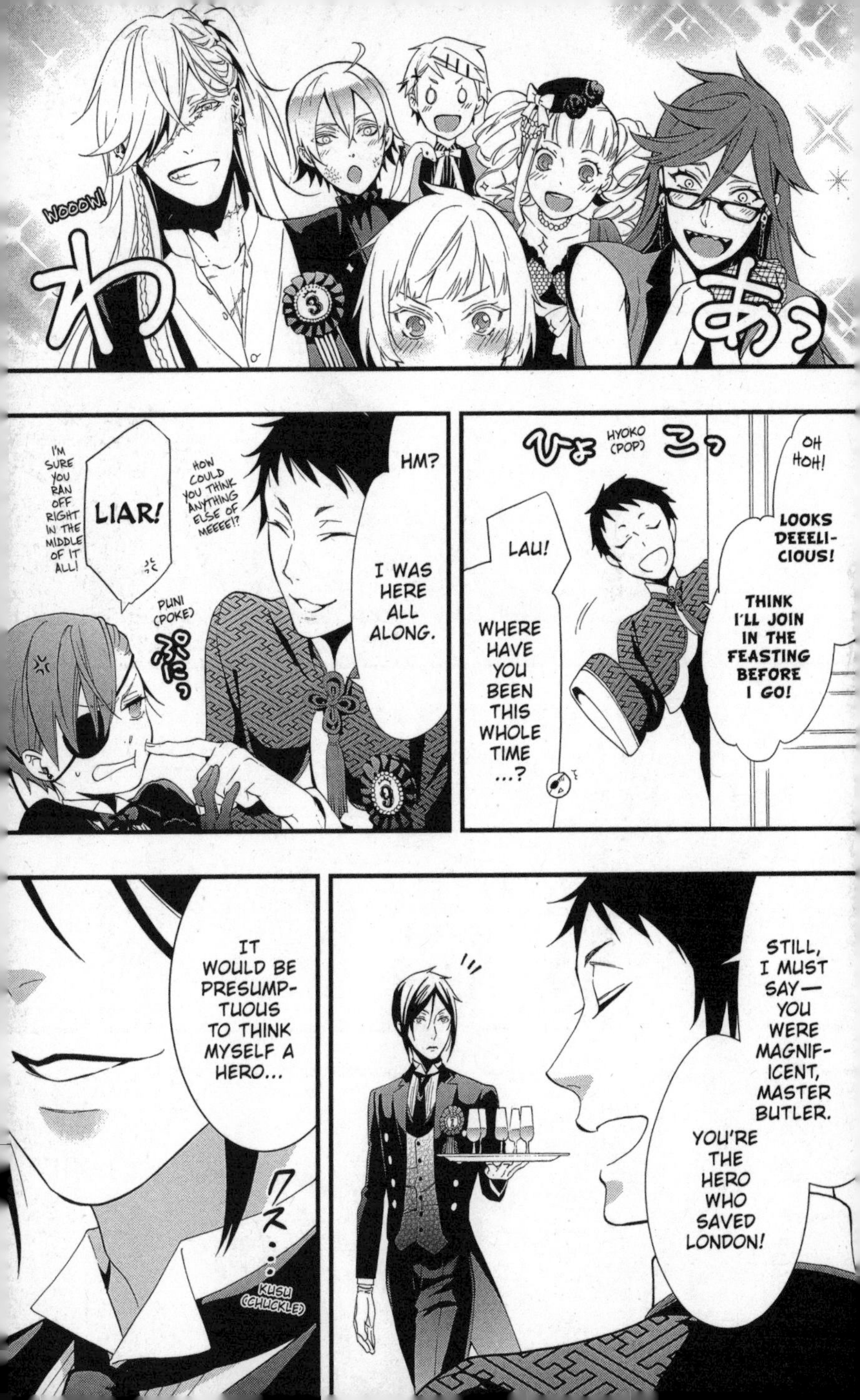
あっ
わっ
WOOOW!
ひょこっ
HYOKO (POP)
OH HOH!
LOOKS DEEELI-CIOUS!
THINK I'LL JOIN IN THE FEASTING BEFORE I GO!
LAU!
WHERE HAVE YOU BEEN THIS WHOLE TIME ...?
HM?
I WAS HERE ALL ALONG.
HOW COULD YOU THINK ANYTHING ELSE OF MEEEE!?
LIAR!
I'M SURE YOU RAN OFF RIGHT IN THE MIDDLE OF IT ALL!
ぷにっ
PUNI (POKE)
STILL, I MUST SAY— YOU WERE MAGNIF-ICENT, MASTER BUTLER.
YOU'RE THE HERO WHO SAVED LONDON!
IT WOULD BE PRESUMP-TUOUS TO THINK MYSELF A HERO...
クス…
KUSU (CHUCKLE)

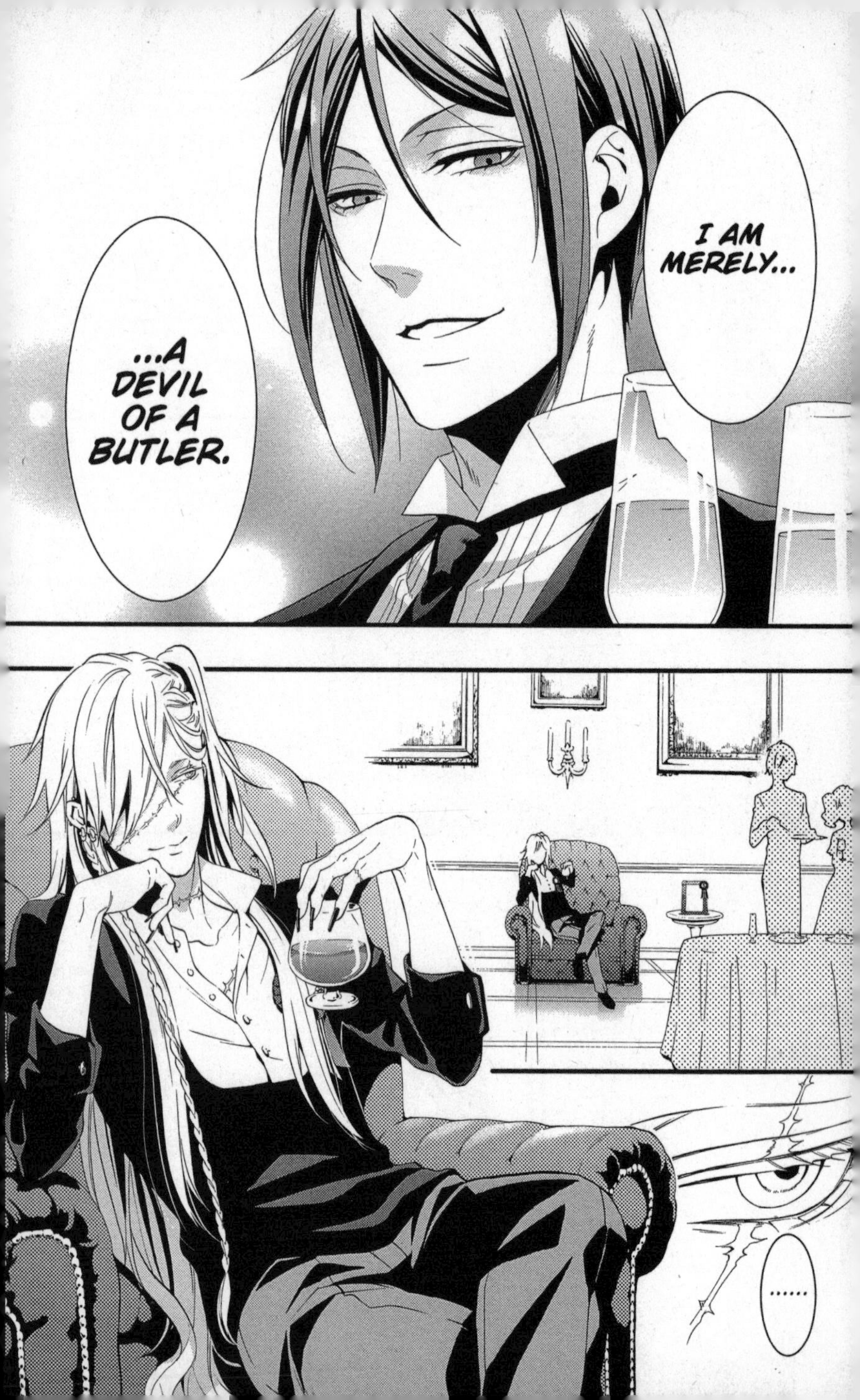
I AM MERELY...
...A DEVIL OF A BUTLER.
......

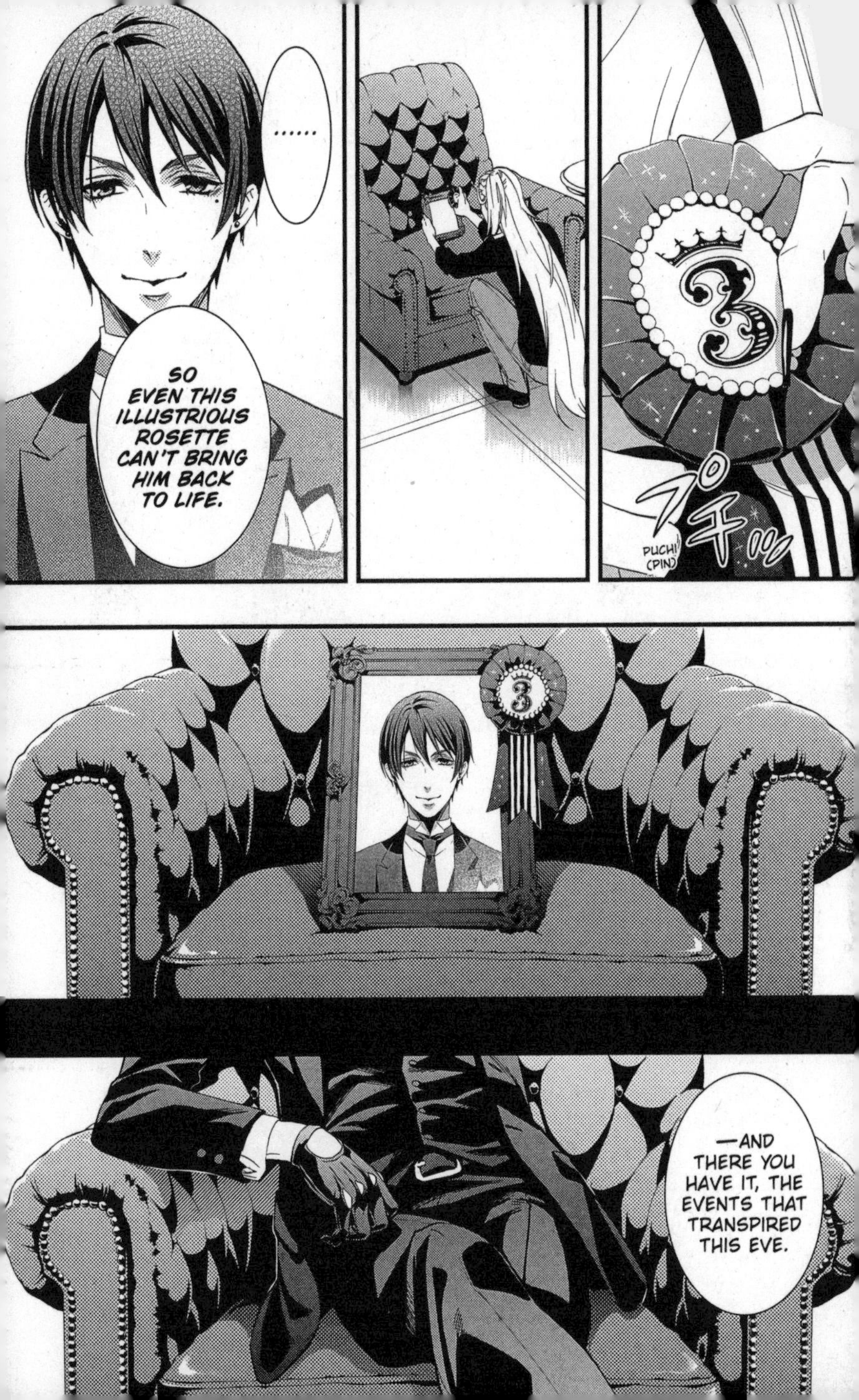
プチッ
PUCHI! (PIN)
......
SO EVEN THIS ILLUSTRIOUS ROSETTE CAN'T BRING HIM BACK TO LIFE.
—AND THERE YOU HAVE IT, THE EVENTS THAT TRANSPIRED THIS EVE.

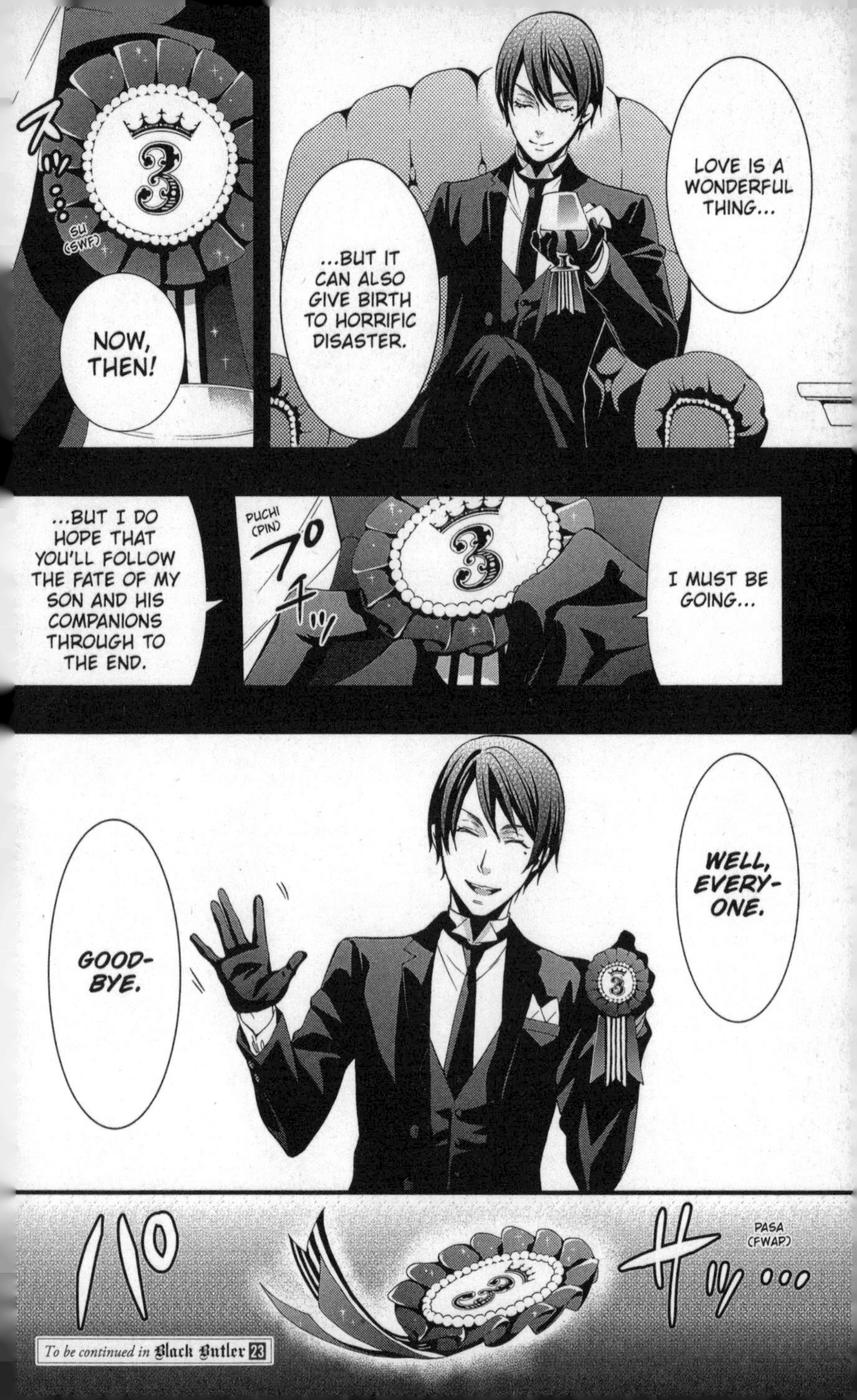
LOVE IS A WONDERFUL THING...
...BUT IT CAN ALSO GIVE BIRTH TO HORRIFIC DISASTER.
SU (SWF)
NOW, THEN!
I MUST BE GOING...
PUCHI (PIN)
...BUT I DO HOPE THAT YOU'LL FOLLOW THE FATE OF MY SON AND HIS COMPANIONS THROUGH TO THE END.
WELL, EVERY-ONE.
GOOD-BYE.
PASA (FWAP)
To be continued in Black Butler 23

➻ Black Butler ➻

黒執事

❧

Downstairs

Wakana Haduki
7
Saito Torino
Tsuki Sorano
Chiaki Nagaoka
Asakura
*
Takeshi Kuma
*
Yana Toboso

❧

Adviser

Rico Murakami

*

Special Thanks

Akira Suzuki

and You!

Translation Notes

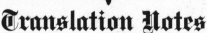

Inside Front and Back Covers

Black Diver

In the original edition, the word used for "diver" is *ama(-san)*, written with the kanji for "sea" and "woman." These divers, part of an historic Japanese tradition, are usually women and are known for diving for pearls.

Page 30

Baden-Baden

Baden-Baden is a resort town located at the foot of the Black Forest in southwestern Germany. With its natural, medicinal springs, the town's tradition as a spa resort dates back to the Romans, but in the nineteenth century, it was de rigueur for members of high society to take the waters in what came to be known as the summer capital of Europe. The German word *baden* means "bath" or "to bathe."

Page 69

Savile Row

Originally an affluent residential street in central London, Savile Row became populated by tailors in the eighteenth and nineteenth centuries. Most notable amongst them was Henry Poole, known for creating the tuxedo. As men of high standing flocked to Savile Row to be outfitted in the latest dinner jackets, the name of this street grew to be synonymous with bespoke, or custom-made, tailoring.

Page 69

Full court dress

A debutante summoned to the Court Drawing Rooms at Buckingham Palace to be presented to Queen Victoria was required to dress in a long gown, typically white in colour, with short sleeves, a low neckline, and a long train of a specific length. White gloves, a certain number of white feather plumes in the hair (the number was dependent on marital status), and a veil, again of specific length, were also compulsory. The carrying of a flower bouquet was also customary, though not mandatory.

Page 77

Alice style

This style of dress has its roots in Lewis Carroll's *Alice's Adventures in Wonderland*, which was published in 1865 with illustrations by John Tenniel. Tenniel's depiction of Alice in a knee-length, puffed-sleeve dress with a pinafore became the definitive Alice in Wonderland.

Page 79

Higgins's Earl Grey

Established in 1942, H. R. Higgins (Coffeeman) Ltd. is an English tea and coffee merchant that holds a Royal Warrant.

Page 85

Formal court curtsy

When a debutante was presented to the queen, she was required to perform the exacting formal full court curtsy. To do this, she would have to bend her knees so deeply that they almost touched the floor, before rising to full height without losing her balance or her headdress or tripping over her train. It was not unheard of for young women preparing for their "coming out" to engage instructors to help them learn just how to succeed at the full court curtsy.

Page 87

Whitehead gag

The contraption Sebastian uses to perfect Lady Sullivan's and Wolfram's pronunciation is actually a medical device used in oral surgery known as a Whitehead dental gag invented in 1877 by Walter Whitehead.

Page 144

Vincent's portrait

The *chiiin* sound effect used on Vincent's portrait is a reference to the striking of a ritual singing bowl (*rin*) with a padded wooden mallet during a Buddhist funeral.

Yana Toboso

AUTHOR'S NOTE

I've written here many times about wanting to visit Great Britain someday, and I finally did. It was my first visit ever, and all I encountered was beyond imagining. The people were nice. The scenery was beautiful. The food was delicious...but sometimes unbelievably awful. I'd like to make the most of my experience and devote myself to creating *Black Butler*. And so this is Volume 22.

The Phantomhive family
has a butler who's almost
too good to be true...
or maybe he's just too
good to be human.
And now you can find
him in two places at once!

Read the latest chapter of

#

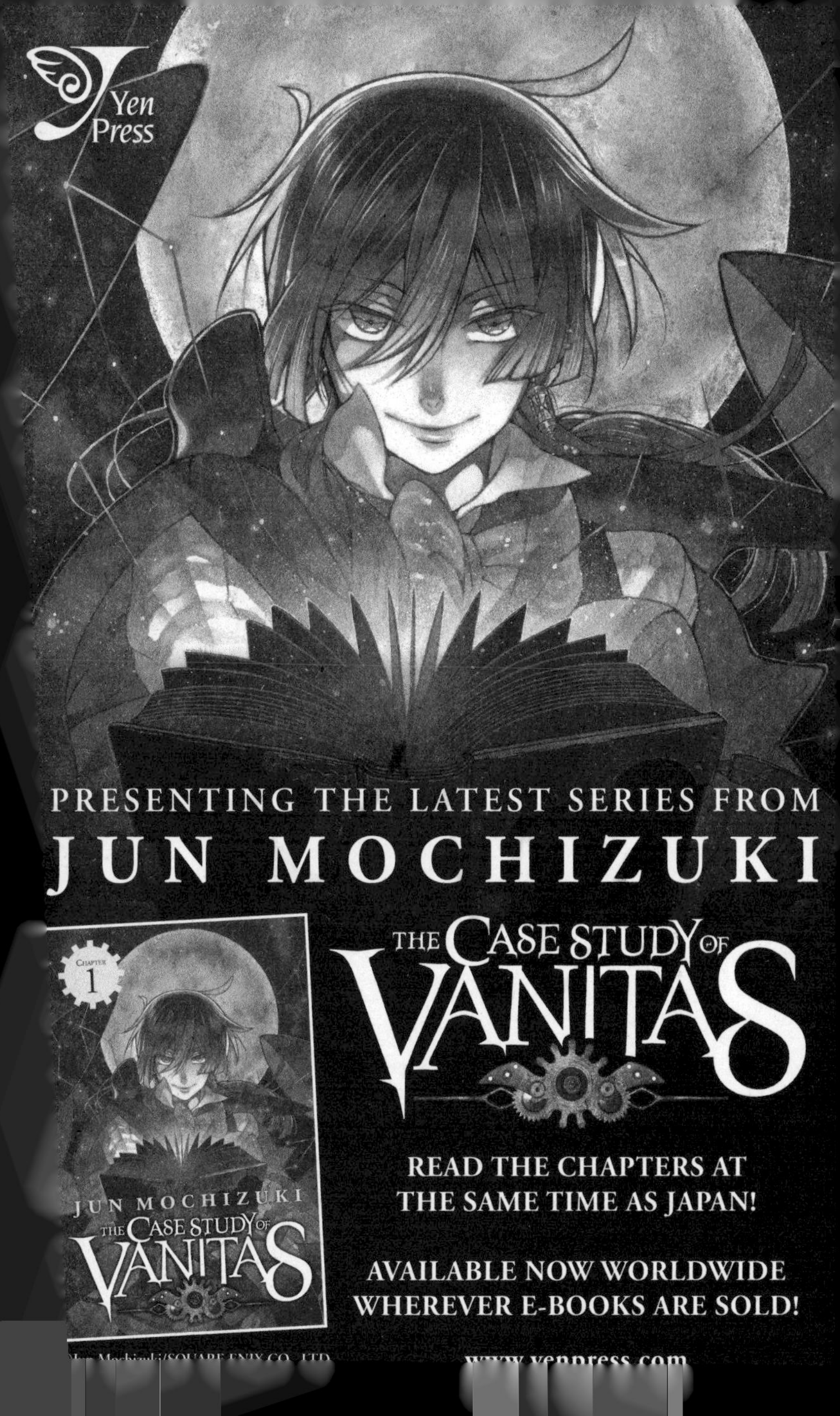

Yen Press
PRESENTING THE LATEST SERIES FROM
JUN MOCHIZUKI
CHAPTER 1
JUN MOCHIZUKI
THE CASE STUDY OF VANITAS
THE CASE STUDY OF VANITAS
READ THE CHAPTERS AT
THE SAME TIME AS JAPAN!
AVAILABLE NOW WORLDWIDE
WHEREVER E-BOOKS ARE SOLD!

BLACK BUTLER ㉒

YANA TOBOSO

Translation: Tomo Kimura • Lettering: Alexis Eckerman

KUROSHITSUJI Vol. 22 © 2015 Yana Toboso / SQUARE ENIX CO., LTD. First published in Japan in 2015 by SQUARE ENIX CO., LTD. English translation rights arranged with SQUARE ENIX CO., LTD. and Hachette Book Group through Tuttle-Mori Agency, Inc.

Translation © 2015 by SQUARE ENIX CO., LTD.

Yen Press
Hachette Book Group
1290 Avenue of the Americas, New York, NY 10104

www.HachetteBookGroup.com
www.YenPress.com

Yen Press is an imprint of Hachette Book Group, Inc. The Yen Press name and logo are trademarks of Hachette Book Group, Inc.

The publisher is not responsible for websites (or their content) that are not owned by the publisher.

Library of Congress Control Number: 2016900913

First Yen Press Edition: May 2016

ISBN: 978-0-316-27226-1

10 9 8 7 6 5 4 3 2 1

BVG

Printed in the United States of America